Future of Business and Finance

The Future of Business and Finance book series features professional works aimed at defining, analyzing, and charting the future trends in these fields. The focus is mainly on strategic directions, technological advances, challenges and solutions which may affect the way we do business tomorrow, including the future of sustainability and governance practices. Mainly written by practitioners, consultants and academic thinkers, the books are intended to spark and inform further discussions and developments.

Roman Becker • Gregor Daschmann

FANOMICS®

Turn Customers into Fans and Profit from it

Roman Becker
2HMforum. GmbH
Mainz, Rheinland-Pfalz, Germany

Gregor Daschmann
Johannes Gutenberg-Universität Mainz
Mainz, Rheinland-Pfalz, Germany

ISSN 2662-2467 ISSN 2662-2475 (electronic)
Future of Business and Finance
ISBN 978-3-658-41238-8 ISBN 978-3-658-41239-5 (eBook)
https://doi.org/10.1007/978-3-658-41239-5

© The Editor(s) (if applicable) and The Author(s), under exclusive license to Springer Nature Switzerland AG 2023

This work is subject to copyright. All rights are reserved by the Publisher, whether the whole or part of the material is concerned, specifically the rights of translation, reprinting, reuse of illustrations, recitation, broadcasting, reproduction on microfilms or in any other physical way, and transmission or information storage and retrieval, electronic adaptation, computer software, or by similar or dissimilar methodology now known or hereafter developed.

The use of general descriptive names, registered names, trademarks, service marks, etc. in this publication does not imply, even in the absence of a specific statement, that such names are exempt from the relevant protective laws and regulations and therefore free for general use.

The publisher, the authors, and the editors are safe to assume that the advice and information in this book are believed to be true and accurate at the date of publication. Neither the publisher nor the authors or the editors give a warranty, expressed or implied, with respect to the material contained herein or for any errors or omissions that may have been made. The publisher remains neutral with regard to jurisdictional claims in published maps and institutional affiliations.

This Springer imprint is published by the registered company Springer Fachmedien Wiesbaden GmbH, part of Springer Nature.
The registered company address is: Abraham-Lincoln-Str. 46, 65189 Wiesbaden, Germany

Preface

Really turn customers into fans ...

When you first open this book, you may think: "yet another book on turning customers into fans." But you'd be mistaken!

In fact, this is the *only* book on really turning customers into fans. Granted: There are numerous publications that promise you the path to turning a customer into a fan. But these approaches use the concept of the fan customer only superficially. They do not deal with the fundamental social-psychological characteristics of fan relationships, but even ignore these connections. For them, the fan customer crumbles into a mere metaphor—an exciting label that, when put into practice, hides nothing more than conventional measures to increase customer satisfaction.

With *FANOMICS,* you *really learn* to turn customers into fans and to profit from this in the long term—regardless of your core markets and products, economic and cultural conditions, your target groups, your industry, and your company size.

Our approach is fundamentally different since we have taken the concept of a "fan" literally. We used scientific fan research to analyze how fan relationships work in principle and, based on this, have designed measurement tools which can identify fans and also fan customers. On this basis, we then developed a comprehensive management concept that enables companies to become more successful with fan customers—and to increase this success even further by gaining new fan customers. Our approach thus *truly enables* companies to turn customers into fans—unlike many others who only pretend to do so. Our approach consists of three key unique and fundamental points:

1. Based on the findings of scientific fan research, we have discovered what the *principle* conditions of a *fan relationship* are. A true fan relationship is created through the interaction of identification and perceived uniqueness. Fans want to recharge this relationship again and again through rituals. We call this interaction the *Fan Principle.* You won't find a second approach in marketing literature that works out what a fan is and why people become fans as deeply and scientifically as the *Fan Principle.*

2. We have applied the *Fan Principle* to the relationship between customers and their suppliers. We prove that there are customer relationships which exhibit the characteristics of fan relationships and can measure this by using the *Fan Indicator* we have developed. In this way, we identify the fan customers and their share of the total customer portfolio, the so-called *Fan Rate, for each company*. We call this transfer of the *Fan Principle* into economic contexts *FANOMICS*—as a term for systematic management, i.e. for the economics of the *Fan Principle*.
3. *FANOMICS means aligning* one's customer relationships—based on the insights of the *Fan Principle*—with the mechanisms of fan relationships: This equates to knowing the core needs of one's customers and making these needs a consistent and regular experience in the customer journey at all points of contact. *FANOMICS* includes numerous management tools that enable you to increase the *Fan Rate* among your customers and thus become demonstrably more successful.

The *Fan Principle* includes all phenomena of genuine fan relationships as they can be derived from social sciences research. *FANOMICS*, on the other hand, is the transfer of these findings to customer relationships and includes the control and analysis tools we have developed which companies should apply if they really want to turn their customers into fans.

The sustainable alignment of a company with *FANOMICS* requires a reorientation. This is because it breaks with many cherished beliefs of conventional management and shows a completely new way to increase customer value and make companies more successful economically in the long term. We use the term "sustainable" deliberately because *FANOMICS* is not only a growth engine, but also at the same time serves basic human needs and thus makes customers simply happier.

In this book, we introduce you to our entire approach—from the definition of the idea of fan to the sophisticated concept of *FANOMICS*. We will present you with the theoretical concept behind our thinking as well as numerous theoretical and empirical evidence for the validity of our approach. In addition, we will introduce you to proven tools for measuring and managing, which you can use to make your company more successful—such as the *Fan Indicator* as a measure of emotional customer loyalty and the *Fan Rate* as a currency for the value of customer relationships.

In the first chapter, we begin by answering some fundamental questions regarding our approach, namely what constitutes a fan or fan customers, how to identify them, and how to align your entire customer portfolio with the idea of the fan customer. In the second chapter, we prove the usefulness of this systematization by showing, based on broad empirical data and what outstanding customer value fan customers have for any company. In the third chapter, we show what we mean by *FANOMICS* as a comprehensive, customer value-based management tool and the central place that Positioning (as an expression of Focusing) and Orchestration have in our approach. In the fourth chapter, we use a structured implementation model to explain how to turn customers into fans and what companies can do to develop their employees into Fan Makers. In the fifth chapter, we go into more advanced areas of application for *FANOMICS*—for example, the strategic acquisition of new customers whose fan *potential can* be determined with *FANOMICS* before they are even customers, or the possible combinations of *FANOMICS* with the *NPS* (*Net Promoter Score*). The sixth and final chapter shows the key success factors of *FANOMICS* and is primarily intended for those who already wish to initiate concrete measures in their company immediately based upon our book.

Our explanations are filled with many vivid examples. We illustrate our fundamental reflections on the question of what fans are and why people become fans of something in the first place with numerous examples of fans and fan behavior from music, sports, and culture from A to Z: From fans of the Swedish pop group *ABBA* to fans of the US hard rock band *ZZ-Top*, from Danish fans of the soccer club *Aarhus GF* to fans of the ice sports club *Zug* from Switzerland. And we will present numerous examples of companies which have been successful thanks to a high *Fan Rate*. This gives you an even deeper insight into how you can use *FANOMICS to turn* your customers into fans and profit from it.

In the end, you will see, by aligning with the *Fan Principle* and implementing *FANOMICS,* your investments in customer relationships will not increase, but decrease. Because you will then target your resources where they really pay off. Our promise is: Regardless of the industry, regardless of the size of your company, regardless of whether you are in the B2B or B2C sector, regardless of whether your company is based in Europe, Asia, or North America—your economic success will increase when you apply *FANOMICS*. But *FANOMICS* has an even more far-reaching effect: if implemented consistently, it places people, their needs, and their relationships at the center of all actions—the return on this focus is then virtually inescapable. *FANOMICS,* as we will show, is not only the path to economic success, but also a detailed guide for every company and its decision-makers on how to align their own actions in a meaningful way.

Implementing the *Fan Principle* consistently with *FANOMICS* promises you progress on numerous levels: It creates company growth and increased profits, it has a meaningful effect owing to the focus on the quality of relationships and thus promotes corporate culture and employee loyalty, and it provides you as a user with knowledge and competence advantages in everyday business. In the end, all of this pays off in terms of your profile as a decision-maker and your personal visibility within the company—and thus in terms of your own personal success. So, we will not only show you how to *really* turn customers into fans—but also how you can profit from it.

Fig. 1 If you would like a short overview before reading, just watch our explainer video. https://fanomics.de/en/#explainer

With this in mind, look forward to expanding your Fan Base (Fig. 1).
Three important notes about this book:

1. The terms used in this book *FANOMICS*, *Fan Principle*, *Fan Indicator*, *Fan Portfolio*, *Fanfocus Germany*, *Fanfocus G7*, *Excellence Barometer* as well as *Motiversum* are protected as word/figurative trademarks of 2HMforum. GmbH, Mainz, Germany.
2. For more information on the *Fan Principle* and *FANOMICS,* as well as videos and podcasts with the authors, visit: https://www.fan-prinzip.de and https://www.fanomics.de/en/.

Mainz, Germany
Roman Becker
Gregor Daschmann

Contents

1	**The *Fan Principle*: Fans and Fan Customers**		1
1.1	What It Is About		1
1.2	What Is a Fan?		1
	1.2.1	The Concept of Fan and its History of Origin	2
	1.2.2	What Does the Word "Fan" Actually Mean?	4
	1.2.3	Why Fan Relationships Are Emotional Relationships	7
	1.2.4	What We Mean by a Fan	11
	1.2.5	The Search for Identification as the Basis of Every Fan Relationship	13
	1.2.6	The Search for Uniqueness as the Basis of Every Fan Relationship	17
	1.2.7	How the Fan Finds His Star	19
	1.2.8	How the Star Finds His Fan	21
	1.2.9	Characteristics of the Fan Relationship: Permanence and Repetitiveness	25
	1.2.10	Characteristics of the Fan Relationship: Resilience and Willingness to Consume	29
	1.2.11	Characteristics of the Fan Relationship: Communication and Community	32
	1.2.12	Summary: What Is a Fan?	34
1.3	From *Fan Principle* to *FANOMICS*: What Is a Fan Customer?		36
	1.3.1	Fans also Exist in Customer Relationships	36
	1.3.2	Beware of Satisfied Customers	39
1.4	The *FANOMICS Basis*: The *Fan Indicator*		46
1.5	The *Fan Rate* as a KPI		49
	1.5.1	The *Fan Rates* of German B2C Companies	54
	1.5.2	The *Fan Rates* of German B2B Companies	57
1.6	The *Fan Portfolio*		59
	1.6.1	The Customer Types within the *Fan Portfolio*	60
	1.6.2	The Validation of the *Fan Portfolio* Through Fan-Specific Behavior	70

	1.6.3	The Complete Segmentation of the Customer Landscape Through the *Fan Portfolio*.............	74
	1.6.4	The Complete *Fan Portfolio* in Industry Comparison: National and International....................	79
References...			90

2 The Value of Fan Customers............................... 95
2.1 The Fan as a Growth Driver........................... 96
2.2 Fans and Market Penetration: Growth with Existing Customers in Existing Business......................... 98
    2.2.1 Fans Are Loyal.................................. 99
    2.2.2 Fans Are Forgiving............................. 101
    2.2.3 Fans Have Confidence.......................... 102
    2.2.4 Fans Are Less Price Sensitive................... 102
    2.2.5 Fans Have the Highest Monetary Customer Value.... 103
    2.2.6 Fans Have the Highest Customer Lifetime Value..... 104
    2.2.7 Growth Through Fans Can Be Planned............ 105
2.3 Fans and Market Development: Growth Through Acquisition of New Customers in Existing Business................... 114
    2.3.1 Fans Are Positive Ambassadors.................. 115
    2.3.2 Fans Are the Best Referrers..................... 116
    2.3.3 Excursus: How Do Word-of-Mouth, Social Media, and Recommendation Work?..................... 118
    2.3.4 Fans and Recommendation Incentives............. 125
    2.3.5 Excursus: Why Opponents Are Dangerous Customers................................... 126
2.4 Fans and Product Development: Growth with Existing Customers Through Expansion of the Product Range......... 128
    2.4.1 Fans Are Innovators............................ 128
    2.4.2 Fans Are Involved............................. 129
2.5 Fans and Product Diversification: Growth by Attracting New Customers for New Products....................... 133
2.6 Summary: The *Fan Rate* as the Key Growth Factor.......... 134
2.7 Increasing Customer Value Through *FANOMICS*............ 136
References... 137

3 *FANOMICS*: The Economics of the *Fan Principle*............. 139
3.1 Focus Generates Identification......................... 141
    3.1.1 Examples I: Successful Focus Through "Freude am Fahren" or "Vorsprung durch Technik"......... 141
    3.1.2 Examples II: Is Flying Really More Pleasant? *Deutsche Bahn* Versus *Lufthansa*........................ 144
    3.1.3 Examples III: The Value of Focus in a Crisis—*ADAC* and the Falsified Survey Results.................. 146
    3.1.4 Examples from Practice IV: When Focus Is Useful and When It Is Not—VW and the Emissions Scandal.. 148
    3.1.5 Examples V: Where *Praktiker* Actually Failed....... 151

		3.1.6	Examples VI: *Deutsche Bank*—How "Passionate Performance" Becomes Performance that Creates Suffering..	152
		3.1.7	Don't Be that "Egg-Laying Jack-of-All-Trades"......	154
		3.1.8	Conclusion: Focus as the Basis for Emotional Customer Loyalty and for Efficient Use of Resources...	156
	3.2	Orchestration Creates Perceived Uniqueness...............		156
	3.3	Definition of *FANOMICS*...............................		159
	3.4	Examples VII: *ALDI*—The Simple Principle...............		160
		3.4.1	Identify Core Customer Needs....................	161
		3.4.2	Identify Key Touchpoints........................	163
		3.4.3	Focusing and Orchestrating on Core Customer Needs......................................	164
	3.5	Examples VIII: *Miele—Orchestration* of Performance and Communication...................................		170
	3.6	*FANOMICS*: From Development to Implementation.........		174
	References..			175
4	**How Do I Really Turn Customers into Fans?**.................			177
	4.1	Positioning...		178
		4.1.1	Instruments and Management Systems in the Positioning Process...........................	179
		4.1.2	Instruments I: Identify Loyalty-Drivers: Customer and Competitor Customer Survey................	181
		4.1.3	Instruments II: Deepening and Locating Customer Needs: The "*Motiversum*"......................	184
		4.1.4	Instruments III: Understanding Identity: The Identity Workshop..................................	187
		4.1.5	Instruments IV: Checking Identity: The Employee Survey.....................................	188
		4.1.6	Instruments V: Checking Processes in Customer Management: The *Maturity Check*................	190
		4.1.7	Instruments VI: Identifying Opportunities for Differentiation: The Communication Analysis........	190
		4.1.8	Derivation of Positioning.......................	194
	4.2	Orchestration.......................................		204
		4.2.1	The Importance of Contact Frequency and Measures to Increase.................................	204
		4.2.2	The Touchpoint-Specific Orchestration............	211
		4.2.3	Management Instrument: The Follow-Up Feedback Survey.....................................	213
		4.2.4	Example VIII: DiBaDu: Perfect Orchestration in Telephone Customer Contact....................	218
		4.2.5	Orchestration of Individual Touchpoints...........	221
		4.2.6	Touchpoint I: Demand-Oriented Offers and Services...	222
		4.2.7	Touchpoint II: Prices in Line with Demand.........	229

		4.2.8	Touchpoint III: Reducing Shortfalls Through Needs-Based Complaint Management.............	233
		4.2.9	Touchpoint IV: Deploying Product Innovations in Line with Demand.........................	239
		4.2.10	Touchpoint V: The Emotionalizing Effect of Digital Channels.................................	241
	4.3	Employees as Fan Makers.............................		242
		4.3.1	The Customer Orientation of the Employees.........	243
		4.3.2	Factors Influencing Customer Orientation...........	244
		4.3.3	Influencing Factor 1: Knowledge and Information About Customers (Customer Insights)..............	245
		4.3.4	Influencing Factor 2: Employee Skills..............	246
		4.3.5	Influencing Factor 3: Identification with the Employer—Fans Among Employees...............	246
		4.3.6	All Employees Are Fan Makers...................	258
	4.4	Customer Value-Based Control.........................		259
		4.4.1	Personalized Assignment in the *Fan Portfolio*.......	260
		4.4.2	Customer Value Specific Measures and Prioritization................................	262
	References...			264
5	**FANOMICS: More than Controlling Relationship Quality**......			267
	5.1	Customer Value-Based Segmentation with the *Fan Portfolio*...		268
		5.1.1	Fan Marketing: How to Turn Fans into Profitable Customers...................................	271
		5.1.2	Potential-Based Segmentation Versus Segmentation with the *Fan Portfolio*.......................	276
		5.1.3	Allocation of B2B Customers in the Context of Value-Based Segmentation with the *Fan Portfolio*..	277
	5.2	*FANOMICS* as an Instrument for Efficient New Customer Acquisition...		280
	5.3	Dovetailing of NPS and *FANOMICS* to Form "*NPSplus-Insights*"..................................		283
	References...			290
6	**Success Factors of FANOMICS**...........................			293
	6.1	Building Awareness and Acceptance.....................		294
	6.2	Validation of Success Effectiveness by Measuring the Customer Value of Fans...........................		297
	6.3	Continuous Measurement and Goal Systems for Managing Success...		301
	Reference...			304

More than "Just" Success: How FANOMICS Gives Meaning to Doing Business.. 305

About the Authors

Roman Becker is founder and managing partner of the market research and consulting company "2HMforum. For best Relationships." in Mainz. He is a pioneer in the analysis and optimization of emotional customer loyalty and employee loyalty. Over the past 25 years, he has helped decision-makers at national and international companies to optimize customer and employee relationships with the help of *FANOMICS* and thus become more successful.

Roman Becker is also the initiator of the benchmark studies "Fanfocus Germany" and "Employee Focus Germany" as well as the renowned company competition "Germanys Customer Champions." Becker studied journalism and economics at Johannes Gutenberg University in Mainz, where he also worked for many years as a statistics lecturer. He is a fan of the football club Mainz 05 and passionate about winter sports.

Gregor Daschmann is Full Professor for Media Effects at the Department of Communication Studies and Dean of the Faculty of Social Sciences, Media and Sports at Johannes Gutenberg University Mainz. He is also an academic advisor to "2HMforum. For Best Relationships." His work focuses, among other things, on media psychology, media effects, and empirical methods. After studying Communication, Politics and Psychology, Daschmann worked as a journalist in various broadcasting stations. After his doctorate, he first became a professor of media and communication studies at the IJK Hanover, from where he went back to the Mainz University. Gregor Daschmann is a fan of the football club Mainz 05 and plays bass guitar in the *Rockin' Blues Band*.

The *Fan Principle*: Fans and Fan Customers

1.1 What It Is About

This book is about Fan Customers. In other words, customers whose relationship with a supplier is just as intense as the relationship fans have with a celebrity, a cult object, or a sports club. In case you were in any doubt as to whether such customers or such customer relationships exist: They do exist, and we will prove that conclusively and convincingly. We will also show that Fan Customers exist for every type of company, every type of product and every type of service all around the world. And we will prove that such customers are the most important factor for the success of any company. Exciting prospects—but we still must ask you for a little patience. Because before we go into such detail about Fan Customers, we need to take another imperative step: We must first explain the nature of the fan. Because the question of what the actual make-up of a fan actually is, was at the forefront of all our considerations. Only those who have understood what a fan is and how a fan behaves are in a position to understand Fan Customers and deal with them appropriately.

1.2 What Is a Fan?

What is a "fan" anyway? Where does the term come from, who does it refer to nowadays, and what characteristics distinguish typical fans as we know them from the fields of sports, music, or the media? What do we mean by the label "fan" in this book? We will answer these questions in the following. The aim is to analyze which characteristics fans have and what actually constitutes fan behavior in order to derive indicators and patterns that can be transferred to the relationship between customers and companies.

1.2.1 The Concept of Fan and its History of Origin

Etymologically, the term "fan," which comes from English, originates from the Latin word "fanaticus," and was used in the Middle Ages to describe extreme zealots, or "fanatics." It was not until the 19th century that the term was secularized: the term "fanatics" was now also used to describe the followers and fellow travelers of the mass political movements who were appearing for the first time. At the end of the 19th century, the term was first used in its abbreviated form "fan" in U.S. newspapers to refer to supporters of certain baseball teams (as well as to theatergoers, who were apparently assumed not to be serious in their reception of what was happening on stage). Fan-like behaviors—of course without reference to today's fan term—are, however, already reported from the audience of the ancient Olympic Games or the Roman Circus.[1]

In the twentieth century, increased time outside of work—i.e., leisure time—became a mass phenomenon for the first time. The consequence was a more extensive use of cultural offerings, from which the development of the film and sports sectors, and later also the gastronomy, music and event industries, profited in the long term. With the expansion and professionalization of these leisure sectors, their players also became increasingly prominent—thus stars or star ensembles and consequently, also fan culture continued to build up.

The English short word "fan" is accepted and adopted in almost all languages today. The adaptation of the borrowed term "fan" into the non-English language area took place in the 1950s through US youth trends such as jeans, twist, hula-hoop or rock'n'roll which spread worldwide. In some cultural circles, the new fan term simultaneously expressed the parents' generation's disdain for the youthful followers of these trends. Before the word "fan" became established, synonymous terms such as admirer or follower were still common in many languages for this phenomenon.[2] Even though even today the two words "follower" and "fans" are mostly used synonymously in everyday language, their different linguistic roots already illustrate an ambivalence that is still inherent in the fan phenomenon today. On the one hand, the "fan" is a "follower," i.e., he follows a movement and thus belongs to the passive followers of a trend whose direction is determined by other actors, however, this passive "follower" is at the same time a "fan," i.e., a highly involved, almost fanatical actor who is committed to his cause to an above-average degree—a cause he does not only passively follow in the bandwagon, but which he also actively advances at the same time through his own commitment at the head of

---

[1] Cf. Göttlich and Krischke-Ramaswamy (2003) and Roose et al. (2017b). Even before the emergence of modern consumer societies and the coining of the term "fan," "fans" probably existed - back to antiquity - albeit not in the mass-like movements of today. The "fan" is therefore not a purely modern phenomenon. Cf. the historical outlines by Schmidt-Lux (2017) and Schlicht et al. (2003, p. 236 ff.).

[2] In some Romance languages, too, the loanword "fan" was adopted into everyday language only through the U.S. model, although the word root "fanaticus" existed there before (e.g., "fanatico" in Spanish).

the movement. This Janus-face as follower and leader at the same time is how fans are nowadays found in almost all cultures. And indeed, as we will show in the following, a fan is neither exclusively a will-less trend consumer nor exclusively an uncontrollable persuader, but a complex hybrid of these two types.

During the so-called *Beatlemania* (cf. Fig. 1.1) of the 1960s, fan behavior first entered the public consciousness as hysterical mass culture. At that time, the term fan still had a widespread negative connotation. This alone proves that the passion experienced positively by the fan alone can also be perceived negatively by outsiders: For non-fans, fans are often perceived as suspicious—as exaggerated enthusiasts as well as quirky or strange followers of an idea. And extreme fans are not infrequently labeled as crazy disciples or even pathologically obsessed. In everyday life, therefore, the term "fan" has more than just a positive connotation (Mikos 2010, p. 108).

In the years that followed, this predominantly negative view changed: On the one hand, postmodernism brought greater tolerance for individual passions and lifestyles, which also expanded the accepted space of articulation for fans. On the other hand, the realization that the many different fan groups also represent a socially relevant economic factor with a high willingness-to-pay prevailed at the same time. Owing to these market potentials, the fan phenomenon successively became part of a cultural industry that is taken for granted today (Akremi and Hellmann 2017; Göttlich and Krischke-Ramaswamy 2003, p. 168). The result was an increasing social acceptance of "being a fan," which in turn led to more freely acted-out and thus more active fan behavior. Fans began to organize their own "fanhood" through associations, gatherings, and their own publications. Over the last 20 years, these creative activities of fans and fan groups have received a decisive communicative boost through Web 2.0 with its possibilities for the worldwide dissemination of *user-generated content*: On social media platforms, fans today have the opportunity for

Fig. 1.1 Fan hysteria as a new mass movement: *Beatlemania* (Courtesy of © picture alliance/ Heritage Images | Keystone Archives 2022. All Rights Reserved)

the first time to network and exchange ideas worldwide and to live out the active-creative side of their fanhood across all borders.

Since the 1960s, the increasing acceptance and marketing of the fan phenomenon triggered new marketing strategies in the culture industry, which now designed stars and cult objects on the drawing board to stimulate fan behavior and thus create or revive sales. For example, in pop music, inventive producers repeatedly created artificial music groups from the 1970s onward: Professional musicians recorded music titles in the studio, which were then marketed by bought-in protagonists with playback performances. Interestingly, the first cases of such conceptualized pop groups, such as "The Monkees" in the U.S. or "Boney M." in Europe, led to great indignation—the fact that the musicians heard on the recordings were not also the actors performing in public was perceived in many places as inauthentic or even as fraud. Nowadays, on the other hand, such divergences are taken note of in a completely unexcited manner: Strategically planned star concepts from the drawing board have become almost a matter of course in pop, mass, and youth culture. If we summarize the changes in the behavior of fans, stars and the culture industry outlined above, it becomes clear that today's fans have three faces. First, they are consumers of a cultural good; second, they are active co-creators of this culture and third, they are also often a product of the associated culture industry.

1.2.2 What Does the Word "Fan" Actually Mean?

The question of who or what a fan is according to today's understanding seems trivial at first glance, because the word has become an everyday term that we encounter in many different forms. When we hear the term "fan," we see very different phenomena before us: *Sports fans who* flock to the stadium in their team's colors; *Beyoncé* fans who cheer along as a screaming horde in front of the stage; *Donald Duck* fans who gather for Duckburg-themed symposiums; *Jaguar E-Type fans* who drive rallies and share stories on their own websites; *Will Smith* fans who wait for hours in front of the red carpet in an attempt to elicit an autograph or even a "selfie" with their star; *Taylor Swift* fans (Driessen 2022) who buy the colored vinyl editions of their star's new album even when they do not have a record player for it themselves; *Lord of the Rings* fans who converse in *Elvish, Harry Potter* fans who meet for *Quidditch tournaments*, *haute couture* fans who attend every fashion show their designer puts on, or *Star Trek* fans who greet each other with the *Vulcan salute*. In everyday life, we refer to them all as fans in the narrower sense, although the way they live out their fanhood is completely different. What unites them is the apparently positive emotional connection to a phenomenon that lies outside their person, as well as the behaviors that result from it. This phenomenon on which the fan focuses can be a real person, such as an actor or a pop star, or a fictional character, such as Spiderman (Havard et al. 2020). It can be a material object such as an automobile, a particular cultural genre such as *Western movies* or *rap music,* or even a pure fantasy product such as a fantasy sports league (e.g. Patera

2013; Billings and Ruihley 2013; Ploeg 2017; Dwyer et al. 2022) or the universe of the *Starship Enterprise*.

In addition to this multiformity of the term "fan" in the narrower sense, a fan in the broader sense has developed in everyday language. In everyday life, we now use the word "fan" as a synonym for the words "connoisseur" or "lover"—just as there is the "wine connoisseur" or the "cake lover." So, you might refer to your child as a "*Nutella fan*," your friend as a "red wine fan," or yourself as a "pasta fan"—but without meaning any overly obsessive behavior. People who "like" anyone or anything on social media platforms by clicking a button, essentially expressing only a vague approval or sympathy, are now also referred to as "fans." And sports journalists often refer to "the fans" when they mean only the entirety of stadium visitors. This broadest use of the term characterizes only harmless preferences, without implying any specific behaviors—in contrast to the narrower fan term. So, at first glance, there seem to be countless different understandings of the term "fan". And the further we investigate everyday language use, the more multifaceted and dazzling the term becomes. In the end, it seems to expand almost arbitrarily—and to be nothing more than a synonym for the word "Sympathizers."

Obviously, the everyday understanding of the term doesn't help us when we want to get to the bottom of the "fan" phenomenon. So, let's look at science instead. Interestingly, this reveals a parallel to the everyday understanding of the term: In the social sciences, too, the term "fan" initially had almost exclusively negative connotations. Until the 1980s, being a fan was regarded in sociological literature as a trivial behavior that was not to be taken seriously, and fans tended to be seen as obsessive loners or hysterical crowds. This understanding did not change until sociologists in the Anglo-American-speaking world began to take a serious look at the phenomena and concepts of popular culture in the 1980s in the context of the *cultural studies* (see, for example, the overview in Winter 2017). These research approaches were also taken up in Europe in the 1990s and led to a more positive reception of the fan phenomenon in the international social science literature. Since then, numerous sociological studies on fans and fan behavior have been published internationally (e.g. Bailey 2005; Duffett 2013; Fritzsche 2011, p. 29 ff.; Gray et al. 2007a; Harrington and Bielby 1995; Hills 2002; Jenkins 2007; Roose et al. 2017a). Many of them—following the tradition of cultural studies—deal with the manifestations, motives and behaviors of special *fan communities* in qualitative analyses. Initially, these were mostly distanced scientific observations—in line with the still questionable acceptance of the fan phenomenon. In more recent ethnographic studies, on the other hand, the researchers are often part of the *fan community* themselves (e.g., Benzecry 2011). Accordingly, there is also a proliferation of works whose basic tenor defends fans against stigmatization or disdain (e.g., Maar 2018, p. 24). Regardless, most of these studies persist in describing the behavior of specific fan groups on a case-by-case basis (e.g. Zhang 2022; Fritzsche 2011). Cross-case studies, on the other hand, which abstract in a theory-building manner and work out what fan-typical behavior patterns and motives are evident across the many different concrete fan *communities,* are just as rare as quantitative studies with large representative samples.

Correspondingly, the definition of the term "fan" in scientific literature is heterogeneous, although it is by no means as diverse as in everyday use. There is no basic, undisputed, and generally accepted definition, although there are numerous proposals for different fan typologies in the literature (e.g. Richards et al. 2022; Harrington and Bielby 1995; Jenkins 1992; for an overview for sport fans see Weber et al. 2022). In places, one even gets the impression that a discussion of the definition of the term "fan" is rather avoided. Some studies which try, due to the definition problem, to identify the fan phenomenon empirically, often fall back on self-assessment as a definitional characteristic: A fan is considered to be someone who describes himself as such (e.g. Wann 2002; Wann and Branscombe 1993; Sutton and Knoester 2022). This may seem convincingly simple, but has a serious lack of validity (as we will show in Sect. 1.6.2). Other studies use fan-typical behaviors such as wearing fan jerseys, attending events, or spending large amounts for fan items (e.g., Roose et al. 2017a, b, c) as discriminating criteria. However, it is doubtful whether fans always have to exhibit such behaviors (see the discussion in Osborne and Coombs 2013, see also Vlada 2022). We will therefore in the first step attempt to define the concept of fan and fan relationship without resorting to behaviors as a criterion.

Despite the heterogeneous literature, however, it is possible to identify settings that have received particular attention. These are the definitions by Hills and Duffett. Hills writes: "Everyone knows what a 'fan' is. It's somebody who is obsessed with a particular star, celebrity, film, TV program, band; somebody who can produce reams of information on the object of their fandom, can quote their favorite lines or lyrics, chapter and verse. Fans are highly articulate. Fans interpret media texts in a variety of interesting and perhaps unexpected ways. And fans participate in communal activities—they are not 'socially atomised' or isolated viewers/readers" (Hills 2002, p. IX). Or, as Duffett puts it: "A person with a relatively deep, positive emotional conviction about someone or something famous, usually expressed through recognition of style or creativity" (Duffett 2013, p. 18). If one summarizes the characteristics of the scattered definitions in an overview, one finds, there are central characteristics that recur as integral elements in many definitions. Most definitions emphasize the moment of the passionate and long-term relationship of the fans to their object of fandom (e.g. König 2002, p. 44). The high emotional quality of the relationship, on the one hand, and its resulting long-term nature or even permanence, on the other, are thus consistently regarded in the research literature as the core of every fan relationship. Both phenomena—high emotional quality and permanence—can be combined under the term emotional *bond*. Thus, according to the currently valid scientific understanding, emotional bond is the central and necessary component of nearly every fan definition.

But why are fan relationships emotional relationships? The assertion that this is the case runs—explicitly or implicitly—through the entire research literature. However, it is hardly ever elaborated or substantiated. We want to close this gap in the following and discuss why fan relationships are emotional relationships. And at the same time show that this does not mean that fan relationships are irrational or based only on feelings. To do this, however, we must first take a brief detoured look at psychology—namely at the question of what emotions are and what purpose they serve.

1.2.3 Why Fan Relationships Are Emotional Relationships

In everyday life, we often use the term emotions synonymously with the term feelings. But this equation is scientifically inaccurate: emotions are much more than feelings. Emotions are states such as sadness, joy, fear, or pride that we usually must consciously experience or cope with and that we can often attribute to concrete external causes such as a misfortune or winning the lottery. Emotions, on the other hand, go far beyond these conscious feelings. They are transient, holistic mind-body states of experience that researchers believe consist of at least six different dimensions: A distinction is made between affective, physiological, cognitive, expressive, motivational, and subjective components of emotions (see, among others, Scherer 2005; Myers 2014; Frenzel et al. 2009) (cf. Fig. 1.2).

The *affective component* is formed by the impulsive, yet consciously perceivable emotional states mentioned at the beginning, which we often mistakenly equate with the emotion as a whole. The *physiological component* is all the physical reactions associated with the emotion. A few of these, such as breathing, can be consciously controlled. Most, however, we cannot control, such as our pulse, the arousal of certain brain regions, or the situationally triggered release of hormones and neurotransmitters. They are subject to control by our central nervous system. The *cognitive component,* so to speak, takes care of situational information processing: it interprets the situational stimuli from the environment that trigger emotions, and it

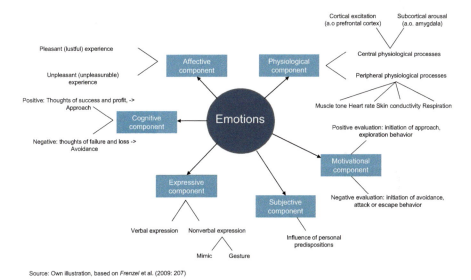

Source: Own illustration, based on *Frenzel* et al. (2009: 207)

Fig. 1.2 The components of emotions—Why are fan relationships emotional relationships?

interprets our own arousal states. We will explain this in more detail in a moment. The *motivational component* performs a matching of the emotional experience with one's own goals: Does the emotion promise reward or gain? Does it fulfill our needs? Such positive stimuli lead to approach or exploration behavior. Negative, threatening stimuli, on the other hand, trigger fear, escape, and avoidance behaviors. We will show later that our motives and needs are central to what emotions we experience. The *expressive component* is the totality of observable behavior that results from emotion experience. This includes conscious, motivation-driven actions such as attention or withdrawal as well as unconscious behaviors (e.g., defense and flight reflexes or gestures and facial expressions). And the *subjective component* ultimately moderates these processes depending on personality: a choleric person, for example, will be much more upset by an insult than a calm contemporary. However, the subjective differences are less significant here than the similarities: Research shows that we humans react surprisingly similarly emotionally to similar environmental stimuli.

In early psychology findings and in our everyday perception, one often finds a simple demarcation between cognitions and emotions: Rational information processing, i.e., perceiving and thinking, is attributed to cognition, while emotional experience, i.e., arousal and sensation, is attributed to emotion—as if these were two completely separate processes. This has long been accompanied by a dispute in psychology: Do cognitions precede and give rise to emotion? Or is the emotion triggered first, which is subsequently processed cognitively? This question was long considered the chicken-and-egg problem of emotion research. From today's perspective, we know that the artificial separation between cognitions and emotions is inaccurate. On the contrary, both processes are closely interwoven: Emotions can be a product of cognitions on the one hand, and on the other hand they can trigger cognitions again. Basically, one can even say: Emotions could not take place at all without the participation of cognitions. And conversely, almost all cognitive processes of our mind are subject to emotional colorations (Myers 2014, p. 498ff.).

The cognitive component has a twofold role in the emotion process: Let's look at the evaluation of a situation by our cognitive system can trigger an emotion. For example, if you observe someone scratching your new car, your cognitive perception and processing system interprets this as an intention to harm by a fellow human being—which for us is always associated with the emotion "anger" and leads to the corresponding reactions. These cognitive situation evaluations, so-called appraisals, are central and, in alignment with subjective motives, control further action in the emotion process (Scherer 2005). However, the cognitive system can not only interpret a situation in the run-up to an emotional arousal and thereby justify emotions, it can also interpret your own physical emotional state after the occurrence of an emotional arousal. In our example this would mean: Your cognitive system perceives that you are excited and interprets this physiological state as "annoyance" about the paint scratch. You could also say: Your feeling is your subjective interpretation of your state of arousal.

This interpretive power is necessary because emotions often occur even before the cognitive system has consciously interpreted a situation. An example that all parents can relate to: Imagine you have picked up your child from kindergarten and are now walking with him or her by the hand along the edge of a busy street. Suddenly and unexpectedly, the child breaks away from your hand and runs into the street. Quick-witted, you intuitively grab hold—and are able to yank your child back at the last moment before they reach the road. Startled and relieved, you press your offspring to you—and only now do you realize how much the situation has shaken you up. Your hands are sweaty, your heart is racing, your pulse is pounding in your temples—you sense that you are afraid. Or to be more precise: You feel an emotional arousal and interpret this in retrospect as fear—because this fits with what you have experienced.

What exactly happened in this example? Your cognitive system has perceived a situation (a child tearing away) and recognized a pattern of danger in the environment (busy road). Although this recognition of action-triggering patterns is a cognitive performance, it still occurs in the process of perception and is therefore completely subconscious. This preconscious pattern recognition alone is sufficient to move the body and mind from a state of relaxation to maximum performance in a fraction of a second. The circulatory system is abruptly ramped up, neurotransmitters and hormones, such as adrenaline, are released, the entire nervous and muscular system goes on alert, and all cognitive resources are immediately focused on the dangerous situation (what we commonly call attention). The alarm readiness is immediately followed by the alarm action: reflexively, an action program is triggered to avert the danger (reaching for the child). It occurs subconsciously—just as you reflexively raise your arm when an object flies toward you. This example illustrates that there are everyday situations in which emotion processes take place even before our conscious mind is involved. And at the same time, it also makes clear why this is so: It ensures our survival, because especially dangerous situations require the shortest possible reaction times to successfully initiate defense programs. And our consciousness is not involved in this for two reasons: First, because it is simply too slow. Or, to put it another way: If there is no time to think about it, thinking about it is the most unwise thing you can do. On the other hand, because emotions are behavioral programs that have evolved evolutionarily long before our cognitive apparatus with its conscious processing procedures. Recent neurological research shows that, at least in more highly developed vertebrates, similar emotional programs run and also take place in comparable brain areas: The spontaneous panic program of a rabbit in a pack hardly differs in its sequence from the panic behavior of humans—at the first sign of fleeing comrades, the program is immediately activated. This drastically increases the chances of survival. The behavior and the panic program behind it are therefore similar, but the subsequent process is different: we humans subsequently think about how and why we behaved and interpret the situation cognitively. The rabbit probably does not have such impulses.

The panic program is not the only emotion program we have. Recent research has distinguished seven such evolutionary action programs, which have been given the plastic labels SEEKING, FEAR, RAGE, LUST, CARE, PANIC, and PLAY (see Panksepp 1998). The SEEKING system tests new stimuli to see if they potentially deliver reward. The FEAR system ensures that threatening situations and dangers are

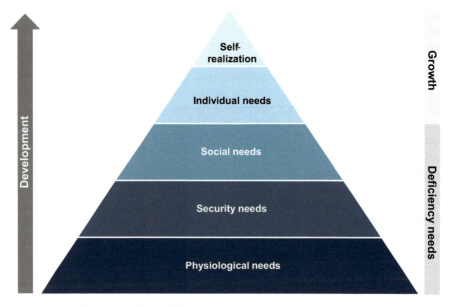

Source: Own illustration, based on *Maslow* (1981)

Fig. 1.3 *Maslow's* pyramid of needs

avoided. The RAGE system is associated with attack behavior, which is particularly evident in competitive behavior. LUST refers to the system that motivates reproduction, while the CARE system performs care functions to strengthen the spread of one's genes via offspring. The PANIC system triggers immediate escape behavior. And the PLAY system allows playful testing of behaviors, especially in social interactions (Müller and Kuchinke 2019, p. 66).

If one reviews these seven different programs, one quickly realizes: All these programs are designed to satisfy basic existential needs as defined in the three lower levels of Maslow's pyramid of needs (cf. Fig. 1.3): Physiological needs (food and prey success through the SEEKING program), safety needs (conflict, protection, and escape programs such as RAGE, CARE, FEAR, and PANIC), and social needs (PLAY and LUST) are assigned to the programs mentioned in each case (Maslow 1981; Myers 2014, p. 440f.). The implementation of the aforementioned emotion programs increases the likelihood that these needs will be met. *Emotion programs thus primarily serve to satisfy core needs*. And conversely, the fulfillment of these core needs puts us in an emotionally positive state, which we perceive as a pleasant feeling.

It now becomes clear how much emotions and needs go hand in hand: We have a basic need, for example, for safety. This means that we desire the absence of danger or threat. If this is not the case and we feel unsafe, our evolutionary FEAR program kicks in: We feel fear—and fear is an extremely uncomfortable feeling that drives us either to flee or avoid or to act with which we try to restore the state of safety. Both serve our self-preservation. If, on the other hand, our basic need for safety is met, we experience a completely different feeling, that of security, and focus our further actions on the next highest need in the pyramid. The need for security as an example makes it clear: Emotions are programs that are basically linked to the fulfillment of needs. If basic needs are met, positive emotions are activated. On the other hand, if important needs are not met, negative emotions are activated, triggering actions to remedy the situation. Emotions are thus an expression of our perceived fulfillment of need.

This connection between emotions and central needs leads us back to our initial considerations: Why is the fan relationship an emotional relationship? The answer is now obvious: because it fulfills central needs of the respective fan. Only in this case, we are no longer talking about the basic existential needs of the pyramid of needs, but rather the needs at the top of the pyramid, which come into play when our existential physiological and our safety needs are met (which is usually the case in affluent societies): These are the needs for social belonging, for individuality, and for self-actualization. In contrast to the existential needs, there are no evolutionarily anchored programs for achieving these goals. It is therefore much more difficult to realize them because there are no patent remedies—which is precisely why many contemporaries fail to do so and become dissatisfied or unhappy.

In the following, we will show that fan relationships fulfill these central needs: They enable self-realization, fulfill the need for individuality and create social belonging. Because of the fulfillment of these core needs, fan relationships are experienced as emotionally fulfilling—and because of this positive experience of need fulfillment, the emotionally controlled behavioral program behind it is reinforced and repeated, so that an attachment to it slowly builds up. For this reason, then, fan relationships are emotional bonds. However, this does not mean that fan relationships are irrational or based only on feelings. Their emotional impact is based on the subjectively perceived unique fulfillment of needs—and these needs can be quite rational.

1.2.4 What We Mean by a Fan

As we already pointed out, in addition to emotional attachment, many fan definitions emphasize their specific behaviors. This may seem plausible, because it is usually precisely the fan-typical, sometimes quite extraverted, exposed, or conspicuous behaviors with which fans are perceived in public. Fans who do not display their fandom outwardly would therefore not be true fans. However, the behavior resulting from the fan relationship can be as diverse as the cult objects of the fan relationship. Criteria such as "investment of time and/or money", therefore, seem to us to be too narrowly guided as a defining component (Roose et al. 2017a, p. 4). For our purposes, it is sufficient to note for the time being that being a fan does not only mean a certain inner attitude towards an object but is also lived out by the respective fan through observable behaviors.

In addition to these two fundamental elements—the emotional bond, as well as the resulting behavior—we believe that a fan definition integrally includes the following four elements: (1) the fan relationship refers in every case to an object external to the fan, whether these are persons, objects, or conceptual objects; (2) this fan object can be different for each individual fan since, as the remarks on emotions have shown, each fan relationship is individually different and in each case central needs are fulfilled; (3) a fan is, as already shown, both a follower and a leader—in other words, he or she is part of the following of a trend that he or she also plays a leading role in shaping; (4) a fan actively distinguishes himself or herself from others who do not share this passion by means of his or her passion.

Based on these considerations, we define the concept of fan as follows:

▶ A fan is a consumer and at the same time a co-creator of a specific cultural good,[3] who experiences the fulfillment of a central need through this and therefore develops a strong emotional bond to this cultural good, which distinguishes them from others and causes them to behave in specific ways.

Thus, fan relationships are characterized by seven fundamental features:

1. The fan experiences the fan relationship as the fulfillment of a central individual need
2. The fan relationship creates social affiliation, individuality, and self-realization.
3. Fan objects are fan-specific: for each fan, only *his or her* individual fan object sufficiently fulfills *his or her* core individual needs.
4. In the relationship with a fan object, a fan is both a passive follower and an active co-creator.
5. The fan has a passionate and long-term relationship (i.e., emotional attachment) to their fan object.
6. The fan distinguishes himself from other consumers through their relationship and actively sets themselves apart from them.
7. Because of this relationship, the fan develops courses of action and behavior that make them identifiable as a fan in the public eye.

This definition not only bundles our understanding of the concept of fans and fan relationships, but also helps us to distinguish them from the diverse everyday meanings outlined earlier. When we speak of fans or fan relationships in the following, we refer to this definition. In essence, it says that fan relationships are emotional relationships because they fulfill central needs for the fan. The fact that fan relationships can fulfill these needs is based on two necessary characteristics that every fan relationship has: Fan relationships are based on identification. And fan

---

[3] In the social sciences, "cultural property" is also understood to mean any man-made product, artifact, or social phenomenon.

relationships are experienced as unique. We will explain this in the following passages.

1.2.5 The Search for Identification as the Basis of Every Fan Relationship

With our definition of a fan, we have now outlined what a fan is and what characteristics make him or her one. However, we have so far left out one pressing, if not the fundamental question: Why do people become fans of anything at all? Why do people get excited about a phenomenon outside of themselves, even outside of their own living environment? Why do they invest resources in a relationship with an actor or object with which they often do not even have direct contact? What needs motivate the subsequent fan to establish such a relationship? And what rewards does he derive from it?

It is obvious that the best way to ask these questions is to ask the fans themselves. This has often been done in research—but interestingly, the answers are not very enlightening. "Because it is fun ...", "because it fascinates me ...", "because the star is so great ...", "because it excites me ..." are the typical responses from those concerned. These answers are bogus explanations because they do not really explain *why being a fan* is fun and what is fascinating or exciting about it. Apparently, and we will return to this phenomenon a little later, many fans are not aware, or it is not linguistically expressible to them, what the central motive of their passion is.

So, if the fans themselves can't provide a convincing reason for their actions, perhaps a look at science will help us again. But this, too, is sobering. Many studies in the field of fan research simply ignore the question "Why does a person become a fan? At least there are some initial theoretical explanations. Roose et al. (2017c, p. 20), for example, discuss whether fan behavior can be explained based upon rational choice theory. This would mean—in short—that the fan makes a conscious, rational, and utility-maximizing decision to be a fan because he or she expects to gain benefits from doing so. The authors show, and this initially supports their assumption, that there are social reward structures of being a fan, e.g., that particularly long-lasting fan relationships provide social recognition in the fan community, or that being a fan increases the chances for repeated positive emotional experiences. However, as the authors themselves admit, this explanatory approach falls short. For it does explain why the fan is repeatedly encouraged to practice his or her fan behavior by these rewards. However, the outlined reward structures are completely unattractive for a non-fan. Therefore, the approach does not explain why a non-fan becomes a fan in the first place—and this was the initial question.

Maar (2018) investigated whether fans exhibit certain psychological personality traits. Even this explanatory approach cannot satisfactorily explain the phenomenon of being a fan—possibly because the underlying premise is dubious: namely, the assumption that only certain people with certain characteristics become fans. At first glance, this assumption may seem accurate because when we think of fans, we often only have certain stereotypes in mind, such as soccer fans. And of course, we do not

Fig. 1.4 "Everybody's got a hungry heart": Why do we become fans?

necessarily imagine the nice elderly lady next door wearing a fan scarf at the stadium. Therefore, we tend to spontaneously assume that only certain people can be fans (cf. Fig. 1.4). In fact, however, the elderly lady may well be a fan of something, e.g., Pilcher novels or the sitcom "Golden Girls" (just to mention clichéd examples—she could of course also ride a *Harley-Davidson* ...). In other words, since one can "become a fan of almost anything" (Roose et al. 2017b, p. 11), by implication anyone can become a fan—because there is a target for every passion, no matter how bizarre. Fans are, therefore, not a specific character type or breed of people (see also Sutton and Knoester 2022; Gemar and Vanzella-Yang 2022). Anyone can be a fan, and it is even possible that everyone is a fan of something without knowing it—which still does not explain *why* one becomes a fan.

In some studies, fantasizing is portrayed as a consequence of the newly emerging phenomenon of leisure time—after all, about 120 years ago, a larger audience emerged for the first time that had time and money resources for cultural performances. This factor certainly favored the emergence of fantasizing, but it is not the only cause. Even then, there were certainly many other ways to spend time and money than investing these resources in a fan relationship.

Thus, the available explanations are unsatisfactory—which prompts us to conduct our own theoretical reflections on why people enter fan relationships. A helpful starting point is the observation mentioned above, according to which the phenomenon of the fan developed only in the twentieth century with the advent of leisure. However, two more serious social changes set in at the same time: First, industrial and postindustrial societies became increasingly affluent. For broad sections of the population, it became increasingly self-evident that basic needs such as hunger, shelter or physical integrity were assured. Accordingly, previously subordinate needs such as social participation, identification, or self-realization (cf. Maslow's pyramid of needs in Sect. 1.2.3) came into focus, especially among the broad middle classes. Parallel to this growing search for identification opportunities, there was a contrary development on the "supply side," as traditionally meaningful objects of identification increasingly disappeared. Above all, it was the churches to which many people first lost their identification and then their emotional attachment. Similar losses of attachment can also be observed regarding state authorities, in the disappearance of family structures and in the loss of homeland. All these objects of reference were gradually lost—and with them identity-forming offerings that were part of the self-image of many people. Thus, at the latest with the onset of postmodernism in Western societies, a triad had emerged that led to an "identification vacuum" and triggered and accelerated the fan phenomenon as we know it today: (1) the need for identification offerings had increased, (2) the existing instances of identification had collapsed, and (3) a broad social stratum had both the time and the money to satisfy its need for identification offerings elsewhere.

For many people, the disappearance of social instances not only led to uncertainty about their own self-concept and identity—it also had social consequences. After all, the need for identity is always also about one's own positioning in the social environment: "In which environment do you place yourself, from whom do you distinguish yourself?" are social questions that go hand in hand with finding one's identity. The loss of identification instances thus triggers not only a search for a new identity, but always also a search for social participation in new social groups. These new social orientations are not without consequences: Social psychologists Tajfel and Turner (1986) show, within the framework of social identity theory, how people and their behaviors change as a result of perceived membership in a social group. Once people believe they have commonalities with certain people that they do not share with others, they build an emotional attachment to that perceived group and begin to rate their membership in that group in a positive manner. They begin to act pro-socially for the group (ingroup bias) while actively distancing themselves from non-group members (outgroup bias, see also Kenny et al. 2015; White et al. 2021). The reason for this is the striving for a more positive social identity. According to George Herbert Mead, the need for cultural identity also leads to similar ingroup effects (internalization of the attitude of one's own group) (Jörissen and Zirfas 2010). A loss of identity-forming offers thus usually leads to social reorientations aimed at gaining new identity anchors.

As a result of the disappearance of instances of identification in the postmodern era, a fundamental human need has remained increasingly unfulfilled: the need to belong and to find one's own self-image, one's own identity through this belonging (Theodorakis et al. 2012). In explaining why fan relationships have such a high emotional quality, we had already worked out that they fulfill the need for social belonging, for individuality and self-realization. If one follows these considerations, the need for identity-forming social affiliation, which is fallow at best in many places today, is the central driver for why fans exist: Because people are in search of precisely fitting values and attitudes—in other words, identity building blocks that they can appropriate and add to their self-image. They need people, statements, objects, or ideas with which they can identify because these stand for their own values and attitudes—and they feel secure when they sense that other people share these values and attitudes with them at the same time. This leads to our central conclusion: The need for identification is the cause of every fan relationship.[4] This derivation is in line with a broad part of the fan literature: many studies elaborate empirically or theoretically on identity formation and identification as the central aspects of fan relationships, e.g. (Amiot et al. 2014; Intezar and Sullivan 2022; Liutikas 2011; Meyer 2014; Newson et al. 2016; Tague et al. 2020; Tarver 2017; Tonetti 2012; Seaton et al. 2022; Wann et al. 2017).

However, such identification can only arise if the fan intuitively feels a maximum alignment, i.e., an optimal fit, between himself and his star. How can this sensation come about, what gives rise to this subjective feeling of fit? For this to happen, there must be a perceived alignment—the recognized defining characteristics of the star must coincide with the fan's central needs and motives. In other words, the star must be outstanding in the eyes of the fan with respect to precisely those criteria that are subjectively of special value to the fan. The needs of the one and the characteristics of the other must correspond with each other. If the image that the fan develops of his star promises this high degree of alignment with his central motives and values, then the star, as the bearer of this image, is a undeniable fan platform (Mikos 2010, p. 116). At its highest level, object, and fan even merge. The star becomes part of one's own identity, one's own personality. It becomes quasi-identity-forming for the fan. It is typical of this maximum form of identification that fans can no longer imagine a world without their star, i.e., without their fan platform (Schäfer 2017; Fritzsche 2011)—recall, for example, the fatal suicide attempts by fans because of the breakup of the boy band *Take That*.

Maximum identification is, therefore, absolutely essential for a fan relationship. It is based on a subjectively perceived match between core needs and motives on the fan side and the perceived strengths of the star on the other side. Becoming a fan is therefore not a conscious, fun-driven hedonistic decision. Rather, being a fan satisfies a deep inner longing—and this longing often leads to a central passion. In a sense, it is about the need for an expanded self—the need to be part of a whole that goes beyond oneself. Noelle-Neumann described this need as man's "social isolation fear" (Noelle-Neumann 1980).

If one accepts the search for objects of identification as an explanation of being a fan, this leads to a significant inverse conclusion that underlines what we mentioned above: Basically, everyone is a fan of something (Gray et al. 2007b, p. 1)—or at least has the potential to be, because everyone is fundamentally looking for social identity: for belonging to an extended self. And there are probably thousands and thousands who are currently walking through the world with their emotional "fan

---

[4]This also makes it intuitively plausible why young people, of all people, often exhibit particularly pronounced fan behavior: they are in the life phase of the search for identity.

synapses" open, waiting with longing to finally dock onto something that is just right for them. Or, to put it more popularly and aptly in the words of *Bruce Springsteen* (1980), *"Everybody's got a hungry heart ... "*.

1.2.6 The Search for Uniqueness as the Basis of Every Fan Relationship

Since identification is the central driver of a fan relationship, the fit between the fan and his or her cult object is crucial (Mikos 2010, p. 115). The projection surface offered by the star or cult object must match the longings of the fan exactly, who is seeking identification objects in its offer of identity-forming content.[5] The more the fan feels such a "fit", the stronger he experiences the identification moment. In other words, the offer must serve the fan's central needs. If this is the case, being a fan is experienced as a reward, because it promises identity formation and social belonging to a community.[6] This moment of identity-creating social affiliation can be seen particularly clearly in the fans of national sports teams: Fans almost exclusively choose the team of their own country as a cult object (cf. Fig. 1.5)—precisely because that is where the cultural and social commonalities are greatest and thus the opportunities for identification are most appropriate (cf. Otte 2017, p. 65f.; Schlicht et al. 2003, p. 140). This seems so self-evident to us in everyday life that it no longer seems worth asking—but, as we will show, it is anything but self-evident.

This perceived fit gives rise to the fan's perceived uniqueness as the second constitutive characteristic of every fan relationship. This is because every genuine fan relationship has an unavoidable exclusivity: within the genre—for example, soccer or pop music—a fan will only choose *one genuine* star (Mikos 2010, p. 117). From the fan's perspective, only *one* fan object ever offers the optimal fit—the fan thus finds *a* unique promise in the person of his or her star. The star occupies an exceptional position in the fan's mind. This uniqueness in turn has an identity-forming effect: being a follower of exactly this star and not of any other star becomes a conscious act for the fan—it becomes part of his personality. And in the long run, the individual image that the fan perceives of his star thus becomes part of his own self-concept (Leistner 2017). The consequence is: You have only *one* soccer club—you can't really be a fan of *Real* and *Barca* at the same time, or of the *San Francisco 49ers* and the *New England Patriots*—or of the *Dallas Mavericks* and the *LA Lakers*. Or you can be a fan of either the *Beatles* or the *Rolling Stones*. Of course, this does not rule out the possibility of finding fans of both the *Beatles* and the *Stones* among *Real fans*—because according to the theory of social identity, it is always

---

[5] Schlicht et al. (2003, p. 140) even speak of the fan building "part of his self-concept from his connection to the star."
[6] Cf. Greenberg et al. (2021).

Fig. 1.5 Identification with the national team: acquired or innate? (Courtesy of © Adobe Stock/ picture alliance (dpa/Revierfoto/Sven Simon | Frank Hoermann) 2022. All Rights Reserved)

only the distinction from the *relevant* outgroup that is interesting; in case of soccer fans the distinction from the other soccer club (Kenny et al. 2015).

Why do several stars of one genre exclude each other? Because they would then contradict the principle of identification, i.e., the optimal fit. The decisive factor for maximum identification with the star, all the way to identity-forming connection, is not only that the star fits the fan's central motives and needs in the best possible way, but also that the star fulfills these needs better than any other star in the eyes of the fan (Mikos 2010, p. 117). In other words, for the fan, the star always occupies an exceptional position—he or she is ascribed a virtual monopoly for the fulfillment of the core fan needs.

In summary, we can say that, in addition to identification, uniqueness is another essential condition of any fan relationship. Because from the fan's point of view, there is no alternative for the fulfillment of his central needs—the star is thus ascribed a claim to sole representation. As a result, the star acquires a "monopoly position in the fan's mind" from the interplay of the two components of *identification* and *uniqueness*.

1.2.7 How the Fan Finds His Star

If everyone fundamentally has the potential for a fan relationship, however, the next question immediately arises: Why do some people become fans of a certain club or star, while other people are completely indifferent to them? What criteria do people use to choose their cult figures?[7] One thing is certain: the selection of the cult object and the establishment of the fan relationship is made by the (later) fan, not by the object offering itself for this purpose. Among numerous possible objects of identification, it is only one of many—a projection surface that offers itself and is chosen.

But even if the "choice" of the star is made by the fan: The decision to enter the fan relationship usually does not appear rational or conscious to the fan himself or to outside observers. Football fans know this. As a habitant of Torino, you love *Juve*, as a Dortmund citizen you love *Borussia*, and as a Madrilenian you might love *Real* (if you are not a fan of Atlético, of course). Why and how this came about is often something the fans themselves no longer know—it simply is the way it is. Most of these "native" fans do not feel they ever consciously chose this fan relationship. It was just there. Being a fan, is not something you can learn. You just are a fan. At first glance, this seems plausible: soccer fans from Madrid are in fact fans of either *Real* or *Atletico*—but, as a rule, of a Madrid club. But does this have to be the case? Let's leave the big cities in Europe with their traditional soccer clubs and go to less densely populated areas. To places where the next first division stadium is more than 100 kilometers away. There, too, we find soccer fans—but mixed: there we find fans of *Real, Barca, Chelsea, Juve, Bayern* or *Milan*. This is not a connection by birth—these fans have obviously chosen their club.[8]

It is a similar story with national identity: Recent studies show that the identification with national teams, which is often taken for granted, is visibly crumbling (Tamir 2014; Tamir et al. 2016; Devlin et al. 2020; Weber et al. 2022) and does not have to be a compelling driver for fanhood, even among soccer fans. There are Danish fans of the *Aarhus GF* soccer club who do not begrudge their great rival in the country, *FC Copenhagen*, a single victory in a European competition. And other fans of *Aarhus GF* who always root for the Copenhageners on the European stage. Both are Danish fans of the same club—but one's fandom is more about regional identification, the other is about national identification. The examples show: In fact, no one is born a fan of anyone or anything. It usually takes an experience to trigger the fan relationship. For example, you might accidentally attend a concert by a musician whose work you had previously considered completely different, and after

---

[7] On the motives of sports fans, see Gabler (2002).
[8] In this context, the choice of the star in a globalized and mediatized world is becoming more and more culture-unspecific, cf. Roose (2017) as well as Ohr (2017).

the evening you are completely enraptured. Or it is a movie in which the main actor suddenly seems to speak to us from the soul. Or one is infected by a passion from one's circle of friends. Numerous interviews with fans reveal two remarkable aspects: First, almost all fan biographies can be traced back to such initial experiences. And second, these triggering events were usually not actively sought out by later fans but experienced passively. A biographical coincidence often provided the initial experience, which then became the basis of a lifelong fan relationship. This does not mean that this trigger event was interchangeable—rather, the special biographical value of the event lies precisely in this rare coincidence of encounter: that a person happens to come across exactly the identification offer that fits his or her needs.[9] Incidentally, this is also true for most soccer fans—they just usually do not know it anymore (Akremi and Hellmann 2017, p. 276f.). Because in their case, such experiences often lie far back in childhood.[10] For example, that they witnessed how the family cheered along in front of the television. Or how their father went to the stadium on Saturdays with a fan scarf.[11] Or experiencing a full stadium for the first time as a child or teenager—that's what happened to us, the authors. Since then, we have lived and suffered with our *Mainz 05* soccer club.

You will not find a fan who at some point decided to become a fan of their star based on conscious planning. Rather, most fan biographies are based on these chance trigger events. The reason for this lies in the fan's perceived uniqueness of the fan relationship: the later fan experiences by chance that an offer of identification by a star serves exactly his search for identity, i.e., exactly his subjective needs. This coincidence is experienced as emotionally overwhelming—almost like a revelation, and results in an immediate devotion on the part of the fan that can then no longer be put into words.

Thus, on the one hand, a fan relationship always has a trigger event. On the other hand, a fan relationship is often a socially mediated relationship (Skrobanek and Jobst 2017). It develops because we become aware of the preferences of reference persons and begin to share these preferences (Tamir 2022). In many fan communities, this social mediation is even fundamental. In some places, it even requires a formal rite of passage by established fans. This is also an initial experience.

As already mentioned, most fans are not able to justify in words why they are fans. Similarly subconscious, as has now become clear here, is the choice of the object of reference, which is often based on a biographical coincidence. If you ask fans what they specifically find "great" about their star and why, you often do not get any conclusive answers either. This is typical of emotional ties. If you were asked

---

[9]This also explains why there are supposedly so few fans, even though anyone can become a fan: Because biographical coincidence is required to come across the corresponding offer.

[10]"Only on father's shoulders, I could see something, and immediately it was done around me ... My new heroes, the eleven in red and white ... Mainz 05, love of my life ... " Piranhas R. (2004)

[11]As Melnick and Wann (2011) show, male socialization agents are frequently the trigger for a fan relationship in sports.

why you love your children, you would shrug your shoulders in irritation. The very question of "Why?" seems downright absurd. You love them because they are your children. Period. No further reason is needed. A real fan feels the same way. He loves his star or his fan object—any further justification would be superfluous. Because you do not become a fan because you are pursuing a rational purpose or want to achieve a certain goal, but because you experience the fulfillment of a central need in it (Stever 2011). Being a fan is an emotional bond (Schäfer 2017).

1.2.8 How the Star Finds His Fan

Let's now look at the other side of the relationship: namely the stars. What do the stars do to create a fan relationship? What are the central mechanisms that stars of art, music, or sports use to achieve the powerful emotional bond that constitutes a fan relationship?

In the media society, stars have also long since learned how they can actively work on shaping their fan relationships. Because shaping them is not solely in the hands of the fan. It is true that the fan "chooses" the star, thus actively opens the emotional relationship with him and fills it with devotion and passion. And yet the stars or the producers of the cult object can play a decisive role in the emergence and maintenance of fanhood. They even must do so (Akremi and Hellmann 2017).

We have shown that a fan relationship can only develop through identification, i.e., when there is a fit intuitively felt by the fan between him and his future star. The star must therefore convey what needs he stands for. And in doing so, he must establish a distinctiveness of his own appearance and thus create the basis for a unique perception of the fan. Only those who offer an identification platform that conveys a clear and unique message will be able to rally a fan community around them in the long run. This means: The star needs a "positioning". On the one hand, the formation of an unmistakable image is of course a necessary basis for this. If you do not make it clear what you stand for, you'll never have a star career. But image alone is not enough for sustained success: on the other hand, the star must also "deliver" accordingly: he must also credibly implement the positioning he communicates to the outside world, otherwise fans will turn away disappointed after a short time because the central promise is not kept. The pop star who is regarded as an eternal bachelor must not marry; the pop singer who gives himself the image of the model son-in-law must not misbehave; the artist, on the other hand, who mimes the enfant terrible must not conform; and anyone who pretends to take great pleasure in smashing musical instruments on stage must actually do so, as we will see in the following. The star is thus, to a certain extent, a Captives of his fan identifications.

This is true even if these fan identifications are based on positionings that the star has deliberately and consciously brought about. The German singer *Helene Fischer*, for example, who is successful far beyond Germany's borders, is one of the world's most commercially successful musicians despite (or perhaps because of) her focus on German-language pop songs. She has professional training as a musical performer and danced in the *Rocky Horror Picture Show*—so she was originally in musical genres far removed from "German Schlager". Her later focus on German-language Schlager was, as she herself revealed in interviews, a conscious decision that she made together with her management, since in this genre—in contrast to pop music, which is almost exclusively sold via the Internet—sound carriers were still much easier to market. This deliberate positioning, which *Fischer embodied professionally* and credibly from the beginning of her career, has brought her high fan numbers. Nevertheless, she is also a captive of this positioning.

Just imagine if *Helene Fischer* were to announce tomorrow that in the future, she would only perform English-language heavy metal songs instead of German Schlager—she would immediately lose most of her long-standing fans, since in their eyes she would be giving up what she stands for: folk German Schlager, which offers emotional security with catchy lyrics and melodies to sing along to. However, despite her numerous performing and musical talents, she would not initially gain any new fans either, since her previous Schlager image would make a positioning as a rebellious heavy-rock lady absolutely implausible for potential heavy fans and would therefore not offer a fit for these fan needs. Or another example: Although there are millions of *ABBA fans* worldwide, the hard and blues rock band *ZZ Top* would probably lose all its old fans and hardly gain any new ones if it were to cover only *ABBA* songs from now on. Conclusion: An image change that touches the core of the fan's identification is always a long and rocky road for a star. And it is not for nothing that some managers sarcastically say that deceased artists are easier to market than living ones—precisely because they would no longer think of changing their positioning without consultation.

The example illustrates how important the positioning of the star is: the fit of the star's offer to the fan's central needs is essential for the fan relationship. This is because the fulfillment of needs generates, as already Sect. 1.2.3 emotional excitement, positive feelings, and ultimately long-term emotional loyalty.

In addition to consistent positioning, the star must make the fan relationship tangible for the fan. Because the fan wants the bonding experience with the star—and he wants it over and over again. It is, therefore, important to create regular, ritually recurring points of contact where the fan can live out his fanhood and where the fan relationship can be emotionally recharged at the same time, because fans want to experience the fit with their central needs again and again. Only those who offer such contact opportunities with a high recognition value on a permanent and regular basis will be able to expand their fan community in the medium term.

The creation of identification and uniqueness could now be left to chance by the star, which was also often the case in the early days of pop music. The *Beatles* themselves, for example, were so surprised by the phenomenon of *Beatlemania that* they did not know how to deal with this hype in the early years. But today, the unorganized Woodstock days of pop music have long since turned into a billion-dollar pop business in which the positioning of stars is no longer left to chance. Instead, these processes are actively initiated, planned on the drawing board, and controlled—right down to the casting shows on television (Daschmann 2007; Schneider 2004). These marketing processes rely above all on a fully comprehensive

1.2 What Is a Fan?

communication strategy. This drives the consistent building of an image that is attuned to the fan community, because it is the image that provides the projection surface that enables the fan to take up the relationship. This image building is often accompanied by a focus. The star communicates not only what he stands for, but also which fans he does *not* want to have. So, it is a mistake to think that the broader a star's positioning, the more fans it collects. It is more important that the positioning of the star clearly communicates which fan target group he serves and which fans he is not interested in at all. Only the demands of a homogeneous fan community can be satisfied in the long run.

The measures on which a sports', film, art, or music star must concentrate if he or she wants to successfully build up a fan community are derived almost inevitably from the catalog of fan and fan relationship characteristics identified above. Enabling identification and being perceived as unique are thus central factors of success for the star. To do this, he must identify the relevant needs of the fans and align himself with them: He must make it perceptible that he precisely serves these needs. In addition, he must create a distinctive image for his own appearance—in other words, he must convey the impression that he fulfills these needs like no other. This is the only way to avoid interchangeability and create perceptible uniqueness.

Even if it is hard to believe from today's perspective, successful stars made use of such concepts decades ago—sometimes unconsciously and without knowing this theoretical background, but sometimes quite purposefully. The pop group *The Who* from England is a good example of this. Founded in 1964, it seemed impossible for the quartet to conquer the British charts against the triumphant success of the *Beatles* and the *Rolling Stones*—and also under pressure from the *Kinks*, who were entering the market at the same time. So, a strategy was needed that enabled identification and promised uniqueness.

Kit Lambert, the manager of *The Who* at the time, knew that there was a lot of tension among young people in England in the early 1960s: poor job prospects, authoritarian parental homes and encrusted social structures caused many young people to despair. Rebelliousness was therefore in high demand. Drawing attention to themselves with outrageous things and rebelling—that was the central need of many young people (Schmidt-Joos and Kampmann 2008). For this reason, the *Stones* had already had a *bad-boy image created for them* on the drawing board— also to distinguish themselves from the *Beatles,* who were considered to be more well-behaved. *Lambert* suspected that he would have to go one step further here: He instructed drummer *Keith Moon* and guitarist *Pete Townshend* to destroy their instruments with brute force at the end of every performance, especially on television (cf. Fig. 1.6) (Winkler 2010).[12] *Lambert* sensed the central desire of young fans

---

[12] In an interview with the *Süddeutsche Zeitung,* singer *Roger Daltrey* explains how it came about in the first place that the destruction of instruments became a trademark of *The Who*: "The people in the club where we were performing suddenly began to stomp as if hypnotized. It made Pete Townshend a little nervous. He was banging the neck of his guitar against the amplifier. Our manager Kit Lambert was pleased. From then on, Pete had to do it all the time for now." (Winkler 2010, p. 2).

Fig. 1.6 Staged repetition: *The Who* in destroy mode (Courtesy of © Getty Images/ Chris Morphet 2022. All Rights Reserved)

to see something so unheard of and unprecedented—and thus intuitively implemented nothing other than what constitutes fan relationships: he aligned the positioning of *The Who with* the central needs of potential fans.

The *BBC* recording of *Townsend* ramming an electric guitar neck-first into a speaker box is still legendary today.[13] And *The Who* were on everyone's lips in one fell swoop. They had highlighted their unique image as rebels. Instinctively, manager *Lambert* coupled this new positioning with a clear target group focus: He gave *The Who* musician the image of a mod band, a youthful subculture movement of the 1960s that was constantly at loggerheads with the simultaneously emerging rocker movement (Winkler 2010).[14] The message was clear: if you're Mod, you listen to *The Who*—rockers listen to something else. A few days later, the blond bass player of the band, *John Entwhistle,* had to dye his hair black on the instructions of the manager (Geisselhart 2008, p. 123 ff.). Only singer *Roger Daltrey* was to appear as a blond so that the fans would know who the band's identification figure was. *Lambert* had obviously intuitively understood the importance of identification and uniqueness for fan relationships. Success proved him right. *The Who* became—despite competition from the *Beatles, Stones* and *Kinks*—one of the most influential and successful rock bands of all time. And *Entwhistle* wore black hair until his death.

Fan relationships are thus based on identification and uniqueness, but they have other characteristics that result from the first two: They are enduring, they are highly resilient, and they lead to specific communicative fan behavior. We will discuss these aspects of fan relationships in more detail in the following chapters.

---

[13] Initially, this approach was anything but profitable: the cost of smashed instruments and amplifiers far exceeded the band's fees, cf. Winkler (2010, p. 2).

[14] From the Süddeutsche Zeitung interview: "But you were a mod!" Daltrey: "No, I played the mod". (Quoted from Winkler 2010, p. 3).

1.2.9 Characteristics of the Fan Relationship: Permanence and Repetitiveness

If a fan relationship is truly deep, the fan is almost at its mercy. This is because a fan relationship is not terminated—one is virtually trapped in it. Just imagine the following situation: A soccer club has been relegated to the second division. Will its fans now make a pilgrimage to the stadium of their local rival to watch first-division soccer? Of course not. This thought seems absurd to any soccer fan—you do not change clubs; you couldn't force yourself to do that. For the fan, the connection to the club is virtually a community of fate—after all, eternal loyalty is precisely the special trademark of this connection (Roose and Schäfer 2017). The fan cannot drop out—and he doesn't want to. After all, fan relationships are long-lasting, if not lifelong. They are entered into as naively and optimistically as we enter other emotional bonds in our lives: They are built to last. At least at the moment the relationship is established, the fan is sure he never wants to give up that bond. He does the same thing we all do when we make a commitment—whether it is the vow of fidelity among friends or at the altar: the fan doesn't commit for a time, but for his entire life. And for some fans, the emotional bond even extends beyond death—as specially established fan cemeteries around the world vividly demonstrate (cf. Fig. 1.7).

FC Barcelona fan mausoleum under Camp Nou (Spain)

Burial in the fan cemetery of Boca Juniors (Argentina)

Feyenoord football club cemetery (Netherlands)

Schalke 04 fan cemetery (Germany)

Fig. 1.7 Emotional loyalty beyond death: Fan cemeteries around the world (Courtesy of Source: FC Barcelona: picture alliance/REUTERS | JUAN MEDINA, Boca Juniors: picture-alliance/ dpa | DB Mareike Aden, Ajax Amsterdam: offen https://www.pc.nl/ajax/, Schalke 04: picture alliance/ Bernd Thissen 2022. All Rights Reserved)

At first glance, this seems to be contradicted by the fact that among young fans in particular, fan relationships are intense but short-lived. On the one hand, young people show particularly conspicuous adoration and devoted rapture for a star. This may hardly be surprising, because in the meaning-seeking phase of life in adolescence, identification with the stars promises support and orientation. On the other hand, some of these fan relationships are obviously only a brief adolescent phenomenon (Fritzsche 2017): The passion for *Nena, Tamagotchis, Britney Spears,* or similar "teen swarms" seems to be a stable and lasting fan relationship among 14-year-olds, which the same fans then suddenly do not want to know anything about a few years later (Fritzsche 2011, p. 56ff.). However, this is not a contradiction to the established permanence of fan relationships. Because in reality, these young fans do not become disloyal, at least they do not feel that way. What actually changes here—and this is the difference to fan relationships in adulthood—is rather the basis of the fan relationship, namely the central needs of the young fans, which inevitably change with personal maturity. Owing to age, the longing for other identity-forming content now increases, as does the need to no longer align oneself with one's original reference group with the choice of one's stars, but to set oneself apart from it. The previous stars are not cast out because of this, but they can no longer fulfill the central promise of a fan relationship, namely, to be a perfect match for the fan's longings.[15]

If we look at it closely, the dissolution of this promise is the only reason why a fan relationship can break down at all. As with any lasting bond, the fan relationship is also based on trust. On trust in the integrity of the star. This integrity does not mean moral integrity, but rather trust that the star will continue to keep the identity-creating promise in the long term. In other words, that the star will remain true to himself, that he will not betray the shared values. A regularly repeated example of such a betrayal is the switch of a professional soccer player adored by the fans to another club—if not to the arch-rival. For example, *Christiano Ronaldo*'s move from Madrid to Turin a few years ago, which surprised his die-hard fans just as much as Lionel Messi's transfer from Barcelona to Paris a little later.[16] For the fans of these soccer personalities, these contract changes may still have been acceptable. For the fans of the clubs they left, on the other hand, it is regularly regarded simply as a betrayal of the values that are regarded as forming their identity. The star must, therefore, under no circumstances, disappoint the expectations placed on him. And when multimillion-dollar soccer clubs try to change the way the entire sport is played without taking the fans with them, it ends in disaster—as the disputes over the introduction of the Super League in the spring of 2021 have shown (cf. Fig. 1.8).

---

[15] For a detailed discussion of fandom over lifetime see Lee Harrington and Bielby (2010), Tamir (2022).

[16] The fact that Ronaldo moved on from Turin to Manchester after a few years, on the other hand, did not smell of betrayal to Turin fans: Ronaldo had come as a Mercenary, and that's how he left the club.

1.2 What Is a Fan?

Fig. 1.8 Our passion must be earned—British fans protest against the introduction of the Super League (Courtesy of © Getty Images (Chloe Knott—Danehouse) 2022. All Rights Reserved)

Fig. 1.9 The Star as prisoner: doomed to repeat (Courtesy of © Spock: picture alliance/Michael_Stephens/epa/dpa, Udo Jürgens: Volker Dornberger, Helene Fischer: Getty Images/Isa Foltin 2022. All Rights Reserved)

If the star wants to keep his fan community together, he must create events, which can be repeated, even ritualistic, that serve the needs of the fans. The star is thus doomed to make the identification experience possible, with which he once won fans, over and over again. For example, the actor *Leonard Nimoy* was never able to escape the role of *Mr. Spock in* his further professional life—until he finally accepted it as his life's work (Nimoy 1977, 1995). (cf. Fig. 1.9). And the German-speaking singer *Udo Jürgens* was condemned for almost 50 years to appear on stage at his concerts for the last encore in a bathrobe—after having done so once in the 1960s. In this respect, stars can even become captives of their fans.

The fan is not looking for variety. Fans do not want surprises. Rather, they expect the ritualized repetition of the initial experience that once made them a fan (Dixon 2013; Mikos 2010, p. 116 f.). Anyone who has ever been to a football stadium (e.g. of the Pittsburgh Steelers, see Cottingham 2012) or a soccer stadium, for example, has an idea of how ritualized fan events can be: From the chants before the game to the collective recitation of the team lineups and the goals scored to the subsequent victory celebration with the so-called "Humba" (a fan ritual that conquered soccer stadiums around the world from Mainz): The entire process is not only completely choreographed—it almost resembles a ceremony. And that does not just apply to sports: pop stars can sing a song about this longing of fans for repetition—in the literal sense of the word. After all, fans demand the big hits, the crystallization points of their identification, over and over again at every encounter. A rock musician who exclusively presents songs from his new album at his concerts without playing the old big hits will disappoint his fans (Fritzsche 2011, p. 259ff.). The Canadian songwriter *Neil Young* once confessed to *Rolling Stone Magazine* about his biggest hit "Heart of Gold" that he hated this song because he had not been able to leave the stage for decades without playing it. *Young* is not an isolated case. Whether it is *Oasis* with "Wonderwall," *Madonna* with "Like a Virgin," *Frank Sinatra* and "Stranger in the Night," *Led Zeppelin's* "Stairway to Heaven," *R.E.M. with* "Shiny Happy People," *James Blunt with* "You're Beautiful" or *Simple Minds* with "Don't You Forget About Me," all of these performers hate their successful global hits because they have to perform them over and over again.

But this ritual repetition is precisely what the fan demands. He wants to relive, conserve, and hold on to the core of his fanhood. When their star releases a new album, some fans avoid any advance information about the upcoming product just to preserve the opportunity to hear the new album unaffected—and to recapture the experience of hearing their favorite artist for the first time (Bennett 2012). He doesn't want *"variety-seeking"*, he wants *"more of the same"*. How else can it be explained that the Kino *Museum Lichtspiele* in Munich has had the *"Rocky Horror Picture Show"* on its weekly program for more than 45 years (which earned it an entry in the Guinness Book of Records) and yet—or precisely because of this—cannot complain about a lack of viewers? The sworn fans, who have all seen the film dozens of times, enjoy the ritual: they come in disguise, sing along loudly and throw rice during the wedding scene. And the evening is only enjoyable if it was the same as always. Fans want to stop the clock—they want to make the irretrievable repeatable, they want events with recognition value. And the more often the star offers opportunities and points of contact to make this felt core of being a fan tangible, the stronger the fans' bond will be.

Our example of the rock band *The Who*, which drew attention to itself by smashing its instruments, impressively illustrates this compulsion to repeat. For all the success of his band's positioning, *The Who manager Lambert* had to recognize: *The Who* never got rid of the ghosts he had called. From now on, the fans demanded the legendary final orgy of destruction on stage at every concert—indeed, a large part of the fans came to the concerts at all only because of this.[17] But the musicians did not want to be bound by this behavior. Because every good instrument is a unique piece—and every guitarist knows: Once you have found the perfect guitar, you do not want to lose it again under any circumstances. *Townshend* felt the same way,

---

[17] *Roger Daltrey*: "They did not come for the music then, but because they wanted to watch Pete sacrifice the guitar," quoted from Winkler (2010, p 2).

hardly feeling like smashing such cherished instruments on stage (Winkler 2010).[18] On the other hand, *Lambert* also knew that the demands of the fans had to be met if *The Who* wanted to remain true to their image as a rebel band and be successful in the long run. *Lambert* solved the problem elegantly: He instructed the stagehands to quickly slip *Townshend* a cheap, second-rate guitar during the last song (Stein 1979), which he could then smash as rebelliously as before—to the thunderous enthusiasm of the fans.

Stars are thus not only stars—their successful positioning also makes them captives of their fans, because they must confirm their positioning over and over again. The fans' demand for repetition of the fan experience forces them to "deliver" again and again—that is, to be what corresponds to the image of the star in the fan's mind at every point of contact with the fan. And only those stars who repeatedly fulfill this call for repetition do fans swear eternal loyalty—because only they do not betray shared values. Repeatability is therefore the central mechanism with which stars bind their fans—and the instrument with which they hold their fan community together. The important thing is that this mechanism only works if the fan experience, the repeatability of which is supposed to be offered, is also offered authentically and credibly. So, to take up the example of *The Who* once again, it is not enough just to have the *image of* a "guitar smasher"—you have to smash guitars on a regular basis if you want to keep fans interested. *The Who manager Lambert* knew that.

1.2.10 Characteristics of the Fan Relationship: Resilience and Willingness to Consume

Since a fan relationship is based on emotional bonding, it can be shaken by very little. And certainly not by dissatisfaction. The example of soccer fans who would never change clubs despite a lack of success illustrates this: For the affective bond of the fan, the "performance" of his cult figure or his stars is essentially secondary. It may be that this initially plays a role for the emerging passion in the early days of the relationship. But once the fan relationship is established, it is irrelevant to the bond whether the star's performance maintains his or her performance level over the long term (Göttlich and Krischke-Ramaswamy 2003, p. 169). Even if the beloved rock star hasn't had a top ten hit in decades, the soccer club is relegated to the third league, or the favorite writer is trying the same plot for the third time in her new book: the fan remains a fan even if the star falls short of expectations. And he has no sympathy for those who turn away from the star because of weaker performances. Spectators, for example, who only show up at the stadium when the team is playing an excellent season, i.e., when the performance is right, are even a thorn in the side of the self-proclaimed "real" fan as fair-weather fans.

---

[18] *Roger Daltrey*: "At some point, however, it became not merely expensive but also troublesome," quoted from Winkler (2010, p. 2).

Another example: An American literary critic once claimed that *Stephen King* could publish his laundry list—his fans would still buy the book. Apart from the fact that this mockery hardly does justice to *King's* work, which is often underestimated in literary terms, it hits the nail on the head as far as the fan relationship is concerned: It is not the recurring delivery of top performance with which the star binds his fans. It is the constantly repeatable possibility of identification. This makes the fan willing to forgive many things and remain a fan even under adverse conditions. Unless, of course, the star's identity is based on top performance. In that case, top performance throughout is necessary to fulfill fan needs. In this context, we recall, for example, of the fans of *Real Madrid* or *Bayern Munich*, for whom even a runner-up championship shakes the foundations of their fan relationship.

In general, the fan is extremely willing and able to suffer[19]: He is prepared to travel long distances to meet his star; he pays overpriced prices for concert tickets or merchandising articles without complaint; he invests time, energy and money in the work of the fan community, or he stands in the stadium in all weathers (Schlicht et al. 2003, p. 141). For the "real" fan, this commitment is a matter of course. Spectators who only visit the stadium when the sun is shining are regarded disdainfully as "fair-weather fans". Even if they support his club, he has no sympathy for them. For in his eyes, they lack the willingness to give their all for this fan relationship (Hornby 1992).

To avoid misunderstandings here: The fact that the fan's emotional tie is not primarily based on performance does not mean that the fan is indifferent to performance. The fan is critical of his star, especially when it comes to his performance.[20] He has above-average demands and expectations of his cult figures. And if the performance fails to materialize, he is just as dissatisfied as other fans and demands this performance (Fitzpatrick and Paddy 2022; Gillooly et al. 2022; Sorek 2022). He desperately communicates with other fans about it, he pleadingly turns to his star via Facebook, or he holds up banners in the corner. When the soccer season is going badly for the club, diehard fans sometimes gather in front of the clubhouse and chant, "We're fed up!" (König 2002, p. 51ff.). And if things get even worse and the season ends in a sporting disaster, fan affection can even turn into aggression (cf. Fig. 1.10; see also Shadmanfaat et al. 2022).

There is no doubt about it: fans are extremely critical and can be uncomfortable, and they can certainly be dissatisfied (Schmidt-Lux 2017). Yet this dissatisfaction, which results from a lack of performance, does not determine their emotional attachment. The critical and demanding attitude of the fan does not detract from his affective adoration—as long as the star does not abandon the core promise that connects them to the fan: to be the "one" with which the fan can identify. So, fans

---

[19] This willingness to suffer even includes health risks, cf. Kohlmann and Eschenbeck (2009, pp. 635–680).
[20] On fear of failure due to spectator influence, see Alfermann (2000, pp. 65–109) and Alfermann and Würth (2008, pp. 719–778); on athlete motivation due to fans, see Daschmann (2014, pp. 46–62).

1.2 What Is a Fan?

Fig. 1.10 Fans endure suffering: protesting football fans in Liverpool (picture alliance/Propagandaphoto/EXPA/picturedesk.com 2022 All Rights Reserved)

remain fans for the time being—even if the expected performance fails to materialize (Seaton et al. 2022; Rullo et al. 2017). Only when their trust is disappointed over and over again in the long term do they perceive their fanhood as a burden and begin to turn away.

Thanks to this devotion, the fan is a first-class consumer (Akremi and Hellmann 2017). He consumes not only the object of his cult, but also numerous other paraphernalia with which he expresses his fanhood and demonstrates his affiliation with the fan. He has a high propensity to buy all offers related to his fan object (Mikos 2010, p. 109; Navarro-Picado et al. 2022). With the increasing importance of the entertainment industry since World War II, this marketing potential of fan cultures has also been recognized. In the meantime, the latter is not only served by merchandising and other cult-related marketing activities, it is virtually ignited and provides for sounding coin on the part of the clubs and the stars. The most famous example of this is probably the shirt of Portuguese soccer star *Christiano Ronaldo*. After *Real Madrid* lured the star away from *Manchester United*, his jersey was sold over 1.2 million times in *Real fan stores*. The 94 million euros in transfer fees for "*CR7*," as fans call him, that Madrid had once paid to Manchester were thus completely refinanced (Mikos 2010, p. 110). And when the news broke a few years ago that *Ronaldo* had moved to *Juventus Turin* for the transfer fee of 105 million (cf. Fig. 1.11), the Italian club sold 520,000 *Ronaldo jerseys* in the first 24 hours alone (20min.ch 2018). Ronaldo's move back to Manchester in the summer of 2021 then broke all records: within one week, ManU sold *Ronaldo* jerseys worth 220-million euros (Bild 2021).

No doubt about it: the increase in "fan" atics that can be observed in all genres cannot be explained solely by the growing search for objects of identification in post-industrial society; it is significantly reinforced by the active business of meeting the needs of fans—and is additionally driven by corresponding marketing interests.

Fig. 1.11 Fans are ready to buy: bestseller *Ronaldo* jersey (Courtesy of © Getty Images/Isabella Bonotto, AFP 2022. All Rights Reserved)

1.2.11 Characteristics of the Fan Relationship: Communication and Community

The fan is not a loner, but part of a true fan culture (Göttlich and Krischke-Ramaswamy 2003, p. 169). He lives in a virtual or actual fan community, which can be understood as a cultural community of taste with shared interpretations and practices. The totality of this fan community and its activities is usually referred to as "fandom" in the literature. It is defined by a shared cultural and social practice. It is based on shared aesthetic, sensory, or affective experiences, shared practices of action, and shared interpretations of the world. The cult and its practices are created by the fans themselves. They are common lifestyle groups that expressively live out their cult action. Fans meet at their own *conventions* and enjoy the bonding of ritual behavior in the group (cf. Fig. 1.12). The commonalities required for this do not have to be negotiated communicatively: They are part of fan culture—and precisely because they are latent and implicit, they create community (Fritzsche 2011, p. 38 ff).

This communal experience is presumably the real social and emotional reward of being a fan: with their commitment to the fan object and the fan community that goes with it, fans create a positive escape and experience space in the middle of their often-sobering everyday lives (Schlicht et al. 2003, p. 141). Through the group process of being a fan, he gains a piece of individually felt identity. He creates a social home and protected spaces of experience (Jasny and Lenartowicz 2022). If we look at the phenomenon from this perspective, it becomes clear that fantasizing is by no means pathological but serves understandable social and emotional needs for identity and security (Mikos 2010, p. 113). It also becomes clear why the fan phenomenon and the fan communities became so popular at the same time as the classic meaning-giving authorities such as the church, the state and the family disappeared.

The increased ingroup feeling of the fan community is accompanied by an outward demarcation. It is about the pleasure of being different and standing out. Fan behavior, which appears to the uninvolved observer from the outside as

1.2 What Is a Fan?

Fig. 1.12 Fans as community: *Star Trek* costume record in Las Vegas (Courtesy of © Getty Images/David Livingston 2022. All Rights Reserved)

conformity and mass behavior, is experienced by the fan himself as a process of identity formation and thus individualization. Through this, the relationship with his star acquires a uniqueness. For him, being a fan thus also always means wanting to be different, to stand out, and to escape normality—and not having to do this in isolation, but in a group of supposedly like-minded people (Gebhardt 2017; Kalman-Lamb 2021). The distinction between one's own peer group, i.e. the fans with whom one shares one's passion, and the "rest" of society is imperative for him.

In sociodemographic terms, therefore, there is essentially no such thing as a "typical" fan of a particular star or cult object. Although fans share a common star, they are not usually a homogeneous sociological group. Although there are fan communities, especially among young people, that are socio-demographically very homogeneous in terms of age, gender or social background, other fan communities, e.g., of sports clubs or movie stars, show that fan communities are usually sociodemographically heterogeneous (Otte 2017).

The fan is invaluable as a communicator and multiplier. He is a constant ambassador for his cult object. Not only does he make his adoration public through insignia that he consciously displays—such as a logo, a T-shirt or even a tattoo. Then there is his *word-of-mouth marketing*, through which he repeatedly brings up the star and his cult in personal conversations in his environment. The importance of this *word-of-mouth* and the fan's ambassadorial role has been significantly enhanced by the advent of social networks (Woods and Lee Ludvigsen 2022). This is because fans need platforms to live out their fanhood—and online platforms enable this in an unprecedented way (Winter 2017). Fans are no longer locally or regionally bound thanks to new communication technologies (Kang et al. 2022). The fan community can now come together virtually in forums, blogs or on Facebook pages—the community can be experienced by the individual daily despite considerable spatial distances, is more capable of acting in its formation of wills and is more perceptible to the outside world. What's more, fans can now get more involved in the public debate about their star or cult object in a variety of ways.

This also applies to communication with the stars or the producers of the cult objects themselves. Because fans are not only recipients, they are also active producers of cultural products. Fans continue to write the books and storylines of their cult authors, they produce their own music videos of their favorite titles, they compose their own fan chants for the fan base, devise stadium choreographies for the moment when the teams enter the stadium or design their own clothing to match their beloved fantasy novel. *Lord of the Rings fans,* for example, not only memorize the fantasy languages that *J.R.R. Tolkien* once created in his trilogy, they even add new vocabulary to them. The fans appropriate the subject matter of their cult and push it further. They are thus active contributors to the star's fantasies, as well as impetus and innovators for his performance.

1.2.12 Summary: What Is a Fan?

We have determined—based on fan research in social sciences—what is meant by a "fan": A fan is a consumer and at the same time a co-creator of a specific cultural good, who distinguishes themselves from other consumers by a strong emotional bond towards this cultural good and consequently develops specific behaviors. We have shown that the search for identification and the need for social connection are the fundamental motives that provide the subconscious impulse to enter a fan relationship, and that it is characteristic of this relationship that it is experienced by the fan as exclusive and unique. The fan relationship endowed with this quality of identification and uniqueness shows numerous subsequent characteristics, which we also elaborated on. You will find all these characteristics listed again below and grouped in a meaningful way in terms of content. We refer to the resulting bundle of characteristics as dimensions of the fan relationship. However, there is a clear hierarchy between these dimensions: while identification and uniqueness are the causal drivers, without which no fan relationship can come into being, the three other dimensions are consequential characteristics, which are also found in every fan relationship, but are not causal for the emergence of the relationship. This catalog of the essential characteristics of fan relationships as well as the identification of the hierarchical relationships between these various characteristics constitute the central discovery content of the *Fan Principle*: It describes which fundamental principles genuine fan relationships follow.

Dimensions and Characteristics of Fan Relationships
Identification and uniqueness as the basis of every fan relationship

1. *Identification as a fundamental motive of every fan relationship*
   - The fan relationship serves needs for identity formation and social belonging.
   - The fan relationship is based on identification: the star embodies the fan's core values.
   - The fan chooses the star based on their individually perceived fit.
   - The fan relationship thus creates maximum affective and emotional bonding.
   - The fan has concrete expectations and demands on the performance of their star.
   - The fan can be emotionally loyal yet dissatisfied.
2. *Uniqueness as a necessary element of any fan relationship*
   - The fan relationship is exclusive. In the eyes of the fan, it is a unique selling point.
   - The fan relationship gives the fan a sense of individuality.
   - The fan distinguishes themselves from other "non-fans" through their fandom.

Characteristics of the fan relationship resulting from identification and uniqueness

3. *Permanence of the fan relationship and the repeatability of the identification experience*
   - The fan relationship is created through initial events.
   - The fan relationship is designed to last.
   - The fan needs frequent opportunities for contact that make being a fan a tangible experience.
   - The fan needs repeating experiences that enable enduring identification.
   - The fan needs events with recognition value: they are looking for "more of the same".
   - The fan perceives any change in the identity-forming characteristics as a threat. It can lead to the termination of the fan relationship.
4. *The fan as ambassador and as member of the fan community*
   - The fan relationship is a socially mediated relationship.
   - The fan is an active ambassador of the star.
   - The fan is a multiplier through *word-of-mouth.*
   - The fan moves in a fan community.

(continued)

- The fan actively communicates in their community.
- The fan needs a platform to live out their fanhood.
5. *The resilience of the fan relationship and the fan's willingness to consume*
   - The fan relationship is characterized by a high level of trust in the integrity of the star.
   - The fan is ready to live out their fanhood even under adverse conditions.
   - The fan forgives a lot and has a high capacity for suffering.
   - The fan is an active contributor to the fandom of his or her star.
   - The fan is an impetus and innovator for the star's performance.
   - The fan is willing to pay a high price for their fan experience.

1.3 From *Fan Principle* to *FANOMICS*: What Is a Fan Customer?

Now that the details of the term "fan" and the typical characteristics of them have been uncovered, we are faced with the crucial question: Can these insights of the *Fan Principle* regarding fans and fan relationships be profitably transferred to customers and customer relationships? Is there anything we can learn from the characteristics of fans that will enable us to retain customers over the longer term and align companies accordingly? Is there even such a thing as "Fan Customers"—i.e., customers whose customer relationship with their provider resembles a fan relationship? This fundamental finding is the prerequisite for the second step of our approach: the transfer of the findings of the *Fan Principle* to economic contexts and customer relationships, and the development of a comprehensive management concept for companies based upon this—which we call *FANOMICS*. We will address the outlined questions in the following.

1.3.1 Fans also Exist in Customer Relationships

Yes, they do exist, the Fan Customers! Granted: The example of motorcycle fans who have the *Harley Davidson* logo tattooed on them (cf. Fig. 1.13) is now old hat in marketing literature. And not every company has such an emotional product to offer as a cult motorcycle. But still, the Harley *example* is spot on at this point, because it vividly illustrates what a fan customer is, and what happens when customers become fans.

Harley-Davidson has such customers, whose relationship with the brand literally gets under their skin. And *Harley* knows the worth of these customers. For decades, the US manufacturer has known how to position its brand accordingly: "Our

1.3 From *Fan Principle* to *FANOMICS*: What Is a Fan Customer?

Fig. 1.13 The fan tattoo: a customer relationship that gets under the skin (Courtesy of © Getty Images/Chicago Tribune 2022. All Rights Reserved)

motorcycles are more of a worldview than a means of transportation,", [21] and they use this brand positioning in every public appearance. The message behind this is clear: if you buy a *Harley,* you buy a philosophy—and you get the motorcycle for free.

What's special about this positioning is that product features hardly play a role. When *Harley-Davidson* advertises its machines, it is not about engine performance, suspension, or frame quality. It's about emotion, about the promise of an experience. And as a result of this positioning, the actual product features fade into the background. It is not the technical quality of the motorcycle that is the issue for the *Harley rider,* but the emotionally charged cult bike.

Obviously, many customers thus have a very special relationship with the *Harley-Davidson* brand. The word satisfaction is hardly sufficient to characterize this relationship. Indeed, these customers are emotionally loyal. So much so, in fact, that they even have the company logo tattooed on them and proudly display it as brand ambassadors. They identify with this motorcycle brand—and for them, no other bike comes into question. Identification and uniqueness—in many *Harley-*

---

[21] *Bernhard Gneithing*, former Marketing Director of *Harley-Davidson* Germany (quoted from Ilg 2009).

Davidson customer relationships, precisely these two central characteristics of fan relationships, are fulfilled. In other words, many *Harley customers* are "fans."

Now you may want to object that such devotion on the part of a customer, right down to the tattoo, is only conceivable with highly emotional products, such as motorcycles. In fact, this is not the case. A few years ago, for example, a young man who won 16,000 euros on the German edition of "Who wants to be a millionaire?" then announced that he would use his winnings to get the logo of his favorite beer brand engraved was the talk of the town. When the moderator asked him why, he replied that it was a cult beer. The internet is full of pictures of tattoos of the brand logos of, for example, Mercedes, Apple, McDonalds or even WalMart. These examples not only indicate that the phenomenon of the fan customer can exist in very different sectors and industries. At the same time, they convey an initial idea that Fan Customers, i.e., customers with a high level of emotional attachment, are invaluable to any company. After all, these are customers who come back again and again, who buy again and again, and who recommend. Having such customers is a longing that drives many corporate decision-makers. After all, stable customer relationships, increasing sales per customer and active recommendations are growth drivers.

To understand what this means in concrete terms, close your eyes for a moment and imagine the following, if a customer, who comes to your business premises or who you visit for a sales meeting, would have your company logo tattooed on them, you would know immediately: This deal is yours for sure. This customer obviously swears by your company and your brand. For the needs he has at this specific moment, he knows of no better provider than you. He will pay your price, he will definitely not buy from the competition, he will recommend you to others and—most importantly—he will come back. The relationship with you gets under his skin—in his mind, you have a monopoly on his needs. And he carries this conviction as an ambassador with his tattoo proudly to the outside and recommends you in an active manner.

A dreamlike idea, no doubt. You think it is unrealistic? You think it is an absurd idea and such customers can't exist for your company? If you think so, you are mistaken. There are such customers. And the example of *Harley Davidson* makes it clear that there are companies that have understood how to maintain such a deep relationship with their customers for decades.

Yet most companies think it is impossible to build such fan relationships with their customers. They are under the misapprehension that such an emotional tie between customers is only possible with emotionally charged products such as motorcycles. Contrary to this assumption, we will show in this book that it is possible for companies in any industry, whether B2B or B2C,[22] to build customer

---

[22] B2B ("business-to-business") refers to a business relationship between companies. Both the supplier and the customer are companies. B2C ("business-to-consumer"), on the other hand, refers to the classic customer relationship between a provider company and a private consumer.

relationships of this emotional quality. Customer relationships that get "under the skin".

Yet although it would be possible for companies to have many such high-quality customer relationships—they do not have them, or they are far from exploiting their potential for them. Why do most companies have so few Fan Customers? Because they are backing the wrong horse in customer relationship management—namely, not emotional attachment, but customer satisfaction. And, as we will see, that is a serious mistake.

1.3.2 Beware of Satisfied Customers

At first glance, the headline may seem irritating: Why should one warn about satisfied customers? Because a satisfied customer—so the widespread assumption goes—is a loyal and thus at the same time a valuable customer. In fact, however, it is dangerous to gear a company's customer relationship management primarily or even exclusively to customer satisfaction. For one thing, customer satisfaction in our highly developed markets does *not* lead to sustained customer loyalty. And on the other hand, the attempt to increase customer satisfaction devours immense corporate resources that could be used much more profitably elsewhere. The following explanations make this clear.

Customer Satisfaction Alone Does Not Create Customer Loyalty
For most companies, customer orientation is a natural part of their corporate strategy. With this in mind, they have been investing intensively in the quality of their customer relationships for many years. This commitment is based on the insight that well-maintained, lasting and loyal customer relationships are a central, if not THE central, business success factor—since on the one hand, stable customer relationships allow more reliable sales planning, and on the other hand, under the conditions of intensifying competition, it is much more profitable to retain an existing customer and maintain the relationship with them, than to acquire and build up a new customer at great expense.

As a type of barometer for measuring the success of their elaborate measures to improve the quality of customer relationships, companies around the world focus primarily on one central parameter: customer satisfaction. This is not surprising. After all, satisfied customers, it seemed for a long time, are more loyal customers with more stable and lasting customer relationships—in the relevant management literature[23] this view, according to which customer satisfaction inevitably leads to customer loyalty, is still widespread. The assumption seems even so natural that it is not questioned in many places. And so, in the pursuit of customer loyalty, customer satisfaction has become the mantra of customer orientation. Accordingly—in

---

[23] The fact that increased satisfaction generates loyalty in the long term is an untested assumption even in the relevant management science literature (cf. e.g., Homburg 2016).

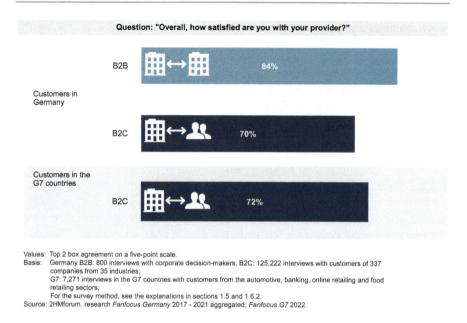

Fig. 1.14 Customer satisfaction scores in Germany (B2C and B2B) and in the G7 countries (B2C only)

Germany as in many other developed markets, there is considerable investment in customer satisfaction. Apparently with success: Fig. 1.14 shows exemplary customer satisfaction scores for B2C and B2B companies in Germany as well as for B2C companies in the G7 countries.

To achieve these outstanding satisfaction ratings, immense efforts were necessary. Huge sums were invested in improving quality and performance to make customers first satisfied and then even more satisfied. Studies on customer satisfaction mushroomed. Advertising claims boasted of "more than 90% satisfied customers". Satisfaction creates loyalty, was the motto—in other words, "keep the customer satisfied"—no matter what the cost. At first glance, this calculation also worked out—the overwhelming majority of highly satisfied customers seems to prove this.

In fact, however, the path taken led astray. Companies may have done their homework when it came to customer satisfaction, but they have not achieved their real goal—higher customer loyalty. On the contrary, many companies are experiencing the opposite: although customers are becoming increasingly satisfied, they are nevertheless migrating to the competition. Obviously, satisfied customers are increasingly behaving just as disloyally as dissatisfied ones. The immense investments made in improving product and service quality have been rewarded less and less by customers. They remained ineffective because they created more satisfaction, but no loyalty.

Clearly, the postulated influence of customer satisfaction merely upon customer loyalty applies only to a limited extent. The reason for this becomes clear when we take a closer look at the construct of customer satisfaction. There are numerous models and approaches to this in research. At their core, they all understand customer satisfaction as the result of a process in which the customer compares his expectations of a product or service with the actual quality of the product or service provided. If expectations are not met, dissatisfaction or anger is the result. If expectations and performance are in balance, the customer is satisfied (Homburg and Stock-Homburg 2016). If the performance exceeds the expectation, he is considered highly satisfied or enthusiastic (Oliver et al. 1997). In the end, it is assumed, highly satisfied customers have higher customer loyalty, i.e., an increase in customer loyalty (Homburg and Bucerius 2016). Rising customer satisfaction, it is also commonly postulated, leads to lower price sensitivity on the part of the customer and to increased willingness to repurchase, recommend and cross-buy. In short, satisfied customers are the customers with the highest customer value.

But this cause-and-effect relationship has long since come to an end. After all, customer satisfaction is based on performance—to be more precise, it reflects the customers' perception of performance. For a company, wanting to improve this means making costly investments in an increasingly higher level of quality and performance. The crux of the matter, however, is that increasing performance makes it virtually impossible to differentiate oneself from the competition. This is especially true if the competitor also aims to increase customer satisfaction by providing more service. What then arises is devastating competition between companies that permanently increase their performance and are nevertheless—or even precisely because of this—hardly distinguishable for their customers. The perceived performance thus does not lead to stronger customer loyalty, but rather to customer uncertainty: customers perceive that they can also obtain the same performance from other providers. For him, it is interchangeable.

Additionally, it is important to consider: In many industries, customers' perception of performance has already reached the maximum. Remember, if performance meets expectations, customers are satisfied. On a five-point scale from 1 (best grade) to 5 (worst grade), this roughly corresponds to a rating of "2". However, many companies are already experiencing that they are rated with the best grade—i.e., "1"—in terms of satisfaction. This means that many companies are already exceeding performance expectations—but they still do not differentiate themselves from their competitors, who offer the same exceptional performance and are therefore also rated as "very good" by their customers. In the customer's perception, the products of the competitors are like two peas in a pod—and can be interchanged at will.

It is precisely this mechanism that means that highly satisfied customers are not automatically loyal but can turn to the competition's offerings just as quickly as dissatisfied customers. Owing to the companies' lack of profile, the willingness to switch is also high among highly satisfied customers—and with aggressively priced offers, the path to the competition is short. So, the customer jumps from offer to offer. Satisfied customers—as recent studies show—are therefore just as disloyal as dissatisfied customers. They behave like mercenaries (Fig. 1.15).

Fig. 1.15 High price sensitivity as a product of non-distinguishing providers (Courtesy of © Tom Fishburne, www.marketoonist.com 2022. All Rights Reserved)

Other positive characteristics such as low-price sensitivity or a high willingness to recommend, which are usually associated with highly satisfied customers, can hardly be demonstrated: Even highly satisfied customers are increasingly adopting a savings mentality and pursuing "smart shopping" strategies. The situation is similar with the willingness to recommend, which is increasingly seen as the key indicator of customer loyalty in many companies: instead of sharing their positive experiences with others and helping to gain new customers by recommending them, many highly satisfied customers are quietly enjoying themselves. Their customer value as ambassadors thus approaches zero.

So, when companies ask themselves why, despite major investments in quality and performance, they have satisfied but not loyal customers, they find the answer in a fatal chain of errors: they have focused singularly on customer satisfaction, which does not create loyalty. And they have relied on performance to increase that satisfaction. However, performance alone can hardly be used to convey differentiating features, because in developed markets the competing products and services are becoming increasingly similar, and in the customer's perception there is always at least one other provider who is "just as good". The consequence of this ruinous competition was not that companies turned away from focusing on customer satisfaction, but that their efforts were further intensified: According to the motto "a lot helps a lot," investments continued to be made in every service area that could influence customer satisfaction—usually without checking whether these measures were truly effective in achieving their goals. A "more is more" mantra was born, which, without any focus, spread equally across all service areas and devoured vast sums in the process.

Customer Satisfaction as a Cost Trap
Our assertion: Due to a one-sided focus on performance, many companies have failed to offer their customers alternative differentiators. This is true for companies large and small and across virtually all industries. With this flawed strategy, companies have virtually driven their customers into "mercenaryism." And in the process, they have driven up costs: Since, due to a lack of alternatives, differentiation only works based on price. The strategy is at the expense of margins and reduces the return on investment. This means that satisfaction management alone not only fails to achieve its goal of increasing customer loyalty, but it is also not profitable. Focusing solely on customer satisfaction inevitably leads to a cost trap.

The following example of a retail chain store shows how serious this cost trap is. The company had implemented a series of quality and satisfaction-enhancing measures in some of its stores. Among other things, the product range was expanded, wider aisles were installed in the stores, more and larger parking spaces were offered, and greater emphasis was placed on cleanliness. All these measures were, by their very nature, expensive: the ever-larger, more diversified range reduced the chances of obtaining even more discounts from producers, and wider aisles made for relaxed shopping, but cost money. Even more cleanliness meant higher costs for cleaning staff, and more parking spaces also had their price. People believed in the "more is more" principle: more use of resources also creates more satisfaction, more loyalty, more sales and higher returns.

At first glance, the expensive measures did not miss their mark. In fact, all this effort increased customer satisfaction in the stores concerned, but this gain in satisfaction did not pay off. On the contrary, it was at the expense of the return on investment. The higher the customer satisfaction, the lower the return on sales per store. Figure 1.16 illustrates this astonishing correlation.

Each point in the diagram represents a single store. The further a point lies to the left in the diagram, the lower the customer satisfaction, the further to the right the point lies, the higher the customer satisfaction. Furthermore, the further down the point lies, the lower the return on sales; the further up it lies, the higher the return on sales in that store. The solid line is a regression line: it describes the relationship between customer satisfaction and return on sales calculated across all stores. In this example, the trend is downward, i.e., the higher the customer satisfaction, the lower the return on sales.

Satisfaction reduces the return on investment. How can that be? The apparent contradiction is resolved if we use this example to once again visualize the mechanisms of action already explained: In the example of our retail chain, investing in performance led to greater satisfaction, but not to better differentiation. This is because the customer experienced the service positively but knew that a comparable range and quality of service also awaited him at the competing provider. As a result, customers continued to react sensitively to aggressively priced offers from the

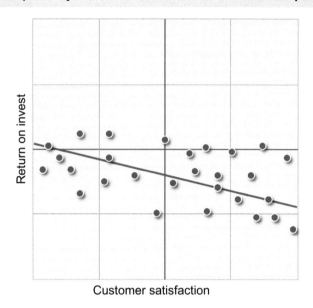

Fig. 1.16 The relationship between customer satisfaction and return on invest

competition. The increase in satisfaction that our provider had created by offering more service did not, therefore, lead to an increase in loyalty. In other words, customers were more satisfied, but they did not buy more or more often as a result. The measures, therefore, did not lead to the intended increase in sales in the stores concerned. However, since at the same time the increased performance in these stores cost money, the return on investment fell—despite increasing satisfaction.

A similar process has taken place in Germany in the furniture sector. For decades, a well-known supplier in the Rhine-Main region was the sole "top dog" for ready-to-assemble furniture. Then, about 15 kilometers away, a competitor opened a new, large-scale store. The long-established supplier reacted reflexively by investing in its performance. At immense expense, the existing building was almost demolished, the sales area was increased from 28,000 to 43,000 square meters by the new building, and 80 additional parking spaces and new access roads were created. The costs for this were in the millions. The building permit alone cost half a million euros. Added to these costs is the drop in sales during the reconstruction phase, during which the "top dog" was only able to offer a reduced range of products under provisional conditions. Certainly, all these measures—a larger and more modern store with more space and more parking spaces—lead to greater customer satisfaction. But they do not create loyalty because there is no differentiation from the new competitor.

1.3 From *Fan Principle* to *FANOMICS*: What Is a Fan Customer?

The explanations illustrate why a one-sided focus on customer satisfaction leads to a cost trap—and that at the same time the widespread approach of wanting to retain customers by increasing satisfaction falls short for the following reasons:

- Satisfaction is based on performance.
- However, performance hardly offers the opportunity to differentiate from the competition anymore.
- As a result, customers' willingness to switch to the competition remains high even when performance increases.
- Consequently, satisfied customers are increasingly behaving just as disloyally as dissatisfied ones.
- Thus, increasing performance does not lead to increasing loyalty.
- Satisfaction is, therefore, not a reliable driver of customer loyalty.
- Satisfaction is unsuitable as the sole indicator of customer behavior.
- Investments in performance simultaneously reduce the return on investment.
- Increasing satisfaction is not profitable.

This means: Customer satisfaction is indeed a necessary and indispensable component of intact customer relationships because no one will seriously claim that a company can be successful in the long term with inadequate performance and correspondingly dissatisfied customers. However, as the sole management parameter of customer relationship management, customer satisfaction obviously falls short. This is because even highly satisfied customers often no longer show any commitment to their provider and instead behave disloyally. For companies that want to achieve customer loyalty, a new, additional benchmark is therefore absolutely essential alongside satisfaction.

In the search for such a new parameter, it makes sense to look again at the *Harley-Davidson example* from the previous section. There, two things became clear: First, the extraordinary relationship of *Harley customers to* their favorite manufacturer is obviously based on something other than satisfaction alone. Second, *Harley customers* are indeed Fan Customers: They have an emotional attachment to *Harley-Davidson* because they find there—corresponding to a fan relationship—a unique identification offer.

What if we were to develop a parameter for this type of emotional tie? A metric, so to speak, that indicates whether a customer relationship is of fan quality? On the one hand, this new metric would have to be able to identify the Fan Customers within a company's customer base, i.e., customers with above-average emotional loyalty. And it would have to do this independently of customer satisfaction, since—as has just been shown—even highly satisfied customers are increasingly behaving in a disloyal fashion. It is therefore essential to be able to use the new parameter to differentiate between customers with high and low loyalty; even within the group of highly satisfied customers.

Such a metric would be superior to other measures of customer relationship quality for two reasons: Firstly, it would measure what constitutes a fan relationship—maximum attachment loyalty, or, as we relate it to customers, maximum emotional customer loyalty. And secondly, it would subsequently enable us to increase this emotional customer loyalty by applying the findings from fan research in social sciences to the relationship between companies and customers. And indeed, we have succeeded in developing such a parameter that can survey and identify the fan-typical emotional bond of customers independently of their satisfaction. We call it the *Fan Indicator*. It is the heart of the transfer of the findings of the *Fan Principle* into our *FANOMICS management* model.

1.4 The *FANOMICS Basis*: The *Fan Indicator*

We had deduced on a theoretical and empirical basis that a fan relationship is a relationship with high emotional connection. And we had subsequently shown that there are Fan Customers who have such a fan-like relationship with their provider. So, it is understandable and necessary to develop a metric for the emotional attachment of Fan Customers based on the characteristics of fan relationships. With this approach we solve a central problem of the manageability of a parameter for emotional commitment. The endeavor to measure emotional customer loyalty directly would have little chance of success. It would mean measuring the customer's emotional connection to the company or brand. Although this is possible and is also being pursued in a few approaches, it is nevertheless empirically difficult and, above all, hardly economically practicable. This is because measuring emotions requires a sophisticated and extremely comprehensive inventory of psychological measurement instruments (Müller and Kuchinke 2019). However, this would exactly contradict our goal. This is because we are not only looking for a valid indicator to measure emotional customer loyalty, but also want to develop *FANOMICS* as a lean management tool suitable for everyday use based on this measurement. So, we are looking for an indicator that can be measured repeatedly and with little effort.

In our search for a streamlined and viable solution to measure emotional engagement, we leverage our knowledge of fan characteristics. To be able to identify customers who show an emotional attachment to their provider, we do not necessarily have to record their emotions. After all, our goal is not to know customers' emotions, but their relationship quality. If we can identify customers whose relationship quality with their provider is of a similar quality to that of a fan's relationship with his or her star, then, since fan relationships always exhibit a high level of emotional attachment, we have also identified the customers with a high level of emotional attachment. It is therefore sufficient to capture those relationship characteristics that we know are also found in fan relationships. And it is precisely these characteristics that we have described as the *Fan Principle* in Sect. 1.2 based on the state of social science research and theoretical considerations: *(1) identification and (2) uniqueness of the relationship.*

The core of our argument is: Fan relationships are relationships with high emotional attachment since they fulfill a central need for the fan. Customers who identify with their provider in a similar way to fans and perceive the relationship with the provider as unique exhibit a comparable emotional relationship quality to fans

1.4 The FANOMICS Basis: The Fan Indicator

and are therefore defined as "Fan Customers". The concept of Fan Customers is to be understood as a transfer: It is irrelevant whether these customers are actually "fans" of the company in the sense of the social science definition. They are customers who have a fan-like relationship with this provider—that is all this label is intended to say.

Thus, our goal was to make the two constituent characteristics of fan relationships—identification and uniqueness—measurable in customer surveys—and to do so with minimal effort. The aim was to transfer the characteristics to be measured linguistically, accurately, and as succinctly as possible to relationships between companies and their customers. Based on numerous empirical surveys and analyses of our own, we operationalize the two characteristics "Identification and Uniqueness" as follows: For the identification potential of the relationship, we measure whether the customer states that the supplier is made for someone like him. For the uniqueness of the relationship, we survey whether the customer considers the provider to be the most attractive in this area. We survey agreement or disagreement with these statements in five-point agreement scales.

Based on numerous empirical surveys and analyses, we have combined these two dimensions into one arithmetical value: a central indicator. The two dimensions are weighted according to their significance for relationship quality. The result is a weighted index value, the so-called *"Fan Indicator"* (cf. Fig. 1.17). The measurement on which it is based captures the necessary and sufficient characteristics it takes to identify Fan Customers. This means that Fan Customers always show these relationship characteristics, and vice versa: relationships that do not show these characteristics are not relationships of Fan Customers.

The *Fan Indicator* is thusly a bivariate construct whose components were first derived theoretically and qualitatively, then condensed and then concentrated in a weighted manner based on empirical analyses. Since it is based on the key characteristics that we had previously identified in the *Fan Principle* as typical of fan relationships with high emotional connection, it is also an indicator of emotional connection—without directly measuring emotions itself. Since this indicator conclusively transfers the fundamental social science findings from the *Fan Principle* to

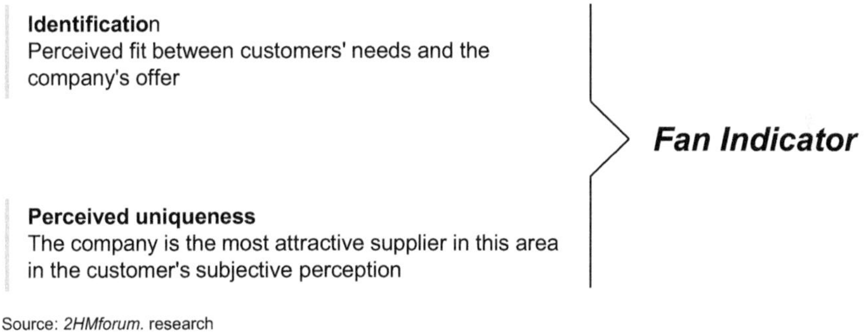

Identification
Perceived fit between customers' needs and the company's offer

Perceived uniqueness
The company is the most attractive supplier in this area in the customer's subjective perception

} *Fan Indicator*

Source: 2HMforum. research

Fig. 1.17 The dimensions of the *Fan Indicator*

customer relationships, through its development we complete the step from the Fan *Principle* into our economic management model based on it. Since it combines theoretical considerations and empirical findings from *fan research* and economics, we refer to this management model as *FANOMICS*. Based on the *Fan Indicator,* it contains the entire corporate toolbox for implementing the *Fan Principle* in customer relationships and is presented in detail in the following chapters.

We had determined in Sect. 1.2 that the fit between the offer of the star on the one hand and the central needs of the fan on the other is decisive for the emotional fan relationship. The *Fan Indicator* measures exactly the same content-related relationships for the relationship between a company's offering (expressed by its positioning) and the central needs of its Fan Customers: Through the constant fulfillment of central needs, customers experience identification and perceived uniqueness. This leads to a fan-like customer relationship and thus to positive emotional experience and bonding behavior. We refer to this indicator below as a measure of emotional customer loyalty. And similar to what has already been evident Sect. 1.2 for the fan relationship, the same applies to Fan Customers: *The relationship has an emotional experience quality because it fulfills central needs.* However, this does not mean that *emotional customer loyalty is* a purely feeling-based, affective, or irrational relationship.

In contrast to the widely used indicator of customer satisfaction, which is based solely on performance perception, the *Fan Indicator* as a measure of relationship quality is based on two components that reflect the degree of fit. While customer satisfaction expresses the degree to which *any* needs are met—from "not at all" to over-fulfillment—emotional customer loyalty expresses the degree to which the *customer's core* need is met in order to create perceived fit. If we relate the two to each other, we obtain a matrix of satisfaction and emotional commitment (cf. Fig. 1.18).

The chart contrasts the "more is more" mantra of satisfaction management with the central characteristic value of *FANOMICS*, which in turn is based on the empirical findings of the *Fan Principle*. The horizontal axis illustrates the result of pure satisfaction orientation: more and more is invested aimlessly in performance areas to increase satisfaction. As a rule, however, this does not create a bond, because it serves *any* needs of the customers—but not their *central* need in a targeted manner. Thus, no emotional experience is created here. The *Fan Indicator* on the vertical axis is quite different: Here, the fit between the *central needs* of the customers and the perceived positioning of the provider is plotted. The more these are aligned, the more emotional satisfaction of needs is experienced and the more an emotional bond is created. It is therefore important for the provider to focus on doing the right thing and to position itself accordingly. When both—focusing on central needs and meeting needs in line with requirements—come together, we speak of "Fan Customers": Customers whose central needs are always met in a focused way by the provider, creating perceived uniqueness. The validity and explanatory power of this approach is extremely high. We prove this in the following through several thousand customer interviews from all over the world.

1.5 The *Fan Rate* as a KPI

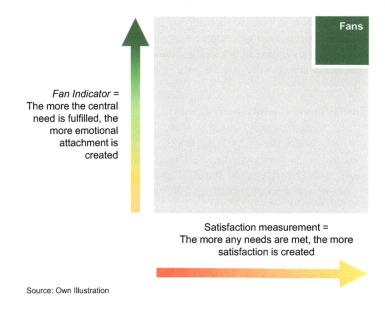

Fig. 1.18 The matrix of satisfaction and emotional commitment

1.5 The *Fan Rate* as a KPI

Let us summarize the previous steps once again: We have first shown that the control variable "customer satisfaction" applied in many companies is primarily based on performance and quality assessments about companies and products, but without considering emotional references of the customer relationship. We have further established that customer satisfaction is not sufficient to explain customer loyalty—because even highly satisfied customers can behave disloyally. We therefore developed a new control variable based on the relationships between fans and their stars, namely the denominated *Fan Indicator*: a measure of relationship quality that captures the degree of emotional connection. This section looks at the progress this new metric makes in analyzing customer relationships and how it can be used to identify fans among a company's customers.

The first step here is to compare this new indicator of emotional customer loyalty with the traditional measure of customer satisfaction. As we have always emphasized, satisfaction is of course a very relevant parameter in customer relationship management since you cannot be successful with dissatisfied customers. It is just not sufficient as the sole control variable since it does not create sustainable customer loyalty. It is necessary to develop an additional metric that differentiates between customers (those truly connected and those not bound to the company) within the segment of satisfied customers. Thereby making it possible to distinguish between valuable and less valuable customers. The converse conclusion is that the indicator we have developed is only an advancement on the conventional measure of customer satisfaction if it enables such further differentiations within the satisfied customers. Our *Fan Indicator* offers precisely this added value. We will illustrate this in the following by means of comprehensive empirical surveys—initially using data from Germany and, building on this, also using international findings.

> **Why Start with the "Germany" Example?**
> The German market is ideally suited to illustrate the analytical added value of the *Fan Portfolio* and the *FANOMICS* approach. "Made in Germany" is still associated with high quality and the art of engineering—this highly advanced production and process quality makes Germany a highly developed and fiercely competitive market in both the B2C and B2B sectors with very high customer satisfaction ratings (cf. Fig. 1.14). This presents every international competitor with particularly high challenges: "If you can make it there, you'll make it anywhere," is the motto. In fact, in Germany it is hardly possible for individual providers to differentiate themselves from the competition merely through performance. This makes emotional customer loyalty even more important for companies. Using Germany as an example, we will show that it is precisely in such highly developed markets that focusing on emotional customer loyalty leads to sustainable success.
>
> Using our fundamental underlying research, we have already been collecting data on the correlations between satisfaction and emotional attachment for hundreds of companies and for almost all industries on the German market for many years and can conclusively prove the validity of our model there—both in the B2C and B2B sectors. For example, we have been measuring the *Fan Rates* of well-known and leading companies in Germany from numerous industries for ten years. The cumulative study now covers more than 35 industries. As a rule, customer interviews are conducted annually in each industry for every provider with at least 2% market share. The results of this research, which in the last five years alone has now covered more than 125,000 customer interviews, are published by us regularly under the name *Fanfocus Germany* and can be accessed online (2HMforum 2021). [24]
>
> Owing to this market situation and this uniquely broad data basis, we will first present the core of our approach based on the German market. We will then use data collected internationally to demonstrate that the insights gained in Germany are transferable to all developed markets in the world and their customers.

Figure 1.19 illustrates the relationship between customer satisfaction and emotional customer loyalty—based on data from more than 125,000 cross-industry

---

[24] For details of the methodological approach, the companies studied, and the complete findings of *Fanfocus Germany*, see also the German edition of this book (Becker and Daschmann 2022, p. 55ff).

1.5 The *Fan Rate* as a KPI

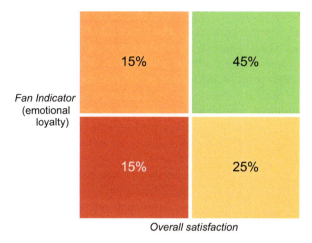

Fig. 1.19 The correlation between customer satisfaction and emotional customer loyalty

Basis: 125,222 customer interviews from about 337 companies of 35 B2C industries
Source: *2HMforum.* research *Fanfocus Germany* 2017 - 2021 aggregated

customer interviews from the B2C sector (for the exact survey method, cf. Sect. 1.6.1).

If, as in Fig. 1.19 vis-a-vis the new *Fan Indicator* as a measure of emotional customer loyalty, it becomes clear how important it is to use both indicators to classify the customer landscape. This is because an exciting differentiation emerges. If the horizontal axis—satisfaction level—is subdivided based on the average value, as we have done here, we can distinguish between customers with above-average and below-average satisfaction. We see that 70% of German B2C customers are satisfied above average. This is exactly the value we had also reported in Fig. 1.14. Accordingly, 30% of customers are only satisfied at a base level. We made the same portion at the mean value on the vertical axis, on which the *Fan Indicator*, i.e., our measure of emotional customer loyalty, is plotted. If we now combine both portions with each other, we obtain four fields that clearly confirm empirically what we suspected theoretically in the previous section: Apparently, among the 70% above-average satisfied customers shown on the right-hand side of the chart, the vast majority also have a high emotional tie to their provider. But equally, there are also highly satisfied customers who show little or no emotional attachment (45 vs. 25%). There are also two camps among the 30% below-average satisfied customers on the left-hand side of the chart: 15% each have high or low customer loyalty.

So, the first thing we can say is: Both indicators obviously measure different things. We learn more about satisfied customers if we also look at their emotional connection. We can now divide them into customers with high and low relationship quality. The observation made in Sect. 1.3 that even satisfied customers do not always have to be loyal customers is thus clearly confirmed. However, we also learn more about emotionally loyal customers because they can be more or less satisfied.

The second observation is that this diagram itself shows that customer satisfaction is useless as an orientation variable in management; Because it does not differentiate in the consideration between content customers, who are bound and therefore loyal, and content customers, who threaten to become unfaithful despite this contentment and because they do not exhibit emotional connection. It is obvious that the approach to both customer groups must be very different to be successful. Anyone who only manages according to satisfaction will not be able to respond adequately to this.

The third observation is: this comparison in the chart enables us to identify the customer type which was the starting point for our entire considerations: the fan customer. The quadrant at the top right (45%) in Fig. 1.19 shows those customers who are more satisfied than average and more emotionally loyal than average. It is intuitively plausible that we will find Fan Customers only in this quadrant. However, it would contradict our previous statements if we were now to declare all customers in this quadrant to be fans. According to our definition, the fans must rather be those customers with a particularly high relationship quality within this segment with above-average satisfaction and above-average loyalty. After all, a "merely above-average" relationship would hardly characterize what a fan relationship is all about. Now and in the following, we consider "Fan Customers" to be those customers who excel in both emotional attachment and customer satisfaction with maximum ratings of their providers. We can identify them in the combination of both characteristics as a very special customer segment which—as we will show in Chap. 2—is characterized by the highest customer value. We have colored it in the graphic in Fig. 1.20 colored in dark green. We will refer to these customers, as we define them, as "fans" or "Fan Customers" in the following. Fans are not only very satisfied with the services, but also have a very high emotional connection to products, services or brands and companies.

In context with Fig. 1.20 we referred to the 45% of customers in the upper right quarter of the graph who are above-average satisfied and at an above-average level loyal. Owing to our high benchmark of Fan Customers, we subdivide this group

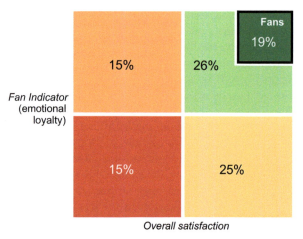

Fig. 1.20 Fan customers: customers with highest satisfaction and highest emotional attachment

once again: into above-average satisfied and connected customers on the one hand versus highly satisfied and highly connected customers on the other, the fans. These Fan Customers can be found in the top right-hand corner of the graphic—because they are the customers who combine the highest levels of satisfaction with the highest levels of emotional commitment. This fraction now also reveals the proportion of fans in the total customer base: 19%, or almost one-fifth of customers, are Fan Customers—on average across all B2C industries. We can thus determine a percentage indicator: the *Fan Rate*. It tells us what proportion of customers are highly satisfied and at the same time emotionally loyal and can thus be considered Fan Customers according to our definition. The *Fan Rate* of 19% shown here is an average value. Depending on the market and the industries or companies included, the *Fan Rate* as well as the values of the four quadrants in Fig. 1.18 can vary significantly—as we will show later. What remains constant, however, is the realization that the comparison of emotional attachment and satisfaction makes it possible to identify five different customer groups—including Fan Customers.

Comparing many companies and industries, the *Fan Rate* provides information on how successful the customer relationship management of an individual company actually is. The higher the *Fan Rate*, the better the management. Because Fan Customers, we will prove this later, have a higher customer value than all other customer segments (cf. Chap. 2). The higher their share, the greater the economic success. It is therefore profitable to gear one's company to a constant increase in this *Fan Rate*—which means nothing less than making it the central control variable for management.

Thus, the *Fan Rate* can be understood as the central KPI of our approach. It is the new control variable for companies that we propose and recommend for the fundamental orientation of management. This is because the *Fan Rate* makes the quality of customer relationships and the associated customer value measurable and thus offers companies a valid and reliable management option. In addition to its significance in terms of content and theory, the *Fan Rate* also has other practical advantages as a key performance indicator: First, it can be measured with little empirical effort. This aspect may seem secondary at first glance, but it is of central importance. After all, to manage a company according to the *Fan Principle*, it is necessary to constantly align it with the *Fan Rate*. So only regular measurements of the *Fan Rate* promise sustainable success here. Secondly, the *Fan Rate* is not an abstract measure, but one that is intuitively comprehensible. The statement that, for example, "23% of customers are fans" can be understood and communicated by every employee, from the trainee to the CEO. This brings us to the third advantage of the *Fan Rate*: It can be communicated easily and emphatically and passionately within the company hierarchy. Those who choose it as a management tool will probably quickly find acceptance among their employees. This is because the *Fan Rate* is vivid, concise, intuitive, concrete, and easy to understand. Knowing the proportion of Fan Customers of one's own company and seeing it increase is much more comprehensible to many employees than, for example, an abstract recommendation score. Especially since the information content of the *Fan Rate* goes far beyond such scores, as we will show in Chap. 2.

1.5.1 The *Fan Rates* of German B2C Companies

We have shown empirically that Fan Customers are a particularly valuable customer segment that cannot be identified via satisfaction measurements alone. And based on this, we had identified the *Fan Rate* as the most important indicator for the quality of customer relationships and thus as a significant control variable for companies. But the *Fan Rate* is not only convincing because of its theoretical derivation and intuitive plausibility—it is also suitable as a benchmark tool for assessing companies.

This results from the customer value of Fan Customers. Fans buy more and they buy more often. They are also more loyal: They remain loyal to "their" company longer than other consumers. Furthermore, they are less price-sensitive and can be an important and helpful partner in external communications as well as product development and positioning for "their" company. We will elaborate and prove all these outstanding advantages of Fan Customers in detail in Chap. 2. Until we deliver on this promise, we ask you, dear reader, to simply assume the following premise: Companies that have more Fan Customers are—all other things being equal—also more economically successful. And it is under this premise that the following results of *Fanfocus Germany should be viewed* and take on their particular relevance: They use the *Fan Rate to show* which industries and companies in Germany are particularly successful—because they know how to turn customers into fans.

Figure 1.21 shows a ranking of the average *Fan Rates* of the 35 industries examined in *Fanfocus Germany* from 2017-2021.

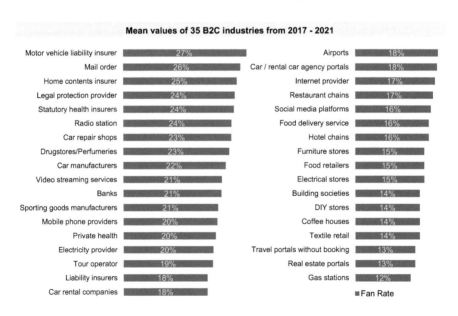

Fig. 1.21 The average *Fan Rates* of 35 B2C industries

1.5 The *Fan Rate* as a KPI

The data show that some intuitive assumptions about the *Fan Rate of* certain industries do not hold true because they are based on product-centric perceptions. Each of us would probably have assumed that you can intuitively name "typical fan industries," i.e., industries with high *Fan Rates*—and also the "less typical" industries, i.e., those with low *Fan Rates*. But would you have guessed that car insurers, with their rather "dry" products such as liability and comprehensive insurance policies, would end up in first place in the ranking? And thus leave the world-renowned German car manufacturers behind, who use more than ten times the advertising budget for what appears to be a much more emotional product?

DIY stores, on the other hand, have a devastatingly low number of fans despite their supposed on-site advice, while mail-order companies, with whom people only have contact via mouse click and parcel service, have more than twice as many Fan Customers. And even the hours of online presence in social media channels do not turn participants into fans of these platforms—not even because *Facebook introduced* the "fan button" back then.

If we take a closer look, it becomes clear that the performance in the *Fanfocus Germany* ranking apparently has little to do with the character of the actual products and service of the respective industries. For example, the first three places in the ranking, as Fig. 1.21 shows, two insurance sectors (motor vehicle liability and household contents). Liability insurers, on the other hand, perform only at an average level. The industry of video streaming services such as *Netflix* or *Amazon Prime* would, one would assume, have the best chances of coming out on top, as numerous customers turn to their emotionally charged offerings for several hours a day. In fact, the streaming services do quite well, but their *Fan Rate* lands on a five-year average behind far less "exciting" industries such as insurance providers for legal issues or health insurers. Travel and real estate portals are in joint second-to-last place, while mail order, whose business model is also based on online portals, has the second-best *Fan Rate*.

Obviously, many of our intuitive and plausible-sounding everyday hypotheses simply do not apply. There is a plausible reason for this discrepancy between our intuitive assessments of "fan industries" and the empirical findings: When we try to estimate the *Fan Rates* of individual industries, we involuntarily think about the emotional potential of the products. A video streaming service seems more emotional to us than car insurance, a sports car more exciting than ordering from *Amazon*. We want to believe that one can be emotionally attached to the designer of a *Harley-Davidson,* but less so to the manufacturer of a washing machine. Because we intuitively and naturally think only from the product. However, emotional customer loyalty is hardly explained at all by the type of product or service offered. The only decisive factor is the management strategy, namely the extent to which a company—intuitively or with guidance—already applies *FANOMICS* and thus achieves high retention quality. Conversely, this also means that anyone can successfully apply *FANOMICS*. And since implementation is apparently more advanced in some industries than in others, these surprising industry differences occur. We will explain the reasons for this in detail later in this book.

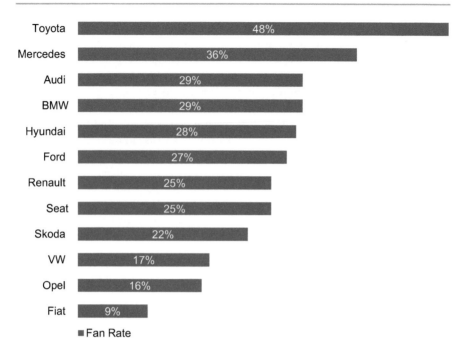

Basis: 21,262 customer interviews, from which 1,200 interviews were conducted with customers of the 12 providers listed
Source: 2HMforum. research *Fanfocus Germany* 2021

Fig. 1.22 *Fan Rates* of the leading automotive brands in Germany in 2021

Let's look at it from another perspective. If the type of product or service offered were causal for the *Fan Rate*, the *Fan Rates* of the individual providers would have to be similarly high or low within an industry. In fact, this is not the case. Within the industries, companies differ distinctly regarding emotional customer loyalty. Let's look at an example together: The *Fan Rates* of the leading car manufacturers in Germany, i.e., in one of the most competitive automotive markets in the world. They are listed for the year 2021 in Fig. 1.22 listed.

Here, too, we can see some remarkable findings. Firstly, we can see that the differences within a sector can be even more distinct than in a sector comparison: there are no less than 39 percentage points between the *Fan Rate* of Toyota in first place and that of Fiat in 12th place. This confirms what has already been said: It is not the product category that is the cause of high or low emotional customer loyalty, but evidently factors which differ between the suppliers in an industry. And since people within the industry operate under the same framework and market conditions, the conclusion is obvious that these are factors that are in the hands of the company management. The decisive factor is obviously not, as can already be seen here, the nationality of the manufacturer. Toyota manages to push ahead of the German flagship brand Mercedes by a wide margin on the German market, and Skoda clearly outstrips its German parent company VW. The differences in *Fan Rates* must therefore be attributable to other causes. The wide range within the industry also confirms the high informative value of our key indicator, the *Fan Rate*: it clearly and distinctly differentiates between the customer loyalty of different companies. Aligning oneself with it puts a provider in a position to prevail against the competition—especially when the products of the industry are hardly distinguishable for the end consumer. An extremely high *Fan Rate* is therefore possible in any industry—regardless of what the emotional bond may look like on average in the industry.

1.5.2 The *Fan Rates* of German B2B Companies

Up to now, we've looked only at the *Fan Rates* of B2C providers—that is, companies that primarily have end consumers as customers. But what about the large number of B2B providers—i.e., those companies that do not have primary end consumers as customers, but other companies? Does emotional customer loyalty play a role there, too? At first glance, one might want to doubt it: The end consumer, one might think, is more prone to emotional decision-making processes and behaviors. They do not always make their purchasing decisions rationally, but often spontaneously based on their gut instinct, and they are susceptible to the emotional coloring of brands and products, which are presented accordingly in advertising. In companies, on the other hand, one could assume that purchasing decisions are made much more systematically and rationally—emotional customer loyalty has no effect here. This speculation seems plausible, but it is incorrect. In fact, emotional customer loyalty also plays an important role in the B2B sector. Because the fact that companies trade with companies here is actually only correct from a legal or fiscal point of view. In fact, however, people also trade with people in the B2B sector—namely the respective representatives of both companies. And that is precisely why emotional customer loyalty and the *Fan Rate also play* an important role in B2B.

The fact that emotional customer loyalty exists not only in the B2C sector but also in the B2B sector is borne out by the findings of another fundamental study which we conducted in Germany. In interviews, we asked 800 representatives of German companies from a wide range of industries about customer relationships with their supplier companies. Figure 1.23 shows the customer loyalty of the company representatives surveyed to their suppliers—divided by supplier sector.

As the example from the German market shows, there are also significant *Fan Rates in* the B2B sector. Again, the differences between industries are less important. Rather, the fundamental message is that it is obviously possible to have Fan Customers in every B2B industry. Regardless of what a provider sells to another company—whether temporary staffing solutions, software, parts and components, or management consulting—it is possible with each of these business models to turn the responsible decision-makers in customer companies into fans. In this respect, the crucial question is not: "Does emotional customer loyalty exist in the B2B sector, and is it comparable to the B2C sector?" Rather, the question must be, "How can

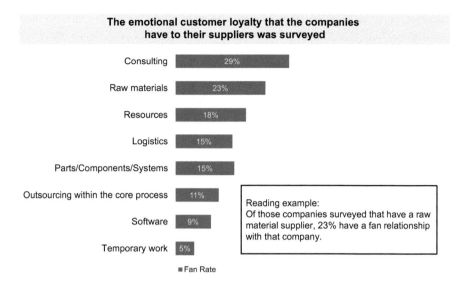

Fig. 1.23 Fan customers also exist in the B2B sector

emotional customer loyalty be increased in the B2B sector as well?" Because the data presented clearly proves that emotional customer loyalty also exists in B2B business, can also be expanded there, and plays a significant role because purchasing decisions are still made by people, even in the overwhelming number of companies.

The results of our empirical findings on *Fan Rates* in Germany can be summarized as follows:

- The *Fan Rate* is a meaningful measure that clearly differentiates between providers in the same industry.
- The *Fan Rates* of different companies and industries can contradict intuitive ideas. Only empirical surveys can provide reliable information here.
- There are no limits to increasing the *Fan Rate*.
- Building emotional customer loyalty is also possible and necessary in B2B industries.
- The level of *Fan Rate* and thus emotional customer loyalty is not a question of the products or services offered or the industry.
- The *Fan Rate* of companies operating under otherwise identical framework and market conditions can diverge greatly. This proves that the triggering factors for this lie in the companies themselves—namely solely in the consistency with which *FANOMICS* is implemented there.

To put it in a nutshell, the findings show that there can be fans everywhere, and every company, regardless of whether it is large or small, B2B or B2C, has the chance to turn its customers into fans—as long as it follows the *FANOMICS approach*. However, the benefits of our approach are by no means exhausted with the identification of fans and the determination of *Fan Rates*. In fact, the comparison of customer satisfaction and emotional loyalty opens numerous other perspectives. For it is not only fans that can be identified. The result is a completely new way of segmenting all customers according to their relationship quality: the *Fan Portfolio*. In the following, we describe this path from Fan Customers to the *Fan Portfolio*—and we show what potential lies in this diagnosis.

1.6 The *Fan Portfolio*

We have seen that all industries and companies have—or at least could have—fans among their customers. Before we delve further into fans, let's take a step back. Do you remember the way we had identified fans among customers? We had developed—based on scientific fan research—an empirical measuring instrument capable of measuring emotional customer loyalty: the so-called *Fan Indicator* (cf. Sect. 1.4). We had subsequently used this (cf. Sect. 1.5) with customer satisfaction and thus identified the fans: We defined Fan Customers as those customers who are highly satisfied and at the same time particularly emotionally loyal. In Fig. 1.20 we also presented this correlation graphically using data from *Fanfocus Germany* and already pointed out an extremely exciting fact—namely that among the remaining "non-fans" there are customer groups in which the interaction between satisfaction and emotional connection is by no means as aligned as among Fan Customers. Obviously, there are also customers with high satisfaction and low loyalty—and vice versa. The interplay between the two parameters therefore varies greatly—as an expression of different forms of relationship quality. The resulting diversity of customer types illustrates the superior explanatory approach of the *Fan Portfolio*, in which relationship quality—in contrast to many other common models—is no longer represented one-dimensionally, but two-dimensionally: as an interaction of loyalty-based and performance-based influences. This opens up completely new perspectives and, as a result, new opportunities to address different customer groups in a more differentiated way according to their relationship status. We will now take a closer look at these different customer groups.

In the following, we therefore consider the "non-fans". And this is the majority of customers in almost all companies: As the individual segments labeled with percentages in Fig. 1.24 show, 80% of the approximately 125,000 customers surveyed in *Fanfocus Germany*—namely all those we have not designated as fans—are spread quite widely across the entire diagram area.

We have divided this area of the diagram into four further areas and marked them with different colors. We already explained how we defined the boundaries of these areas in Sect. 1.5 It is the average satisfaction and the average emotional commitment, respectively, that divide the measured values into "below average" versus "above average" on both axes. The division is thus based on empirical findings. It results in four equal-sized boxes—minus the fans, who occupy a special role in every

Fig. 1.24 The customer types in *Fanfocus Germany*

respect and occupy the extreme values of the upper right quadrant. The percentages within each of the four fields are not values for area integrals; they therefore do not reflect what percentage of the diagram area is occupied by the respective segment. Rather, they reflect—as seen in *Fanfocus Germany*—the proportion of respondents that we were able to allocate to the respective segment across all 35 industries surveyed. It is therefore possible, for example, that the area with 15% of respondents is just as large as the area with 25% of respondents. We will now take a closer look at and explain the individual customer groups within the diagram. In this way, we create the basis for a target group-specific, cause-adequate approach.

1.6.1 The Customer Types within the *Fan Portfolio*

The Sympathizers
The first type we will focus on is the light green quadrant in the upper right: the field that, with 26% of respondents, directly borders the already identified and extensively discussed group of fans (cf. Fig. 1.24). These individuals appear to be very similar to fans: they are apparently above-average satisfied customers who also exhibit above-average emotional connection. As in the case of fans, customer satisfaction and emotional attachment are therefore equally positively aligned. However, both values are not as pronounced among them as they are among Fan Customers. These are customers who in many respects like the company and its products, but do not (or not yet) express this in fan-typical behavior. We therefore call them "Sympathizers". Such Sympathizers are valuable to any company because, on the

one hand, they are particularly loyal and very satisfied—just like fans—and, on the other hand, they form the group from which further genuine Fan Customers can emerge in the short term. But despite their above-average loyalty, their identification with the company and its products is not as high as that of the fans. This is particularly true of their external behavior: While fans live out their fanhood in a communicative and extraverted manner and are thus active ambassadors for "their" brand, this only applies to a limited extent to Sympathizers. They tend to be more reserved in their external communication. Sympathizers tend to be the "silent" connoisseurs among loyal customers—with considerable consequences for their customer value (see Chap. 2).

The Mercenaries
While the correlations for Fans and Sympathizers are still easy to understand, since satisfaction and loyalty are equally positive, we find Fig. 1.24 two other customer groups that are more difficult to understand because they apparently combine contradictory characteristics. On the one hand, we see—below the Sympathizers—customers who are highly satisfied but still not emotionally loyal. And on the other hand, we find—to the left of the Sympathizers—customers who are emotionally loyal but nevertheless dissatisfied. Both are customer types who live in a certain conflict: In their case, satisfaction and emotional attachment obviously do not coincide.

The first of these two customer types that we are more interested in are the people in the lower right quadrant, colored yellow, of the Fig. 1.24: highly satisfied customers with no ties. Across all B2C industries, about 25% of all customers correspond to this type. Almost every company has such customers. They are those who state in surveys that they are highly satisfied with the service, but then suddenly and apparently without reason migrate to the competition. The reasons for this are obvious, and we have already discussed them in one of the opening chapters (cf. Sect. 1.3): These customers appreciate the performance of a provider, but—for reasons which we will elaborate on later—they have not built up an emotional relationship with the products and services of the brand. And because they are not committed, they have no qualms about switching providers and migrating to the competition if the latter offers them what they consider to be a comparable service.

So, if the competitor is no different in terms of performance, or if this difference is barely perceptible, all that is needed for these uncommitted customers is a small cause, a minimal impulse, to actually switch to the competition. This impulse is usually the price. As soon as a competitor acts aggressively on price with comparable product quality, these customers will defect to him. This is because they cannot identify any other differences between their old provider and the competition. The service seems the same to them, they do not see any differences in the image, they do not have any emotional attachment—and then the promise of a price advantage is enough to trigger their migration. These customers are, therefore, not loyal—rather, mercenary-like, they leave at the first opportunity as soon as a financially more attractive offer beckons. This is why we refer to them as "Mercenary customers" in the following.

Mercenaries, then, are highly satisfied, but fickle customers. And it is precisely because of them that we warned at the beginning of our book: "Beware of satisfied customers!" Because these Mercenaries customers cost every company dearly. They are virtually an indicator that a provider is investing its resources in the wrong way. After all, a large percentage of Mercenary customers means nothing more than that a company has repeatedly put the bulk of its efforts into costly performance improvement to further increase customer satisfaction. And at the same time, it has failed to build emotional loyalty. The result: customers remained mercenaries—i.e., customers who, despite a high level of satisfaction, behave just as disloyally as dissatisfied customers—with devastating effects for economic success.

These Mercenaries create short-term revenue, but this revenue is a Pyrrhic victory. It is the result of a customer relationship management that has a one-sided focus on satisfaction and is thus misguided. This is because revenue from Mercenary customers is, first, unattractive because it is "bought" with a distinct cost of the high investment in the company's performance coupled with low prices. Secondly, this revenue is deemed short-term and not sustainable—despite all efforts, the Mercenaries will soon leave the ship, so that the high-performance investments cannot be counter-financed even in the long term. And thirdly, mercenary customers put every company in a vicious circle: because a provider, who has geared his customer relationship management solely to satisfaction and in this way has created a large mercenary army among his customers, will have to compensate for the disloyalty of this type of mercenary customer. As soon as the company realizes that the customers are threatening to migrate to a competitor because of lower prices, firms will try to retain these customers by offering even lower prices—which will lead to even greater price aggressiveness on the part of the competitor and ultimately result in a price battle that will be ruinous for both companies. Or the supplier will try to compensate for the already existing churn of Mercenary customers by in turn poaching customers from another supplier. However, since the provider's image is overwhelmingly based on performance, his attempts to poach customers will only appeal to those customers of the competition who are price-sensitive and willing to switch—in other words, his mercenary customers. These then become his Mercenary customers, for whom he now must provide more service in order not to lose them. If you play out these relationships in full, you can understand why some industries, such as telecommunications providers or the electrical appliance trade, are drowning in price and discount battles.

Mercenary customers cost money in the end. This raises the question of how companies can effectively counter the development of mercenaryism. Can they do anything at all to turn their Mercenaries into Sympathizers—i.e., customers with real loyalty—and then perhaps even into fans? Or is mercenaryism an unchangeable personality trait of certain consumers, as one might assume with equal plausibility? Are Mercenaries perhaps so price-sensitive because they are under greater economic pressure? Or: Are they so disloyal because they are a product of the zeitgeist of postmodern society, in which loyalty counts for little and permanent change (*variety-seeking*) is an end in itself? If these explanations were correct, it would mean that certain socio-demographic, personal or psychological characteristics inevitably lead

1.6 The *Fan Portfolio*

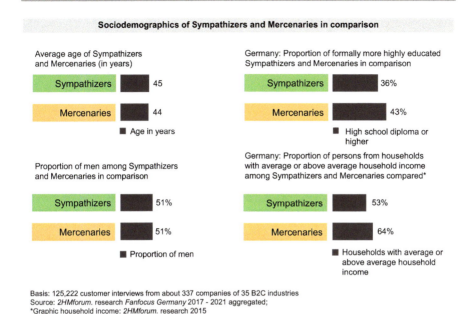

Fig. 1.25 Mercenary customers are more educated and wealthy

to the mercenary phenomenon. Mercenary customers would then be destiny, so to speak—a certain type of consumer that appears in all industries and is unavoidable. *FANOMICS* as a management program would then amount to nothing or would be reduced to identifying from the mass of potential customers those who are already Fans or Sympathizers based on their personality and behavioral characteristics. Influencing and thus developing Mercenaries into Sympathizers or Fans would therefore be less promising. This would be tantamount to an "acquiescence" for marketing and relationship management: the companies would be virtually blameless for the constant increase in the mercenary's rate.

So, are Mercenary customers a destiny or a self-inflicted problem? To answer this question, we systematically examined the various customer groups in terms of their socioeconomic profiles and their demands on suppliers as part of our basis research. We were particularly interested in answering the question of being a Mercenary are more likely to be found in structural characteristics or are indicative of corporate mismanagement. To answer this, we contrasted Mercenaries and Sympathizers— that is, the two customer types with identical satisfaction scores but different levels of loyalty. Comparing their sociodemographic and socioeconomic characteristics then suggests whether these characteristics are potential determinants of mercenaryism. The results are shown in Fig. 1.25 depicted.

First, we look at the left side of the graph: As is evident, Mercenary customers and Sympathizers do not differ from each other in average age or gender distribution. Initially, this argues against the thesis that sociodemographic characteristics are responsible for becoming a Mercenary customer. On the right-hand side of the chart, however, we see small discrepancies between Sympathizers and Mercenaries: among Mercenary customers, the proportion of people with higher educational qualifications is somewhat larger—and their average income is correspondingly higher. So, we find a distinct difference between Sympathizers and Mercenaries. However, this difference runs counter to the initial hypothesis: We had shown that Mercenary customers are particularly price-sensitive due to their performance orientation combined with a lack of loyalty. This raised the question of whether there might be financial reasons for this—in other words, whether Mercenary customers are price-sensitive because they must watch every penny, so to speak. The available data shows the opposite: Mercenary customers do not act out of economic need—they even have the somewhat greater financial resources available to them.

Thus, the price sensitivity of Mercenary customers does not stem from any financial motive. They look at the price, although their economic success does not dictate this. What might be the reason for this? The answer: Mercenaries perceive little to no "fit" between their central needs and the provider's services—hence they are not emotionally loyal. Correspondingly, they are disloyal in their purchasing behavior. They buy here today and there tomorrow because they ultimately do not care: because the supplier and its competitors appear interchangeable, owing to a lack of fit. Because of this perceived interchangeability, Mercenary customers resort to the only differentiating performance criterion in their purchasing decisions; namely price.

The desire to buy as cheaply as possible is, therefore, often not a conscious fundamental purchasing strategy on the part of Mercenaries, but a decision-making heuristic: a stopgap to be able to make a purchasing decision at all in the flood of offers. In other words, Mercenary customers behave like Mercenaries because their central needs are not (sufficiently) addressed by the supplier. It follows that being a Mercenary customer is not destiny. Mercenary customers are not mercenaries because they can't help it. They are Mercenaries because they are made to be. Suppliers themselves have trained them to be Mercenaries—by failing to understand or ignoring the core need of these customers, driving them into price comparison. The cause of customers' mercenary behavior, then, is mainly to be found in the providers' failure to focus on the needs of these customers. However, as we will show in detail in Chaps. 3 and 4, companies do have levers at their disposal to significantly reduce mercenary behavior among their customers.

The Captives

The next contradictory customer type has a relatively high level of loyalty to the company but is nevertheless dissatisfied. We are talking about the orange quadrant at the top left in Fig. 1.24, which comprises 15% of customers. At first glance, one might think that such customers are contract customers, for example, who—although dissatisfied—are tied to a provider by long-term contracts. But this is not the case for this customer type. When we talk about commitment, we do not mean legal or contractual commitment, but emotional commitment. In other words, we are talking about customers who have built up an emotional relationship with a provider's brands, products or services, but for whom the provider's performance does not, or no longer, meet expectations. How can this be?

In order to better understand this, it is important to once again visualize how we measure emotional commitment. We measure emotional commitment by using the *Fan Indicator*: It does not measure emotions, but rather the two central indicators of fan-typical relationships that we have derived from scientific fan research: namely, identification and perceived uniqueness of the fan relationship. Customers for whom we measure high values with this indicator thus show fan-like relationships, from which we can conclude their emotional attachment. For the group discussed here, this means: We are dealing with customers who have a fan-like relationship with their provider but are dissatisfied with the performance. Presumably, these customers used to be both highly engaged and also highly satisfied. They are, in other words, disappointed Sympathizers or even disappointed Fans.

How does it happen? Do you still remember our section on Fans? That Fans can also be dissatisfied with performance and still remain fans? That they chant wild protest slogans in front of their favorite club's home—which does not mean these fans are no longer fans, but on the contrary just proves that they are real fans. Such disappointed fans do not experience the situation that their soccer club or company does not perform as expected as pleasant. They suffer because they are trapped in the relationship with this player. They have invested emotionally in this relationship, and they cannot easily give up this investment. They are trapped in that relationship—regardless of whether the performance continues to be right or not. That's why we call these customer types "captives."

So, what happened to turn these customers from Sympathizers or Fans into Captives? Originally, they were very fond of the provider: their expectations were met, so satisfaction was high, and at the same time the brand and the company appealed to them emotionally and made them emotionally loyal. Then the provider's performance or service declined—at least that's how these customers perceived it. Incidentally, it is irrelevant whether the provider's performance actually deteriorated or whether it is "only" a perception. For the customer, this is irrelevant. The only thing that matters to him is that he is subjectively convinced that performance has declined. And no performance statistics from the provider can take away this impression.[25]

What happens now due to this perception of a supposedly worse performance? Will the customer immediately turn his back on the company and go to the competition? No, he won't do that. Because they have a comparatively high emotional attachment, they are Sympathizers of the company or even a Fan. And Fans, as we explained in detail at the beginning, forgive mistakes. This customer, because he no longer saw his expectations fulfilled, probably contacted the company, and demanded the expected performance. In other words, he complained. And thus, the decisive key to avoiding "captivity" was in the hands of the company: successful

---

[25] In the social sciences, this subjective absoluteness of judgment is called the Thomas theorem: "If men define situations as real, they're real in their consequences" (Thomas and Thomas 1928).

complaint management would have brought service delivery back in line with expectations, and this customer would have remained a Sympathizer or Fan. However, if complaint handling is not successful, he becomes a Captive: A customer, who still has a relatively high level of loyalty, but who is currently dissatisfied; a customer who has a high potential for sustainable business, but who has currently been carelessly squandered. We will discuss these relationships and the importance of complaint management in more detail in Sect. 4.2.

But what will become of the Captives? Will they remain eternally loyal and—like soccer fans to their club—figuratively forgive relegation to the Third League? Will they accept a permanent performance deficit? Hardly. Even the phrase "relatively high emotional attachment" deliberately chosen in the previous explanations about Captives should make it clear that a slow erosion of emotional connection is taking place among captive customers. If the company does not get a grip on the performance deficits or does not convey to the captive customer that it is doing everything it can to get a grip on the perceived problems, he or she gradually turns away—in the worst case, the original, now unfulfilled love turns into dislike: The Captives "migrate" to the bottom left of our diagram—to the Opponents.

The Opponents

This last group, shown in our diagram (cf. Fig. 1.24) is identifiable in the red quadrant at the bottom left with 15% of customers. These are people who—like the Fans or Sympathizers—obviously have a fairly consistent relationship between satisfaction and emotional attachment with regard to their provider, although in their case this is anything but reassuring. After all, these are customers who are dissatisfied and not emotionally loyal. To be clear, this is a group of current company customers. They may not be for much longer, but they still were, at least at the time of the survey. In terms of loyalty and satisfaction, these customers are the exact opposite of Fans—and they behave like them. Because these customers are more than just disappointed. They have become true adversaries of the company (cf. Sect. 4.4). They actively communicate this antagonism to the outside world and can thus seriously disrupt the acquisition of new customers by a company through negative word-of-mouth. They are adversaries who, like guerrilla fighters, suddenly and unexpectedly crossfire when a company tries to position itself via communication and marketing. We therefore call them Opponents. In our model, an Opponent customer is not simply someone who talks badly about a company, but only a (still) customer who does so.

Opponents are not worse or more antisocial than other customer groups. They are not sourpusses, complainers or destructive contemporaries who only want to make life difficult for a company out of resentment. And they were not always opponents. After all, no one becomes a customer of a company as an Opponent. Opponents are customers who have presumably gone through a long journey through the entire customer portfolio—during which they slowly turned from being initially satisfied new customer with long-term potential into an opponent. The Opponent customers make it clear what happens when companies fail to satisfy customers in the long term and fail to retain them emotionally—and even annoy them massively in their

1.6 The *Fan Portfolio*

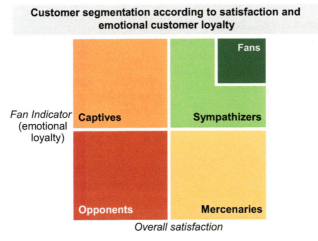

Fig. 1.26 The *Fan Portfolio*

perception. These customers do not "just" leave, which in itself represents considerable damage if you consider that they may be former Fans or Sympathizers, i.e., customers whose original emotional affection has turned into the opposite due to sustained performance deficits. Instead, these Opponents customers also actively work against the company to express their disappointment. Owing to their negative communication, they become a sensitive disruptive factor and trouble spot and actively advise many potential or actual customers against the provider in question. This makes them a real pain for any company (cf. Sects. 4.2 and 4.4).

If we now consider the customer types described—Fans, Sympathizers, Mercenaries, Captives, and Opponents—together, we see that the comparison made in Sect. 1.5 bears much more fruit than "just" the identification of the Fans. Rather, a comprehensive segmentation of a company's entire customer landscape is laid out before us—a complete portfolio of customer types. Figure 1.26 now shows the *Fan Portfolio* once again.

The classification of the entire customer landscape into the *Fan Portfolio* as shown (Fig. 1.26) has been theoretically derived, and also empirically substantiated with customer data from hundreds of companies exclusively for the German market. But what about other developed markets? Does the *Fan Portfolio* also work there? And indeed, using our *Fan Indicator* it is possible to measure the emotional attachment of customers worldwide in developed markets. There, too, we can make the important distinction of whether a satisfied customer is emotionally loyal—and in this way differentiate profitably between Mercenaries, Sympathizers and Fans. As empirical evidence, we specifically conducted the *Fanfocus G7*, an international pilot study, the results of which are published here for the first time.

The *Fanfocus G7:* Markets and Method

The study is similar in approach to *Fanfocus Germany*, which is why we call it *Fanfocus G7*: It surveys the relationship between emotional customer loyalty (i.e., the *Fan Indicator*) and customer satisfaction in seven countries for four industries. The seven countries selected are the G7 countries France, Great Britain, Italy, Japan, Canada, the USA, and Germany: all leading economic nations with highly developed markets in partly different cultural environments, in which the correlations we have postulated should be confirmed. Together, the G7 countries account for about one third of global economic output. The four sectors: automobiles, banks, online retail, and food retail were selected because, on the one hand, they represent comparable markets with similar market maturity across the G7 countries and, on the other hand, because there are some multinational companies that offer their products in all seven markets surveyed.

For each respondent, the relationship with their current provider in each of the four industries was surveyed. The customer interviews were conducted via an online panel; a total of more than 7000 interviews were conducted. As the *Fanfocus G7* is limited to seven countries and four industries, its findings can only be representative of the international market to a limited extent. However, the data basis is sufficient to illustrate the international validity of our argument.

Figure 1.27 presents across all G7 countries and aggregated across the four surveyed industries (automobiles, banks, online retail, and grocery) the interaction between overall satisfaction and the *Fan Indicator* in the *Fan Portfolio* and shows the

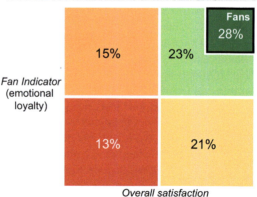

Fig. 1.27 The *Fan Portfolio* in the G7 countries

Basis: 7,271 interviews in the G7 countries with customers from the automotive, banking, online retail and grocery sectors
Source: 2HMforum. research *Fanfocus G7* 2022

percentages for the five customer groups (Fans, Sympathizers, Mercenaries, Captives, and Opponents). The presentation thus follows the same logic that we used in Fig. 1.24 in which we presented the data from *Fanfocus Germany* for the German market.

If you recall, we had already established with a view to the *Fan Portfolio* that the situation for the four sectors investigated in the G7 countries is comparable with the German market. This is because in the G7 countries there is a comparably high proportion of highly satisfied customers at 72% (cf. Fig. 1.14). In these markets, too, it is therefore hardly possible to set oneself apart from the competition by offering more service—and this makes it all the more important to look at the emotional customer loyalty. Figure 1.27 shows that many of the providers in the industries studied have apparently already adjusted to these *conditions*, since the *Fan Rate* aggregated across all the industries and countries studied is 28%. In the four remaining customer segments of the *Fan Portfolio*, however, the differences from the German measurements are marginal (2 to 4 percentage points).

As already mentioned in the presentation of the German data, the *Fan Rate* reflects industry- and market-specific differences with regard to the quality of customer relationships. The same applies to the influence of different cultural framework conditions. The deviations between the German and G7 portfolios should be assessed accordingly: they are an expression of a differently pronounced relationship quality in the industries and markets studied. This is precisely why the *Fan Rate is suitable* as a management tool, since it measures what is essential; namely customer value, and reacts sensitively to differences in customer loyalty.

For both *Fan Portfolios,* from Germany as well as from the G7 countries, it is true that all five sectors of the *Fan Portfolio are represented* in both cases. This confirms what we had already postulated on the basis of the findings from Germany: The *Fan Indicator* has a high added value for segmenting the customer landscape because it enables us to differentiate within the satisfied customers: between high and low loyalty customers. And it does this differentiation not only in Germany, but obviously also in central international markets of the most diverse cultural groups.

The data for the G7 countries also impressively illustrate that the *Fan Indicator* developed based upon our fan definition makes it possible to identify fans in a wide variety of cultural circles. This is shown by the further differentiation of the G7 findings by industry, similar to the German data, in Fig. 1.28.

Here, too, the industry differences—as with the German results—do not correspond to intuitive expectations. The fact that among the four industries studied, online mail order, i.e., an industry which has no products of its own and largely does without personal customer contact, achieves the highest *Fan Rate* and is able to leave the car manufacturers in the dust with its emotionalizing "high-involvement" product, is surprising at first glance. At the same time, food retail, which supplies customers with essentials on a daily basis, has a weaker *Fan Rate* than the banking industry with its tarnished image. Once again, the *Fan Rate* of an industry has nothing to do with the character of the products, but with the quality of the customer relationship. As already mentioned, you do not have to build motorcycles to have a

Fig. 1.28 Average *Fan Rates* of four industries in the G7 countries

high fan rating. Conversely, building motorcycles does not automatically mean that customers are also Fans.

The *Fan Rates* shown are a remarkable finding because they prove that the *Fan Indicator,* we have developed is capable of producing conclusive and differentiating results in international markets as well. In the next step, we will demonstrate that the fans identified in this way also show the fan-typical behavior we predicted across all countries—and in this manner prove that our fundamental considerations regarding fan relationships are of international and cross-cultural validity.

1.6.2 The Validation of the *Fan Portfolio* Through Fan-Specific Behavior

Now that we have validated the German findings on the various customer types of the *Fan Portfolio using* international data, it is time to once again check and prove the accuracy of our theoretical preliminary considerations. We had derived the *Fan Indicator* from our review of the research on fans by showing that identification and uniqueness are the central drivers behind every fan relationship. Therefore, based on empirical evidence we formed the *Fan Indicator*, which serves to identify Fan Customers, only based on these two constructs.

However, we had shown in the theoretical analysis at the beginning that fans have numerous other characteristics and show some fan-typical behaviors: For example, they make their fanhood publicly visible and deal with it freely, or they invest a lot of time and money to live out their fan relationship. Likewise, they show wholehearted trust in their star and regard their relationship with him or her as long-lasting and

1.6 The *Fan Portfolio*

permanent (cf. the list in Sect. 1.2). All these characteristics typically occur among fans, as social science studies on fan behavior have shown. Nevertheless, we have not included these behaviors in our definition since, in contrast to the characteristics of identification and uniqueness, they are not the reason behind then fan relationship. However, these behaviors are certainly useful indicators of fanhood. So, what could be more obvious than to contrast these indicators with our definition of Fan Customers? If our identification of Fan Customers by the *Fan Indicator* is valid, then Fan Customers identified by our method should exhibit these fan-typical behaviors more frequently than other customers. To test this, we surveyed four fan-typical behavioral indicators across all customers, namely (1) their willingness to talk positively about the supplier, i.e., to communicate the relationship to others, (2) their willingness to invest, (3) their willingness to have a long-lasting relationship, and (4) their trust in the relationship. We linguistically adapted these fan-typical behavioral indicators to a customer relationship, since we are dealing with Fan Customers, and asked the customers about their willingness to *recommend* (= willingness to communicate aggressively to the outside world), willingness to *cross-buy* (= willingness to invest), intention to have a lasting relationship, (= willingness to have a long-lasting relationship), and their *trust in the provider.* Figures 1.29 and 1.30 show the results—initially again only for the German market—separated according to B2C and B2B customers.

How Figs. 1.29 and 1.30 show, the identification of Fan Customers by our *Fan Indicator* has been successful in several respects. Fan customers, as we have defined them, almost without exception show the highest level of trust in their provider; they have the intention of a lasting customer relationship and have an extremely high

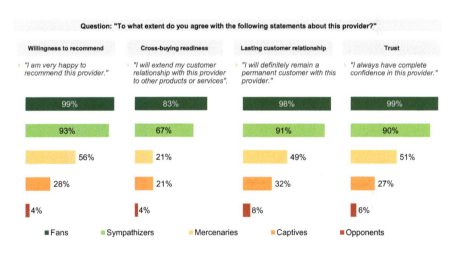

Fig. 1.29 B2C fan customers show fan-typical behaviors

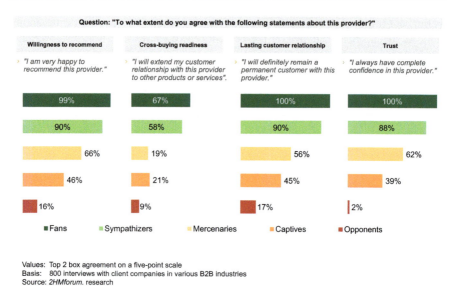

Fig. 1.30 B2B fan customers show fan-typical behaviors

willingness to recommend and cross-purchase. This applies to both B2C and B2B customers.

Following the same logic, we validate the data from the G7 countries. Here, too, we examined below whether the Fan Customers we have identified show more fan-typical behavior than other respondents. As in *Fanfocus Germany,* we used the *willingness to recommend* (= willingness to communicate aggressively to the outside world) and the *cross-purchasing willingness* (= willingness to invest) as indicators. We also surveyed customers' *product knowledge* (familiarity with the supplier's product range) and *loyalty* (loyalty in the event of quality problems). Figure 1.31 shows the results for the customers of the four industries studied in the G7 countries.

The result is clear. The Fan Customers identified by our *Fan Indicator* also show the strongest fan-typical behavior patterns in the G7 countries—they actually lead a fan-typical customer relationship and are therefore particularly valuable. In addition, the graphs show Figs. 1.29, 1.30 and 1.31 that fan-typical behavior always declines across the different segments of the *Fan Portfolio*: Sympathizers customers always follow in second place, Mercenary customers in third place, and so on. This suggests that our *Fan Indicator* is not an arbitrary construct but identifies Fan Customers—not only in Germany; but across all markets and cultures studied.

Our *Fan Indicator* thus has a very valid theoretical and empirical basis. Our measurement is able to conclusively distinguish fans from non-fans according to objective criteria. It forms solid and reliable criteria that is even more valid than customers' self-assessment. This is borne out by additional data from Germany. Since we asked customers—both Fan Customers and others—whether they consider themselves to be fans. (cf. Fig. 1.32).

1.6 The *Fan Portfolio*

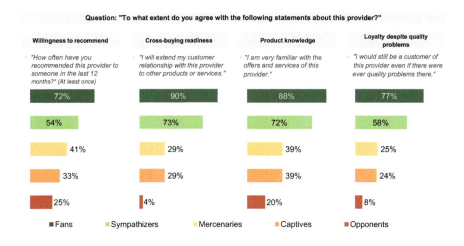

Fig. 1.31 Fan customers in G7 countries show fan-typical behaviors

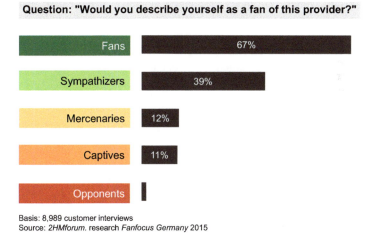

Fig. 1.32 The fuzziness of fan self-assessment

As the chart Fig. 1.32 indicates, there is admittedly a large overlap between the classification by our *Fan Indicator* and the customers' self-assessment. Around two-thirds of Fan Customers also describe themselves as "fans" and thus do so more frequently than any other customer group. The everyday understanding of the term fan distinctly has a lot of overlap with our empirical measurement. More important than the similarities, however, are the differences: nearly one-third of fans do not describe themselves as fans, which means they are not aware of how emotionally loyal they are to their provider. Conversely, almost 40% of Sympathizers consider themselves Fan Customers, although their emotional attachment is not sufficiently pronounced for this, and even 12% of Mercenaries, who lack any attachment, consider themselves to be in fan mode. To identify Fan Customers, it is therefore not sufficient to ask the customers themselves about their subjective classification—because on the one hand, this would not identify almost a third of the fans and on the other hand, it would incorrectly label a large proportion of the non-fans as Fans.[26]

1.6.3 The Complete Segmentation of the Customer Landscape Through the *Fan Portfolio*

With a view to the previous section, we can therefore state overall: The *Fan Indicator* is a stable and valid measure for identifying Fan Customers and thus also the other customer groups in the *Fan Portfolio*. Essentially, this classification forms the fundamental analytical platform of our approach.

The *Fan Portfolio proves* that the two indicators of satisfaction and loyalty obviously reflect different customer characteristics, because there are both satisfied and dissatisfied customers in the portfolio, each with high or low emotional loyalty. And at the same time, it provides fascinating evidence of the added value of our approach of deriving the indicators for emotional commitment from the fan concept in the first step and segmenting the customer landscape according to their emotional commitment in relation to customer satisfaction in the second step. The resulting customer segments differentiate themselves in terms of their relationship quality and customer value (cf. Chap. 2). This means: The *Fan Portfolio provides companies with* a completely new, highly economically relevant customer segmentation and thus access to target group-specific control of all customer-related processes. They can deploy resources in sales, marketing and service in a more differentiated way. They will achieve greater impact with reduced effort because their measures can be tailored to the characteristic features of the customer groups from the *Fan Portfolio*.

One or the other methodologically savvy reader may ask: How were the boundaries between the various customer segments drawn or defined? Solving this problem was indeed not easy, because of course the boundaries between the segments are fluid. Nevertheless, it is necessary to draw such boundaries: Because only the formation of the different segments in connection with the assignment of the customers results in the decisive information advantage, as one urgently needs it for the successful control of enterprises. So, to achieve the clearest possible delineation between the segments, we have repeatedly looked at the empirical findings in hundreds of customer studies for companies in a wide range of industries over a

---

[26] Due to this fuzziness, research approaches which identify fans by self-assessment always have a limited construct validity (e.g. Wann and Branscombe 1993; Wann 2002).

period of more than ten years. We looked for patterns in customer behavior and analyzed exactly where, for example, Fan behavior ends, and Sympathizer behavior begins. We identified where there were significant jumps and breaks in the distribution of customers within the *Fan Portfolio* and derived the segment boundaries on which our classification is based on the interpretation of these empirical findings. This allows the customers of each company to be classified reliably and accurately.

We have drawn the segment boundaries of the *Fan Portfolio* based upon empirical findings—and we applied them in this stable and fixed form as a classification grid for our analyses to all companies from all industries. Therefore, as already mentioned, the different area sizes of the differently colored segments must not be misunderstood as integrals: The areas and their sizes result from the defined boundary drawings. They say something about which customer type an individual customer can be assigned to, if he could be designated to a certain area based on his satisfaction and loyalty within the *Fan Portfolio*. However, the areas do not correspond to the size of the individual customer segments, so they say nothing about the number of customers behind each of the individual areas at a concrete company.

The *Fan Portfolio*—and it is essential to keep this in mind—is a segmentation of a company's customers, but not of the entire market. It does not therefore reflect how "non-customers" rate a company or whether they have an emotional attachment to it. The totality of all potential customers must be imagined as a type of environment around the *Fan Portfolio*. These include former customers who have turned their backs on the provider—for whatever reason—potential new customers who are yet to be recruited, customers of the competition—those who are willing to switch as well as those who are loyal—and consumers who are outside the target group and are, therefore, only of interest as an observing public, but do not represent a potential customer segment. If one visualizes this connection, it becomes clear that changes in the *Fan Portfolio* of a company cannot only occur through shifts and migrations between the five different customer types. Equally important is that migration from the surrounding population of potential customers into the individual customer types (or, conversely, migration out of the customer types) can—and usually does—occur at any time.

The *Fan Portfolio* clearly demonstrates the conclusiveness of our previous argumentation and its derivation: On the one hand, it shows that satisfaction is not enough to turn customers into fans—rather, that this requires additional emotional attachment. On the other hand, the *Fan Portfolio* shows that even high retention quality, expressed by the *Fan Indicator*, is not enough on its own. Only the maximum satisfaction that goes hand in hand with loyalty ensures that we can really call customers Fans. The significance of this described interaction of satisfaction and emotional customer loyalty can be well illustrated if we now—knowing the entire *Fan Portfolio* and the different customer types—take another look at the findings of our empirical basis studies, which we have previously discussed in Sect. 1.5 para. Figure 1.33 first shows the *Fan Portfolio* shares of the various customer groups for the *Fanfocus Germany*. However, the five customer types from Fans to Opponents are not arranged in segments here, but horizontally in a bar chart. Therefore, in contrast to the representation in the *Fan Portfolio,* we can also directly see the

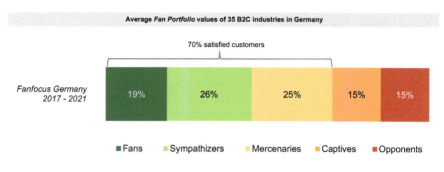

Fig. 1.33 70% are satisfied—but only one in five customers is a fan

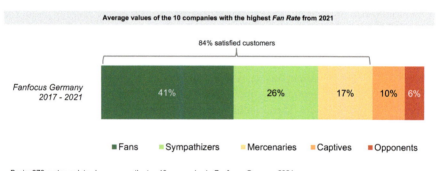

Fig. 1.34 The *Fan Portfolio* average of the top ten companies in 2021

proportions of the individual customer types according to the different sizes of the colored blocks. However, the definition of the various customer groups, the color assignment, and their differentiation from one another are identical to the segmentation within the *Fan Portfolio*.

By changing the representation from the *Fan Portfolio* to the bar chart in Fig. 1.33 we can now clearly see: The leading B2C companies in Germany are doing a decent job. In addition to the 19% true fans, which we already detailed, they have an average of 26% Sympathizers. So nearly half of their customers are satisfied and emotionally loyal. Another 25% are Mercenary customers who are satisfied; but not emotionally loyal-and only 15% each are Captives or Opponents. But what at first glance appears to be satisfactory in the overall findings still holds enormous potential for improvement. This becomes clear when looking at the portfolios of the top ten companies from *Fanfocus Germany* with the highest *Fan Rate*s across all sectors (cf. Fig. 1.34). The positively charged customer segments of Fans and Sympathizers are much larger among them—and on average they have correspondingly fewer Mercenaries customers and only slightly problematic customer segments such as

1.6 The Fan Portfolio

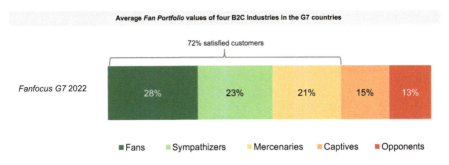

Fig. 1.35 G7 countries: 72% are satisfied—but not even one in three customers is a fan

Captives or Opponents. This comparison with the best demonstrates how great the potential for improvement is that German companies still have in improving their customer relationships.

Again, let's look at the data from the G7 countries. Figure 1.35 shows the *Fan Portfolio* shares of the various customer groups of the *Fanfocus G7*.

The data from Figs. 1.33–1.35 prove one of our core statements as to why customer satisfaction as a control variable for corporate success and the customer satisfaction management based on it can only be successful to a limited extent. Take another look at the proportions of satisfied customers marked in brackets in the figures. Here it becomes clear: Across the industries studied, 70% of German B2C customers (G7: 72%) are already satisfied—but not even one in five customers (G7: not even one in three customers) is really a Fan. So, the *Fan Rate* can still be increased—but customer satisfaction is already very high. A company's attempt to further increase customer satisfaction by costly improvements in performance is therefore bound to fail for two reasons: Firstly, customer satisfaction will eventually reach a ceiling effect (if it has not already done so in some companies): It will then simply no longer be possible to increase it. On the other hand, it will no longer be possible to position oneself and set oneself apart from the competition through satisfaction: After all, how can you stand out if all companies have excellent satisfaction scores?

If, on the other hand, emotional customer loyalty is added as a control variable, we can see how powerful this approach is, since loyalty does precisely what was not possible before: separating the wheat from the chaff within the mass of highly satisfied customers and aligning oneself in such a way that one not "only" has satisfied customers, but as many Sympathizers or, even better, Fans as possible. This is particularly impressive in the B2B sector, for which we present exemplary data from Germany (cf. Fig. 1.36).

Two remarkable correlations stand out here: First, in Germany, we measure 55% emotionally loyal and simultaneously satisfied customers in the B2B sector—Fans and Sympathizers considered together. This means that the majority of B2B

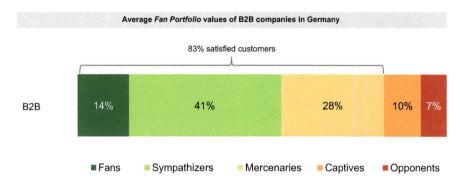

Fig. 1.36 The *Fan Portfolio* in the B2B area

customers already feel emotionally loyal to their suppliers. So, it is not just theoretically wrong to claim that emotional customer loyalty doesn't play a role in B2B. On the contrary, the data prove that this assertion completely misses the point of empirical reality. Emotional customer loyalty is even—as the data shows—a prerequisite for success in the B2B sector. Because when so many companies seem to know how to build an emotional bond with their customers by recognizing their core needs and meeting them in a focused manner, it is hardly possible to impress as a provider in this environment if you aimlessly focus only on increasing satisfaction.

Secondly, it is worth noting that this proportion of emotionally loyal customers in the B2B sector is around 10 percentage points higher than in many German B2C companies. Correspondingly, the proportion of Captives and Opponents is significantly lower among them than among B2C companies. This is not only a further indication of how important emotional ties are in the B2B sector but is also an indication of where the common misconception comes from that there are no Fan Customers in the B2B sector: It is probably due to the clearly different relationship between Fans and Sympathizers in the two areas. While Fans and Sympathizers are almost equal in the B2C sector, the proportion of Sympathizers is much higher in the B2B sector—only one in four of the emotionally highly committed customers is also a Fan. In other words, B2B companies have just as much, if not more, potential for emotionally loyal customers. It's just that these customers exhibit fan-typical customer behavior to a lesser extent, such as active recommendation or a focus on one provider. The reason for this is clear: These behaviors are ruled out for some B2B customers, for example, owing to a multi-supplier strategy for risk hedging. In this respect, there are certain limits to the level of *Fan Rate* in B2B, but not to emotional

1.6 The *Fan Portfolio*

customer loyalty. Here, therefore, a high rate of Sympathizers is almost as valuable as the *Fan Rate*—and this is precisely what many German companies in the B2B sector are evidently already relying on.

1.6.4 The Complete *Fan Portfolio* in Industry Comparison: National and International

Let's take another look at the B2C sector. In Fig. 1.21 we had already presented the *Fan Rates* from *Fanfocus Germany* of 35 consumer sectors examined. Figure 1.37 now completes the picture and shows the values of the entire *Fan Portfolio* in an industry comparison.

The bar chart allows for a quick intuitive comparison of numerous *Fan Portfolios* at a glance—of industries as well as companies—and thus allows for further conclusions. We had discussed how surprising the *Fan Rates of* some industries are in Sect. 1.5 discussed in more detail. With the knowledge of the customer groups of the entire *Fan Portfolio,* the picture is now completed. And here it becomes clear: High or low rates among fans, Mercenaries or Opponents do not come about by chance. Rather, there are explainable processes behind them, which we will take a closer look at in the further course of the book. We have already selected a few noteworthy aspects in advance:

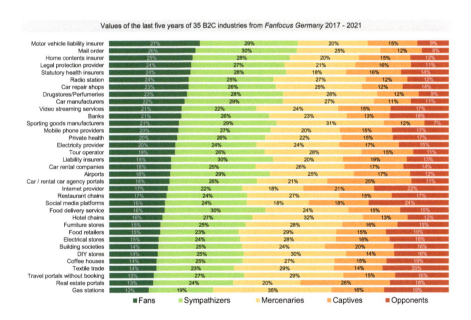

Fig. 1.37 The *Fan Portfolio* of over 300 German companies in an industry comparison

– The five leading sectors in the ranking are not only at the top in terms of *Fan Rate*. If Sympathizers are included in the analysis, more than half of their customers have a high emotional connection to their provider. These include insurers, legal protection providers and mail order companies—industries with complex products and little personal contact with customers, which at first glance one might not have expected such high loyalty values.
– It is no coincidence that gas stations are in last place. They have the highest percentage of Mercenary customers. At first glance, this is not surprising—the choice of a gas station is often made involuntarily by the fuel gauge. But these constraints aside: Many motorists choose the nearest fuel provider solely based on the prices visible from the road. After all, in decades of marketing, the oil companies have not really succeeded in positioning themselves in any way other than through price. The result is an army of Mercenaries.
– Health insurers in Germany are often seen as authoritarian, less customer-oriented institutions. Our data show that this image is long outdated. Health insurers have a high retention rate—and only an average proportion of Captives.
– Social media platforms are often believed to have all their users be Fans, as tools like the thumbs up button have made the concept of "Fan" omnipresent. The data paints a different picture: social media channels have a below-average *Fan Rate* and the highest proportion of Opponents. The negative everyday experiences and frustrations of many users are becoming a burden for the industry.
– Despite software scandals, car manufacturers still enjoy a fairly high level of emotional customer loyalty: 51% fans and Sympathizers speak for themselves.
– On average, video streaming services have several hours of screen contact with their customers every week—but they do not make enough of it. They are clearly unable to convert their reach into above-average satisfaction and loyalty: One in three of their viewers is dissatisfied and feels no attachment to the brand.
– The banks may have suffered an image blow owing to the financial crisis, but the emotional connection of their customers has obviously barely suffered. The industry is in the top third in this respect.
– And Internet providers, with 43% Captives and Opponents, have more than just an image problem: Here, customer care processes apparently do not match expectations.

These examples illustrate the additional insights into successful and problematic customer relationships that can be gained with just a first look at the *Fan Portfolio*. Let us therefore look again at our international data from the *Fanfocus G7* with this perspective. In Fig. 1.35 we showed how the *Fan Portfolio* looks in bar form across the four surveyed industries and seven countries in the overall result. This picture can be further differentiated by industry and country. Let us first look at the various industries (automobiles, food retail, online retail, banks) in comparison across the seven countries (Fig. 1.38).

We looked in more detail at the differences between the *Fan Rates* of the various sectors and the possible reasons for this in connection with Fig. 1.28. Figure 1.38 now shows the complete *Fan Portfolio* for the different industries—and immediately

1.6 The *Fan Portfolio*

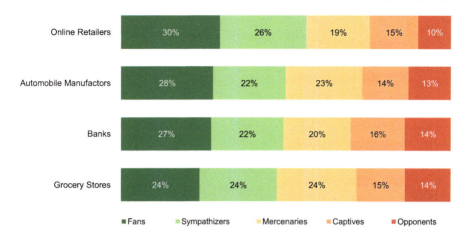

Basis: 7,271 interviews in the G7 countries with customers from the automotive, banking, online retailing and grocery sectors
Source: *2HMforum.* research *Fanfocus G7* 2022

Fig. 1.38 The *Fan Portfolio:* industry comparison across the G7 countries

further insights can be derived. The two industries with the lower *Fan Rates*—i.e., banks and grocery stores—simultaneously have the higher proportion of dissatisfied customers, i.e., of Captives and Opponents (this observation seems trivial at first glance, but we will see later that one does not necessarily follow from the other). This means: Something is obviously wrong here at the performance level compared to the other two sectors. At the same time, we see: Online retail—Sympathizers and Fans combined—has more emotionally loyal customers overall among satisfied customers than the other industries. Which means that these providers understand better than car manufacturers, banks, and grocers how to turn their satisfied customers into emotionally loyal customers. The optimization opportunities for grocery retailers and banks are consequently two-pronged: companies in these industries must initially reduce performance deficits to create more customer satisfaction, and they must secondly increase customer loyalty among these satisfied customers.

Even more revealing than the differentiation of the G7 findings by industry, however, is the breakdown of the G7 findings by country. We showed at the beginning of Sect. 1.6.2 that the *Fan Portfolio* also yields substantial findings on international markets. Now it is even more interesting to compare the individual markets and to investigate to what extent the *Fan Portfolio* unfolds the same explanatory power in other economies as in Germany. (cf. Fig. 1.39).

What becomes particularly clear here are the extremely small differences overall between most of the countries analyzed. Germany, Italy, Canada, Great Britain, and France present an almost congruent picture with only negligible deviations—the customers surveyed in the four sectors are distributed almost identically across the

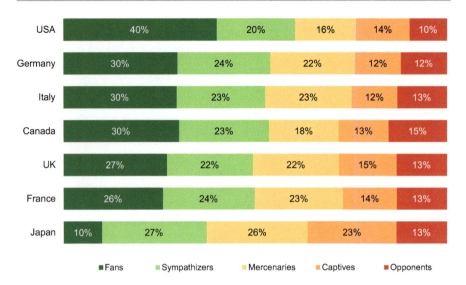

Fig. 1.39 The *Fan Portfolio*: comparison of G7 countries across all four sectors

five categories of the *Fan Portfolio*. The shares of Fans, Sympathizers, Mercenaries, etc. in the portfolio do not diverge by more than two percentage points around the common mean in all these countries. This is a remarkable finding, since it proves that the *Fan Indicator* is not only capable of producing valid, conclusive, and differentiating results in international markets. It also shows that it actually produces comparable measurement results in comparable cultural environments and markets.

There are only two clear differences between the countries: In Japan, the average *Fan Rate* of the four industries studied is much lower and, in the USA, much higher than in the other G7 countries. At the same time, the proportion of Captives customers is unusually high in Japan, while the proportion of Sympathizers and Mercenaries customers is unusually low in the USA. This raises the question of whether there are fundamental cultural differences in mentality between nations that are reflected in emotional attachment and thus in the *Fan Portfolio*. It is conceivable that these differences in the measured values are due to individual industries that play a special role in the respective countries. Or they may be country-specific differences caused by culture and mentality. If the latter were the case, however, these differences would also have to show up within each industry. To investigate this, we break down the findings by country and industry at the same time. Cf. Fig. 1.40. The overall picture is multifaceted.

There are indeed specific differences for Japan and the U.S. across all industries that are consistently evident. Japan's outlier values are the most striking: in all four industries, the proportion of Fan Customers in Japan is significantly lower than in the

1.6 The *Fan Portfolio*

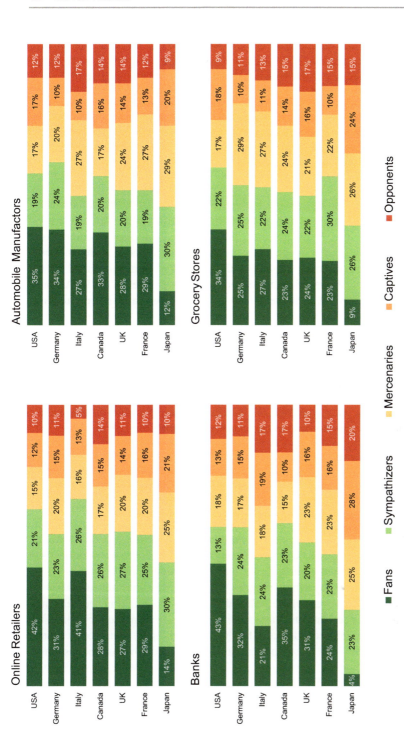

Fig. 1.40 The *Fan Portfolio*: four industries in seven countries

other countries. At the same time, the proportion of Sympathizers in Japan is not significantly higher, making Japan the country with the lowest proportion of satisfied and emotionally loyal customers (= Fans and Sympathizers). At the same time, the proportion of Captives is also consistently highest in Japan. The Japanese figures for the banking industry are particularly striking: only 4% of Japanese bank customers are Fans of their bank, but 28% feel trapped in this customer relationship. Since captives are also emotionally loyal, this results in an unusual finding: Japan hardly has fewer customers with high loyalty (= Fans, Sympathizers and Captives) on average, but fewer satisfied customers: In terms of the proportion of satisfied customers (Fans, Sympathizers and Mercenaries), Japan brings up the rear in all four sectors.

The other striking country-specific finding relates to the USA: it has the highest *Fan Rate in* all four sectors, and its high proportion of satisfied and emotionally loyal customers (= Fans and Sympathizers) puts it in second place (behind Italy, Germany, Canada or France, depending on the sector). Clearly, high emotional loyalty values are the order of the day in the USA. This is accompanied by the lowest proportions of Mercenaries in three out of four industries in the USA. Since the proportion of satisfied customers (Fans, Sympathizers and Mercenaries) is therefore not significantly higher overall in the USA than in European countries, this means nothing other than that companies in the USA apparently find it easier to turn satisfied customers into emotionally loyal customers.

Thus, the interaction of satisfaction and loyalty in the two countries mentioned explains the specific peculiarities: Japan has the fewest satisfied customers on average, and the USA is better at turning satisfied customers into emotionally loyal customers than other countries. We will examine the possible culture-specific reasons for these two phenomena in the following excursus.

Excursus: What Is Different in Japan and the USA?
Before we go into this in more detail, a preliminary remark: It is not possible to describe the mentality of a nation or the population of a country without making gross generalizations. Of course, each person is an individual—"Japanese" as a homogeneous group who all behave similarly does not exist—just as there is no such thing as "the Germans" or "the Americans" as a homogeneous group. However, there are ways of thinking and behaving in every culture that are more prominent and more common there than elsewhere. In Germany, for example, more value is placed on punctuality than in many other countries. However, this does not mean that all Germans are always and everywhere punctual. Such ways of thinking and behaving, which are typical of a certain national mentality, are what we want to focus on in the following. Based on our special findings for the USA and Japan, we talked to experts in these markets about how these findings can be explained. Overall, the responses paint an exciting picture:

Internationally, the Japanese are considered extremely polite and reserved. For a Japanese, it is important to always keep one's composure and not lose one's composure even in the greatest consternation. Exposure or embarrassment is the worst thing that can happen to a Japanese person in public. Because of this mentality,

Japanese people are usually reserved: they do not come out of their shells, tend to be introverted in front of strangers, and rarely show emotions like anger or euphoria openly. This is also reflected in the fan behavior of the Japanese: It is true that there are also fans in Japan in sports, music and culture who are enthusiastic about certain stars. But they show this affection with more restraint and less extroverted fan behavior. After Japan's victory over Germany at the 2022 World Cup in Qatar, for example, the Japanese fans left their block only after they had disposed of all the garbage there. The Japanese remain disciplined—even as fans.

Now, one might think that the proverbial Japanese restraint and politeness should also be expressed in the behavior of Japanese customers toward their provider—for example, that the Japanese do not complain or complain out of politeness. The opposite is the case. The roles of courtesy between provider and customer are clearly distributed in Japan. The customer is king (or maybe even higher)—and the supplier must court him. Even a stop at the gas station illustrates the characteristic conditions in Japan: Here, the service that fell victim to rationalization in Europe 50 years ago still exists. A gas station attendant refuels the vehicle, cleans the windows during the process and checks the oil. Customers take this for granted. But the service goes much further: the gas station attendant stops the flowing traffic to make it easier for his customers to thread their way in—not, of course, without then thanking the stopped motorists for their cooperation with a bow.

So, anyone who wishes to sell in Japan has to go to great lengths to woo customers—and because this has been the case for decades, this has educated the Japanese to be extremely demanding customers. The anecdote about a customer returning a Mercedes because the ashtray seems too small, which is considered a joke in Europe, can become reality in Japan. For example, the Japanese complain about intact deliveries of goods if only the packaging is damaged. The fact that the packaging only has the purpose of protecting the goods is not an argument for Japanese customers. All suppliers on the Japanese market know this. For them, the basic rule is that if you satisfy one Japanese, you will hardly have any customer complaints anywhere in the world. If you can make it there, you'll make it anywhere.

These high expectations of Japanese customers are difficult for many providers to meet. Because of this, satisfaction ratings in Japan are comparatively low. And the powerful role of the wooed customer makes the Japanese willing to switch: they like to try out other providers, so they display much less customer loyalty. To counteract this, many companies in Japan rely on elaborate sales measures: High personnel deployment, personal customer contact and even door-to-door visits are not unusual means in Japan, even for large international suppliers, to keep customers in line.

The fact that specifically banks in Japan have fewer fans than average is not surprising. For decades, there have been virtually no interest on credit balances and high bank fees in Japan. Switching providers is extremely costly and cumbersome for customers, and many complain about the inadequate service orientation of the financial institutions. Many Japanese therefore do not even conduct their daily money transactions via banks, but rather in the *convenience store* around the corner, where they can make their transfers at the checkout in cash together with their groceries.

So much for the Japanese situation. In the U.S., on the other hand, things are completely different: US-Americans are often outgoing, extroverted, wear their hearts on their sleeves and also like to "come out of their shells." A large part of the population goes through life with a fundamentally positive world view: When in doubt, US-Americans find the conditions they encounter "O.K." for now. For them, the glass is usually half full, not half empty. The skeptical view of Germans, for example, who like to see problems everywhere and make them a topic of discussion, is unusual to them. In doubt, they see more opportunities than risks.

US-Americans also live out their fanhood with this worldview—and it is no coincidence that the USA is the country where the term "fan" in its current international meaning first saw the light of day some 130 years ago. Americans love to be enthusiastic about things. This is based on a certain, one might say, rational hedonism: US-Americans have understood that they have a much higher emotional quality of experience when they are enthusiastic about the things and events around them. Accordingly, they quickly show commitment to a cause and fan-typical behavior: For example, US-Americans enjoy cheering along at sporting events—regardless of whether it is the Super Bowl or a third-class match in a regional league.

In the U.S., it is almost good manners to be a fan of someone or something. Anyone who answers the question, "What's your team?", with an apathetic "I do not prefer any team", is often met with perplexity and disbelief: often in the opinion of an US-American, a heart must beat for some team. So being a fan and being enthusiastic is an everyday occurrence for Americans (see also Allison and Knoester 2021). And because there are fans of everything and everyone in the U.S., on the one hand there is a great deal of tolerance for fan behavior in public, and on the other hand the framework for fan behavior is also socially defined: riots by fan groups (although they do occur) are more rare in the U.S. than in Europe, for example. With this openness, positive world view and enthusiasm, it is no longer a long way for a satisfied customer in the USA to become a fan customer: Once a customer is satisfied with a provider, it only takes a little impetus to become a fan.

The data from Fig. 1.40 confirm the finding that *Fan Rates* cannot simply be predicted intuitively: For example, across five countries, the values for car manufacturers and for grocery stores are quite similar, while the scatter in online mail order and for banks is somewhat larger. It is worth noting that in each sector it is a different country that can claim the highest *Fan Rate*: For mail order it is Italy, for car manufacturers it is Germany, for banks it is Canada and for grocers it is France. It is possible that one might have expected the findings from France and Germany because of the internationally common stereotypes of "savoir vivre" and "Made in Germany". But the fact that the Italians are fans of mail order, and the Canadians of their banks is surprising. This confirms what we said at the beginning: *Fan rates* can't be predicted with a crystal ball or estimated from reading three social media posts. Intuition also often lets you down. You have to measure it regularly to be able to control it with *FANOMICS*.

The analysis so far has illustrated—in addition to the common features of many countries—that on the one hand there can be culture-specific differences in the

1.6 The *Fan Portfolio* 87

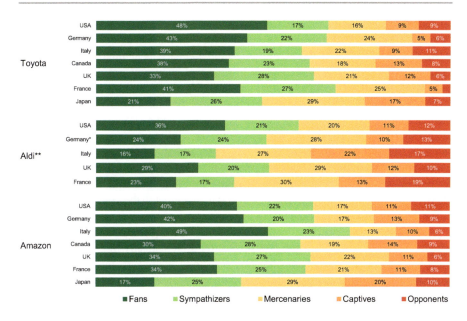

Values: *Average of Aldi South and Aldi North; **No values available for Aldi in Japan and Canada.
Basis: 7,271 interviews in the G7 countries with customers from the automotive, banking, online retailing and grocery stores sectors;
Source: 2HMforum. research *Fanfocus G7* 2022

Fig. 1.41 The *Fan Portfolio* of selected companies in a country comparison

characteristics of the *Fan Portfolio*, which either express the country-specific differences in the maturity of relationship management or are culturally conditioned—or both at the same time. On the other hand, these national characteristics can be identified through country-specific industry benchmarks. This second point is particularly important for internationally oriented companies when it comes to *Fan Portfolio comparison of* different countries. It is precisely in this comparison that the superior benefit of the *Fan Portfolio* lies for international companies: based on the central control variable, the *Fan Rate*, the various national markets can be compared with each other without ignoring the different cultural conditions. This then immediately yields indications of control options. We present in Fig. 1.41 exemplary such data from the *Fanfocus G7* for three large international companies that have a nearly nationwide presence in the markets studied: The car manufacturer *Toyota*, the grocery chain *Aldi* (not present in Japan and Canada), and the mail order company *Amazon*.

Figure 1.41 illustrates how the selected companies fare in terms of customer loyalty in the seven markets listed. For each of these companies, it can be seen across the various countries where relationship management is more or less effective (if we exclude the consistent outliers Japan and the USA). For example, carmaker *Toyota* scores high in *Fan Rates in* Germany, France, Italy and Canada, but is less popular in the UK. The grocer *Aldi* has many fans in the UK, but fewer in France or Italy. And the mail order company *Amazon* has a particularly large number of fans in Italy and Germany, while the proportion of Fan Customers in Canada is significantly lower. If the management also has country-specific industry benchmarks for the *Fan Portfolio,* as we have presented them in Fig. 1.41 they will not draw the wrong conclusions: One will be able to weight and classify the particularly high or low *Fan Rates* in the USA and Japan with this country-specific bias, because one recognizes that the competition there also performs significantly better (USA) or worse (Japan) than in the other countries. The decisive factor for a reliable cross-country comparison is the result in relation to the respective competition. With regular measurement in all countries, the *Fan Portfolio* is a permanent, lean and sustainable instrument for international comparison and customer value-based management.

The comparison of the customer groups thus documents the central added value of the *Fan Portfolio*: emotional attachment and satisfaction create a completely new segmentation of the customer population here. This segmentation makes it clear which customer groups exist and how they differ systematically in the interaction of both parameters. In addition, the *Fan Portfolio* makes it possible to think strategically about how best to treat these different groups in a differentiated way in order to turn them into Fans if possible. In this way, it provides the first indications for *FANOMICS*, i.e. for controlling corporate activities on the basis of the *Fan Principle*. Simply knowing the proportion of true Fan Customers, Mercenaries or Captives can be directly and successfully translated into entrepreneurial strategies. A few fictitious examples may illustrate this:

- **Example 1**
  One company already is on the road to success: The *Fan Portfolio* has an above-average *Fan Rate* compared to the rest of the industry. There is therefore a large segment of customers who are not only highly satisfied, but also identify emotionally with the company or the brand. The signs are good for expanding the business model and extending it to other market segments. After all, thanks to the Fans, there are many existing customers with a high propensity to cross-buy. The introduction of line extensions, merchandising articles or new product families under the same brand umbrella seems particularly promising in this constellation.
- **Example 2**
  A company has high sales, but also feels high customer turnover and strong price pressure: the *Fan Portfolio* has an above-average Mercenary rate compared with the rest of the industry. So, there is a large segment of customers who are highly satisfied but do not have sufficient identification—they are rather disloyal and price-sensitive. This is where a fundamental turnaround makes sense: instead of continuing to invest costly sums in increased performance or price reductions, the focus must instead be on building emotional customer loyalty to retain these Mercenary customers in the long term. This is tricky, but not impossible and—as we will show—has a lot to do with the right positioning of a company.
- **Example 3**
  A company is under economic pressure: The *Fan Portfolio* has a higher-than-average Captive rate compared to the industry. So, there is a large segment of

customers who have a relatively high level of identification and loyalty, but at the same time are dissatisfied with current services. Firstly, it is important to invest more in quality management, to put our own processes to the test and to question whether the performance parameters are still right. Secondly, customer service urgently needs to be improved: First-class complaint management can help to turn these valuable—because (still) connected—Captives back into Sympathizers or even Fans.

- **Example 4**
 A company is under pressure to communicate: Some blunders in quality management have caused bad press, and as a result one wave of indignation after another is raging in the social networks. The *Fan Portfolio* shows an above-average Opponent rate compared to the industry average. There is a negative spiral, because there is obviously a large segment of dissatisfied customers who have no emotional attachment to the company, and who are therefore happy to communicate these negative messages to the outside world. Here, it is important to use the *Fan Portfolio* to identify and activate the positive antipole: in other words, to determine where the fans are located and how to motivate them to intervene with positive messages on social media platforms and thus stop the negative spiral. These communicative contexts will also occupy us in the further course.

- **Example 5**
 A company is looking for areas of expansion: It has a *Fan Portfolio* created not only for its own clientele, but also for its most important competitors. In this way, it can identify the customer segments of the competition that are loyal and committed, as well as those that are less loyal and willing to churn. In the aggregate, it is possible to estimate how great the potential for market expansion actually is, and in conjunction with individual customer data, it is even possible to clearly identify the target groups for poaching. The acquisition effort is thereby used in a much more targeted and efficient manner, since, for example, one does not work in vain on fans of competitors.

In this chapter, we have derived the *Fan Indicator*—based on the findings of scientific fan research—and, building on this, developed the *Fan Portfolio*, which makes it possible to segment the entirety of a company's customers into five groups according to emotional connection and satisfaction. We have elaborated the specific characteristics and peculiarities of these groups and illustrated them with findings from a wide range of industries. And we have presented numerous empirical examples of the analytical added value of the *Fan Portfolio* as well as initial content-related considerations and strategic indications of the indispensable insight value that the *Fan Portfolio* provides as a basis for corporate management with *FANOMICS*—because it enables decision-makers to derive the right measures to turn customers into fans. However, all of these considerations and measures are based on a central premise, which we have already touched on several times in the course of this article: namely, that fans have a higher customer value and thus actually make a company more successful. We will prove the accuracy of this assertion in detail in the following Chap. 2.

References

20min.ch (2018) Millionen verdient: Juve hat schon 520.000 Ronaldo-Trikots verkauft [Millions earned: Juve has already sold 520,000 Ronaldo jerseys]. https://www.20min.ch/story/juve-hat-schon-520-000-ronaldo-trikots-verkauft-808069671351. Accessed 24 June 2021

2HMforum (2021) Fanfocus Germany. https://2hmforum.de/leistungen/branchenfokus/fanfocus-deutschland/. Accessed 24 June 2021

Akremi L, Hellmann K-U (2017) Fans and consumption. In: Roose J, Schäfer MS, Schmidt-Lux T (eds) Fans. Soziologische Perspektiven [Fans. Sociological perspectives]. VS Verlag fuer Sozialwissenschaften, Wiesbaden, pp 273–292

Alfermann D (2000) Social processes in sport. In: Gabler H, Nitsch JR, Singer R (eds) Einführung in die Sportpsychologie [Introduction to sport psychology]. Teil 2: Anwendungsfelder [Part 2: Fields of application]. Karl Hofmann, Schondorf, pp 65–109

Alfermann D, Würth S (2008) Group processes and intergroup relations. In: Schlicht W, Strauß B (eds) Grundlagen der Sportpsychologie [Foundations of sports psychology]. Encyclopedia of psychology, area D, series V, vol 1. Hogrefe, Göttingen, pp 719–778

Allison R, Knoester C (2021) Gender, sexual, and sports fan identities. Sociol Sport J 38(3): 310–321

Amiot CE, Sansfacon S, Louis WR (2014) How normative and social identification processes predict self-determination to engage in derogatory behaviours against outgroup hockey fans. Eur J Soc Psychol 44(3):216–230

Bailey S (2005) Media audiences and identity: self-construction in the fan experience. Palgrave Macmillan, New York

Becker R, Daschmann G (2022) Das Fan-Prinzip. 3rd edn, Gabler Verlag, Wiesbaden

Bennett L (2012) Music fandom online: R.E.M. fans in pursuit of the ultimate first listen. New Media Soc 14(5):748–763

Benzecry CE (2011) The opera fanatic. Ethnography of an obsession. University of Chicago Press, Chicago, IL

Bild newspaper (2021) 220 Millionen Euro. Ronaldo-Trikot bricht alle Verkaufs-Rekorde [220 million euros. Ronaldo jersey breaks all sales records]. https://www.bild.de/sport/fussball/fussball-international/cristiano-ronaldo-cr7-trikot-bricht-alle-verkaufs-rekorde-77644220.bild.html. Accessed 20 September 2021

Billings AC, Ruihley BJ (2013) Why we watch, why we play: the relationship between fantasy sport and fanship motivations. Mass Commun Soc 16(1):5–25

Cottingham MD (2012) Interaction ritual theory and sports fans: emotion, symbols, and solidarity. Sociol Sport J 29(2):168–185

Daschmann G (2007) Der Preis der Prominenz. Medienpsychologische Überlegungen zu den Wirkungen von Medienberichterstattung auf die dargestellten Akteure. [The price of celebrity. Mediapsychological considerations about the effects of media coverage on the actors portrayed]. In: Schierl T (ed) Prominenz in den Medien. Zur Genese und Verwertung von Prominenten in Sport, Wirtschaft und Kultur [Prominence in the media. On the genesis and exploitation of celebrities in sports, economic success and culture]. Von Halem, Cologne, pp 184–201

Daschmann G (2014) Schneller, Höher, Weiter, Twitter? [Faster, Higher, Further - Twitter?] Der Einfluss des Social-Media-Kontakts zu Fans auf die Motivation von Spitzenportlern [The influence of social media contact with fans on the motivation of top athletes]. In: Schmidt H, Schmidt J (eds) Kommunikationsmanagement und Markenstrategien im social web [Communication management and Brand strategies in the social web]. Eimo, Berlin, pp 46–62

References

Devlin MB, Brown KA, Brown-Devlin N, Billings AC (2020) "My country is better than yours": delineating differences between six countries' National Identity, fan identity, and media consumption during the 2018 Olympic games. Sociol Sport J 37(3):254–263

Dixon K (2013) Learning the game: football fandom culture and the origins of practice. Int Rev Soc Sport 48(3):334–348

Driessen S (2022) Campaign problems: how fans react to Taylor Swift's controversial political awakening. Am Behav Sci 66(8):1060–1074

Duffett M (2013) Introduction. In: Understanding fandom: an introduction to the study of media fan culture. Bloomsbury Academic, New York, pp 1–34

Dwyer B, Larkin B, Goebert C (2022) Fantasy sports participation and the (de)humanization of professional athletes. Sport Soc 25(10):1968–1986

Fitzpatrick D, Paddy H (2022) From fanzines to foodbanks: football fan activism in the age of anti-politics. Int Rev Soc Sport 57(8):1234–1252

Frenzel AC, Götz T, Pekrun R (2009) Emotions. In: Wild E, Möller J (eds) Pädagogische Psychologie [Educational psychology]. Springer, Berlin, pp 205–234

Fritzsche B (2011) Pop fans. Study of a girl culture, 2nd edn. VS Verlag fuer Sozialwissenschaften, Wiesbaden

Fritzsche B (2017) Fans and gender. In: Roose J, Schäfer MS, Schmidt-Lux T (eds) Fans. Soziologische Perspektiven [Fans. Sociological perspectives]. VS Verlag fuer Sozialwissenschaften, Wiesbaden, pp 201–218

Gabler H (2002) Motive im Sport. In: Motives in sport. Motivational psychological analyses and empirical studies. Karl Hofmann, Schondorf

Gebhardt W (2017) Fans and distinction. In: Roose J, Schäfer MS, Schmidt-Lux T (eds) Fans. Soziologische Perspektiven [Fans. Sociological perspectives]. VS Verlag fuer Sozialwissenschaften, Wiesbaden, pp 161–180

Geisselhart C (2008) The Who - Maximum Rock: Die Geschichte der verrücktesten Rockband der Welt [The story of the craziest rock band in the world]. Hannibal Publishing House, Innsbruck

Gemar A, Vanzella-Yang A (2022) The measure of a fan: social patterns of voracious sports following in Canada. Can Rev Sociol 59(1):76–95

Gillooly L, Medway D, Warnaby G, Roper S (2022) 'To us it's still Boundary Park': fan discourses on the corporate (re)naming of football stadia. Soc Cult Geogr 23(9):1275–1293

Göttlich U, Krischke-Ramaswamy M (2003) Event/experience culture, leisure culture/fan. In: Hill HO (ed) Handbuch populäre Kultur [Handbook of popular culture]. J.B. Metzler, Stuttgart, pp 167–172

Gray J, Harrington CL, Sandvoss C (2007a) Fandom. Identities and communities in a mediated world. University Press, New York

Gray J, Sandvoss C, Harrington CL (2007b) Introduction: why study fans? In: Gray J, Harrington CL, Sandvoss C (eds) Fandom. Identities and communities in a mediated world. University Press, New York, pp 1–16

Greenberg DM, Matz SC, Schwartz HA, Fricke KR (2021) The self-congruity effect of music. J Pers Soc Psychol 121(6):137–151

Harrington CL, Bielby DD (1995) Soap fans: exploring pleasure and making meaning in everyday life. Temple University Press, Philadelphia, PA

Harrington CL, Bielby DD (2010) A life course perspective on fandom. Int J Cult Stud 13(5):429–450

Havard CT, Grieve FG, Lomenick ME (2020) Marvel, DC, and sport: investigating rivalry in the sport and comic settings. Soc Sci Q 101(3):1075–1089

Hills M (2002) Fan cultures. Routledge, London

Homburg C (ed) (2016) Kundenzufriedenheit [Customer satisfaction]. Concepts – methods – experiences, 9th edn. Gabler Verlag, Wiesbaden

Homburg C, Bucerius M (2016) Customer satisfaction as a management challenge. In: Kundenzufriedenheit [Customer satisfaction]. Concepts - methods - experiences, 9th edn. Gabler Verlag, Wiesbaden, pp 53–92

Homburg C, Stock-Homburg R (2016) Theoretical perspectives on customer satisfaction. In: Homburg C (ed) Kundenzufriedenheit [Customer satisfaction]. Concepts – methods – experiences, 9th edn. Gabler Verlag, Wiesbaden, pp 17–52

Hornby N (1992) Fever pitch. Ball fever - the story of a fan. Kiepenheuer and Witsch, Cologne

Ilg P (2009) Goldene Geschäfte mit dem wilden Leben [Golden deals with wild life]. http://www.stern.de/auto/service/harley-davidson-goldene-geschaefte-mit-dem-wilden-leben-652234.html. Accessed 25 June 2021

Intezar H, Sullivan P (2022) Metamorphosis from exalted person to cultural symbol: a case study of the GOAT in tennis. Cult Psychol 28(3):395–412

Jasny M, Lenartowicz M (2022) A war between football fans and the government from the perspective of Herbert Blumer's collective behaviour theory. Sport Soc 25(10):1805–1830

Jenkins H (1992) Textual poachers: television fans and participatory culture. Routledge, London.

Jenkins H (2007) The future of fandom. In: Gray J, Cornell S, Lee HC (eds) Fandom: identities and communities in a mediated world. University Press, New York, pp 357–364

Jörissen B, Zirfas J (eds) (2010) Schlüsselwerke der Identitätsforschung [Key works in identity research]. VS Verlag fuer Sozialwissenschaften, Wiesbaden

Kalman-Lamb N (2021) Imagined communities of fandom: sport, spectatorship, meaning and alienation in late capitalism. Sport Soc 24(6):922–936

Kang J, Kim J, Migyeong Y, Eunil P, Minsam K, Lee M, Han J (2022) Behind the scenes of K-pop fandom: unveiling K-pop fandom collaboration network. Qual Quant 56(3):1481–1502

Kenny DA, Gomes SB, Kowal C (2015) The intergroup social relations model: ISRM. Group Dyn Theory Res Pract 19(3):152–165

Kohlmann KW, Eschenbeck H (2009) Stress and stress management. In: Schlicht W, Strauß B (eds) Grundlagen der Sportpsychologie [Fundamentals of sport psychology]. Encyclopedia of psychology. Area D, Series V, vol 1. Hogrefe, Göttingen, pp 635–680

König T (2002) Fankultur: Eine soziologische Studie am Beispiel des Fussballfans [Fan culture: a sociological study using the example of the soccer fan]. LIT, Münster

Leistner A (2017) Fans and violence. In: Roose J, Schäfer MS, Schmidt-Lux T (eds) Fans. Soziologische Perspektiven [Fans. Sociological perspectives]. VS Verlag fuer Sozialwissenschaften, Wiesbaden, pp 219–246

Liutikas D (2011) Manifestation of identity in sport fans' journeys. Filosofija Sociologija 22(2):214–225

Maar S (2018) Fan segmentation and fan psychology. Nomos Verlagsgesellschaft, Baden-Baden

Maslow AH (1981) Motivation and personality, 12th edn. Rowohlt, Reinbek bei Hamburg

Melnick MJ, Wann DL (2011) An examination of sport fandom in Australia: socialization, team identification, and fan behavior. Int Rev Sociol Sport 46(4):456–470

Meyer D (2014) Social identity complexity and sports fans. Dissertation: University of Pretoria, South Africa

Mikos L (2010) The fan. In: Moebius S, Schroer S (eds) Divas, hackers, speculators: social figures of the present. Suhrkamp, Berlin, pp 108–118

Müller CJ, Kuchinke L (2019) Can emotions be measured? Emotion concepts in physiology. In: Kappelhoff H, Bakels JH, Lehmann R, Schmitt C (eds) Emotionen [Emotions]. An interdisciplinary handbook. J.B. Metzler, Wiesbaden, pp 65–72

Myers DG (2014) Psychology, 3rd edn. Springer, Berlin

Navarro-Picado JF, Torres-Moraga EI, González-Serrano MH (2022) How are fans teams' consumption behaviors impacted by their federations' innovativeness perceived organizational legitimacy. Sport Soc 25(8):1545–1564

Newson M, Buhrmester M, Whitehouse H (2016) Explaining lifelong loyalty: the role of identity fusion and self-shaping group events. PLoS One 11(8). https://doi.org/10.1371/journal.pone.0160427

Nimoy L (1977) I am not spock. Celestial Arts Publishing, Milbrae

Nimoy L (1995) I Am Spock. Hyperion, New York

Noelle-Neumann E (1980) Die Schweigespirale [The spiral of silence]. Public opinion - our social skin. Piper, Munich

References

Ohr D (2017) Fans and the media. In: Roose J, Schäfer MS, Schmidt-Lux T (eds) Fans. Soziologische Perspektiven [Fans. Sociological perspectives]. VS Verlag fuer Sozialwissenschaften, Wiesbaden, pp 293–318

Oliver RL, Rust RT, Sajeev V (1997) Customer delight: foundations, findings, and managerial insight. J Retail 73(3):311–336

Osborne AC, Coombs DS (2013) Performative sport fandom: an approach to retheorizing sport fans. Sport Soc 16(5):672–681

Otte G (2017) Fans and social structure. In: Roose J, Schäfer MS, Schmidt-Lux T (eds) Fans. Soziologische Perspektiven [Fans. Sociological perspectives]. VS Verlag fuer Sozialwissenschaften, Wiesbaden, pp 57–82

Panksepp J (1998) Affective neuroscience: the foundations of human and animal emotions. Oxford University Press, New York

Patera CM (2013) The hyperactive fan: characteristics of online fantasy football players. Dissertation: Minnesota State University, Mankato

Piranhas R (2004) Mainz 05 – Liebe meines Lebens [Mainz 05 - Love of my life]. Label: Suppenkazper Noise Imperium, Mainz

Ploeg AJ (2017) Going global: fantasy sports gameplay paradigms, fan identities and cultural implications in an international context. Eur J Cult Stud 20(6):724–743

Richards J, Parry KD, Gill F (2022) "The guys love it when chicks ask for help": an exploration of female rugby league fans. Sport Soc 25(5):927–944

Roose J (2017) Fans and globalization. In: Roose J, Schäfer MS, Schmidt-Lux T (eds) Fans. Soziologische Perspektiven [Fans. Sociological perspectives]. VS Verlag fuer Sozialwissenschaften, Wiesbaden, pp 367–388

Roose J, Schäfer MS (2017) Fans and participation. In: Roose J, Schäfer MS, Schmidt-Lux T (eds) Fans. Soziologische Perspektiven [Fans. Sociological perspectives]. VS Verlag fuer Sozialwissenschaften, Wiesbaden, pp 319–342

Roose J, Schäfer MS, Schmidt-Lux T (eds) (2017a) Fans. Soziologische Perspektiven [Fans. Sociological perspectives]. VS Verlag fuer Sozialwissenschaften, Wiesbaden

Roose J, Schäfer MS, Schmidt-Lux T (2017b) Introduction. Fans as an object of sociological research. In: Roose J, Schäfer MS, Schmidt-Lux T (eds) Fans. Soziologische Perspektiven [Fans. Sociological perspectives], 2nd edn. VS Verlag fuer Sozialwissenschaften, Wiesbaden, pp 1–18

Roose J, Schäfer MS, Schmidt-Lux T (2017c) Fans in theoretical perspective. In: Roose J, Schäfer MS, Schmidt-Lux T (eds) Fans. Soziologische Perspektiven [Fans. Sociological perspectives]. VS Verlag fuer Sozialwissenschaften, Wiesbaden, pp 19–38

Rullo M, Presaghi F, Livi S, Mazzuca S, Dessi R (2017) Time heals all (shallow) wounds: a lesson on forgiveness of ingroup transgressors learned by the Feyenoord vandal fans. Soc Sci 6(3):83

Schäfer MS (2017) Fans and emotions. In: Roose J, Schäfer MS, Schmidt-Lux T (eds) Fans. Soziologische Perspektiven [Fans. Sociological perspectives]. VS Verlag fuer Sozialwissenschaften, Wiesbaden, pp 93–114

Scherer KR (2005) What are emotions? And how can they be measured? Soc Sci Inf 44(4):695–729

Schlicht W, Strauß B et al (2003) Social psychology of sport. An introduction. In: Strauß B (ed) Sportpsychologie [Psychology of sport]. Hogrefe, Göttingen

Schmidt-Joos S, Kampmann W (2008) Rock-Lexikon 1 and 2. Rowohlt Verlag, Hamburg

Schmidt-Lux T (2017) The history of fans. In: Roose J, Schäfer MS, Schmidt-Lux T (eds) Fans. Soziologische Perspektiven [Fans. Sociological perspectives]. VS Verlag fuer Sozialwissenschaften, Wiesbaden, pp 37–56

Schneider UF (2004) Der Januskopf der Prominenz. Zum ambivalenten Verhältnis von Privatheit und Öffentlichkeit [The Janus face of celebrity. On the ambivalent relationship between privacy and publicity]. VS Verlag für Sozialwissenschaften, Wiesbaden

Seaton W, Cranmer GA, White C, Bober J, Humphrey K, Obeng A (2022) "That's it. I'm done with this team!": public reactions to NFL teams' racial activism as a function of social identity management. Commun Q 70(5):585–607

Shadmanfaat SMS, Kabiri S, Solensten B, Willits DW, Cochran J (2022) A longitudinal study of fan aggression: a test of general strain theory. Deviant Behav 43(5):543–555

Skrobanek J, Jobst S (2017) Fans and socialization. In: Roose J, Schäfer MS, Schmidt-Lux T (eds) Fans. Soziologische Perspektiven [Fans. Sociological perspectives]. VS Verlag fuer Sozialwissenschaften, Wiesbaden, pp 181–200

Sorek T (2022) Sports and boycott: attitudes among Jewish Israelis. Int Rev Sociol Sport 57(8): 1197–1213

Springsteen B (1980) Everybody's got a hungry heart. The River. Columbia Records, New York

Stein J (1979) The kids are alright. Shepperton Studios, Shepperton, UK

Stever GS (2011) Fan behavior and lifespan development theory: explaining Para-social and social attachment to celebrities. J Adult Dev 18(1):1–7

Sutton FS, Knoester C (2022) U.S. women's sport consumption and self-identified fandom: an exploration of social structural and sociocultural antecedents. Int Rev Sociol Sport 57(8): 1321–1349

Tague AM, Reysen S, Plante C (2020) Belongingness as a mediator of the relationship between felt stigma and identification in fans. J Soc Psychol 160(3):324–331

Tajfel H, Turner JC (1986) The social identity theory of intergroup behavior. In: Worchel S, Austin WG (eds) Psychology of intergroup relations. Nelson-Hall, Chicago, IL, pp 7–24

Tamir I (2014) The decline of nationalism among football fans. Television New Media 15(8): 741–745

Tamir I (2022) The natural life cycle of sports fans. Sport Soc 25(2):338–352

Tamir I, Galily Y, Yarchi M (2016) "Here's hoping we get Pummeled": anti-nationalist trends among Israeli sports fans. J Sport Soc Issues 40(1):3

Tarver EC (2017) The I in team: sports fandom and the reproduction of identity. University of Chicago Press, Chicago, IL

Theodorakis ND, Wann DL, Nassis P, Luellen TB (2012) The relationship between sport team identification and the need to belong. Int J Sport Manag Mark 12(1-2):25–38

Thomas WI, Thomas DS (1928) The child in America. Behavior problems and programs. Knopf, New York

Tonetti LJ (2012) The experience of being a sports fan: a qualitative, phenomenological analysis of the causes and impact of sports team identification. Dissertation: Chestnut Hill College, Philadelphia, PA

Vlada B (2022) Periphery fandom: contrasting fans' productive experiences across the globe. J Consum Cult 22(4):889–907

Wann DL (2002) Preliminary validation of a measure for assessing identification as a sport fan: the sport fandom questionnaire. Int J Sport Manag 3:103–115

Wann DL, Branscombe NR (1993) Sports fans: measuring degree of identification with the team. Int J Sport Psychol 24:1–17

Wann DL, Hackathorn J, Sherman MR (2017) Testing the team identification-social psychological health model: mediational relationships among team identification, sport fandom, sense of belonging, and meaning in life. Group Dyn Theory Res Pract 21(2):94–107

Weber R, Brand A, Koch F, Niemann A (2022) Cosmopolitans and communitarians: a typology of football fans between national and European influences. Int Rev Sociol Sport 57(4):532–551

White FA, Newson M, Verrelli S, Whitehouse H (2021) Pathways to prejudice and outgroup hostility: group alignment and intergroup conflict among football fans. J Appl Soc Psychol 51(7):660–666

Winkler W (2010) Roger Daltrey "we probably prevented a world war," p 2. Sueddeutsche.de, May 17, 2010. https://www.sueddeutsche.de/kultur/roger-daltrey-wir-haben-vermutlich-einen-weltkrieg-verhindert-1.429001. Accessed 24 June 2021

Winter R (2017) Fans and cultural practice. In: Roose J, Schäfer MS, Schmidt-Lux T (eds) Fans. Soziologische Perspektiven [Fans. Sociological perspectives]. VS Verlag fuer Sozialwissenschaften, Wiesbaden, pp 141–160

Woods J, Lee Ludvigsen JA (2022) The changing faces of fandom? Exploring emerging 'online' and 'offline' fandom spaces in the English premier league. Sport Soc 25(11):2234–2249

Zhang X (2022) Why most Chinese fans of American superhero movies are girls: a gendered local fandom of a global Hollywood icon. J Int Intercult Commun 15(2):148–164

The Value of Fan Customers 2

Segmenting the customer landscape by *Fan Portfolio*, identifying fan customers, and increasing their share of the total customer base—in other words, focusing on the *Fan Rate*—only makes sense if they sustainably promote the central goal of any company. And that goal is: increasing economic success. In this chapter, we will show that our approach precisely achieves this: Fans make companies more economically successful, in several ways at once. In the following, we will present numerous empirical examples from companies in the B2B and B2C sectors—including companies that have already successfully applied *FANOMICS* and increased their sales and returns as a result. In doing so, we draw—as in Chap. 1—on data from our extensive fundamental research in Germany, which spans several years, as well as upon data from the international pilot study which we collected specifically for this book.[1] However, we do not stop at this empirical yet still exemplary evidence. We go a decisive step further: we look at the customer value of fan customers from the strategic perspective of management. In the following, we will conclusively demonstrate the contribution of fan customers to successful corporate development and show that—regardless of which growth strategies a company pursues on which international market—each of these growth strategies is more successful and sustainable due to fan customers.

---

[1] This chapter presents the customer characteristics that we collected in the G7 countries. Unfortunately, it was not possible to collect data on all the customer characteristics described here on an international basis. In these cases, findings from Germany only are presented. Details on the samples and survey methods used in both studies can be found in Chap. 1.

2.1 The Fan as a Growth Driver

If companies want to increase their success, i.e. their return on investment, this cannot be achieved in the long term through cost reduction and rationalization alone. Instead, companies must grow by opening up new additional sales opportunities. They must therefore either increase their market share within the target groups they have already tapped, i.e. achieve greater penetration of the existing market, or open up new markets—either by gaining new customer segments or by expanding the product range—or by doing both at the same time. All four strategies involve varying degrees of additional effort and risk. Ansoff (1965) contrasted these different growth strategies and their risks in the *product-market matrix* that has become famous and well-established (cf. Fig. 2.1).

The starting point for all companies' growth considerations is usually the lower left quadrant of the *Ansoff matrix*: *Market Penetration. This is because increasing market penetration* is always the simplest and least risky strategy, as it requires the least investment. It aims to increase market share by increasing sales to existing customers or by gaining new customers in the same market segment. The advantage of this strategy is that it is cost-effective since it does not require modification of the existing product range. However, its effectiveness is limited because market saturation will be reached at a foreseeable point in time. At the latest when the market

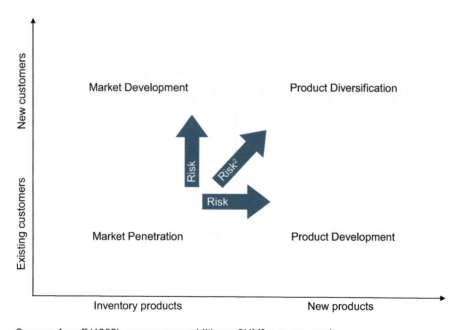

Source: *Ansoff* (1965); arrows: own additions; *2HMforum.* research

Fig. 2.1 Product-market matrix according to *Ansoff* (1965)

becomes saturated, every company will have to try to open and develop further sales areas—either through market or product development.

Market development aims to expand the potential sales areas for the given product range, i.e. to open up new markets for it. This is the vertical upward movement within the matrix in the direction of "new markets". This can be done by addressing completely new target groups or market segments that were not previously the sales focus for these products, or by expanding the sales market geographically. This is advisable for companies whose strength is based primarily on a special and limited product family for which sales opportunities are also seen in previously unserved markets. Since this growth strategy enters a new and previously unknown market, the investments are higher and the prospects of success lower than with the market penetration strategy. The risk is therefore correspondingly higher.

Product development, on the other hand, aims to use existing customers to sell additional products or new variants of conventional products. This is therefore the horizontal sideways movement within the matrix in the direction of "new products". This is advisable for companies whose strength lies in their existing market position and customer loyalty, and whose product range permits meaningful expansion and variation. Since product innovation must first be achieved, the investments are also higher and the prospects of success lower than with the market penetration strategy. Here, too, the risk is therefore correspondingly higher.

In principle, it is also possible to combine market and sales development at the same time: product *diversification*. This aims to generate new sales areas with newly developed products in previously untapped markets. This is, therefore, a diagonal upward movement within the matrix in the direction of "new markets" and in the direction of "new products" in equal measure. Since high returns are possible here, it may make sense in individual cases for companies that see great innovative potential to use their own house for a newly accessible industry. *Apple*'s entry into the cell phone market with the simultaneous invention of the smartphone may be such an example. But this is a rare exception. The rule is that companies do not succeed on this path but fail—because the enticingly profitable but unlikely chance of success à la *Apple is* offset by exponentially high risks. This is because the market entry and innovation costs, i.e., the risks of the combined strategy of market and product development, must be multiplied by each other because they occur simultaneously, so that if the two risk components have similar values, the overall risk quasi squares compared to each of the individual strategies. Basically, every company should be advised not to pursue this combined strategy, but to first occupy one of the neighboring quadrants by a horizontal or vertical movement in the matrix, and then from there to reach this last quadrant of product diversification by another vertical or horizontal movement with reduced risk.

In line with these considerations, we have made an adaptation of the product-market matrix (cf. Fig. 2.2), in which we have differentiated the growth strategies—similar to Ansoff—according to current customers or new customer orientation on the one hand and according to existing products and new products on the other.

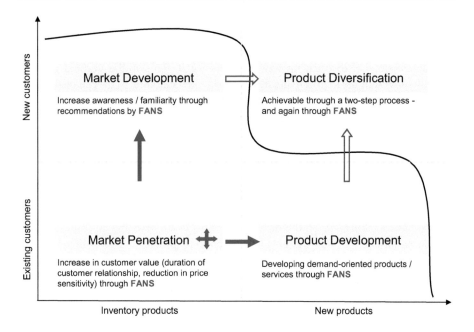

Source: *2HMforum.* research; adapted from *Ansoff* (1965)

Fig. 2.2 Growth strategies supported by the *Fan Rate*

In line with our preliminary considerations, we will limit ourselves to the growth strategies of the first three quadrants mentioned, symbolized by the green-colored arrows. In the following, we will show that a high proportion of fan customers, i.e. a high *Fan Rate*, makes each of these three growth strategies described less risky and more successful financially.

2.2 Fans and Market Penetration: Growth with Existing Customers in Existing Business

Let us first turn to the strategy of market penetration (cf. Fig. 2.3). It aims at increasing market shares in the already occupied market segment with as little effort as possible. The first prerequisite for this type of growth is to prevent the contrary process of shrinking market shares. After all, if you have a high customer turnover, i.e., you regularly acquire new customers but constantly lose customers of the same size, you have to invest permanently in acquisition, but will hardly increase your market shares on balance despite these new customers. On the other hand, if you have a large proportion of loyal existing customers, so that your customer portfolio hardly shrinks, you can regard almost every investment in new customer acquisition as an actual investment in growth.

2.2 Fans and Market Penetration: Growth with Existing Customers in Existing Business

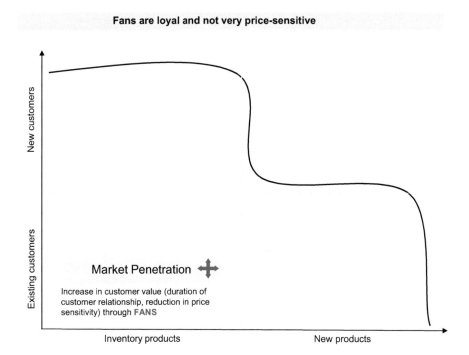

Source: *2HMforum.* research; adapted from *Ansoff* (1965)

Fig. 2.3 Fans as a growth factor: Market Penetration

2.2.1 Fans Are Loyal

Permanently loyal customers are therefore less costly than acquiring new customers and are also an excellent prerequisite for a growing customer base. And it is precisely this prerequisite that fan customers fulfill like no other customer group: because fan customers show almost unconditional loyalty. Do you remember what we said about the characteristic behavior of fans toward their soccer club, for example? Fans are loyal—and not willing to change even in the deepest crisis. Fan customers show exactly the same behavior.

As Fig. 2.4 proves, almost nine out of ten fan customers in Germany say that they definitely want to remain a customer of their provider in the long term. This loyalty is a constituent feature of fan customers: Sympathizer and Mercenary customers do not show such loyalty—even though they are just as satisfied with the provider as the fans. It is not satisfaction that they lack, but loyalty. The higher the *Fan Rate*, the

Fig. 2.4 Fans are loyal

more secure and stable the existing customer base—and the more profitable new customer acquisition becomes, because it actually promises growth.[2]

Back to the loyalty of fan customers: It is also expressed in the fans' immunity to all negative external influences that could jeopardize the customer relationship. Across all industries, 57% of fan customers "completely agree" with the statement that they would still buy from "their" provider even if friends or acquaintances dissuade them to do so (cf. Fig. 2.4). In contrast, such commitment is hardly found among Sympathizer or Mercenary customers. Fans are therefore resistant to the effects of negative word-of-mouth campaigning—even if it is carried out by credible persons such as friends or acquaintances.

However, there is more to the term "dissuade" than just negative campaigning: "Dissuading" does not always have to mean that others speak negatively or derogatorily about the provider. Even the tip from a friend to choose another provider because it offers better service or is cheaper in price (which essentially means the same thing) can be seen as "advising against". Such "advice" can basically only ever be aimed at the performance level of a provider: for example, that the self-appointed "advisors" think there are quality deficiencies with the provider in question. Or they think the prices are "too high". The fan is immune to such suggestions—because his loyalty is based primarily on the emotional quality of the relationship and not primarily on the service provided. Asking a real Fan Customer of a car brand why he doesn't switch to the competitor brand because it is more powerful or cheaper is like asking a Manchester City fan if he doesn't want to become a Manchester United fan because ManU has won the league title more often.

---

[2] Here, we would like to make a brief remark on the further procedure: Similar to Fig. 2.4, we will also construct a large part of the following charts: We primarily contrast and compare the three highly satisfied customer groups of Fan customers, Sympathizer customers, and Mercenary customers. This is because it allows us to show that high emotional loyalty is the factor that turns highly satisfied customers into economically profitable customers.

2.2 Fans and Market Penetration: Growth with Existing Customers in Existing Business

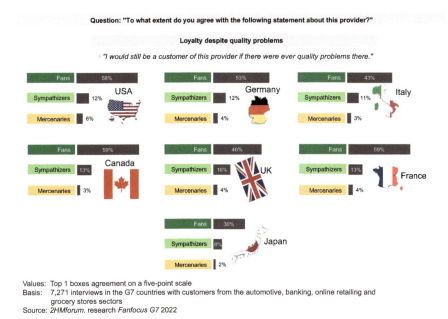

Fig. 2.5 Fans forgive mistakes

2.2.2 Fans Are Forgiving

However, the fan relationship is not only robust against hostility from outside: Even if "their" supplier makes mistakes, many fans do not leave the ship. On average, more than 50% of the Fan Customers surveyed in the G7 countries "fully agree" with the statement that they would still want to remain loyal as a customer even if there were ever quality problems with "their" provider (cf. Fig. 2.5). Among the Sympathizers, only 12% agree with this statement on average, and among the Mercenaries, only a vanishing minority still hold this opinion. What is remarkable here is that we can observe these serious differences between Fans, Sympathizers and Mercenaries equally in all G7 countries.

To prevent misunderstandings: This statement does not mean that Fan Customers will accept defects without complaint. On the contrary, they will certainly complain. But they do not immediately terminate the customer relationship because of it. In the fan relationship, faults are curable—in contrast to a Mercenaries customer, who can be lost due to a small scratch in the quality of the product or service. The reason that the fan is forgiving of mistakes is the same reason that makes him resistant to negative recommendations: because of the emotional quality of his customer relationship, the performance evaluation is secondary—although, mind you, not insignificant. The fan is emotionally loyal—he remains loyal because of this relationship quality, even if he subjectively feels the need for improvement. Just as soccer fans remain loyal to their club even in the most serious crises.

2.2.3 Fans Have Confidence

Are fans naïve or less demanding because they let "their" supplier get away with the occasional blunder or performance dent? No, certainly not. Rather, they assume that their loyalty will not be disappointed in the first place. 86% of fan customers have "complete trust" in their provider. The other highly satisfied customer groups do not even begin to share this view (cf. Fig. 2.6). In this respect, this tolerance of fans toward quality defects is not naive good nature, but nothing more than a further expression of their loyalty.

To sum all this up: Fan customers have the highest level of customer loyalty imaginable. They declare consciously and open-heartedly that they want to remain customers in the long term, they have complete trust in their provider, and they do not question this relationship even if the provider weakens for once or if attractive competitor offers beckon. These characteristics of fan customers pay directly into your customer value because fans ensure that the customer base remains secure and stable—and this reduces the cost of customer care on the one hand and increases the profitability of new customer acquisition on the other. Through their high loyalty, fan customers thus indirectly create the prerequisite for further market penetration of the provider.

2.2.4 Fans Are Less Price Sensitive

Fan customers are less price-sensitive than other customers. There are two reasons for this: First, fans tend to have a slightly distorted perception when assessing the performance of "their" provider: they perceive its conditions much more positively than other customer groups do (cf. Fig. 2.7). Accordingly, they also judge the pricing less strictly.

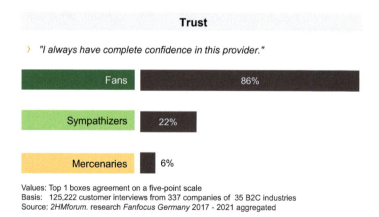

Fig. 2.6 Fans have confidence

2.2 Fans and Market Penetration: Growth with Existing Customers in Existing Business

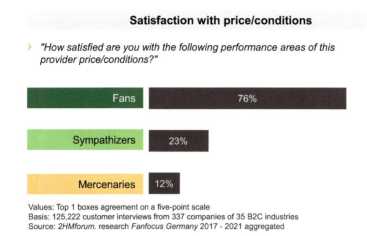

Fig. 2.7 Fans rate conditions better and are therefore less price-sensitive

Secondly, from the customer's point of view, a price that is too high is basically nothing other than a performance deficit. Fans, however, as shown, define their relationship with the company in less performance-based terms. Their high relationship quality is not primarily attributable to the company's performance. Accordingly, they are also less sensitive to such performance parameters than the other customer groups.

In addition, price is often a heuristic decision-making aid for other customer types, such as Mercenaries: When differences between suppliers are not discernible, price becomes the decisive criterion. In the eyes of the fan, however, the supplier world looks completely different: For him, there are clearly perceptible differences between "his" provider and the less "beloved" competition. So, the fan is no longer looking for a criterion for deciding which provider to choose—he has long since made up his mind. The price, which is often the decisive criterion for the Mercenary customer in choosing a provider, is no longer the focus of the fan's considerations. The fan is not a customer of the company because of the price but remains a customer despite the price. And this price tolerance of the fans is directly reflected in the margin on the supplier side. But you should *not* infer from this that you should demand higher prices from fans (cf. Sect. 4.2).

2.2.5 Fans Have the Highest Monetary Customer Value

This is by no means an exhaustive description of the customer value of fan customers. Another important factor is that fan customers are a direct guarantee of revenue for every company. This is because fan customers buy more frequently and spend more money on the products of "their" companies—more than any other customer group. Fans, therefore, have a directly higher monetary customer value. Figure 2.8 illustrates this impressively with the example of the sales figures of a

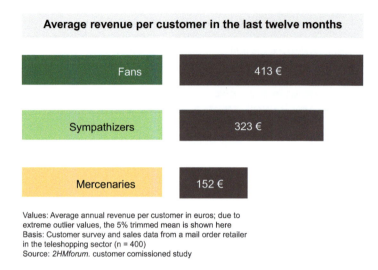

Fig. 2.8 Average revenue per customer of a B2C mail order retailer

medium-sized B2C mail order company from Germany. From a representative sample of its customers, we had both survey data on individual customer loyalty and satisfaction as well as information on customer-specific sales in the year before the survey. This enabled us to assign average factual annual sales to the customer types in the *Fan Portfolio*. The result shows a clearly superior monetary customer value of fan customers compared to other customer groups.

The fan customers in Fig. 2.8 invest nearly 30% more in the vendor's products than Sympathizer customers and well over two and a half times the amount spent by Mercenaries customers. Here, a single fan customer alone turns over nearly as much as a Mercenary and Sympathizer customer combined. This finding is not an isolated case. We find this correlation in many other B2C as well as B2B industries: Fan customers provide significantly higher sales and contribution margins than all other customer groups (cf. e.g. also the following Figs. 2.12, 2.14, and 2.16) and thus have the highest customer value for any company. There are many reasons for this: Fans identify with "their" provider; they have complete trust in him and whenever they are faced with a relevant purchase decision, they will first try to conclude the transaction via "their" provider. This is because the provider occupies a quasi-monopoly position in their minds. Correspondingly, they buy more frequently and spend more per purchase.

2.2.6 Fans Have the Highest Customer Lifetime Value

This unsurpassed customer value of fan customers goes hand in hand with the above-average loyalty of a fan already described: no customer stays in the business relationship with his provider as long as a fan customer. This is where the highest willingness to invest and the longest customer relationship merge. It follows that fan customers are the customer segment with the highest customer lifetime value for all companies and industries. Companies that fail to identify these customers within their customer base are not aware of their revenue guarantors and are not consistently tapping into their greatest growth potential—because owing to the unique customer lifetime value of fans, an increase in the *Fan Rate* is a reliable guarantor of increasing economic success and should be the primary and clear goal for every company.

2.2.7 Growth Through Fans Can Be Planned

The economic success of a company increases with the *Fan Rate*, which is why the measurement of the *Fan Rate* can be used to assess retrospectively whether and which business decisions were effective. The *Fan Rate is* therefore suitable as an indicator of the effectiveness of measures. However, it is much more than that. It is also a control instrument for strategic success planning, the first tool for entering the *world of FANOMICS*, so to speak, because it can be used to forecast how a company's sales will increase if the *Fan Rate is* increased by means of strategic measures. On this basis, reliable cost-benefit calculations can be carried out and thus secure growth-oriented investment decisions can be made. The growth opportunities that can be tapped by increasing the *Fan Rate* are described in the example of the mail order company mentioned above. Figure 2.9 using the example of the mail order company mentioned above.

The figure shows our analysis path step by step. The upper colored bar of the chart first shows the company's current *Fan Portfolio*, determined based on the representative customer sample: including 24% fan customers, 35% Sympathizers as well as 21% Mercenaries, to name just the most important proportions.

Now we transfer the knowledge gained in this way about the shares of the various segments of the *Fan Portfolio* to the basis population of all the company's customers. Let's assume a customer base of one million customers. We now transfer the size shares of the individual customer segments specified in the *Fan Portfolio to this absolute* number: 24% fans out of one million customers makes 240,000 fan customers; and 35% Sympathizers makes 350,000 Sympathizer customers, etc. These absolute customer numbers per segment are shown in the second bar from the top.

The next step is the real trick: these absolute customer numbers are now multiplied by the value of an average customer in the respective segment. This customer value corresponds to the average annual sales of each customer type as shown in Figure 2.8. The results of this calculation are shown in the third bar from the top (in the unit € thousand): Thus, each of the 240,000 fan customers of the mail order company has an average annual turnover of €413. This leads to total annual sales of €99,120,000 across all Fan customers. For Sympathizer customers with a turnover of €323 per customer, this results in annual sales of €113,050,000 and for Mercenary customers €31,920,000. In total, the company's annual revenue with these three customer groups amounts to €244 million (this does not yet

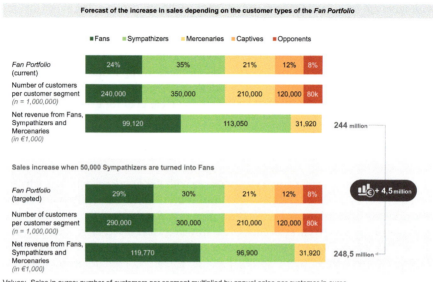

Fig. 2.9 B2C/mail order retailer: More sales through higher *Fan Rate* I

correspond to the total annual revenue, as the lower revenue with Captives or Opponents must still be added, but we can neglect these for the present consideration).

What happens now if the mail order company targets higher market penetration as a growth strategy, i.e. growth with the given product range within the already occupied market segment? With the help of the *Fan Rate,* this strategy can be easily planned. Let's assume, for example, that the company wants to increase sales by increasing the *Fan Rate.* This means: the company must "turn (more) customers into Fans"—the phrase has never been more apt. The easiest way to do this is, of course, to turn Sympathizer customers, i.e., customers who are already highly satisfied and already emotionally loyal to an above-average degree, into Fan Customers (more details on the *FANOMICS strategies required for this* in Chaps. 3 and 4). The company therefore decides on a campaign with targeted measures toward Sympathizer customers. The goal is to increase the *Fan Rate* by 5 percentage points to 29%, which would simultaneously reduce the rate of Sympathizer customers by 5 percentage points to 30%. This targeted new *Fan Portfolio* is shown in the lower half of Figure 2.9 in the large gray rectangle. These target percentages are now again converted into absolute figures for the given one million customers using the same logic as before (second bar) and then again multiplied by the average customer value of the customers in each segment from Figure 2.8. At the end, the total revenue can be displayed, which is achieved if 5% of the total customers, i.e., 50,000 customers who are currently Sympathizers, are successfully converted into Fans. The resulting increase in sales per year is €4.5 million.

4.5 million euros increase in sales on current sales of more than 240 million euros—this increase in sales of a good 2% seems small at first glance for companies that are used to success. However, anyone judging the figures from this perspective is overlooking four significant positive aspects of the operation: Firstly, this is a sales increase that draws its added value entirely from the company's already developed customer landscape. Not a single new customer has to be acquired for this, not a single non-customer has to be reached by cold calling. This means that the effort required is significantly less than the return on the targeted increase in sales. Secondly, the aim of this effort is not to increase customer satisfaction, but to increase the emotional loyalty of highly satisfied customers. The usual performance-based incentives aimed at satisfaction, such as price reductions, discounts or similar, which in the end only eat up the margin, are not at issue here. On the contrary, *FANOMICS* means turning away from the investment-intensive "more is more" of satisfaction management and toward clearly focused measures—and the expenditures required for this are incomparably lower. Increases in relationship quality can be achieved with lower, but properly managed, resource input, so that the effects on the company's results are even more dramatic than those on sales growth. Thirdly, if the plans are implemented successfully, the increase in sales in question is permanent: once a Fan is a Fan, he or she remains loyal for years—the return on investment is therefore sustainable and foreseeable. And fourthly, the newly created Fan customers in turn bring with them the additional indirect customer values explained here, which also contribute to the success of the company in the long term. The creation of new Fan customers therefore always means a market penetration and growth increase that goes far beyond the directly measurable increase in sales.

Of course, the effects postulated in Fig. 2.9 postulated effects can be scaled arbitrarily according to effort and target sizes. Figure 2.10 for example, illustrates the predicted result if the same provider wants to increase its *Fan Rate* not only by five, but even by ten percentage points, other things being equal.

As the figure shows, the targeted *Fan Rate* also doubles the achievable increase in sales from €4.5 million to €9 million. To achieve this, not just 50,000, but 100,000 Sympathizers must be converted into Fans. However, the cost of this does not increase proportionally: since the lion's share of the costs is based on the strategic implementation of the measure (e.g., focused customer care) and not on rolling it out across the board, the costs per customer are usually significantly reduced. The bottom line is that the more you scale up the measure, the more profitable it becomes. But the effects shown cannot just be scaled up—depending on how fundamental the changes in the *Fan Portfolio which* you are targeting, you can achieve much greater effects. After all, our first two examples, which we described regarding the mail order company's customer base, illustrated the "least intervention" in the *Fan Portfolio* that can be chosen: namely, turning Sympathizers into Fans. And Sympathizer customers already have a certain emotional attachment and therefore already have a high monetary customer value, so that the revenue gain that can be achieved

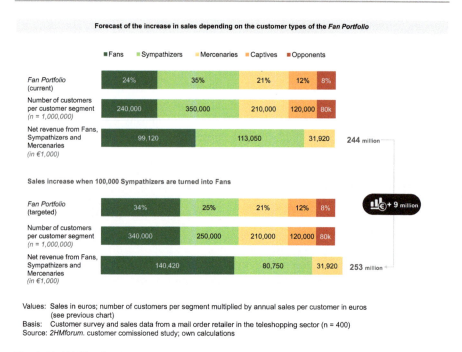

Fig. 2.10 B2C/mail order retailer: More sales through higher *Fan Rate* II

through this is less significant. The situation is quite different if you succeed in turning Mercenary customers, who are highly satisfied but not loyal, into Fans. This is, admittedly, somewhat more complex, but also much more attractive, as Fig. 2.11 illustrates.

The figure depicts the revenues that arise if the company attempts to reduce the share of Mercenary customers by 15 percentage points and at the same time strengthen the camp of Fans and Sympathizers by ten and five percentage points, respectively. Owing to the greater difference in monetary customer value between Mercenaries and Fans, the sales increases here are much more significant: 35.5 million euros in annual sales growth are achieved if the company succeeds in turning 15% of the previously only highly satisfied customers into emotionally loyal customers. At this point, it becomes evident what enormous economic success can be achieved by increasing emotional customer loyalty. And we are still not talking about new customer acquisition here, but growth through market penetration effects and optimization of existing customer business alone.

The three scenarios described by the shipping service provider also illustrate once again the analytical value of the *FANOMICS approach:* The optimizations just shown target only highly satisfied customers—Mercenaries, Sympathizers, and Fans—and aim to improve emotional loyalty there. If the provider had categorized its customers exclusively according to customer satisfaction, it would not be able to see the existing differences in the loyalty of its customers, nor could it address the

2.2 Fans and Market Penetration: Growth with Existing Customers in Existing Business

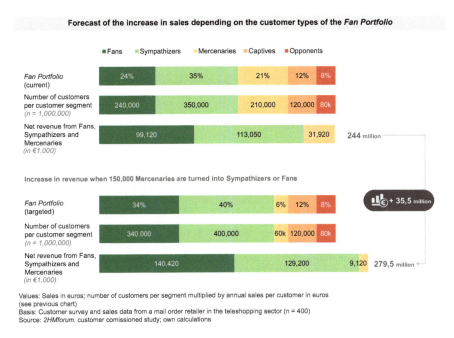

Fig. 2.11 B2C/mail order retailer: More sales through higher *Fan Rate* III

groups differently to trigger the intended loyalty effects in Mercenaries or Sympathizers.

The described development of prognostic scenarios with the help of the *Fan Portfolio* can be applied not only to companies from the B2C sector with mass customer numbers—B2B companies with a comparatively small, but hand-picked customer base can also benefit from it. Let's look at the data of a European personnel service provider with a base of around 2000 customers as an example. Figure 2.12 first shows that the higher monetary customer value of Fan customers can also be empirically proven in the B2B area.

As the figure shows, more than three times the revenue can be generated with Fan customers in the B2B sector than with Mercenaries. The monetary added value of Fan customers is therefore a given—and it follows conclusively from this that an increase in sales can also be achieved here with an increase in the *Fan Rate*. Figure 2.13 illustrates this according to the same logic as in the preceding example of the B2C mail order company.

As the chart shows, the staffing service provider has only 220 Fan customers among its 2000 customers—a rate that can certainly be increased, especially since there is great potential for development: 780 highly satisfied Mercenary customers are literally just waiting to finally become emotionally loyal as well. If the service provider now succeeds in turning just 200 of these Mercenaries into Fans, this would result in an increase in sales of no less than €22 million. This example shows that it always makes sense to consistently align a company with the *Fan Rate*—regardless

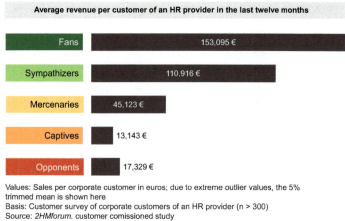

Fig. 2.12 B2B/HR provider: Customer value of fan customers

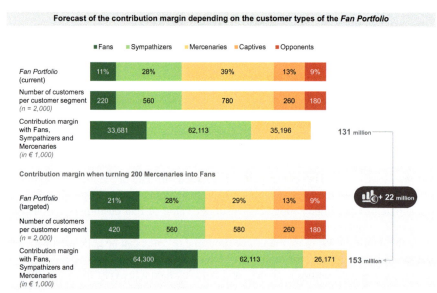

Fig. 2.13 B2B/HR provider: More sales through higher *Fan Rate*

of whether you are operating in the B2B or B2C sector. And it also shows that the higher the company-specific monetary customer value of the fan customer, the more promising it is for a company to increase its *Fan Rate*.

2.2 Fans and Market Penetration: Growth with Existing Customers in Existing Business

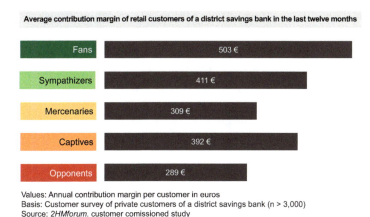

Fig. 2.14 B2C/Banks: Customer value of fan customers by contribution margin

It is not only possible to predict a change in revenue figures by modifying the *Fan Portfolio. It is also possible to forecast* revenues or contribution margins, provided that corresponding data are available at the individual customer level or at least for each customer segment of the *Fan Portfolio*. The Figs. 2.14, 2.15, 2.16, and 2.17 illustrate this using the example of the retail portfolio of a medium-sized bank with around 850,000 retail customers. As Fig. 2.14 shows, this time it is not sales figures but contribution margins per customer that are shown. For this parameter, too, Fan customers show the highest monetary customer value.

Figure 2.14 shows the pattern already familiar from the preceding cases: the monetary customer value continues to increase across the *Fan Portfolio* in the direction of Fans. However, there is one exception here: Captive customers have an above-average contribution margin that almost reaches the values of Sympathizers and Fans. The reason for this is presumably long-term contractual commitments that retail customers enter, especially for real estate financing, and to whose terms they are still bound even if they are overpriced or outdated by the standards of the current credit market. Figure 2.15 now shows how the contribution margins would be affected if the bank in question were to reduce its share of Mercenary customers by 80,000, i.e. by about ten percentage points, and at the same time increase its share of Fan and Sympathizer customers by five percentage points each.

Here, too, the economic success is impressive: If the bank were to succeed in building an emotional bond with 80,000 of its current satisfied but unengaged Mercenary customers, it could expect an annual increase in contribution margin of €12 million. And again, this increase could be realized from existing customer potential alone, without acquiring a single new customer. And in the corporate customer business, too, the same bank could generate around one million euros more in annual contribution margin just by increasing the *Fan Rate*, as Figs. 2.16 and 2.17 illustrate.

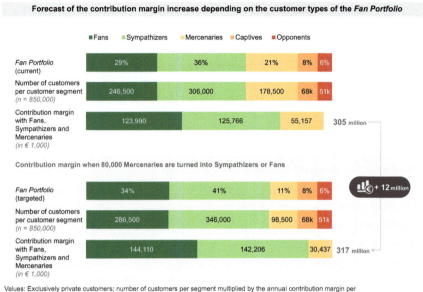

Fig. 2.15 B2C/Banks: Economic success through higher *Fan Rate*

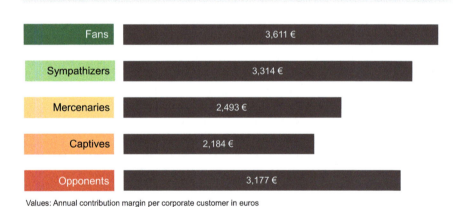

Fig. 2.16 B2B/Banks: Customer value of fan customers by contribution margin

The considerations and findings described so far can be summarized as follows: Fans are the best guarantee of growth for companies, regardless of the industry. This is because Fan customers have the highest monetary customer value, which they will

2.2 Fans and Market Penetration: Growth with Existing Customers in Existing Business

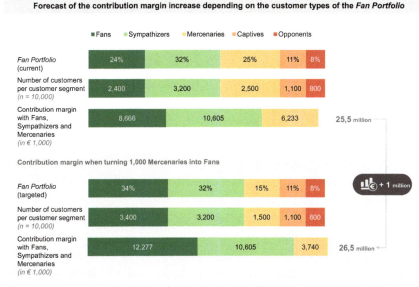

Fig. 2.17 B2B/Banks: Economic success through higher *Fan Rate*

continue to realize for years owing to their high level of loyalty. They are a guarantee of sales and revenue for every company—especially for providers who initially shy away from the risk of expanding into new markets or products and seek their growth opportunities in penetrating market segments that have already been addressed. After all, it is possible to sustainably increase business results by increasing the *Fan Rate* solely through appropriate measures to promote loyalty within the company's own customer base—i.e., without any acquisition of new customers. Even if it may be difficult to acquire new customers since the market is already saturated, a growth strategy can be implemented in this way with low-threshold investments.

What is true for prosperous economic success is, of course, equally true in times of crisis. When—for whatever reason—the global, national, or industry-specific environment becomes difficult, so that growth is out of the question, Fans become the rock of the company. Because Fan customers remain loyal even when other customers have long since left the fold. An example of this is provided by the results of a recent customer survey conducted by a B2B supplier of gearboxes and motors in southern Germany. In 2022, there had been numerous supply bottlenecks in the industry—due to the Covid and Ukraine crises. This supply crisis also affected the supplier mentioned here. In a customer survey, he therefore wanted to know whether his customers had ordered services or products that they had otherwise purchased

Fig. 2.18 Fans remain loyal even in the crisis

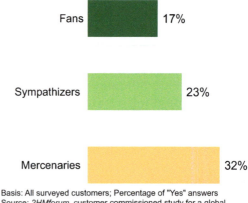

from him from another supplier in 2022 due to the supply crisis. Figure 2.18 shows the responses differentiated by Fan customers, Sympathizers and Mercenaries.

As the figure shows, among Mercenary customers, almost one in three customers was lost to the competition—among fans, on the other hand, the figure was only one-sixth. More than 80% of Fans, on the other hand, remained loyal to the provider even during the crisis. This example illustrates the point: Those who have an above-average *Fan Rate* and can identify their fan customers are stronger than the competition in any recession. After all, even the Covid crisis, record inflation or exploding energy costs can hardly harm a true fan relationship. Moreover, such companies also have lower expenses in bad times: Because with *FANOMICS* they do the right thing in a focused way and do not burn money with superfluous measures according to the "shotgun approach" or "watering can" principle.

2.3 Fans and Market Development: Growth Through Acquisition of New Customers in Existing Business

Despite all the positive effects of a high *Fan Rate* on market penetration described above, there will be a moment during the development of almost every company when the step of acquiring new customers will have to be taken in order to open up additional growth opportunities. In the product-market matrix, this means, as Fig. 2.19 shows, a shift of the business area to the upper left quadrant of market development.

Yet even companies that take this bold stride of stepping out of the comfort zone of the customer base they already address and seek their growth in acquiring new

2.3 Fans and Market Development: Growth Through Acquisition of New...

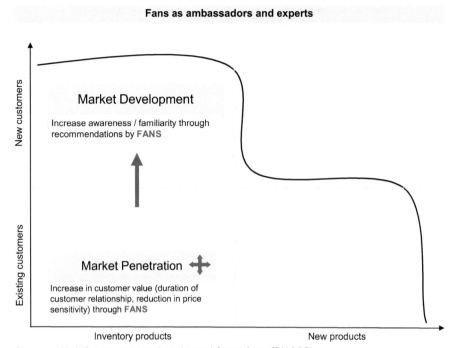

Fig. 2.19 Fans as a growth factor: Market Development

customers can take this path with lower risks and greater chances of success if their portfolio shows a solid *Fan Rate*.

2.3.1 Fans Are Positive Ambassadors

The key advantage of Fan customers, when expanding into new markets, lies in their particularly extraverted communicative behavior: They are the perfect ambassadors for a company or brand—and indispensable trailblazers when it comes to winning new customers. We also prove this fan-specific communication behavior with survey data from Germany and the other G7 countries (cf. Fig. 2.20a–d).

The data impressively show the value of Fans as ambassadors: Around 60% (Germany) to 70% (G7 countries) of them talk positively about "their provider." In all other customer segments—i.e., even among the highly satisfied Sympathizers and Mercenaries—the silent majority is the rule, however. The fans are quite different: the majority proactively speak up—and those who do speak up also comment positively about their provider significantly more often than all other customer types, on average once a quarter—an exceptionally high value. Fans and Sympathizers differ significantly here: on average, fans act as ambassadors twice

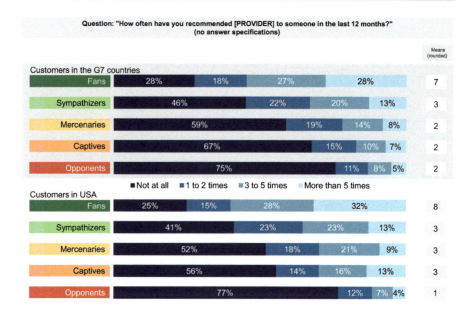

Fig. 2.20 (**a–d**) Fans express themselves positively more often

as often as Sympathizers (cf. the mean values in Fig. 2.20a–d). Fans want to actively implement and live out their identification with their provider in their behavior. Their intensive communication and ambassadorial activity are therefore hardly surprising. Sympathizers, on the other hand, are the quiet connoisseurs: although they often show a similarly high propensity to buy compared with fans, they are nowhere near as willing to take on the extraverted role of ambassador.

2.3.2 Fans Are the Best Referrers

However, the communicative advantages of Fans are not limited to their positive reputation for the company. Active recommendation, which many companies regard as the yardstick of good customer relations, is also particularly pronounced among them. As Fig. 2.21 fans are more likely than all other customers to actively recommend their company to others; thus, providing lasting support for new customer acquisition: Nine out of ten Fans not only recommend their favorite company to others—they also say they are happy to do so.

As Fig. 2.21 shows, all other customer types are clearly behind the fans in their recommendation behavior—including the Sympathizers, who, as already

2.3 Fans and Market Development: Growth Through Acquisition of New...

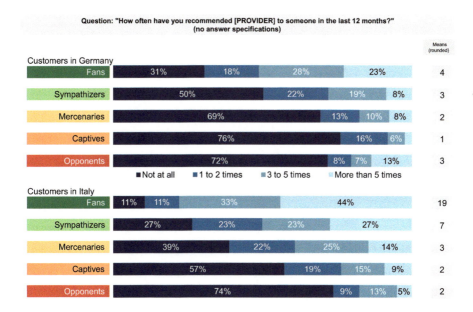

Fig. 2.20 (continued)

mentioned, are much more reticent than the Fans when it comes to communication. This difference between fans and Sympathizers reveals how important it is not to base relationship quality solely on recommendation behavior, but to look at it in a more differentiated way. Otherwise, Sympathizers, in particular, are misclassified: They then appear to be customers of merely average value—only because of their restrained recommendation behavior. In fact, however, they are close to the fans in terms of their relationship quality with the company and thus represent an indispensable resource for expanding the *Fan Rate*. So, we learn that factual recommendation behavior is not sufficient as the sole indicator of relationship quality. Anyone who does not comprehensively map emotional customer loyalty in their analyses, but only relies on recommendation behavior as an indicator, will segment their customer landscape inadequately and ultimately make the incorrect management decisions (cf. Sect. 5.3).

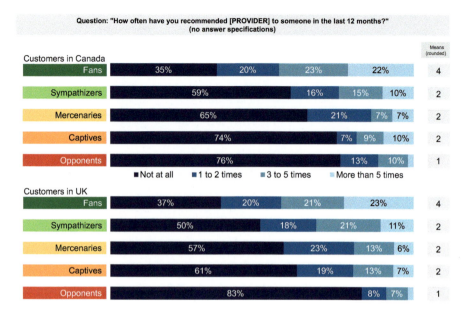

Fig. 2.20 (continued)

2.3.3 Excursus: How Do Word-of-Mouth, Social Media, and Recommendation Work?

But why is recommendation considered to be so important? Customers are already well provided for in terms of communication. Thousands of advertising claims and PR messages pelt them every day. How is word of mouth supposed to prevail in this flood of stimuli? The answer is quite simple: word-of-mouth can prevail not despite, but precisely because of this flood of stimuli. Because the flood leads to disorientation since the customer can no longer differentiate between the providers. Every day, customers are confronted with an incredible number of promises of rewards, all perfectly presented and placed. Almost all of them—as we have already shown—entice the customer with an "ever more" level of performance. In this wooing/pursuing situation, the customer is overwhelmed—he needs help in making decisions and orientation. And those who need orientation and help in making decisions are looking for an advisor. Someone whose judgment they can trust and whom they consider competent and credible. The official advertising and PR communications of providers are rarely afforded these qualities. Hence, advisors from the personal environment are becoming increasingly important since they offer orientation owing to their credibility.

2.3 Fans and Market Development: Growth Through Acquisition of New...

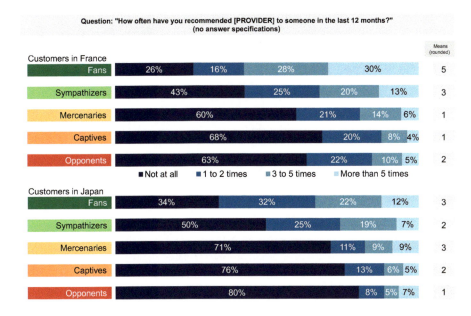

Fig. 2.20 (continued)

But irrespective of the credibility of the person recommending the product, there is another central reason why word-of-mouth is so important: testimonials are a particularly convincing form of communication—they have an exceptionally high persuasive effect. This is proven by findings from media effects research, which became known as "exemplification research" (cf. as an overview Daschmann 2008; Zillmann and Brosius 2000). They show that testimonials in media reports, such as statements by everyday people in street surveys, have a strong effect on the audience. This is even though the statements have virtually no value based on knowledge—they are neither representative nor do they have general validity.

Nevertheless—and this is the fascinating result of research—these statements have a disproportionally large influence on the audience: Most readers, listeners or viewers tend, in fact, to change their views based on a few such statements. They believe that the few statements they hear represent the majority view. They continue to believe this even when they are simultaneously presented with representative survey statistics that say the opposite (Daschmann 2000). Obviously, many people prefer to rely in their judgment on a few witness statements they hear with their own ears rather than on data from valid and representative statistics. Because they now consider the view, they have heard to be the majority view, and majorities always

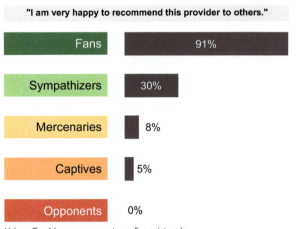

Fig. 2.21 Fans are best referrers

have something convincing about them, this view suddenly seems more convincing to them themselves.

This effect has been proven by more than 60 experimental studies. The exciting thing about this research is that the cause of this effect has been identified across many studies. The testimonials are not effective because they are particularly lively or because the people who say them are particularly credible, convincing, or likeable. The answer is much more banal: they are effective because they are individual cases. Because our brains are evolutionarily designed to draw conclusions from such individual case information—i.e. for inductive reasoning. All human learning is basically based on this (Daschmann 2001).

A child, who accidentally puts his hand on the stove top and burns himself or herself, will never again put his hand on any stove top—regardless of whether it is a gas stove, induction, or ceramic cooking surface. The child learned from this single event and immediately drew a general conclusion: "Be careful! These things are always hot on top!" This mental strategy of generalization, even though it may not always be logically true, ensures our survival and is thus an evolutionary advantage. It is precisely because the human brain is able to derive general conclusions from a few observations that humans have been able to prevail as a species in evolutionary terms. This is why our thinking is so receptive to single-case information—this is also referred to as the "episodic affinity of judgment formation." Intuitively, we all follow this judgment strategy in everyday life. Imagine, for example, that you are a traveler arriving in a foreign city. Your navigation system is down, and you ask for directions at the first intersection. A passerby helps you, and he is remarkably friendly about it. When you ask for directions again two intersections down the road, another friendly person comes to your aid. And should this happen again at your third stop, the matter is clear to you: you will rave at home about what a friendly city this is. Essentially, you know nothing about the city and its inhabitants. You happened to talk to three passers-by, that's all. But you are convinced by these individual cases—and add them up to an overall judgment. And if someone were to come to you with statistics about supposedly unfriendly people in this city, you would gruffly reject them—even though they would probably be much more meaningful than your three random encounters.

Individual statements by everyday people—thus the conclusion of this line of research—have a highly persuasive influence on the formation of our judgments since they are evolutionarily particularly suitable material for us to learn and draw conclusions. The connection with the topic of recommendation is obvious: If individual testimonials are so persuasive, this also explains why recommendations—from friends as well as from strangers—can have such a great effect. As already shown at the beginning, however, this effect increases considerably if testimonials are particularly credible, as can be seen, for example, in the discussion about credible and less credible influencers. With a view to credibility, it becomes clear why fan customers are the ideal referrers as testimonials:

1. Fan customers have a high level of credibility. They use the products, services, and providers they recommend themselves—and their high level of identification with the provider and its products is not imposed, but comes from within, as we will see in a moment. Fan customers are therefore advertising out of conviction and not because they are enticed to do so by incentives. Their advice, therefore, has a high degree of authenticity.
2. Fan customers have a high level of expertise. In some cases, they are more familiar with the products and services in question than the provider itself. Their advice is therefore not only credible. It is also competent. And thus bears twice as much weight.
3. Credibility, authenticity, and competence give the Fan customer's recommendation messages special weight in the great stream of advertising and PR communication. From the perspective of non-customers, his statements stand out qualitatively, so that they receive attention and care. This creates awareness and familiarity for the brands and products to be introduced, especially when entering new markets (cf. Fig. 2.19).
4. Fans are extraverted. No other customer group is as willing to talk as Fans. This means that fans not only have the aforementioned positive communicative qualities, but also the necessary willingness to share.

The conclusion is clear: The Fan offers a perfect symbiosis of characteristics with credibility, competence, and willingness to talk: He or she becomes a valuable multiplier who creates awareness and familiarity for brands and products to be introduced. And this makes the Fan an indispensable instrument for market development. What's more, the Fan's impact is no longer limited to word-of-mouth communication. Today, the central platform for customer testimonials is the Internet. Through user-generated content, especially through social media platforms, the testimonials described have undergone a serious revaluation (cf. Berger 2014). This is based on the following noteworthy changes:

1. Through social media platforms, every customer has the opportunity to provide positive or negative testimonials.
2. Often this can be done from the anonymity of the Internet and without consequences.
3. Through social media platforms, every customer can access such testimonials as needed—even from people he or she does not know personally.
4. Through social media platforms, each testimonial thus potentially has mass media reach.
5. Through social media platforms, testimonials—both positive and negative—remain permanently visible and thus become part of the external perception of a provider.
6. Through social media platforms, people can endorse, support, or reject testimonials from others—by clicking "Like" buttons.
7. Social media platforms not only present testimonials—but they are also usually accompanied by a quantitative overview of how many other users "like" or even "dislike" something—an indication of quantities about the customers and users themselves that never existed in this way in the traditional mass media.

These last two points, in particular, led to the misunderstanding among many private users of counting the "likes" of their own posts and seeing them as a secret indicator of popularity or influence. Some social media platforms have now put a stop to this misguided development and no longer make the number of "likes" of a "post" public. The communications departments of many companies also began to reflexively count "likes" around the turn of the millennium. Not so much because they really knew what they meant, but above all because they finally had a key figure that they could present to the CEO as the person responsible for communications. And so the "likes"—especially the Facebook thumb—developed into the secret currency of social media success. This led to a central misunderstanding: Because the number of "likes" was considered meaningful within the company, it was intuitively believed that web users viewed it similarly, and that visitors to one's own pages could be impressed by high "like" numbers. Experiments from communication science proved that this assumption is incorrect: Visitors to websites or Facebook profiles are completely indifferent to the number of "likes". They notice them, but they are not impressed by them. What, on the other hand, does have a decisive impact on the assessment of the company is the tenor of the testimonials that are visible on the page. A company can have tens of thousands of "likes" on its page—if there are only three or four prominently visible negative user comments on the same platform at the same time, the perception of the company is already damaged. You recall—individual opinions do impress, and statistics fade. This is the anecdotal affinity of forming judgments.

Speaking of Facebook thumbs: even though the Facebook "Like" is often colloquially referred to as a "fan thumb"—this has nothing in common with the concept

Fig. 2.22 Fans visit the *Facebook* page

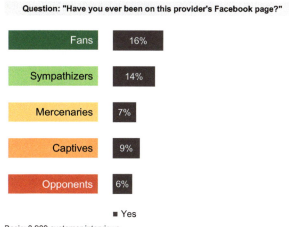

of the Fan that we have developed. Clicking the "fan thumb" can be explained by many different user motives or customer behavior—including mercenary behavior. Under no circumstances, however, can Fans in our sense be identified via such social media "likes"; since these do not express lasting loyalty, merely spontaneous sentiment.

Back to the changes brought about by Web 2.0: These have resulted in a considerable upgrading of testimonials—because every statement made by a customer now has potential mass reach. And this is precisely the source of many companies' fears of Web 2.0: it is the fear of negative testimonials and vituperative criticism that can build up into a wave of indignation. At first glance, this seems plausible, as we have just shown that Opponent customers in particular like to spread negative messages. But in fact, this fear is completely unfounded.

As Fig. 2.22 indicates it is not the Opponents who visit a provider's communication platforms to trigger a wave of indignation. The real visitors to a company's Facebook page, for example, are: the Fans. They visit such pages much more frequently than any other customer groups. That's not surprising. After all, Fans need a platform to live out their fanhood. And what better place to do this than a company's website, a provider's Facebook page, or a subject relevant forum? We can conclude: Fans are not only potentially the best referrers—they are also on precisely those communicative platforms where these recommendations can be disseminated excellently. If we now consider what missionary and at the same time inspiring characteristics Fans bring with them, it becomes clear what incredible opportunities lie in fan communication via social media (cf. Sect. 5.1).

The first opportunity is to bring fans together with other customer groups. Companies can let Fans speak for themselves—and use this communication for their own purposes. Those who bring fan customers together with other customer groups and allow free exchange in the process have nothing to fear—Fans will always fly the company's flag of their own accord. Incidentally, this concept is not an invention, but has been around a while. A U.S. company made it its sole form of distribution: the company in question is *Tupperware* with its Tupper parties. Fan customers, suppliers and new customers come together in a common communicative circle—with resounding sales success. Nowadays, numerous software providers basically do nothing else on the web: they set up forums in which fan customers look after newcomers and beginners with credibility and expertise—and introduce them to the fan community right away.

The second chance consists of authentic positive messages that the Fans can bring to the table. If you have motivated fans, fear of the wave of outrage is out of place—because fans provide positive messages. Fans can, when trouble threatens somewhere on the social media platforms, go online and build a positive counter-current there—and do so much more authentically than any corporate communications department ever could. The key here is to deal with your fans properly and support and motivate them accordingly to live out their fandom profitably on social media platforms. Some companies are already doing this very successfully (see Sect. 4.3).

How successful are companies in mobilizing their fans on social networks? As Fig. 2.22 shows, the proportion of Fans who are active on social media platforms can be determined by survey—and can therefore be shown in benchmark to the industry or to individual competitors. This makes it possible to measure how actively a company mobilizes Fans on social media platforms compared to its competitors. Those who regularly conduct such surveys can identify changes in the behavior of their multipliers before the competition and win the net-public debate, which is reflected with a delay of one to two weeks later in the high-reach media such as television and newspapers—and no longer must be afraid of social media posts.

If we take the significance of fans for social media communication a step further, numerous prospects come to light with incredible potential. On the one hand, appropriately designed web monitoring and content analyses of social media content can be used to determine the proportion of fan posts on the web and relate this to the company's own *Fan Rate*. *In* this way, it is easy to identify where there is room for improvement in terms of fan motivation for web communication. On the other hand, it is possible to identify the content that is of particular interest to fans and bind them to the company's own website. Skillful content marketing can then increase the fans' motivation to become more present on the web platforms. And finally, appropriate analysis tools could be used to determine from the users' posts whether they are Fans or Mercenaries, Captives or Opponents—who could then also be addressed in a target group-specific manner. All of this clearly shows that the *Fan Portfolio* is an instrument with great potential for the future—because it helps like no other instrument to identify the customers who are decisive communicative guarantors of dissemination and success, even under digital conditions—not only through recommendation, but also due to their authenticity and credibility.

The explanations show what considerable potential there is in the customer value of the Fan as an ambassador—and that social media specifically is causing a rapid shift from monetary to non-monetary customer value. We have calculated this for many companies. In addition to the monetary customer value (based on the contribution margin), we also "monetized" non-monetary aspects of the customer value of the Fans, for example, by evaluating how many new Fans a Fan customer activates through his or her recommendation. The result surprised us ourselves: the "monetized" value of the Fan customers' referral activities can significantly exceed the direct monetary customer value of the original fan customers, depending on the frequency and intensity of referrals and the duration of the customer relationship of the newly acquired fan customers.

This leads us to a key insight: conventional customer value or customer classification models, which regularly only take direct monetary returns into account, not only fall short, but they are also even frequently misleading. This is because they may automatically classify Fan customers with less purchasing power as unattractive due to the limited monetary perspective. As a result, these Fan customers are often unjustly neglected or even noticeably discriminated against—to the detriment of the company. After all, just imagine how great the contribution of a Fan customer with less purchasing power, and thus his customer value, really is if three to four new customers per year are acquired for the company based on his positive statements and his targeted recommendation, and what might happen if he senses that his love is not reciprocated in the long term.

These considerations illustrate why customer value should not be reduced merely to monetary potential. This limits the view to the perspective of how attractive a customer currently is for a company. What is often forgotten is that the opposite perspective, i.e. the attractiveness of the provider for the customer (which is expressed in his emotional attachment), also has decisive consequences for the true customer value (cf. Sect. 5.1).

2.3.4 Fans and Recommendation Incentives

Only the Fan customers are therefore noteworthy ambassadors of any company who make genuine recommendations. With this in mind, how promising is it for companies to actively try to turn customers into ambassadors by creating incentives for referrals or new customer acquisition? Figure 2.23 illustrates that such blanket attempts promise little success.

Overall, only around 8% of customers feel motivated at all by incentive systems to become active as ambassadors (cf. Fig. 2.23). Interestingly, Fans do not deviate from the customer average here—even though, as already shown, they have the most pronounced recommendation behavior of all customer segments (cf. Figs. 2.20a–d and 2.21). Obviously, Fans do not let monetary incentives take the decision out of their hands as to when and whom they recommend. Although the majority regularly recommends "their" provider and are happy to do so, only 10% of them accept incentives for doing so. With this low percentage, they are no different from the other groups. Clearly, the Fans are not interested in the take-away effects of the incentives on offer. But it is not only the Fans who seem to ignore the incentives: The incentives also trigger only a low willingness to recommend in the other customer groups. Incentives are unlikely to turn silent Sympathizers into ambassadors at a

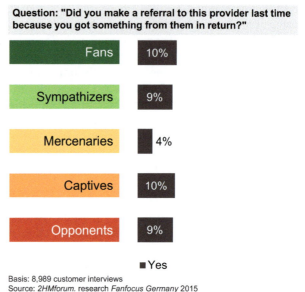

Fig. 2.23 Recommendation incentives do not differentiate

greater rate, and the mere satisfaction of Mercenaries is evidently not enough to turn a silent customer into a recommending ambassador by means of an incentive. In summary, the data thus show: "Recommendation Marketing" via incentives to force is minimally effective. This is because the incentives miss the actual target, namely, to motivate the passive but highly satisfied customer groups of Mercenaries and Sympathizers to recommend the company to others. In the case of Fans, on the other hand, they ultimately have a counterproductive effect: revenue is reduced, because Fans already recommend others—albeit out of intrinsic motivation.

2.3.5 Excursus: Why Opponents Are Dangerous Customers

The other side of the coin, the counterpart to recommendation, is less pleasing for companies, but nevertheless cannot be ignored: when damaging word-of-mouth is spread, whether justified or unfounded from the provider's point of view. This "negative word-of-mouth phenomenon," as it is also called, repeatedly fills many companies with concern. It is not for nothing that a nearly century-old classic of customer advocacy goes, "If you're dissatisfied, tell us—if you're satisfied, tell others!" Negative word-of-mouth should be avoided at all costs. But who is actually spreading these negative messages? We have findings on this, too. Figure 2.24 shows which customer types really work actively against the company's interests (cf. Sect. 4.3).

Here it becomes clear that we have indeed quite rightly given the segment of dissatisfied and disengaged customers the label of Opponent customers: More than

Fig. 2.24 Why opponents are dangerous customers

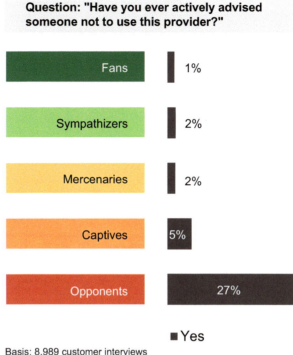

one in four of them actively works against the company's interests among their acquaintances or even in public—and thus counteracts with guerrilla actions and criticism often full of vitriol that which companies previously tried to establish in terms of image in small steps, laboriously and at great expense. It becomes clear: Opponent customers are not only lost, their negative word-of-mouth advertising costs further customers and thus cash money. Company reflexive efforts to improve the relationship with Opponents by paying a great deal of attention and making intensive efforts rarely prove promising, because the "fit" with these customers is simply not there. We will go into more detail elsewhere on how to proceed with Opponent customers instead (cf. Sect. 4.4).

At the same time, however, with a view to Fig. 2.24 to note: It is exclusively the Opponents who work so explicitly against the company's goals. All other customer types hold back on negative word of mouth. On the one hand, this confirms how important and useful it is to identify customer types by means of the *Fan Portfolio*—and on the other hand, it again underlines the selectivity of our empirical classification: since the negative word-of-mouth can be clearly assigned to the Opponents, while the positive testimonials come from the fans.

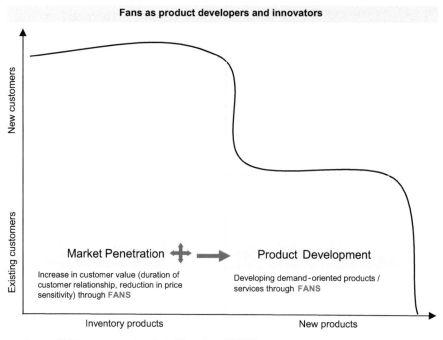

Fig. 2.25 Fans as a growth factor: Product Development

2.4 Fans and Product Development: Growth with Existing Customers Through Expansion of the Product Range

The alternative to opening new customer markets is to expand the product range with the aim of generating additional sales with existing customers. In the product-market matrix, the company thus moves horizontally in the direction of the lower right quadrant (cf. Fig. 2.25).

2.4.1 Fans Are Innovators

Fan customers can also play an indispensable role in this growth strategy: after all, they will be the first to purchase, use and recommend the new products with which the company wants to be successful. This is because Fans show an extraordinarily high willingness to cross-purchase, as Fig. 2.26 impressively illustrates.

Around two-thirds of all Fan customers surveyed in the G7 countries candidly state that they intend to extend their customer relationship to other products or services from their favorite provider. Again, we find the same clear differences

2.4 Fans and Product Development: Growth with Existing Customers...

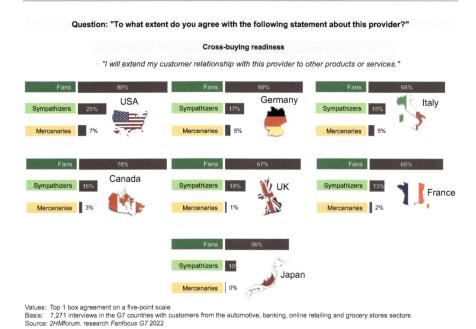

Fig. 2.26 Fans are the innovators in the diffusion process

between Fans, Sympathizers and Mercenaries across all countries surveyed. Fan customers are thus receptive to cross-selling or up-selling. This willingness is not surprising, but a fan-typical behavior. We explained in the sociological derivation of our Fan definition in Chap. 1 that Fans are willing to spend high sums for their fanhood. And if they love and trust a provider, they will queue up when the new product line is released—no matter how much the iPad, the concert ticket or the stadium attendance may now cost. Fans thus take the lead role of initial adopters when their "star provider" launches new products. Classical diffusion theory divides customers into five different groups depending on the timing of their product acceptance when new products are introduced into a market: Innovators are the initial adopters, followed by early adopters, up to mass implementation in the market by other groups (Rogers 2003). Fans are thus the so-called innovators in the diffusion process: They are the first to acquire the products and then promote them in their environment—so that the spillover to the early adopters greatly facilitates the exponential rise of the diffusion curve (cf. Sect. 5.1.1).

2.4.2 Fans Are Involved

But it is not only the innovator role that makes Fans so significant in the context of (new) product development. There is also a specific characteristic that is basically only found in fans: Involvement. This is because the Fan's connection is not only reflected in his loyalty. Fan customers are also highly involved customers—owing to their intensive relationship with the provider, they are anything but indifferent to how the company behaves on the market, whether it is successful or not, what products it develops and how it is perceived. The Fan is interested in his supplier and his actions—and therefore observes his favorite company with a particular intensity (cf. Fig. 2.27).

Fans follow their provider's steps very closely: the vast majority has a high level of product knowledge, which means the Fans are very familiar with their provider's offerings and services. This knowledge is no coincidence: we know from surveys in Germany that most Fans actively and regularly inform themselves about new offers and services from their provider on their own initiative—much more than any other customer segment. But the Fans' commitment does not stop at this interest alone. They do not simply passively absorb information. They want to have their say and do have the necessary expertise to do so. On average, almost every second fan in the G7 countries believes he or she would be able to advise his or her provider well on the further development of products and services (cf. Fig. 2.28). Here again, Fans in all countries differ equally from the other customer groups. This assessment on the part of Fans is not even presumptuous. In fact, some Fans are more familiar with the products or services of "their" providers than their employees. This may be one of the reasons why Fans remain loyal to their provider even when others advise against it: Their view is so well-founded and so solidified that it is difficult to shake.

Companies should take advantage of the great expertise of their Fans: They can improve products and processes in a very needs-oriented and efficient manner if they involve their Fans in optimization and (new) product development. Many companies are now making targeted use of this knowledge of their Fans via online platforms: In so-called crowdsourcing, they take up the suggestions, test uses, improvement requests and development ideas of their Fans and thus use the free "swarm intelligence" of the fan community, which they at the same time bind even more strongly to themselves through these activities (cf. Sect. 5.1).

But where does the Fan's motivation, even desire, to participate actively and even gratuitously in the company's value creation process come from? The answer is simple: it's the typical fan behavior that can be observed among fans in all areas of life and culture. For the Fan, being a Fan is not enough. They must live out their fanhood, they want to shape it, they want to actively participate in it. And they want to belong to something. To a community of fans and to the product world of their provider. Companies that have understood this are already exploiting some of the potential of their fan community. But only companies that also know how to increase their *Fan Rate* can increase this crowdsourcing potential many times over.

The willingness of fan customers to cross-buy, the product expertise they have acquired through involvement, and their willingness to communicate all of this proactively, as described above, also make fan customers valuable supporters in the growth strategies of product development.

2.4 Fans and Product Development: Growth with Existing Customers... 131

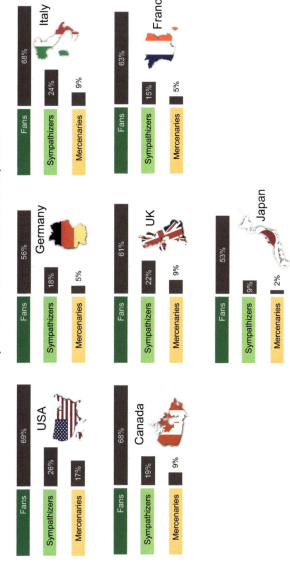

Fig. 2.27 Fans are involved and therefore experts I

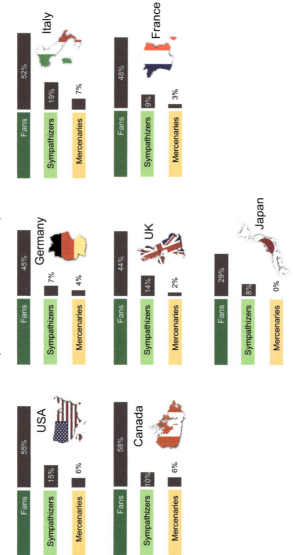

Fig. 2.28 Fans are involved and therefore experts II

2.5 Fans and Product Diversification: Growth by Attracting New Customers for New Products

Up to this point, we have been able to show that Fan customers offer an almost inexhaustible support potential for all growth processes covered by the market-product matrix, which is basically indispensable for strategic management. But the matrix still contains a fourth quadrant in the upper right-hand corner, which stands for the introduction of new products in markets which have not yet been tapped, and which Ansoff has given the perhaps not entirely accurate label of "product diversification." Figure 2.29 again illustrates the context.

At the outset, we already advised against companies taking the diagonal growth path indicated in the matrix, because the risks are multiplied here. But based on what we have said so far, this hasty step no longer seems necessary. We have been able to show that each of the other growth strategies in the matrix, in the upward as well as in the sideways movement, will probably be promising and successful with a high *Fan Rate*. This also makes it possible to combine both methods with an appropriate time interval—and in whatever sequence. Both possible combinations ultimately lead to the quadrant of product diversification, which can then also be mastered thanks to fan support. The two non-colored arrows in Fig. 2.27 are intended to illustrate this connection.

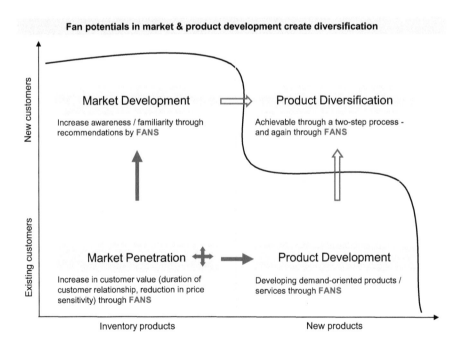

Source: *2HMforum.* research; adapted from *Ansoff* (1965)

Fig. 2.29 Fans as a growth factor: Product Diversification

2.6 Summary: The *Fan Rate* as the Key Growth Factor

With the *Fan Portfolio,* we have presented an instrument in Chaps. 1 and 2 which we have developed from fan research, and which can be used to segment the entire customer portfolio according to relationship quality. We have described the characteristic features of these customer groups in the *Fan Portfolio* and have also provided evidence that the various customer segments in the *Fan Portfolio* differ not only in terms of their relationship quality but also in their customer value. While increasing satisfaction has virtually no effect on customer value, it virtually explodes if the company succeeds in increasing emotional attachment. Thus, the previous findings can be summarized in one sentence: The *Fan Rate* is the key growth factor of every company.

Anyone who ensures an increasing *Fan Rate* will be successful in business. This is because Fan customers buy more frequently and spend more money on the products of "their" companies—more than other customer groups do. Fan customers are also less price-sensitive and thus generate more revenue through upselling and cross-selling. They, therefore, have the highest monetary customer value and at the same time maintain the longest business relationships with "their" company. Fans therefore have the highest customer lifetime value. Fans also indirectly increase sales and revenue because they support their company through their behavior in numerous areas. Fans are more forgiving of poor performance and resistant to poaching and negative advice. Fans also actively recommend their company to others and thus support the acquisition of new customers as multipliers. In this way, they reduce the costs of acquiring new customers and at the same time generate an increase in sales through their communication. Fans get involved with ideas and innovations and, owing to their above-average involvement, form an excellent basis for crowdsourcing—i.e., collecting impulses and ideas from the Fan community for the company's own product development—which also significantly reduces internal development costs and increases the chances of success for innovations. Through all these mechanisms, Fan customers directly and indirectly increase both sales and revenue. Therefore, companies with a higher *Fan Rate* have a more stable economic foundation and greater success. Those who create Fan customers thus not only build a basis for short-term profits, but also ensure sustainable economic success for their company. Figure 2.30 visualizes the various success factors that Fan customers bring to a company; both for customers on the German market and for international customers in the other G7 countries.

We have illustrated all these positive effects of fan customers on corporate success so far, primarily using examples from the B2C sector. However, the explanations apply equally to the B2B area without restriction. There, too, Fan customers have the highest customer value, the highest customer lifetime value, are the best recommenders and have the highest involvement. For illustration purposes, we present—comparable to the data in Fig. 2.30—some data from B2B customers in Fig. 2.31 from our consulting activities. They show that all the success factors of Fans that apply in the B2C area also unfold in the same form in the B2B area.

2.6 Summary: The *Fan Rate* as the Key Growth Factor

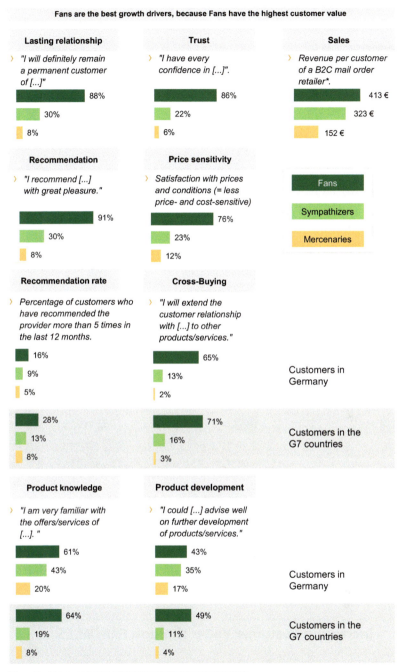

Fig. 2.30 The *Fan Rate* as a key growth factor in B2C

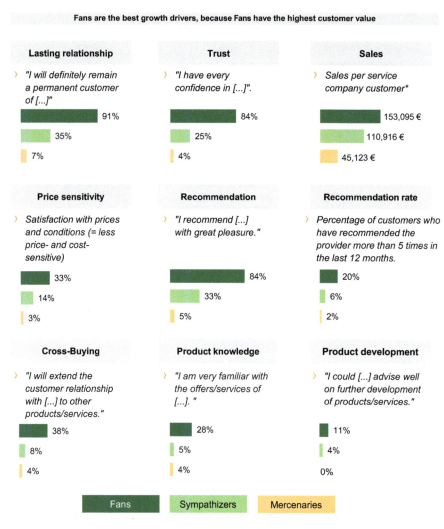

Fig. 2.31 The *Fan Rate* as a key growth factor in B2B

2.7 Increasing Customer Value Through *FANOMICS*

The high customer value of Fans, which we have been able to demonstrate in these explanations, impressively illustrates why every company that wants to be successful should apply *FANOMICS* and thus focus on increasing the *Fan Rate*: The goal

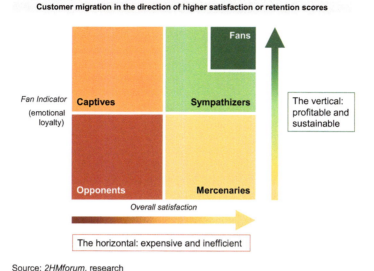

Fig. 2.32 Optimization movements in the *Fan Portfolio*

must be to move highly satisfied customers without maximum emotional attachment, i.e., Sympathizers and Mercenaries, from the bottom to the top, i.e. vertically, in the *Fan Portfolio*. The resource input required for this creates new loyal Fan customers with high customer value, which is profitable and sustainable. Figure 2.32 illustrates this movement.

By contrast, a company that focuses only unilaterally on increasing customer satisfaction merely tries to make dissatisfied customers satisfied, i.e., to move them from left to right in the logic of the diagram. This is expensive and inefficient, since increasing satisfaction presupposes a permanent increase in performance—but it creates no loyalty and no additional sustainable customer value. How to achieve the upward movement in the *Fan Portfolio*, on the other hand, i.e., to turn customers into Fans, is the core of *FANOMICS*—and the subject of the following Chaps. 3 and 4.

References

Ansoff HI (1965) Checklist for competitive and competence profiles. In: Ansoff HI (ed) Corporate strategies. McGraw Hill, New York, pp 89–99

Berger J (2014) Word of mouth and interpersonal communication: a review and directions for future research. J Consum Psychol 24(4):586–607

Daschmann G (2000) Vox pop & polls: the impact of poll results and voter statements in the media on the perception of a climate of opinion. Int J Public Opin Res IJPOR 12(2):160–181. https://doi.org/10.1093/ijpor/12.2.160

Daschmann G (2001) The influence of case studies on reader judgments. Experimental studies on media effects. UVK Media, Constance, Amsterdam

Daschmann G (2008) Effects of exemplification and exemplars. In: Donsbach W (ed) The international Encyclopedia of communication. Wiley-Blackwell, Oxford, UK, pp 1632–1636

Rogers EM (2003) Diffusion of innovations, 5th edn. Free Press, New York

Zillmann D, Brosius H-B (2000) Exemplification in communication: the influence of case reports on the perception of issues. Routledge, New York

FANOMICS: The Economics of the *Fan Principle*

3

In the previous sections (Chaps. 1 and 2), we completed seven important analytical steps:

1. Based on social sciences research, we have discovered the *Fan Principle*, which describes the basic mechanisms of Fan relationships from sports, music or art
2. From the two central characteristics of fan-typical behavior, we have developed the *Fan Indicator* as a measure of emotional customer loyalty.
3. We related the *Fan Indicator* to customer satisfaction and then defined those customers as fans who have an extremely high emotional attachment and, at the same time, an extremely high level of satisfaction.
4. This enabled us to identify the *Fan Rate* as a key indicator and test variable for the relationship quality of companies and thus demonstrate that customer satisfaction alone is not sufficient as an indicator for managing customer relationships.
5. At the same time, we have created a completely new segmentation of the entire customer landscape along the way with the *Fan Portfolio*.
6. We have shown the potential that lies in this breakdown by demonstrating that the various customer segments of the *Fan Portfolio* differ not only in terms of their relationship quality, but also in their customer value, and that it is the Fans who make companies more successful economically in the long term through their customer value.
7. Using data from an international comparative study for the G7 countries, we were able to show that these basic mechanisms of the *Fan Principle* function across markets and cultures, and that we can therefore speak of a global system.

These analytical steps are important to better understand customer relationships and identify the value of customers—but they would be useless if they could not be used to derive management control strategies that actually make a company more economically successful. We have developed such a management control model and called it *FANOMICS*. Its derivation and explanation is the subject of this chapter.

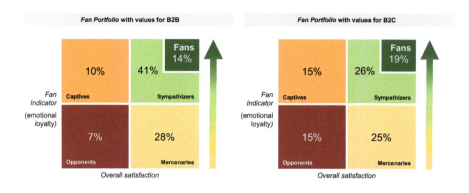

Basis: B2B: 800 interviews with corporate decision-makers, B2C: 125,222 interviews with customers across 337 companies of 35 industries
Source: 2HMforum. research, B2B: *ExBa* 2006, B2C: *Fanfocus Germany* 2017 - 2021

Fig. 3.1 Vertical movement in the B2B/B2C *Fan Portfolio*

With *FANOMICS,* we are giving the entire customer relationship management a new direction. What we mean by this is made clear by a look at the Fan Portfolio: For the majority of companies, it does not make economic sense to try to turn dissatisfied customers into satisfied ones, which corresponds to a horizontal movement in the *Fan Portfolio.* This is because, as explained in detail in Sect. 1.3 and also intuitively identifiable, most companies have already achieved this goal to a large extent. It is a matter of turning highly satisfied customers into those with high emotional attachment, which corresponds to a vertical movement in the *Fan Portfolio.* And how exactly this vertical movement works is explained by *FANOMICS* (cf. Fig. 3.1).

Successful implementation requires a complete change in management thinking. Half-hearted implementations are not enough. It is not enough to look at the *Fan Rate* as a parameter in an analysis or to segment the customer landscape once by the *Fan Portfolio.* A realignment of customer relationships toward emotional customer loyalty can only work if the entire customer relationship management is aligned with this idea. Only those who redesign their customer relationship management and use the instruments presented here—*Fan Indicator*, *Fan Rate* and *Fan Portfolio*—in interaction on a regular basis in a targeted, systematic, and coordinated manner will lead their company to sustainable growth. Success will only come if a company understands emotional connection, i.e., what makes the fan a Fan, as a central parameter of its mission statement and consistently aligns itself with it.

To develop *FANOMICS* as a management model, we have consistently oriented ourselves to the *Fan Principle,* i.e., to our findings in fan research in social sciences. If we succeed in transferring these findings to the management of customer relationships, we will have found the key starting points for our management model.

As explained in detail in Sect. 1.2, the *Fan Principle* is primarily about *identification* and perceived *uniqueness*: Fans want to experience over and over again what once made them fans. They want; indeed they need, the repetition, the ritual. In order for companies to succeed in the "translation process" of identification and perceived uniqueness, two factors are essential: firstly, the Focus within the framework of the company's positioning, and secondly, the Orchestration, i.e., the concrete translation to the customer experience. We explain this in more detail below.

3.1 Focus Generates Identification

Why is focus an crucial element? Every management of a company must be focused on the core needs of the customers. This is because the mechanisms of fan relationships, which were intensively examined in Sect. 1.2, are decisively based on the experienced fit between the motives and desires of the Fan and the central characteristics and messages of his or her star, since it is precisely this fit which generates identification. The following three essential conditions must be met for fit to occur:

1. Companies recognize and understand the key needs of their customers.
2. Companies focus on these core customer needs in their service delivery and communication.
3. The aspects of this service delivery and communication that are relevant to customer needs are experienced as strengths by customers.

Conversely, this means that no fit occurs as soon as one of the three conditions mentioned is not fulfilled. Because then the following undesirable developments occur:

1. Companies do not focus.
2. Companies focus, but do not know the relevant customer needs.
3. Companies focus on relevant customer needs, but then fail to meet them.

We now want to take a closer look at focusing in the context of "Positioning," by using some examples from practice. In doing so, we will look at examples of success, explain the value of high identification as a result of experienced "fit", and take a look at the typical mistakes that we often encounter in companies.

3.1.1 Examples I: Successful Focus Through "Freude am Fahren" or "Vorsprung durch Technik"

What is the basis of *BMW*'s success? It is the consistent focus on customers' core motivational structures (cf. Fig. 3.2). *BMW recognized as early* as the 1960s that there is a broad target group among drivers worldwide for whom driving pleasure ("Freude am Fahren") and sportiness are paramount. This target group has needs that can be optimally harmonized with the strength of the German engine manufacturer, namely the development of high-torque and high-performance power drive systems.

142   3   FANOMICS: The Economics of the *Fan Principle*

Source: BMW Group, with kind permission

Fig. 3.2 "Freude am Fahren ": consistent positioning and coding. (Courtesy of © BMW Group 2022. All Rights Reserved)

Consequently, even if the claims within the various markets slightly differ, *BMW* has made "driving pleasure" its worldwide brand essence and ensures that customers can feel and experience this promise.

We would like to take a closer look at a particularly striking example of this focus in the following. It is about how *BMW* translates a new technology to the central motives of its target groups and at the same time differentiates itself from the competitor perceived as the pioneer of this technology. The technology in question is all-wheel drive. And who do you think is the established competitor?

Similarly, we have been asking our listeners this question during presentations for many years: "Which car brand do you think of when you hear the word 'all-wheel drive'?" In Germany, in nine out of ten cases, the spontaneous association is: "*AUDI*. "To the follow-up question, "And what image do you have in mind when you think of an *AUDI Quattro*?" the listeners answer just as spontaneously: "Of an *AUDI Quattro* driving up a ski jump ." (AUDI USA) This advertising campaign is legendary, its origins date back to 1986, and even though it has not been broadcast for several years, it still shapes our image of the all-wheel drive of an *AUDI* (cf. Fig. 3.3). We maintain: This translation of the positioning at the time decisively explains *AUDI's* success today, as it made the brand promise "Vorsprung durch Technik" ("Progress through Technology") visible to every car driver in a way that was both intuitively understandable and impressive. "Vorsprung durch Technik" reached a competitive, performance-oriented, dominance-seeking type of driver and has retained that type to this day: Anyone who has ever driven up a mountain pass

3.1 Focus Generates Identification   143

Fig. 3.3 Creating fit by focusing on core customer needs (Courtesy of © AUDI: Corporate Archives of AUDI AG 2022; BMW: Jung von Matt/Alster Werbeagentur GmbH 2022. All Rights Reserved)

road as an *AUDI Quattro driver in* heavy snowfall, watching the pitiful drivers of other car brands put on their snow chains from the comfort of the vehicle's interior, knows what this dominance feels like.

AUDI's translation of all-wheel drive technology as a symbol of "Vorsprung durch Technik" was thus centrally and dominantly positioned in the market. Against this background, how did *BMW* present its all-wheel drive technology xDrive to the public? A striking commercial from the launch phase illustrates how *BMW* succeeded in translating the same technology—drive on four wheels—to the needs of its customers through clever storytelling and intuitive visual language and sounds: There, we see a colorful jumping jack that alternately raises its arms and legs and teasingly sticks its tongue out at us again at the end, the whole thing accompanied by melodic sounds from a children's series (cf. Fig. 3.3). The message is clear: "Dear customer, here is the *xDrive*: your new toy." There is no better way to translate the result of highly complex engineering into intuitively tangible customer benefits—and at the same time clearly set yourself apart from the established competition.

The example shows what consistent focus on core customer needs means: The same interchangeable technical feature "all-wheel drive" is communicated in a benefit-oriented manner by two different companies for two different driver and customer types in a completely different way—creating the perfect feeling of fit for the respective target groups.

3.1.2 Examples II: Is Flying Really More Pleasant? *Deutsche Bahn* Versus *Lufthansa*

This example is about the way the right or wrong focus on one and the same customer need affects the relationship quality and thus the company's success.

Let's look at Deutsche Bahn, the state-operated German railroad: Hardly any German, whether a rail customer or not, will seriously deny that *Deutsche Bahn* has a problem with punctuality. In the perception of most contemporaries, delays are as much a part of train travel as fireworks on New Year's Eve. After all, on almost every train journey, one experiences loudspeaker announcements on the platform or in the carriage—sometimes formulated in a very peculiar way—that inform the passengers several times about delays. The unpunctuality of *Deutsche Bahn* has become so self-evident and legendary in the general perception that there are various book publications and caricatures on this subject (cf. Fig. 3.4).

Works or caricatures similar to those in Fig. 3.4 do not exist about *Lufthansa, the German airliner*. Why not, actually? Is *Lufthansa* so much more punctual than *Deutsche Bahn*? Our data says otherwise: Based on so-called follow-up feedback from travelers directly after their arrival at the station and the airport, respectively, the two mobility giants differ only marginally: *Lufthansa* is just as unpunctual as *Deutsche Bahn* (cf. Fig. 4.17).

The different perceptions therefore have other causes. We approach these by looking at the aspect of punctuality from a different customer perspective: For if we ask representative regular and occasional users of both transport companies in general about their punctuality and reliability, a completely different picture emerges: *Deutsche Bahn* trails *Lufthansa* by a long way in the perception of

Source cartoon: Janson
Sourve book cover: Spörrle / Schumacher, "Senk ju vor träwelling". How to travel with Deutsche Bahn and still arrive. With kind permission.

Fig. 3.4 *Deutsche Bahn*: As unpunctual as its reputation or customer needs just misunderstood? (Courtesy of © Caricature: Jürgen Janson 2022. Source Book Cover: Spörrle/Schumacher, "Senk ju7 vor träwelling" 2022. All Rights Reserved)

3.1 Focus Generates Identification 145

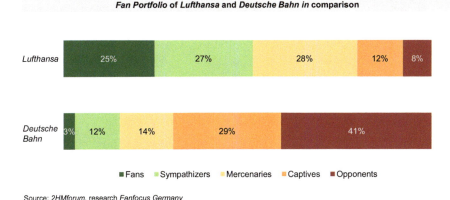

Fig. 3.5 The consequences of right and wrong focus: The *Fan Portfolios* of *Lufthansa* and *Deutsche Bahn* in comparison

punctuality. (cf. Fig. 4.16). And with consequences (although the causes are certainly not one-dimensional): If you look at the distribution of customers of the two transport giants in the *Fan Portfolio*, *Lufthansa* has many more Fans, *Deutsche Bahn* practically none, but plenty of Opponents (Fig. 3.5).

Where do these—obviously inaccurate—different perceptions of *Deutsche Bahn*'s punctuality compared to *Lufthansa come from*? At first glance, one is inclined to assume that the answer lies in communication errors on the part of *Deutsche Bahn*. Every traveler in Germany is familiar with the often awkwardly delivered, in several languages and in high frequency, information about delays and the effects on connecting trains. But anyone who looks for the reasons only in communication is merely scratching the surface. The reason for the different customer perceptions lies much deeper: Both companies understand the core need of customers in connection with punctuality completely differently.

Deutsche Bahn assumes that both departures and arrivals on time are key customer needs. That's why it communicates its offer to the minute—and accordingly tries to keep to this meticulous timing. At the same time, it calculates travel times to be as short as possible—because it believes it must compete with flights and cars. As a result, travel times are optimized to the hilt and reserves are exhausted, leaving no room for maneuver in the planning. As a result, it practically never happens that a *Deutsche Bahn* train arrives too early. But anyone who constantly tries to operate at the time limit and communicates this time limit as their average performance standard inevitably cannot always meet the expectations that this raises. In addition, *Deutsche Bahn*'s own performance statistics consider all trains to be on time if they are less than six minutes late (Schumacher 2012). The internal benchmark of service delivery is therefore "softer" than the external benchmark that is communicated to the outside world and that determines customer perception. Inevitably, this cannot work: This is because expectations are raised here (to-the-minute

Source DB: Getty Images (Thomas Lohnes). Source LH: Deutsche Lufthansa AG (© Photographer: Jens Goerlich - © Models: Cowunder).

Fig. 3.6 Same performance—different perceptions... (Courtesy of © DB: Getty Images (Thomas Lohnes) 2022. Source LH: *Deutsche Lufthansa AG* (© Photographer: Jens Goerlich—© Models: COwunder) 2022. All Rights Reserved)

timing) that one cannot and does not want to fulfill at all according to one's own standards (six-minute tolerance window).

Lufthansa is quite different. It has understood that it is immaterial to its customers whether a flight takes off on schedule or a little later, and that it is equally insignificant in the eyes of the passenger how long his plane is in the air. For the customer, only one thing is important: when he actually arrives—because his further travel or daily planning usually depends on this. Consequently, the airline communicates its departure times only every five minutes and regularly provides its domestic flights with a time buffer of about 15 minutes. In this way, *Lufthansa is* able to meet customers' punctuality expectations much more frequently than *the Deutsche Bahn.* The airline seems to be on the right track with its strategy. Because studies show that air travelers often do not know at all when they took off and how long they were in the air—but they do know when they arrived (cf. Fig. 3.6).

This vivid example documents how important it is to really know the core customer needs—and what impact it has on emotional commitment if this is not the case. And last but not least, as the *Lufthansa* example shows, you can certainly "afford" weaknesses in partial aspects that are less important to customers if you "deliver" on the relevant needs.

3.1.3 Examples III: The Value of Focus in a Crisis—*ADAC* and the Falsified Survey Results

What is the value for a company to sustainably focus on core customer needs and thus generate a broad fan base? The benefit becomes particularly visible at the moment of crisis. We will explain this using the example of the Allgemeiner Deutscher Automobil-Club e. V. (ADAC), Europe's largest motoring association with around 21 million members. You will see that a company need not fear even a self-inflicted crisis if it has successfully focused and continues to focus even after the crisis (cf. Fig. 3.7).

Source: © ADAC/Beate Blank

Fig. 3.7 Sensing what matters to fans: *ADAC* roadside assistance (Courtesy of © ADAC/Beate Blank 2022. All Rights Reserved)

At the beginning of 2014, there was a great deal of media excitement surrounding the *ADAC in* Germany: The automobile club was forced to publicly admit that in recent years the numbers of votes cast for the "Yellow Angel" prize, which was awarded annually to the Germans' favorite car, had been inflated by the club and that rankings had also been manipulated. There was talk in the media of shaken confidence, irreparable damage to the image and a credibility crisis. Politicians and decision-makers from the business community quit, and numerous commentators predicted a huge wave of membership resignations. There was no doubt about it: public opinion saw *ADAC* heading for a long and severe crisis.

But none of that came to pass. In the first half of 2014, "only" 385,000 members turned their backs on *ADAC*. In the same period, however, around 370,000 new members joined. As of summer 2014, *ADAC* had 15,000 fewer members on balance. With a membership of more than 18 million at the time, this is a negligible loss of less than one per thousand. What journalists and many experts had predicted as a result of the "yellow angel" scandal therefore did not materialize: There were no mass departures, not even a real wave of departures. There was nothing except a small dent in the membership figures—a small scratch for *ADAC,* but anything but threatening its existence.

Why did this self-inflicted crisis pass over the club with virtually no loss of members? Why did it not come to the dramatic wave of departures predicted by many? The answer has two facets:

On the one hand, the strong emotional bond of its members has saved *ADAC* from greater damage. This tie is not a product of chance, but the logical result of the excellent focus, i.e., the first-class work that the association performs in its core function: In roadside assistance and in protection and advice on all aspects of automobiles.

On the other hand, because of the manipulated ranking, there could not be a total loss in the member relationship, because this topic is irrelevant for the members and thus much too far away from the brand core of the *ADAC*. The low level of participation in the reader polls, which after all had prompted those responsible to fudge the results in the first place, speaks a clear language: "What does this have to do with *ADAC*'s daily performance in providing roadside assistance?" asked *ADAC* member Thomas Z. on the automobile club's Facebook page at the height of the crisis. And another member wrote: "The true "yellow angels" are the ones who get the car running again on the highway at night, who rescue people and help in emergency situations. (…) To cancel the *ADAC* membership now, hits the wrong ones and in the end also everyone himself. (…) Fire the fools and carry on" (Facebook 2014).

We learn from this example how valuable it is to know the core customer needs and to fulfill them in a focused and credible way. Even in a self-inflicted crisis, the Fans remain loyal as long as their "star"—in this case "their" *ADAC*—does not break the fundamental value promise that creates the fit (cf. Sect. 1.2). And for the Fan, *ADAC*'s fundamental value promise lies neither in the credibility of rankings nor in its awards for car manufacturers. The true *ADAC fan is* almost completely indifferent to these activities of his club. For him, only one thing counts: excellent breakdown assistance on the hard shoulder—that is the brand essence of *ADAC* (cf. Fig. 3.7). And that is also the only reason why its members once joined it and became Fans.

As long as the ADAC continues to provide this basic service, its fans will remain loyal to it—manipulated automobile awards or not. But if the ADAC were to start charging money for every assistance provided on the hard shoulder tomorrow or were to offer this service only on a regionally restricted basis—the club would be dead in just a few years.

3.1.4 Examples from Practice IV: When Focus Is Useful and When It Is Not—VW and the Emissions Scandal

Another example of how a company in a self-inflicted crisis initially benefits from its successful focus up to that point is the VW emissions scandal.

In the fall of 2015, the public learned that *Volkswagen AG* had used an illegal device in the engine management system of its diesel models. This deactivation device was used to manipulate the test emissions of the vehicles in order to be able to advertise the vehicles as particularly "clean". No sooner did the full extent of *VW*'s emissions cheating become apparent in 2016 than prophecies overflowed predicting a bleak future for the automotive group. Every day we read and heard new assessments of what *VW would* face after the emissions manipulation became known: recalls, repair costs, recourse claims, economic success in the billions,

3.1 Focus Generates Identification

long-term damage to its image, and much more. (Reuters Staff 2016). Yet few talked about an issue that was much more crucial for the future of the Volkswagen Group: the truly lasting and long-term threat in this scandal was the endangerment of customer relationships. The central question at the time was: how do *VW*'s customers react to the news from Wolfsburg, the company's German headquarters)? Will they turn away disappointed forever, or can *VW* count on their loyalty?

In view of the bad news that came to light every day as the scandal was unraveled, the news at the time about stable, and in some cases even rising, order intakes for new *VW* cars in Germany did not seem to fit in very well with the picture. The explanation for this is based on the same mechanics as before in the *ADAC example*: our representative benchmark study *Fanfocus 2015* showed that almost three quarters of *VW customers* in Germany had a high emotional attachment to the manufacturer at the time of the emissions scandal. Such a high level of attachment results from a perceived match between the customer's own motives and needs and what he receives from his supplier. In other words, the experienced fit was a key stabilizing factor. In concrete terms, this means that many customers felt that their requirements of a car manufacturer in terms of safety, reliability, longevity, and a large dealer network were fulfilled to a particularly high degree by *VW*—and this was both an opportunity and a danger for the Wolfsburg company.

The opportunity: The emissions scandal did not affect essential core needs of *VW customers*. This explains why the slump in sales in Germany predicted by many did not occur. *VW* had cheated, but in doing so it had not violated the brand core in the sense of the values of its customers described above. If the reason for the scandal had been a technical defect with a direct impact on driving safety, customers would have felt "betrayed" by *VW* and probably left in droves.

So it played into *VW's* hands that driving an environmentally friendly vehicle was apparently a rather secondary need for many *VW drivers* at the time. The supposed experts who predicted the demise of the company had massively overestimated this customer need. As strange as this may sound, especially from today's perspective: Whether a passenger car had low nitrogen oxide or carbon dioxide emissions hardly played a role as a motive for buying a *VW*. It was therefore not surprising that the emissions scandal had little impact on the quality of customer relationships and that the widely predicted waves of customer churn did not initially occur.

The danger: Even back then, we pointed out in a publication that the declining resale value of the affected vehicles represented a major potential danger for *VW*. After all, the high resale value of a vehicle was and is a particularly important need of *VW customers*. "*VW* will have to take countermeasures here, for example through a modified 'scrappage premium', i.e., incentive schemes for customers to replace the affected vehicles with new ones. This will have a negative impact on sales and especially on profitability but will bind customers to *VW* for years to come," we argued in 2016 (Becker 2016).

In fact, the opposite has happened since then. For years, *VW* refused to compensate customers financially, especially in Germany. In addition, there was (non-) communication which, instead of building long-term stable relationships with customers, focused one-dimensionally on reducing the financial damage. And this

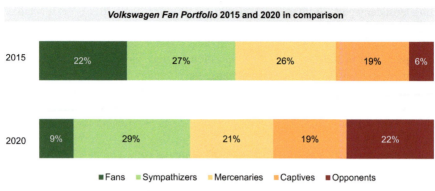

Fig. 3.8 The consequences of ignored customer needs: Since 2015, *VW*'s *Fan Rate* in Germany has been in a nosedive, while the Opponents rate has exploded

even though the *VW Group* was still earning good money despite immense penalties and compensation payments. The foreseeable long-term damage to the company's reputation, which is so important for *VW customers,* was ignored: As we know from various studies with automotive customers, *VW customers* in Germany are often drivers for whom buying a car is not a particularly important purchase decision and who are not particularly familiar with cars. This is mostly due to only occasional use. Particularly in the case of such low relevance purchasing decisions, the reputation of a brand plays an essential role. Brand is nothing more than a stereotype that makes complex considerations superfluous, conveys a high degree of certainty and thus simplifies purchasing decisions.

What this leads to when a company like *VW* neglects its reputation in such a way under these circumstances, and thus the "fit" can no longer be experienced by customers at an essential point, we can see in our *Fanfocus Germany data*: *VW*'s *Fan Rate in* Germany has decreased from 22% in 2015 to 9% in 2020, while the Opponents rate has almost quadrupled from 6% to 22% in the same period. (cf. Fig. 3.8).

Even if this is not yet clearly reflected in the economic success, *VW* will sooner or later have to pay the bill for this betrayal of the central needs of its customers.

This example shows very clearly that the previously successful focus in self-inflicted crises only helps if the causal deficits do not affect the ideals—i.e., the central needs of the fans. As shown, this was the case at the beginning of the emissions scandal. This changed abruptly when the resale value of the affected vehicles dropped and—even more fundamentally—when *VW* permanently damaged its brand image through poor crisis communication and refusal to pay damages, without understanding how important this was and is for the perceived fit of its customers. Instead, a countermeasure, a return to the roots, analogous to the approach of the *ADAC* described above, would have been purposeful.

3.1.5 Examples V: Where *Praktiker* Actually Failed

The previous examples may have given the impression that it is very easy to create a high level of identification through focusing as a result of perceived fit, and that consequently most companies also succeed. This is not the case: With the following examples, we address scenarios that prevent the success of focus strategies.

First, we show what can happen to companies that focus; but misjudge customer needs: They can simply become insolvent—as happened to the *Praktiker* DIY chain (Becker 2014).

Praktiker AG was a listed holding company of several European DIY chains. With around 20,000 employees, the company most recently generated sales of around three billion euros per year and gained fame in Germany through its advertising slogan "20 % off everything (except pet food)". On July 10, 2013, the company declared itself over-indebted and bankrupt. (Deutsche Welle 2013).

Why did *Praktiker* fail? At the height of the insolvency, expert contributions mushroomed, blaming the failure primarily on insufficient profit due to the low-price strategy. But these superficial analyses are fundamentally wrong. Because *Praktiker* was nowhere near as cheap as is commonly believed. In fact, customers at *Praktiker* paid the same prices at the checkout for comparable products as they did at other DIY stores. *Praktiker* was not actually cheaper than others—*Praktiker* just positioned itself that way. And it was precisely this positioning that caused the company to fail.

Praktiker had initially done a lot right with its aggressive "20 percent off everything" message. After all, there were and are many, indeed too many, DIY stores in Germany with an almost interchangeable product range. In this situation, it is vital for suppliers to position themselves clearly: Only with a clear focus, only with a clear message will customers notice you. *Praktiker* had implemented this in a textbook manner: The distinctive sound of the *Bruce Willis dubbed voice* made the aggressive price war image credible: "except pet food" became the unmistakable claim. And when competitor *Obi* set "We will rock you" by the group Queen to music, *Praktiker* countered with "Others let their employees sing, we lower the prices!" The result was a perceived unique position: If you asked who the cheapest supplier in the industry was, *Praktiker* was named before all others.

But if the focus strategy was right, why did it still not work? The answer may surprise some: *Praktiker* had ignored the core customer needs of the industry with this positioning (cf. Fig. 3.9). After all, the core need of the typical German DIY customer is not the price advantage. It is the emotional experience promised by the products. The feeling of happiness at creating something themselves. The sense of achievement of mastering a project on one's own, from planning to completion. In other words, self-realization. That is what the "do-it-yourself products" promise. Those who sweat to build their garden house experience something that today's alienated working world often no longer offers them: Self-efficacy and pride of creation. It follows from this: Many DIY products are so-called *high-involvement products*. The customer is interested in an emotionally significant experience, and it therefore becomes important which materials, and, above all, which tools he works

Source: Dirk Bauer / WAZ

Fig. 3.9 "20% off on everything": *Praktiker* has not understood central needs. (Courtesy of © Dirk Bauer/WAZ 2022. All Rights Reserved)

with. What is required is a high-quality range of products, matching, highly competent advice, and a sales atmosphere that already makes the approaching experience of self-realization tangible. *Praktiker did not* offer, promise, or understand all this, but the competition did—at least in terms of communication. There, the focus was on consulting, quality, and emotional experience: "What counts is the project," was the claim of the competition. *Praktiker, on the other hand, focused* almost exclusively on price in its positioning—and failed to recognize that only a minority of customers were addressed by this: The price-sensitive customer segments, i.e., the potential for price positioning, are simply too small in the DIY sector in Germany.

Now you may object that positioning via the lowest price is part of everyday life in many industries, where it opens large customer segments. Why did the concept of low-price positioning not work at *Praktiker,* while it works excellently in the food industry, for example at *ALDI*? The succinct and perhaps perplexing answer is that customers, especially many Germans, attach more importance to quality in tools than in food. In fact, the food sector is not a *high-involvement industry*. Only a few consumers in Germany buy food with quality in mind. Most customers here are primarily bargain hunters, and the price-sensitive customer segment is large. We will come back to this in detail later (cf. Sect. 3.4).

3.1.6 Examples VI: *Deutsche Bank*—How "Passionate Performance" Becomes Performance that Creates Suffering

Just as fatal as *Praktiker*'s focus on an aspect that has no relevance for customers is when a company focuses on the relevant needs of customers, but then fails to deliver on this focus in terms of performance, instead weakening precisely in this central area. For the emergence of a perceived fit, it is crucial that fans also perceive corresponding strengths in their star or provider in the aspects relevant to them. For example, a soccer club that is constantly playing against relegation in the first

3.1 Focus Generates Identification

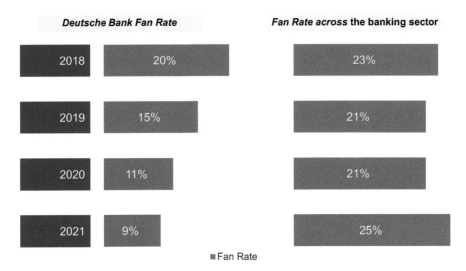

Fig. 3.10 *Fan Rate* of *Deutsche Bank* compared over time

division will hardly have fans who are particularly success oriented. These are more likely to be found at Real Madrid or Bayern Munich (cf. Sect. 1.2).

A striking example of a focus without perceptible performance fulfillment is *Deutsche Bank*, the largest German credit institution in terms of total assets and number of employees.

Since 2003, *Deutsche Bank* has positioned itself with the claim "Performance with Passion. This addressed a central need very well that basically reached the performance-oriented clientele striving for dominance. In order for this focus to be experienced by the addressed customers, highly motivated employees filled with pride and a distinct performance culture are required. The dubious business practices, the many scandals throughout the ensuing years (Scherbaum 2020), the constant changes in management board positions and the strategic lurching course—all this led to great uncertainty and increasing distancing among employees. In surveys, one increasingly overheard employees and customers who perceived a bank whose "performance caused pain"; distinctly the opposite of the intended message.

As a result, *Deutsche Bank* ruefully abandoned its focus on "Performance through Passion" in 2017 (Osman 2017). The new focus on "#PositiveContribution" was intended to reinvigorate the badly battered pride and motivation of employees in order to gradually win back the unchanged performance-oriented clientele. As our current figures show, *Deutsche* Bank is not more successful even with this new orientation; on the contrary, *Deutsche Bank*'s fan *rate* has been falling steadily for several years and is moving further and further away from the industry average for banks in Germany (cf. Fig. 3.10). It is reasonable to assume that past events and the many scandals continue to resonate with employees and that the corporate culture is not perceived as authentic in relation to "#PositiverBeitrag".

3.1.7 Don't Be that "Egg-Laying Jack-of-All-Trades"

Finally, we would like to discuss the effects of a lack of focus: resources are not bundled and concentrated on the decisive strengths but are distributed with a watering can—in other words, investments are made in many or even all potential customer needs in equal measure. Behind this is the conviction that one wants or needs to shine in all areas at the same time—out of concern that one or two customer needs could remain unsatisfied and customers with these needs could be lost. At first glance, this approach may seem quite sensible, and it continues to be pursued by most companies—after all, it corresponds to the "more is more" mantra of satisfaction management that we have already described in detail (see Sect. 1.3). In fact, however, this strategy is inefficient and does not achieve its goals.

Let us illustrate this with an example from sports: Take the French decathlete *Kevin Mayer, who in* 2018 raised the world record in this so-called supreme discipline of athletics to a fabulous 9126 points (Spiegel 2018). No one will deny that *Mayer* is an exceptional athlete. But of course—as with any other decathlete—his individual performances in the ten disciplines of the all-around are significantly weaker than those of the specialists in the respective individual disciplines (cf. Fig. 3.11). Even the best decathlete will never run the time of *Usain Bolt* or reach the distance of *Mike Powell* in the long jump. On the contrary: even in his strongest discipline, the pole vault, *Mayer* would not even have reached the final competition of the best twelve specialists at the last Olympic Games in Tokyo—he is "only" mediocre in the individual disciplines. So, a track and field athlete has two choices: Either he decides on a particular discipline that corresponds to his strengths and specializes there—or he tries, as a multi-discipline athlete, to perform passably in all areas at the same time, but by no means at the top. As an all-rounder, however, he then always pays the price that the fame of the best, the world record in the individual discipline, will always go only to the specialists. It is not possible to excel in all areas at the same time—and anyone who attempts to do so is attempting the impossible.

Nevertheless, one could now argue: Companies that try to achieve outstanding performance perceptions in all areas are doing nothing other than emulating a decathlete—and this is, after all, the supreme discipline of athletics, i.e., associated with special fame. Those who make this comparison must realize what is truly special about the athletic all-arounder. What is a decathlete awarded for? The answer is simple: not for his top performances, but for his versatility. Competitive sports have turned mediocrity into a discipline, so to speak. But here's the difference between our sports metaphor and the business world: among customers, there is no prize for versatility—only for focus. Because every customer has an individual need that is particularly central to him and whose fulfillment is more important to him than the fulfillment of all other needs. And it is only this core need that

3.1 Focus Generates Identification

Discipline	World record decathlon 	World records individual discipline
100 m	10.55 sec.	9.58 sec.
Long jump	7,80 m	8,95 m
Shot put	16,00 m	23,37 m
High jump	2,05 m	2,45 m
400 m	48.42 sec.	43.03 sec.
110 m hurdles	13.75 sec.	12.80 sec.
Discus throw	50,54 m	74,08 m
Pole Vault	5,45 m	6,18 m
Javelin throw	71,90 m	98,48 m
1500 m	4:36.11 min.	3:26.00 min.

Source: Own representation
Source Mayer: Erik van Leeuwen / Wikimedia Commons

Fig. 3.11 Whoever occupies all topics sinks into mediocrity (Own illustration/Image Mayer: Courtesy of © Erik van Leeuwen/Wikimedia Commons 2022. All Rights Reserved)

determines the customer's emotional tie. You will not find a customer who becomes your fan precisely because he perceives you as good average in all areas. Companies may be able to stay afloat with this kind of positioning—but it will not increase emotional customer loyalty. Successful customer relationship management is not a decathlon. And where the athlete has two options, there is no alternative for companies.

If you want to be the star everywhere at the same time, you won't win any fans. Because anyone who tries to excel in all areas of performance perception does not sharpen their profile, but rather dilutes it. Ultimately, such a company then tries to be nothing other than a legendary mythical creature from German proverbs: the "eierlegende Wollmilchsau". This "egg-laying wool-producing lactating sow"/ "Jack of all trades" does not and will never exist, in nature just as little as in the corporate landscape. Nevertheless, there are numerous companies that orient themselves to this model—that is, that try to be perceived as this mythical creature: Companies that indifferently invest their resources in all areas according to the "more is more" principle, in the hope that this will serve every potential customer need and create lasting customer loyalty. But these expensive investments do not create uniqueness; on the contrary, they ensure that you are lost in the mass of companies pursuing the same indifferent strategy. In the end, you are one of many in an unmanageable herd of "egg-laying woo-giving lactating pigs".

3.1.8 Conclusion: Focus as the Basis for Emotional Customer Loyalty and for Efficient Use of Resources

The examples thus impressively demonstrate how important it is for companies to harmonize core customer needs and their own strengths through consistent focus: Otherwise, sustainable customer identification as the basis for emotional customer loyalty cannot develop. Failure to recognize core customer needs damages the quality of customer relationships and thus produces considerable economic damage—as does the failure to provide relevant services or the attempt to provide top performance in many areas in order to serve as many different customer needs as possible.

This latter aspect of the still widespread "more is more" strategy opens the door to another positive economic aspect of focus. This is because a well-founded alignment of service provision and communication helps to do the right things and to do things right; in other words, it has an equally efficient and effective effect. If core customer needs are understood as a fixed point to which everything should be aligned, and thus as a guard rail that provides orientation for investment decisions, this also makes it easier for companies to decide not to do something. According to our many years of consulting experience, this is one of the main benefits of implementing *FANOMICS*. A company decision maker once expressed this as follows during a feedback meeting: "Not that we didn't do things we had to do before. It's that we've relearned to leave things alone. " Of course, this "leaving things alone" has an immediate economic success. But it also has other benefits: Omitting the wrong actions also avoids mistakes. Because as we will recognize with the further representation of *FANOMICS*, introduced measures, if they stand in the goal conflict to the core customer need, can damage the emotional customer loyalty even (see. Sect. 3.4).

3.2 Orchestration Creates Perceived Uniqueness

In Sect. 1.2, we explained in detail that fan relationships are based on experienced repetition—that is, that fans want to experience again and again what once made them a fan. This leads to a feeling of uniqueness, i.e., to precisely that perception of differentiation that can often no longer be generated by performance alone. How can this mechanism of fan relationships best be transferred to corporate relationship management? How can companies make the core needs of their customers come alive again and again so that their customers become fans? Obviously, it is not enough for a company—as explained in Sect. 3.1 to focus its positioning on core customer needs. Because then the strategic goal has been formulated, but not yet how it is to be achieved. To ensure that customers repeatedly experience what turns

3.2 Orchestration Creates Perceived Uniqueness

them into fans, it is imperative that there is intensive understanding and mutual coordination between all relevant responsible persons and corporate units. The image of Orchestration has proven to be particularly intuitive and comprehensible for this purpose. This image is also suitable for differentiating between Focusing and Orchestration. In addition, it makes the fundamental conceptual difference between *FANOMICS on the* one hand and the "more is more" mantra of satisfaction management on the other hand visible in a very vivid way.

Imagine a renowned orchestra for this purpose. We all take it for granted that the musicians of an orchestra coordinate with each other before a performance. But for the sake of illustration, let's run through the absurd case that such an alignment does not take place before the start of a performance. If we think this scenario through to its logical conclusion, we must distinguish between two cases in this thought experiment:

1. **There has been no understanding of *what is* being presented at all**
   The first case seems completely absurd to all of us. Imagine each of the musicians playing his or her favorite piece at the same time, and untuned. Depending on temperament and preference, light works such as Vivaldi's "Allegro" from the "Spring of the Four Seasons" or sustained pieces such as Grieg's "Morning Mood" from the "Peer Gynt Suite" or dramatic works such as Orff's "Carmina Burana" or Stravinsky's "Le Sacre du Printemps" would be sung simultaneously. Performed in this form, the overall impression would become an unbearable cacophony for the listener, despite the excellent performances of each individual musician, in which he would not be able to identify any of the pieces presented at all. The situation would be similar, but probably even worse for the music-lover, since it would be acoustically unbearable to the highest degree, if the musicians had agreed beforehand on the work to be performed, but not on key. Even the most passionate classical music fan would find it difficult to hear the agreed upon music piece at all under such dissonant conditions. You've surely already recognized what's happening here: Although each individual gave a professional performance, the orchestra as a whole did not align itself with the central need of the audience, but with its own preferences. The discord here would therefore be a product of *a lack of focus*. We have already explained the consequences in detail using the fabulous creature of the egg-laying Jack-of-All-Trades.
2. **There has been no understanding of *how* a piece will be presented**
   Similar, but far from identical, is the second case: Everyone plays the same piece in the same key, i.e., the orchestra has definitely focused. But each plays his or her part at any volume, at his own tempo, does not listen to the other and does not follow the conductor's instructions. Thus, by deciding together with his fellow musicians on a particular piece, everyone has aligned themselves with a fundamental need of the audience as a common goal, i.e., focused, but everyone nevertheless simply does in an uncoordinated way what they consider to be meaningful for reaching the goal. The resulting action may well be worth hearing in isolation—perhaps the flute plays its own passage beautifully to heartbreak—but because the strings are playing themselves into the foreground at that

moment, the audience will never be able to make that determination. The discord here would therefore be a product of a lack of coordination, i.e. a *lack of Orchestration.*

In fact, in many companies, things are similar to the scenario described with second orchestra, if you compare the individual musicians with the employees—or alternatively with the individual contact points at which customers can experience this company: While the common goal in terms of focus is clear, there has been no coordination on how to implement this goal. Instead, in each department, at each customer contact, everyone simply does what they believe will best meet the customer's central need on which they have previously focused. Let's assume that at *BMW, for example,* the salesperson focuses on the effect of his competence, the service employee believes in the importance of accessibility, and the communication conveys the joy of driving instead of acting in a coordinated manner. In this context, we also speak of a pronounced silo thinking (Luchsinger 2021). For the customer, the overall work is incoherent and hardly recognizable (i.e., he does not know what the company stands for), and at best, the brass section will prevail—i.e., those who play the loudest. Translated into corporate contexts, this would mean, for example, that the employee with the most frequent customer contact will prevail in the customer's perception.

The orchestra example illustrates on the one hand that focus is the mandatory prerequisite for increasing emotional commitment, but that focus does not lead to the goal if the resulting measures are not orchestrated. In other words, it is not enough for all activities to be focused on the goal of fulfilling the core customer needs. To create a coherent overall arrangement and thus ensure repetition, these activities must also be perfectly coordinated with each other—both "across instruments" and in relation to each individual "instrument".

On the other hand, the example very aptly illustrates the operating mechanism of the "more is more" mantra of satisfaction management, which we have already criticized several times: Because there, too, everyone is doing their best at the same time with their respective "instruments" (i.e., in their function, e.g., as a salesperson, service employee, communications manager). But they do it in an uncoordinated manner and with full commitment: everyone plays their own tune at full volume—in other words, they do what they believe is best for the customer with a lot of effort, instead of acting in a coordinated manner and refraining from certain activities that are either superfluous or even counterproductive since they do not contribute to fulfilling needs or are even harmful in this respect.

FANOMICS, on the other hand, is about real Orchestration, i.e., not only do they all play the same piece in the same key, but they also tune it down to the smallest detail—sometimes the winds are in the foreground, sometimes the strings, and so on. Only the interwoven arrangement of the different instrumental genres and volumes creates the total work of art. And if, figuratively speaking, the timpanist in Joseph Haydn's symphony "with the timpani beat" forgets this very timpani beat, then the work is not complete for the practiced listener.

This image of Orchestration helps us to transfer the mechanics of perceived uniqueness from fan research to the corporate world and to use it to develop an action manual for companies. But what is this call to action? What does "Orchestration" mean for companies? How can this image be translated to everyday business and the shaping of customer relationships?

To illustrate this, we would like to use another image that is now widely used in customer management, namely that of the customer journey. It describes how customers, like travelers, reach various stations during their customer relationship, the so-called contact points or touchpoints. This customer journey begins with the initiation of business and the sales/distribution process. It equally includes service delivery (typical "stations" are e.g., the product, delivery, service or complaint management)—and communication channels (e.g., website, print advertising, newsletter) (cf. Kuehnl et al. 2019; Følstad and Kvale 2018). Successful Orchestration requires a sound understanding of the customer journey with its different touchpoints. Even if there is a great deal of commonality across companies and industries regarding the customer journey, it is worth taking a look at company-specific characteristics. Orchestration in customer relationship management then means that the core customer needs are brought to life across the customer journey at all touchpoints. In the following, we will completely run through the entire process of focusing and Orchestration along the complete customer journey using a company you are familiar with as an example. Before we do that, however, we would like to briefly catch up on something that has been neglected so far: namely, we would like to present you with a definition of *FANOMICS*.

3.3 Definition of *FANOMICS*

In Sects. 3.1 and 3.2 we have transferred the essential characteristics of fan relationships—identification and perceived uniqueness—to the customer relationship management of companies and, in doing so, have worked out, with focus and orchestration, the two relevant levers of how companies can turn customers into fans. Finally, with reference to the customer journey model, we have explained what Orchestration means for companies in concrete terms. With this, we have gathered all the essential building blocks for a definition of *FANOMICS:*

▶ *FANOMICS* means that by focusing and Orchestration, companies make central needs in the perception of customers at all contact points of the customer journey experienceable again and again in terms of performance and communication. This creates a monopoly in the minds of customers, turning them into fans.

This definition not only includes the essential levers "Focusing" and "Orchestration". It equally clarifies with reference to the customer journey model that *FANOMICS is a management program* and *not* exclusively a marketing, communication, customer management and sales management program. *FANOMICS* therefore concerns the entire company, including service delivery and everything related to it.

In the following, we would like to explain how *FANOMICS* is successfully used by means of a concrete best-practice example. We have chosen the discount grocer *ALDI Süd for* four reasons:

1. *ALDI* has a high profile and market penetration, and no longer just in Germany, but virtually throughout Europe and even in the USA. Virtually every reader is either a customer or has had concrete experience with the company at some point. This clarifies the implementation steps: Even if the mechanisms described relate specifically to the German grocery market and the key needs of German grocery customers, ALDI is also positioning itself in many other target markets in the same or similar way.
2. *ALDI does not* stand for an exciting product. Thus, we illustrate that, contrary to widespread prejudices, product characteristics are *not a* relevant success factor for the successful use of *FANOMICS*.
3. Within the food industry, *ALDI is* not commonly associated with high customer focus. Therefore, we use this example to disprove common customer relationship management beliefs.
4. To counteract the impression of self-promotion: There is not and has *never been* a business relationship between the book authors and *ALDI*. Our review of the two company founders, the Albrecht brothers (cf. Sect. 3.4), will show that *ALDI had* already intuitively observed and implemented the underlying rules long before we discovered the *Fan Principle* and developed *FANOMICS* from it.

3.4 Examples VII: *ALDI*—The Simple Principle

While the average fan rate in the German grocery trade is 16%, *ALDI* has 26% fans (cf. Fig. 3.12), making it the industry leader. (*Fanfocus Germany* 2021).

Why is this result surprising for many? Because they intuitively equate "high customer orientation" with "particularly friendly". *ALDI is* an excellent example of the fact that this blanket understanding of customer orientation is incorrect—as well as of the added value of *FANOMICS* as a customer value-based management tool. Because *ALDI* manages its customer relationships according to the idea of *FANOMICS*, and the understanding of "customer orientation" is a central success factor here. In the following, we will look at exactly what this understanding looks like and what it is characterized by, considering other success factors of the implementation. In doing so, our explanations refer throughout to the German food trade and its customers to derive the basic mechanics of FANOMICS.

3.4 Examples VII: *ALDI*—The Simple Principle 161

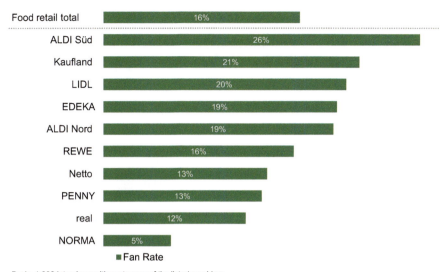

Fig. 3.12 *Fan Rates* in food retailing

3.4.1 Identify Core Customer Needs

The first success factor of *FANOMICS* is the identification of core customer needs. And indeed: *ALDI* serves the central need of many food customers in Germany. Measured as a share of all consumer spending, people in hardly any other Western country spend less money on food than in Germany (Statistisches Bundesamt 2020). Anyone who has visited a wholesale food market in another European country, be it France, Spain, Italy or Switzerland, and compared its prices with those of German food retail chains, will have a vivid impression of how the importance of food and beverages is reflected in the variety of goods, product presentation and shopping experience. Quality also has a different status there, and people are happy to pay a reasonable price for it. In Germany, on the other hand, people only talk about the quality of food when a scandal has once again brought the issue temporarily to the attention of the public. Otherwise, Germans do not often want a shopping experience when they go grocery shopping, they do not want friendly small talk at the checkout, and they do not need anyone to pack their groceries in bags, as the American retail giant Walmart tried in vain (Grabitz and Seidl 2006). For most Germans, buying groceries is apparently a classic *low-involvement issue*, i.e., it's primarily about "cheap and fast." After all, we want to spend as little effort as possible on unimportant issues. *ALDI*'s positioning meets this need exactly—and thus hits the bull's eye.

Price positioning of this kind is not a guarantee of success per se. We have already been able to show this on the basis of the bankruptcy of the *Praktiker* DIY chain, which was analyzed in detail (cf. Sect. 3.1.5): No other DIY store was perceived as being so low-priced. But this strategy ultimately proved to be *Praktiker's* undoing.

Perception	Relevance for emotional attachment
is very fast	high
is very favorable	high
stands for relief	high
offers high quality products	medium
is very varied	medium
is very service oriented	medium
is very successful	low
is very competent	low
is very fair	low
is very sustainable	low

Source: *2HMforum.* research

Fig. 3.13 Excerpt from *ALDI's Fan Traffic Signal*: "fast" and "inexpensive" are the most important loyalty-drivers

After all, do-it-yourselfers are looking for the premium product—price plays a secondary role for them. The situation is completely different in food retailing: Many Germans want cheap food—and they get it at *ALDI*. As the following explanations will make clear, *ALDI* not only "serves" the need for "cheap" in an expert manner—but also the need for "fast".

These remarks on *ALDI* and *Praktiker* illustrate how necessary secure and reliable information regarding core customer needs is for building successful customer relationships. After all, nothing is as fatal and serious as a misjudgment of core customer needs: All subsequent activities, namely the Orchestration of service aspects and communication, then literally come to nothing. This not only costs companies a great deal of money but will inevitably put a strain on the relationship with their customers—churn is the inevitable consequence. As in the case of *Praktiker, the* very existence of the company can be at stake.

So to enable reliable decisions about customer needs, we have developed a special analysis tool with the logic of a traffic signal (red, yellow, green): *The Fan Traffic Signal*. A simplified model representation for *ALDI* (cf. Fig. 3.13) illustrates—based on a customer survey—which needs are particularly important for the development of the emotional bond of *ALDI* customers and which are less important. We therefore call these core needs "loyalty-drivers" in the following. The two most important loyalty-drivers among *ALDI* customers are "is very fast" and "is very cheap". The example shows how necessary valid survey results are in order to create a reliable basis for the further implementation process of *FANOMICS*.

At this point, we would like to motivate you to reflect briefly: What is it like at your company? What is the core customer need at your company, analogous to the "is very fast" at *ALDI*? What is your assessment based on? And how do other decision-makers in your company see this? In the same way as you? Because only then can orchestrated mediation work.

3.4.2 Identify Key Touchpoints

Now that we know the central needs of *ALDI Süd customers*, the next step is to identify the stations of the customer journey, i.e., the touchpoints. This sounds simple at first, but if done thoroughly, it is a major challenge: The representative of a German premium car manufacturer, for example, began his presentation at our Fan Principle conference a few years ago with a chart showing about 220 squares, nothing else. What did this initial chart have to do with customer relationship management and *FANOMICS*? The solution: The squares were the approx. 220 touchpoints that this automobile manufacturer had identified along the customer journey of its customers, from the first potential touchpoint through the pre-sales and sales process to after-sales and all accompanying communication measures. And a mouse click on the squares revealed a detailed description of the respective touchpoint, as well as a precise explanation of how the contact at this touchpoint should be designed in order to fulfill the core customer needs.

Many companies feel overwhelmed by this perfect but strongly theory-driven approach, especially in the introductory phase of *FANOMICS*. It also does not correspond to a pareto-optimized implementation that takes into account the varying importance of the touchpoints. After all, the different touchpoints are not equally important for the emergence of emotional customer loyalty. But how can we find out which ones are particularly important so that we can focus our resources on these touchpoints first? We have developed our own analysis tool for this purpose as well, the *Touchpoint Traffic Signal*. The basis for creating the *Touchpoint Traffic Signal* is also a comprehensive customer survey (see Sect. 4.2).

In our *ALDI* example, the *Touchpoint Traffic Signal* shows in a highly simplified form (i.e., reduced to a few touchpoints) which contact points in the customer journey are particularly important for the overall perception of the central loyalty-driver "*ALDI* is very fast" (cf. Fig. 3.14). In doing so, we build on the findings from *ALDI's Fan Traffic Signal*.

In the column headed "Relevance to core need is very fast", we can see that the touchpoint "Checkout" is the most important. The *touchpoints* with the second or third most important effect on the central loyalty-driver can also be taken from the Touchpoint traffic signal; in our example, these are prices and store layout.

At this point, we would like to invite you to reflect briefly, as we did after presenting the *Fan Traffic Signal* (see Sect. 3.4.1): What is it like at your company? What are the most important touchpoints for you, analogous to the checkout at *ALDI Süd*? What is your assessment based on? And how do other decision-makers in your company view this?

Finally, the question arises as to whether the information on the relevance of the touchpoints alone is sufficient to optimally control the measures for increasing the

Touchpoint	Relevance to central need "is very fast"	Customer review
Checkout	high	good
Prices	high	medium
Branch (structure)	high	good
Assortment diversity	medium	medium
Service	low	bad

Source: 2HMforum. research

Fig. 3.14 Extract of the *Touchpoint Traffic Signal* of *ALDI:* At the highly relevant contact point "checkout", fit arises because *ALDI* is rated well

Fan Rate. In fact, it is advisable to also take the performance at the respective touchpoint into account for this decision—from the customer's point of view. In our *ALDI* example, these ratings are shown in the column headed "Customer Evaluation". We see that the checkout is rated as good, the prices are rated as mediocre, and the store (assortment) is rated as good again. In this specific case, it would be worth checking whether untapped potential can be leveraged more easily and more cost-effectively where the high relevance is accompanied by a poorer customer rating, i.e., in our *ALDI* example at the "Prices" touchpoint.

3.4.3 Focusing and Orchestrating on Core Customer Needs

Once the core customer needs and touchpoints have been identified, the essential step in the implementation of *FANOMICS follows*: It is important to focus on the core customer needs as part of the positioning, then to orchestrate these along the customer journey and specifically, to make them tangible at the highly relevant touchpoints.

This brings us to the actual recipe for success because *ALDI* succeeds—as described in the definition of *FANOMICS*—in optimally serving the customers' central need for "cheap and fast"—i.e., for an economically efficient shopping process—at all relevant contact points: Many *ALDI* customers want "cheap and fast"—and that's exactly what they get. That, and nothing else. *ALDI* therefore deliberately says "no" to all aspects of performance that do not serve customers' core needs. In doing so, *ALDI* also consciously accepts selective dissatisfaction.

As we have shown with the *Touchpoint Traffic Signal*, the checkout is a particularly relevant point of contact, a so-called "moment of truth," when it comes to the orchestrated satisfaction of the customer's core need for speed. Here, an interaction of targeted employee behavior and process optimization ensures a coherent customer experience.

3.4 Examples VII: ALDI—The Simple Principle

Let's look at employee behavior first: You may have already noticed it if you've observed an *ALDI* checkout—the cashier's demeanor is engaging, but by no means effusively friendly. You may have even been annoyed by the fact that, unlike many retail competitors, *ALDI* cashiers, for example, frequently dispense with extensive greetings—even eye contact is discouraged in many cases (Feurer 2021).

In view of the core customer needs, why is it even necessary for this employee to behave "only" obligingly at the checkout, and why does *ALDI* obviously accept a certain annoyance on your part for this? Asked the other way around: What would happen if the cashier behaved in a particularly friendly manner? Surely some customers would feel encouraged by this and see it as an invitation for small talk—with disastrous consequences for the customers in the queue behind him, who "only" want to get out again quickly. So, *ALDI* accepts the dissatisfaction of this customer with the need to talk (and deliberately says "no" to the topic of "particularly friendly cashiers"), knowing that this is the only way to protect the interests of the other customers. We derive five key insights from this example:

1. First of all, this example shows very strikingly that, against the background of the focus on core customer needs, the often-generalized understanding of "customer orientation" must be differentiated. Customer orientation is not automatically a friendliness and charm offensive. Customer orientation means being attuned to customer needs. And wherever customers are concerned with speed (and this is much more often the case than is generally thought), "less friendliness" actually means "more customer orientation".
2. The conscious "no" to more friendliness at the checkout also means the conscious "no" to customers for whom friendliness is particularly important when buying food. *ALDI* thus deliberately takes the risk of losing these customers (or not winning them in the first place). This is the (obviously) acceptable price for offering an attractive customer potential what they expect.
3. Initiating measures in customer management without reflection (e.g., according to the aforementioned "more is more" mantra of satisfaction management) may not only be of no use but may even damage the customer relationship. Imagine that *ALDI* did not know about the central relevance of "fast" for its customers or did not understand the trade-off between "friendly" and "fast". In this case, the employees in the stores would possibly be trained at great expense to act in a particularly friendly manner. This would then not only be wasted money but would harm the relationship quality.
4. If employees are to fulfill their function as brand ambassadors, this means that, if necessary, specific attention must be paid to an appropriate "fit" already during their selection. It is also essential to formulate the rules of conduct very clearly and transparently, to train them and to regularly check that they are being observed.
5. This example highlights the diametric difference between satisfaction management and *FANOMICS*. In the doctrine of satisfaction management, the inevitably poor ratings of the friendliness of the checkout would not be acceptable. One would powerfully work against it. In this context, think of the metaphor of

Orchestration: in satisfaction management, everyone plays their tune at full volume, without regard to the impact on the customer's experience and expectations.

Another striking aspect regarding the experience of "fast" is that no grocer reacts as flexibly and quickly as *ALDI* to rising and falling crowds at the checkouts by opening and closing them. The prerequisites are not only clearly formulated process specifications but also flexible staff deployment—as well as employees who also implement these specifications sensitively and attentively because they have understood what is at stake if they keep customers waiting too long at the checkouts.

Let's now look at some selected processes at the checkout that also contribute to the perception of "*ALDI* is very fast":

- The cashier also plays an important role in the processes. *ALDI* employees report that they have to scan 3400 to 3500 items per hour at the checkout—this corresponds to around 55 items per minute or almost one item per second (Heidenfelder 2018). The high level of commitment to this target can be seen from the fact that it is possible to track in the computer how many items were actually scanned. In addition, a 15-second rule is reported: According to this rule, it must take no longer than 15 seconds to complete a purchase at the checkout, including scanning the items and collecting the change. This rule also has an effect: a study concluded that a checkout process at *ALDI Süd* takes between 20 and 25 seconds on average and is thus completed around 17 seconds faster than at the best competitor (Schlautermann 2009).
- Likewise, the checkout setup helps speed up the payment process. Admittedly—if you're used to the convenience of the merchandise catch basin at the checkout at other grocers, you'll quickly be overwhelmed at *ALDI*. While there the purchased goods collect in an opulent catch basin and wait there until you have collected and stowed them after paying, at *ALDI* you have to hurry. Because if you don't keep up with the pace the cashier sets when scanning there, your products will end up—in the worst case—on the floor. A circumstance which can certainly lead to stress and annoyance, but which many *ALDI* customers in turn accept—knowing full well that this affects the customers in the queue in front of them just as much and therefore shortens their own waiting time as desired (Feurer 2021). This connection between the goods collection area and the speed of the checkout process was already known to the company's founders and was consistently considered by them from the outset (Ley 2018).
- Finally: Loyalty promotions, lottery tickets and the like—as popular as they may be with one or the other customer—are rather a rarity at *ALDI*, because these take up additional time to ask for, count, book or hand out loyalty points, for example.
- If current tests prove successful, there will be no more checkouts at *ALDI in the foreseeable future*; they will be replaced by the "smart" shopping cart: This automatically records the prices of the goods in the shopping cart and adds them to the receipt, which can be seen on a display. At the exit, the receipt is printed out from the shopping cart, which is scanned at a terminal and paid for by

card. (Schuldt 2021). This would save an enormous amount of time during the payment process.

We have used the example of *ALDI* and the "checkout" touchpoint to explain to you how targeted and effective the customer experience can be developed if you know which direction to think in. With that, let's leave the "checkout" touchpoint and turn to the second most important touchpoint, namely prices.
One or the other may ask how the touchpoint "prices" can be optimized in the direction of "fast". This is because many intuitively associate the touchpoint "prices" with the absolute amount and reduce it to this. However, there are many other levers that can be used to optimize the price perception of customers in the direction of "fast". You can find a few selected ones implemented at *ALDI*, whereby the cashier or the checkout also plays a certain role here:

- Before the introduction of scanner technology, *ALDI* cashiers had to memorize all item prices and type each one in by hand. This also suggests that the pioneers at ALDI were aware of the extreme importance of speed in the shopping process for their customers long before the discovery of the *Fan Principle* and the development of *FANOMICS* (Ley 2018). In addition, the number of different prices at *ALDI* was limited to make it easier for employees to memorize them.
- By using an elaborate reading system, the barcodes on the purchased products can be read without the employee having to hold the numerical code directly up to the scanner. With the help of mirrors and scanners, the barcodes, which are kept as large as possible at *ALDI, can be* recognized from any position—even if the product is already heavily wrinkled.
- *ALDI* also makes no compromises when it comes to the payment methods it offers. When cashless payment had long been part of the service offering at many competitors, the motto "cash is king" still applied at *ALDI Süd for a* long time. Behind this was the realization that plastic money usually prolongs the payment process. It is only since *ALDI has had* a uniquely fast transaction process that EC cash and, for some years now, that credit cards have been allowed.

Now, after the checkout and prices, let's take a cursory look at the next relevant touchpoints and answer the question of how the core customer need for "fast" is implemented there:

- The layout of the stores has a high recognition factor: While customers usually must find their way around again completely when visiting different stores operated by the competition in Germany, *ALDI*'s stores are always structured according to the same principle. The customer immediately feels at home and wastes little time searching for the desired items.
- If you are used to the variety on the shelves of full-range retailers, the depth of the assortment is very low. The selection is often reduced to two to three different brands per product category. However, if one assumes that buying groceries is not a major priority for *ALDI* customers, they experience this limited selection option

as highly relieving, because *ALDI* has, as it were, made a sensible pre-selection for them, thus making their own decision easier and faster. We know this pattern from many industries: If it's all about speed for the customer, it's not the depth of the assortment that leads to high satisfaction. Often, under these conditions, suppliers with a limited, needs-based and transparent range are rated better. This has a positive side effect for the provider: A reduced range also has a relieving effect on service and sales staff. They need to know fewer products and are better informed about the products on offer.

Finally, it should be noted that the focus on the core customer needs "fast" at *ALDI is* also reflected in the corporate strategy, namely in the definition of the relevant target groups. There, the guideline supposedly applies that the range of *ALDI* stores does not address older target groups over the age of 75, on the grounds that older people no longer have the required process speed. In fact, this target group is rarely seen in *ALDI stores* (Schlautermann 2008).

We have used the example of *ALDI to illustrate* how the process of focusing and orchestration takes place in detail within the framework of *FANOMICS, focusing* on the performance processes. So, the question is how the orchestration of the communication processes takes place. The approach is analogous. Here, too, based on the findings of the *Fan Traffic Signal,* a *Touchpoint Traffic Signal* is used to analyze how strongly which communication and advertising medium (for example, website, print advertising, trade shows, radio advertising, and advertising brochures) serves the core customer needs (cf. Sect. 4.3). In this way, the highly relevant touchpoints can also be orchestrated accordingly on the communication side. *ALDI* pursues this consistently. Without presenting this in the same depth of detail, we would like to address one aspect of communication at *ALDI*, namely the claim. *ALDI* has been committed to the *"Simple Principle"* since 2015. We would like to explain what this means exactly with a quote from an *ALDI* press release:

> "Every day, we make countless decisions. Orientation is needed—even when shopping. And that's exactly what ALDI offers .... Here you can "simply shop"—straightforward and uncomplicated for more quality of life. To illustrate this core message, the ALDI Group ... will be running outdoor advertising for the first time in large parts of southern and western Germany from September 22, 2015. A total of four different motifs underline the "simple principle" with which the discounter remains true to its proven line: focusing on the essentials.
>
> <u>Decisions made easy</u>
> What does "easy shopping" at ALDI ... mean? On the one hand, a careful pre-selection. Decisions should not be complicated by an overabundance of choices—unnecessary headaches are eliminated. ALDI ... also always has the best products and offers. This principle is also reflected in the stores. A friendly and helpful service is a matter of course at ALDI ... as a matter of course. This also includes that goods are simply presented clearly. This way, shopping is simply done quickly and customers still have everything they need. That leaves more time for family and hobbies, and more money for nice things. Life is already

3.4 Examples VII: *ALDI*—The Simple Principle

Perception	Relevance for emotional attachment	Customer review	Compared to the competition, Aldi is ...
is very fast	high	good	better
is very favorable	high	good	better
stands for relief	high	good	better
offers high quality products	medium	good	same
is very varied	medium	medium	bad
is very service oriented	medium	medium	same
is very successful	low	good	better
is very competent	low	medium	same
is very fair	low	bad	same
is very sustainable	low	medium	same

Source: *2HMforum.* research

Fig. 3.15 Fan Traffic Signal from *ALDI illustrates the emergence of identification*: central loyalty-drivers are rated well and differentiate from the competition

complicated enough, so we want to make it as easy as possible for our customers, at least when it comes to shopping," says Sandra-Sibylle Schoofs, Head of Marketing at ALDI ... "Quality at the best price remains our top priority. So, customers don't have to think long when making their choice, we've already done the work in advance. That saves time and money." (Aldi 2015)

The campaign was implemented through four different ad motifs and commercials and continuously updated. The chosen motifs all focus on the core need of *ALDI customers*; namely, to complete the tiresome grocery shopping with as little expenditure of resources as possible and to use the resources thus saved for more important topics such as hobbies and family.

The final question is whether this consistent Orchestration of *ALDI* according to the concept idea of *FANOMICS has a* positive effect on customer feedback, and equally on perceived fit and perceived uniqueness. To verify this, we look at the full *Fan Traffic Signal*, which, in addition to the relevance of loyalty-drivers for emotional engagement, now also includes information on "customer rating" and "competitor comparison" (Fig. 3.15).

When looking at the middle column "customer rating" of the *Fan Traffic Signal,* one can see that *ALDI is ascribed* strength by customers in the central need "*ALDI* is very fast", which provides the basis for experienced fit and thus for identification.

And finally, the right column of the *Fan Traffic Signal* illustrates that *ALDI* succeeds in being perceived better than the competition in terms of speed. The result impressively shows how the consistent Orchestration according to the *Fan Principle* contributes to the perception of fit and the feeling of uniqueness and why *ALDI has* the highest *Fan Rate* in food retailing.

3.5 Examples VIII: *Miele—Orchestration* of Performance and Communication

"These guys have it all figured out from front to back."—When a brilliant entrepreneurial personality like *Steve Jobs,* co-founder, long-time CEO and, until his death, the "face" of *Apple,* talks like this about the German household appliance manufacturer *Miele,* it deserves a closer look in a book about the *Fan Principle* and its transformation to customer relationships. Because this quote could mean that *Miele* has precisely understood core customer needs and is specifically serving these needs at all points of contact—in other words, is consistently working according to the concept of *FANOMICS.* If this were the case, it would have to be reflected in a high Fan *Rate. We were able to verify* this easily for Germany because we also surveyed the relationship quality of the customers of the leading household appliance manufacturers as part of our basic research. And indeed, the results are impressive: *Miele* is not only the supplier with the most fans—the household appliance manufacturer from Gütersloh with its legendary long-lasting washing machines leaves major competitors such as *Bosch, Liebherr, AEG* and *Bauknecht* far behind. The fan *rate* of 38% is also a top result across all industries (cf. Fig. 3.16). To this day, this

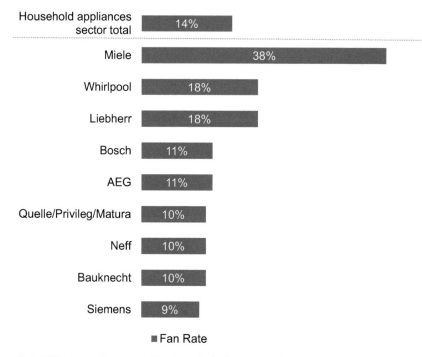

Fig. 3.16 *Fan Rates* in the household appliances sector

outstanding relationship quality enables *Miele to charge* significantly higher prices than the competition—a key prerequisite for profitability and growth.

The data proves it: *Miele* is a company that intuitively practices the *Fan Principle* successfully, and strictly speaking has been doing so for over one hundred years. When the two founders *Carl Miele* and *Reinhard Zinkann* wanted to launch their first milk centrifuges in 1899, there were already established competitors in large numbers in the wider area. In their search for a clear differentiation, the founders had to choose between the attributes "better" or "cheaper", to put it crudely. They opted for "always better"—and accepted the additional expense in terms of design and materials. The aim was to become and remain number one on the market in terms of durability, reliability, quality of results and ease of operation. The claim of quality and innovation leadership was born—brought to the point by the founders at that time by the brand promise "Always better", which still characterizes the company today.

Before we go into more detail about how *Miele* makes this brand promise tangible for customers at all points of contact, both on the performance side and on the communication side, we would like to take a brief moment to consider the question of what need *Miele* serves with this promise. Diametrically opposed to the already outlined demands of *ALDI customers, for* example (cf. Sect. 3.4), we are dealing with typical *Miele customers* for whom the decision for household appliances—and especially for the washing machine, *Miele*'s flagship product—goes hand in hand with a high level of involvement. The high standards of quality and innovation reflect *Miele customers*' need for security, not just to do something good for themselves and their families, but to do the best possible. Whether in the traditional family image of the housewife who defines herself by the quality of her housework, or in the modern understanding of the family with two working parents: They are all united by a longing for relief, in other words, for a household appliance that won't let them down. They want to be able to rely one hundred percent on the appliances they use, because tidy and reliable housework and associated attributes such as cleanliness and hygiene are of great importance.

To put it bluntly, this is not the core need of *all* customers of household appliances. Otherwise, the success of suppliers like *Neff* or *Whirlpool*, which position themselves more strongly on price, would be inexplicable. But obviously, the potential of customers in Germany with a pronounced need for quality and innovation and a corresponding willingness to pay in the household appliance sector is sufficiently large to offer *Miele* attractive growth opportunities to date. But how does *Miele* serve this clientele? How does *Miele* consistently orchestrate its service delivery with regard to the quality and innovation needs of these customers?

First and foremost is the product policy: Over the decades, *Miele shifted its* focus from a broad-based equipment supplier for the agricultural sector to electrical appliances for kitchens, laundry and floor care in private households—as well as related electrical appliances for use in commercial enterprises or medical facilities. Formerly successful product areas such as dairy technology, bicycles, mopeds, cars or kitchen furniture were discontinued in order to be able to concentrate all production capacities, innovative strength and marketing resources on these appliances.

Also, as a consequence of this *Focus, Miele is* able to invest 5 to 8% of its sales, and thus more than all relevant competitors, in research and development—an important prerequisite for credibly serving customers' need for quality.

Brand management corresponds to this restrictive product and range policy: Marketing is carried out exclusively via the *Miele* brand, which is consistently positioned in the premium segment. There are no second brands, low-cost lines, bought-in brands or production for private labels. In addition, numerous quality features from production are to be listed:

- *Miele is* the only manufacturer in the industry to use stainless steel (rather than plastic) caustic tanks on its washing machines.
- The drum crosses and balance weights are made of cast iron (manufactured by an in-house foundry at the Gütersloh headquarters) instead of concrete. These provide additional stability, prevent imbalance during spinning, and are more durable than concrete parts.
- Other components that are subject to mechanical stress are also more solidly constructed than the corresponding products of competitors. At first glance, this can be seen, for example, in the springs and dampers on which the unit comprising the drum, caustic tank and drive is suspended.
- *Miele* is the only manufacturer in the industry to enamel the fronts of its washing machines and dryers. This ensures special hardness and lasting shine.
- The high metal content ensures that *Miele washer-extractors* weigh an unrivalled 100 kilograms instead of 50 to 75 kilograms for competitor products and have an unsurpassed recycling rate of around 90%.
- *Miele* tests products such as washing machines, dryers, dishwashers, refrigerators, and ovens for 20-year durability using demanding load and endurance tests.
- The clear commitment to "Made in Germany" is also an essential facet of service provision: *Miele* continues to stand for German engineering, German workmanship, and predominantly German manufacturing. 90% of productive value creation still takes place in Germany. This distinguishes *Miele* from the competition and helps it credibly fulfill its promise of quality and innovation leadership.

Among numerous other aspects, one particularly striking piece of evidence for the Touchpoint-specific Orchestration towards "quality of service delivery" is the commitment to specialist dealers: In Germany, *Miele marketing is carried out* exclusively by authorized sales partners who guarantee demanding minimum standards in presentation, advice, and service. In return, *Miele* supports its sales partners in a variety of ways, protects them as far as legally and practically possible from those forms of distribution that precisely do not meet these standards, and does not sell its appliances directly to end customers itself.

The attentive reader will not have missed it, and the sales strategy just described is a perfect example of this: Also, at *Miele*—just like at *ALDI* (cf. Sect. 3.4)—the focus on core customer needs goes hand in hand with a consistent "yes to no" approach:

3.5 Examples VIII: *Miele*—*Orchestration* of Performance and Communication

- Despite profound changes in the retail landscape in Germany (steadily increasing market shares of specialty store chains and the Internet, declining number of specialty retailers), *Miele* stands by the "specialty store" sales channel—and refrains from supposedly fast growth via other sales channels that is not in line with its positioning and therefore not sustainably profitable.
- With its *focus on* domestic appliances, *Miele* resisted the temptation to use its enormous brand strength to expand into other product areas. On the contrary: Over the decades, the product range has been systematically throttled. Here, too, the renunciation of quick additional profit results from the realization that a credible communication of quality and innovation leadership can only be achieved by concentrating resources.
- The production quality features described are also an expression of a clear "yes to no," namely a "no" to cheaper materials and production processes that would increase returns in the short term but quickly prove damaging to the brand image in the medium term.

As impressive as these individual aspects are, what is crucial is the Orchestration, and in the *Miele* example, the interplay with an equally orchestrated communication. Let's take a look at this with a few examples:

- First and foremost, the brand promise "Always better" should be mentioned here, which goes back to the two company founders and has not been changed since. As already mentioned elsewhere (cf. our comments on *BMW* and *AUDI* in Sect. 3.1), the constancy of the brand message over a long period of time in conjunction with consistent tangibility is the essential prerequisite for a brand identity to emerge and be felt—and thus create a basis for identification for fan customers.
- The central characteristic of the family company is very pointedly elaborated by *Miele*, namely thinking in generations and not in quarterly reports. This conveys sustainability and reliability. In addition, the company leaders from the founding families are identification figures who have personified and conveyed the values for generations—to employees and customers.
- The statement that *Miele washing machines* last 20 years may prove authentic for many in reality. But the fact that everyone—customers and non-customers alike—almost spontaneously associate *Miele washing machines* with the attribute of longevity is primarily a credit to communication—even those who have never had this experience themselves believe in the longevity of a *Miele machine.*
- *Miele's positioning* as a quality leader is given a valuable boost by the independent awards and test seals that are permanently awarded to *Miele*. *Miele* makes very focused use of these seals and concentrates on particularly prominent or resilient ones. This sustainably serves the customers' discharge motive since it conveys security.

The yield from this perfectly orchestrated customer journey in terms of performance and communication is visibly reflected in the *Fan Traffic Signal* (cf. Fig. 3.17).

Perception	Relevance for emotional attachment	Rating Miele	Compared to the competition, Miele is ...
is very innovative	high	medium	better
is very flexible	high	medium	better
is very credible	high	good	better
is very fair	medium	medium	better
is very reliable	medium	good	better
works very professionally	medium	medium	better
is very serious	low	good	better
is very successful	low	good	better
has a great market recognition	low	good	better

Source: 2HMforum. research *Fanfocus Germany* 2013

Fig. 3.17 The Fan Traffic Signal of *Miele* shows in particular the pronounced perceived uniqueness

In terms of attributes such as "innovativeness" and "credibility", which are essential for positioning as a quality and innovation leader, *Miele* clearly outperforms its main competitors. Even if the initial situation, namely the core customer needs, is fundamentally different from that of *ALDI*, the example of *Miele* also shows how sustainable growth can be realized through consistent alignment with the concept ideas of *FANOMICS*. Since the possibilities are limited to differentiate oneself in a technologically mature market by factual service provision, the decisive effect at *Miele* only and especially arises from the interaction of orchestrated service provision and communication. The high quality of service is the essential foundation, the customer experiences the claim "Always better" as authentic—but only the correspondingly orchestrated communication provides this focused positioning with the necessary identification and uniqueness.

3.6 *FANOMICS*: From Development to Implementation

The *Fan Portfolio* has opened our eyes to the true challenge in customer relationship management: Instead of trying to turn dissatisfied customers into satisfied ones, one should turn highly satisfied customers into those with high customer value—i.e., into fans—which corresponds to a vertical movement in the direction of emotional commitment in the *Fan Portfolio* (cf. Sect. 1.6).

This made it clear that, in addition to the new control parameter of *Fan Rate,* we also needed a control concept that would help us trigger this vertical movement in the *Fan Portfolio in* order to make customer relationship management more successful in the long term. The aim was to present *FANOMICS,* a new management program of this kind, and to explain it using best-practice examples. In doing so, we have consistently oriented ourselves to the *Fan Principle. In developing* this new management system, we transferred the two central characteristics of the *Fan Principle*—identification and perceived uniqueness—to the relationship between companies and their customers. In this way, we were able to work out the mechanism that turns customers into fans and thus enables emotional customer loyalty. This mechanism has been reflected in the definition of *FANOMICS*.

With the *Fan Traffic Signal* and the Touchpoint *Traffic Signal,* we have presented instruments with which companies can generate the essential information for implementing *FANOMICS.* The *Fan Traffic Signal* identifies the loyalty-drivers and thus opens a view of the central demand and motive structures of the customers. By additionally depicting the strengths and weaknesses in a competitive comparison, it is the essential information and control basis. This is because it illustrates the actual state of fit and perceived uniqueness. And the *Touchpoint Traffic Signal provides companies with* concrete information about which touchpoints within the customer journey are of particular importance for the central need. As such, it provides a guide to action on which key touchpoints should be started with Orchestration to proceed efficiently.

With *FANOMICS, it's no* longer about looking at individual customer experiences in isolation and shining everywhere. Rather, *FANOMICS* opens a view of the big picture and shows companies where they need to shine—and where they would be better off saying "no", even having to say "no", in order to promote customer relationship quality. Implemented in this way, the economic success of *FANOMICS* unfolds in two directions:

- The growing identification and perception of uniqueness increases emotional attachment and triggers the desired vertical movement in the *Fan Portfolio*: the *Fan Rate* increases, and customer value rises noticeably.
- Those who focus and orchestrate accordingly are more economical with their resources, which leads to a sustainable reduction in costs.

It thus becomes clear why *FANOMICS has a massive impact* on economic success—and why the necessary investments during introduction and implementation will quickly pay off (cf. Chap. 2).

In the past chapters (cf. Chaps. 1–3), we have presented our comprehensive findings on *FANOMICS*, its derivation from the Fan Principle, its benefits and its mechanisms of action. If you find this an incentive to use *FANOMICS in* your company and want to take the implementation into your own hands, the following Chap. 4 will tell you how to proceed in detail.

References

Aldi Süd (2015) ALDI Süd startet Kampagne zum "Einfach-Prinzip" und schaltet erstmals Außenwerbung. https://unternehmen.aldi-sued.de/de/presse/pressemitteilungen/unternehmen/2015/pressemitteilung-aldi-sued-startet-kampagne-zum-einfach-prinzip/. Accessed 7 December 2022

AUDI USA YouTube Channel Audi Quattro Campaign: "Ski Jump". https://www.youtube.com/watch?v=25u80sQkkkM. Accessed 7 December 2022

Becker R (2014) How false advertising drove the Praktiker DIY store into bankruptcy. https://www.focus.de/finanzen/experten/becker/20-prozent-auf-alles-wie-falsche-werbung-praktiker-in-den-ruin-trieb_id_3009969.html. Accessed 25 May 2021

Becker R (2016) Emissions scandal: For this one reason, customers will remain loyal to VW. Focus Online. https://www.focus.de/finanzen/experten/becker/umweltschutz-ist-ueberschaetzt-abgasskandal-warum-die-kundenvw-trotzdem-die-treue-halten-werden_id_5074996.html. Accessed: May 20, 2021

Deutsche Welle (2013) DIY stores chain bust https://www.dw.com/en/praktiker-diy-stores-to-file-for-insolvency/a-16944612, Accessed 7 December 2022

Facebook (2014) ADAC. https://de-de.facebook.com/ADAC. Accessed 20 May 2021

Fanfocus Germany (2021) Fanfocus Germany: who is the best in his industry? https://2hmforum.de/en/services/industry-focus/fanfocus-germany/. Accessed 30 May 2023

Feurer S (2021) Hat Aldi die schnellste Kasse der Welt? Was hinter der 15-Sekunden-Regel steckt. https://www.chip.de/news/Hat-Aldi-die-schnellste-Kasse-der-Welt-Was-hinter-der-15-Sekunden-Regel-steckt_179387969.html. Accessed 31 May 2022

Følstad A, Kvale K (2018) Customer journeys: a systematic literature review. J Serv Theory Pract 2018:196–227

Grabitz I, Seidl H (2006) Festung Deutschland. https://www.welt.de/print-wams/article145447/Festung-Deutschland.html. Accessed 1 July 2021

Heidenfelder E (2018) Kassiererin berichtet: Als ich einen Kunden verarztete, musste ich mich rechtfertigen. https://www.focus.de/finanzen/karriere/arbeitet-im-discounter-seit-sie-15-ist-fast-jede-sekunde-ein-produkt-scannen-aldi-kassiererin-packt-ueber-ihren-job-aus_id_9139347.html. Accessed 31 May 2021

Kuehnl C, Jozic D, Homburg C (2019) Effective customer journey design: consumers' conception, measurement, and consequences. J Acad Mark Sci 47:551–568

Ley R (2018) Die Aldi-Brüder (aka Aldi - Eine deutsche Geschichte) (working title). AVEpublishing Argon Verlag AVE GmbH, Berlin

Luchsinger C (2021) Kundenzentrierung statt Silodenken. https://www.linkedin.com/pulse/kundenzentrierung-das-silodenken-durchbrechen-cyrill-luchsinger/. Accessed 20 July 2021

Osman Y (2017) Deutsche Bank löst "Leistung aus Leidenschaft" ab. https://www.handelsblatt.com/finanzen/banken-versicherungen/banken/neuer-slogan-positiverbeitrag-deutsche-bank-loest-leistung-aus-leidenschaft-ab/19769814.html. Accessed 16 June 2021

Reuters Staff (2016) Volkswagen emissions scandal deepens as prosecutors probe chairman. https://www.reuters.com/article/us-volkswagen-emissions-idUSKBN1310E9. Accessed 12 January 2023

Scherbaum C (2020) Epstein, Schwarzgeld, Zinsbetrug: Die größten Skandale der Deutschen Bank. https://www.rnd.de/wirtschaft/deutsche-bank-die-grossten-skandale-HB2SV474SBCWTMU3XVDJ454QOM.html. Accessed 31 May 2021

Schlautermann C (2008) Lebensmitteldiscounter – Demographe schadet. https://www.handelsblatt.com/unternehmen/handel-konsumgueter/lebensmitteldiscounter-demografie-schadet/2983984.html. Accessed 16 June 2021

Schlautermann C (2009) Aldi hält Wettbewerber auf Abstand. https://www.handelsblatt.com/unternehmen/handel-konsumgueter/supermaerkte-aldi-haelt-wettbewerber-deutlich-auf-abstand/3162820.html. Accessed 16 June 2021

Schuldt R (2021) Pilot Projekt: Shopping ohne Kasse: Aldi testet smarten Einkaufswagen. https://www.computerbild.de/artikel/cb-News-Smart-Home-Shopping-ohne-Kasse-Aldi-testet-smarten-Einkaufswagen-30661835.html. Accessed 01 September 2021

Schumacher O (2012) Pünktlichkeit: Komplexe Größe zwischen öffentlicher Wahrnehmung und betrieblichen Rahmenbedingungen. https://www.deutschebahn.com/resource/blob/1170754/fba6b918410fff5a6640bcab87205c52/Themendienst-Puenktlichkeit-data.pdf. Accessed 19 May 2021

Spiegel (2018) Mayer bricht Zehnkampf-Weltrekord. https://www.spiegel.de/sport/sonst/zehnkampf-kevin-mayer-stellt-neuen-weltrekord-auf-a-1228377.html. Accessed 16 June 2021

Statistisches Bundesamt (2020) Einkommen, Einnahmen und Ausgaben privater Haushalte - Fachserie 15 Reihe 1 - 2019 (December 16, 2020). https://www.destatis.de/DE/Themen/Gesellschaft-Umwelt/Einkommen-Konsum-Lebensbedingungen/Einkommen-Einnahmen-Ausgaben/Publikationen/Downloads-Einkommen/einnahmen-ausgaben-privater-haushalte-2150100197004.pdf. Accessed 31 May 2021

How Do I Really Turn Customers into Fans? 4

In the first three chapters, we have shown why it is worthwhile for companies to use *FANOMICS* to manage customer relationships according to the *Fan Principle*. *FANOMICS* stands for the fundamental orientation of your company towards emotional customer loyalty—it represents, as it were, the new maxim of your entrepreneurial actions. In this chapter, we now want to show you how you should proceed in implementing the basic ideas of *FANOMICS* on your own. Our implementation concept is based on our experiences from several hundred customer projects. With it, we describe an ideal way that promises maximum success when using *FANOMICS*. Not all elements can be implemented in exactly the same way in every company. It will therefore be crucial that you scrutinize the following explanations for their suitability for your company and, if necessary, take suitable alternative paths. And even if you cannot or do not want to implement certain building blocks currently, do not let this discourage you: Get going, start now—the examination of *FANOMICS* will inspire you, and the first successes will come quickly, and from this you will gain the energy and creativity to tackle even previously postponed steps.

To get you started, we will use a model from *FANOMICS to* introduce and briefly explain the individual building blocks (Fig. 4.1).

1. Emotional loyalty increases when customers identify with their provider, i.e., when there is a match between relevant customer needs and what a provider stands for. The basis for this is created by the right positioning: it focuses on core customer needs and, as a basis for identification, creates the best possible fit with the corporate strategy, corporate culture, strengths, and unique selling propositions.
2. Emotional attachment increases when this fit between the relevant needs of customers and the company's positioning can be experienced repeatedly along the customer journey. It is all about Orchestration**,** and it is all about,

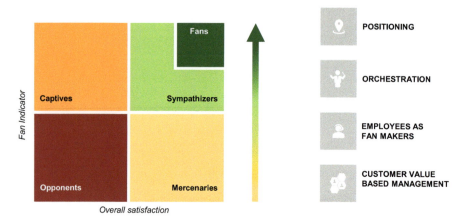

Source: Own illustration

Fig. 4.1 The building blocks of *FANOMICS* (short version/overview)

  (a) Orchestration **across touchpoints,** i.e., all structural, personnel, or systemic measures that—once initiated—ensure the desired fit at many touchpoints along the customer journey,
  (b) **touchpoint-specific Orchestration,** i.e., all complementary measures to align individual touchpoints with core customer needs to further improve the sense of fit.
3. Emotional loyalty is created by the "Company Lifeblood Factor **Employees**": Fan employees are Fan Makers because they create a sense of uniqueness among customers.
4. Emotional loyalty increases when a lack of fit is counteracted in a targeted, customer-specific manner. This means **personalized measures depending on the current allocation in the *Fan Portfolio*.**

4.1 Positioning

Positioning should focus on core customer needs and, as a basis for identification, create the best possible fit with the corporate strategy, corporate culture, strengths and unique selling propositions (Kotler and Armstrong 2020; Homburg et al. 2013).[1] In doing so, it should ideally differentiate from key competitors. Finally, it should provide orientation and planning security in the long term, since key strategic and operational (investment) decisions should be guided and controlled by the positioning.

---

[1] Even though in marketing science "brand" is equated with "positioning", we deliberately do *not* use the terms synonymously in the context of *FANOMICS*, since "brand" in the common understanding is limited to the communicative part, while we are concerned with the orchestration of communication *and service* delivery.

4.1 Positioning

Based on these fundamental considerations, in this section we present criteria that you can use to assess how promising positioning options are within the framework of *FANOMICS*. After all, for the overwhelming majority of companies, there is *no one* correct positioning. We will explain why this is the case later.

4.1.1 Instruments and Management Systems in the Positioning Process

Valid and comprehensive information about core customer needs, your own strengths and weaknesses, and your current position in comparison with the competition are essential prerequisites for a successful positioning process. It is about setting the strategic course because the decisions you make based on this information should be resilient for many years and create the basis for sustainable growth—even, if necessary adjustments to framework conditions repeatedly occur. The defined DNA of the company, and its positioning, remain the same—continuity is one, if not *the decisive* success factor for creating a monopoly in the minds of customers.

Let's take the example already cited in this book of the automobile manufacturer *BMW*—a company with an outstanding *Fan Rate* even across industries (cf. Sect. 3.1). Of course, the general conditions in the automotive sector have changed constantly in recent years and decades. Customer expectations, the competitive environment, new technologies, and social and political conditions have repeatedly challenged the Munich-based automotive group. In the process, *BMW* has been able to rely on one thing: Within the heterogeneous mass of car drivers, there was and still is a target group for whom "driving pleasure" and the associated attributes such as "sportiness" or "excitement" play the central role—a motive that *BMW* serves more consistently and comprehensively than any other automaker. So, the challenge is "merely" to keep adapting customer contacts as conditions change so that this central motive can still be experienced.

Imagine if *BMW* could not rely on the data that provided the way in this direction. To ensure that you can make equally secure and resilient decisions and that your strategic positioning bears fruit in the long term and does not become a blind flight, you need well-founded information and management tools:

- Well-founded information about the core loyalty-drivers[2] (as the key to understanding customer motives) is elementary. This information is absolutely indispensable so that you do not make the same mistake as *Praktiker* (see Sect. 3.1) and position your company "past" the need or market potential.
- Information regarding perceived strengths and weaknesses is also necessary in order to avoid betting on the wrong horse—i.e., on weaknesses—as did *Deutsche*

---

[2] We speak of loyalty-drivers because the *Fan Traffic Signal shows* the relevance of certain characteristics of companies on the emotional attachment of customers.

Bank, for example (see Sect. 3.1), and also to be able to continuously measure the success of measures initiated.
- Finally, comparisons with competitors are particularly important when developing the positioning (cf. Sect. 4.1.2), so that you can select from otherwise equivalent positioning options those which are also most likely to show potential for differentiation from the competition.

This information is generated via a customer survey. The findings, from the *Fan Traffic Signal* (cf. Sect. 3.4), reflect the current positioning of a company from the subjective viewpoint of the customers and open the view, in particular, to the central loyalty-drivers which represent the starting point of successful positioning. Therefore, in-depth qualitative customer surveys should be used to strengthen the understanding of the identified loyalty-drivers and to better understand underlying customer motives.

Let's illustrate this with a concrete example: The *Fan Traffic Signal* of a fictitious company in the IT sector shows that buying from a market-leading company is of central importance for the emotional loyalty of its business customers. But why? What specific motive generates the feeling of fit with this IT provider? Do customers want to use it to document their own claim to power in the sense of "A company like ours only buys from the best (which is equated with the market leader)?" Or is it an expression of a security motive along the lines of "If we buy from this provider, nothing can go wrong" (surely one or the other still remembers *IBM's* earlier positioning in this context, "Too big to fail," which was geared precisely to this customer motive). Qualitative customer surveys are very valuable for answering such questions. To locate the findings regarding the underlying motive structure of customers, we recommend and use the *Motiversum*, our model of emotion-guiding motive structures derived from psychological research (cf. Fig. 4.3).

In the search for a promising positioning, it is crucial that core customer needs and corporate strengths correspond, since only then will the company be able to create a feeling of fit among customers. Therefore, in addition to the customer perspective, information is also needed about how the company perceives itself, what its strategic orientation looks like, its culture and values, and what competencies and unique selling points the company has, but also what weaknesses stand in the way of fulfilling certain positioning aspects. This information can be obtained through various instruments, which should ideally be combined with each other:

- The *identity workshop* provides insight into the strategic direction, values, and desired strengths and differentiators from a management perspective.
- The *employee survey* validates the findings from the identity workshop. It shows how well the company management succeeds in making core values and processes, which are essential for fulfilling the positioning, tangible.
- From the point of view of the relevant decision-makers, the *maturity check provides information on the extent to which* the processes in customer management are suitable for successful implementation of the positioning. If, for

example, a company wants to make life easier for customers, then an up-to-date database containing essential information, including contact history, is an essential basis. If the result of such a maturity check is that the database does not meet this requirement to a sufficient degree, then urgent improvements should be made at this point.

All these instruments serve to mirror the customer perspective, i.e., an external view of the company, with the internal view from different perspectives. This approach also provides initial clues as to the causes of customer ratings.
The information required for successful positioning is rounded off by a look at the competitive environment and the differentiation opportunities that can be derived from it:

- Competitor customers are also surveyed as part of the customer survey. In this way, the company's own strengths/weaknesses profile can be compared with that of its key competitors to identify areas for profiling.
- A communications analysis is used to examine the positions currently occupied by key competitors in addressing their customers. The results can be used to determine which customer-relevant needs are being communicated by competitors and to what extent, and where there may be unoccupied relevant topic areas that offer opportunities for differentiation.

Figure 4.2 provides an overview of the various instruments for obtaining information as part of the positioning process. They are presented in more detail in the following section.

4.1.2 Instruments I: Identify Loyalty-Drivers: Customer and Competitor Customer Survey

This is not a textbook on market research. That is why we want to focus on answering key questions in this chapter that arise when implementing customer and competitor surveys and to show you proven solution options:

- **What topics should be highlighted?**
  In regard to the Positioning implementation field, you will need the following information from the customer/competitor survey:
  - Emotional attachment to and satisfaction with the provider. Based on this information, the *Fan Indicator* and the *Fan Portfolio* are created. The *Fan Indicator* maps the emotional attachment of the customers and serves as the basis for dividing the customers into the *Fan Portfolio*. It is also essential for identifying the relevant loyalty-drivers. Only if the emotional attachment of the customers is known, can the fulfilled core needs, which underline and charge this connection, be depicted by the *Fan Traffic Signal*. In particular, the

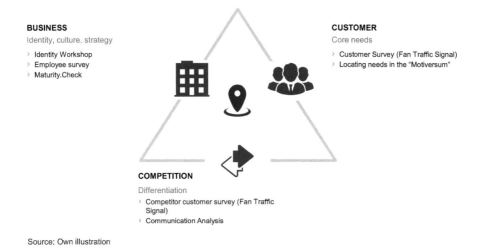

Fig. 4.2 Instruments for obtaining information as part of the positioning process

Fan Rate determined is the basis for measuring the success effectiveness of the positioning.
– Potentially relevant loyalty-drivers for the identification of central needs, the strengths/weaknesses profile, and the perceived differentiation. This information is condensed in the *Fan Traffic Signal*.

The fundamental question is how the catalog of drivers to be queried is developed. On the one hand, there is a high degree of agreement across companies and industries regarding the relevant loyalty-drivers, which speaks in favor of a standardized approach. On the other hand, in our experience, company-specific aspects are so significant that individual adjustments or additions are worthwhile. Responsible employees, but also the customers themselves (e.g., within the framework of qualitative interviews) can help to identify these specific aspects.

– **How complex should the customer survey be? How many countries, regions, target groups do we need to map in order to draw the right conclusions?**
Especially in large companies with complex business areas, numerous customer groups and international orientation, the question often arises to what extent the customer survey must reflect this complexity. Since *FANOMICS* is about finding the common denominator, the answer is simple: focus on your core business, i.e. on the most important markets and the central target groups. Less is more! Once you have found the right message in this manner, translate it for all relevant contact points (countries, markets, target groups). The following thought excurses will illustrate what this means:

Let's assume for a moment that *BMW* had not already recognized its customers' central motive ("joy of driving") for decades and had achieved a monopoly position in their minds through appropriate *Focus* and *Orchestration*. In that case, one would be faced with the challenge of deriving the central customer motive from several product lines, numerous sales markets and correspondingly heterogeneous customer groups when surveying customers *and competitors*. One would probably look at a core product line (e.g., the 5 Series) and core markets (e.g., Germany and the USA). With the insight distilled from this, one could derive differentiated messages for other product areas. Presumably, "joy of driving" translates differently for a 1 Series driver than for an X Series driver. The same applies, of course, to translation to different sales markets. However, all these translation tasks are quite manageable once the message has been discovered: The example from Sect. 3.1 has already made it clear that even technical features of the models such as all-wheel drive can be translated into the motive world of the typical *BMW driver*.

- **How often should the *customer survey* be repeated?**
  There is no clear answer to this question. Since the derivation of the central motive structures is intended and made for a permanent orientation and alignment, there is no need at all for a follow-up measurement from this perspective. The situation is different with the question of one's own strengths and weaknesses and the perception of the competition. Depending on how dynamically your own appearance or that of key competitors changes, significant differences in perception and thus shifts in the color symbolism of the *Fan Traffic Signal* can even occur during the year. As a general rule, the sooner you recognize shifts to your disadvantage, the sooner you can react. It is therefore advisable to check at least the loyalty-drivers from the *Fan Traffic Signal* and the emotional customer loyalty on an annual basis.

- **For B2B companies: Which people in the client companies should be interviewed?**
  Larger customer companies usually have so-called *buying centers*, i.e., purchasing-relevant decisions are usually not made by one person alone, but rather several decision-makers are involved—e.g., a technical manager, a buyer and a managing director. In this case, the question arises as to who should be surveyed as a representative of the customer company, because it is quite conceivable that the technical manager is a Fan and the purchaser a Mercenary customer. The needs structures of the decision-makers involved from the various functional areas can also differ. It is therefore advisable to take a close look at the decision-making process in the customer company in advance of the customer survey and to identify typical relevant decision-makers. If there is a well-founded suspicion (which can also be validated in an upstream test) that the decision-makers involved from different functional areas differ systematically either in their needs structures or in their relationship quality, they should be considered in a differentiated manner in the customer survey. However, in doing so, have the courage to leave gaps. We are not aware of any cases in which more than three people from different functional areas in a customer company have proven to be truly relevant decision-makers.

– **Are there alternatives to customer surveys to generate the information you need?**
If companies cannot or do not want to survey their customers[3] to generate the information they need, they must obtain it by other means. Working out the necessary information together with employees who have contact with customers or with top management has proven to be pragmatic. Using leading questions such as "What do you think are the characteristics that have a particularly strong influence on the emotional attachment of customers?" and then subsequently "Which touchpoints are particularly important for experiencing speed, for example?", information processes can be simulated, as they are also used in the customer survey to derive the *Fan Traffic Signal* and the *Touchpoint Traffic Signal*. *It goes* without saying that the findings obtained in this way should be viewed with caution. Perhaps there will be an opportunity to validate them in informal personal discussions with customers.

4.1.3 Instruments II: Deepening and Locating Customer Needs: The *"Motiversum"*

If we want to understand the central needs as well as the underlying motivational structures of customers, it is important to recall what we had already discussed in detail in Sect. 1.2 in connection with emotions: Needs create psychological motives, i.e., provide motives for our actions. And these motives in turn cause trigger emotions that help us to implement the corresponding actions. Thus, evolutionarily, each of us has several emotion programs embedded in us that are triggered by important needs and serve the goal of fulfilling those needs (cf. Panksepp 1998; Scherer 2005; Myers 2014; Häusel 2016). For example, we all have both an emotional fear program and an emotional fight program. The fear program triggers flight behavior: It ensures the avoidance of danger and thus secures our survival-critical need for integrity. The motives behind this emotional program are "safety & security". So, the need is survival, the motive is safety, the associated emotion program is fear, and the action is flight behavior. The fight program, on the other hand, triggers aggressive behavior: It ensures that we prevail in a competitive struggle and thus secures our need for resources, which is essential for survival. The motives behind this emotion program are "autonomy & power". So, the need is assertion, the motive is autonomy, the associated emotion program is struggle, and the behavior is aggression. Needs, motives and emotions are thus inextricably linked.

The fact that needs and motives are primarily triggered by emotions and that the rational mind alone does not control our behavior is functional in evolutionary terms: Only emotions ensure that physiological processes take place in such core need

---

[3] Reasons can be e.g., data protection hurdles, institutional refusals of customers to participate or overlapping with other customer surveys.

4.1 Positioning

situations that increase the chances of success of our actions—such as the release of hormones and neurotransmitters. Emotions are precisely holistic physical behavioral programs. The example of the fight and flight program also shows the role of the triggering need. If we get into a conflict situation with a rival, both programs give contradictory signals: The fear program advises us to surrender the field without a fight, the fight program advises us to defend our claims. Which program prevails depends decisively on the significance of the underlying need and whether it is located more strongly in the area of the security motive or the autonomy motive.

Emotions thus serve the fulfillment of needs and the realization of motives. And on the other hand, the achievement of motives as well as the fulfillment of needs trigger positive emotions in us, which we perceive as rewards and thus as desirable. Therefore, as we have shown, a fan relationship is a relationship with emotional attachment: Because it fulfills central needs and thereby triggers positive emotions.

If you want to understand the central needs of your customers, it is therefore important to identify the motive structures that lie behind their needs and whose fulfillment triggers positive emotional experiences in them. To facilitate this, it helps to keep in mind the basic different directions and manifestations of motives—in a kind of map of motive structures, as it were. We have created such a map—the *"Motiversum"*. It presents the universe of possible motive structures in a descriptive and exhaustive way, makes it possible to experience it graphically, and thus helps to visualize it (cf. Fig. 4.3).

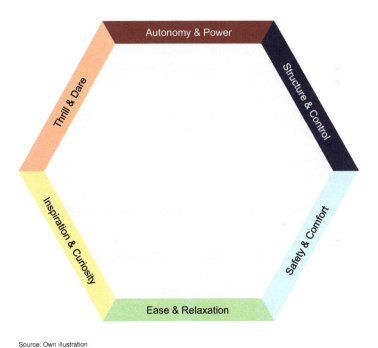

Source: Own illustration

Fig. 4.3 The *"Motiversum"*: Map of emotion triggering motive structures

In deriving the "Motiversum", *we followed* the basic evolutionary emotion programs according to Panksepp (1998), which we have already explained in more detail in Sect. 1.2: SEEKING, FEAR, and RAGE are among them the central evolutionary programs that govern our daily behavior. The SEEKING system looks for new stimuli and rewards, the FEAR system avoids danger and tries to establish safety. And the RAGE system is associated with assertiveness in competition. Accordingly, the underlying motivational structures can be named: The SEEKING system focuses on *"inspiration and curiosity,"* the FEAR system stands for *"safety and security,"* and the RAGE system strives for *"authority and power."* Thus, the first three basic building blocks of the human emotional cosmos are named. At the same time, the interplay of these three basic currents in turn gives rise to nameable mixed forms: Between the motive of *"safety and security"* on the one hand and the striving for *"autonomy and power"* on the other hand hides the desire for *"structure and control"* of all circumstances. Towards the other dimension, between *"safety and security"* on the one hand and *"inspiration and curiosity"* on the other hand, there is the desire for non-binding and danger-free stimulation, i.e., for *"ease and relaxation"*. And the desire for *"inspiration and curiosity"* in turn meets on the other side with the striving for *"autonomy and power" in* the motive field of willingness-to-take-risks, i.e., in *"tension and daring"*.

The *"Motiversum"* with its six segments resembles several similar nomenclatures from the psychological literature, all of which attempt to order and structure the motives underlying emotions. For example, Scheier and Held (2007, p. 145ff.) also present six emotion dimensions: They start from the three "basic rewards" of security, autonomy, and excitement, which they extend by the three intermediate dimensions of pleasure, discipline, and adventure. Faßbender and Thanhoffer (2011, p. 135ff.) adopt five of these dimensions, but replace the term "arousal" with "stimulation." Similarly, Häusel (2016, p. 38ff.) assumes three central emotion systems balance, dominance, and stimulation, which also here stand for safety, curiosity, and power. They are complemented by the mixed forms adventure, fantasy, and discipline. Barden (2013) presented a similar classification for the English-speaking world. What all these taxonomies have in common is that—based on findings from psychology and neurology—they derive the entire emotional motive cosmos from the three basic motives of security, assertiveness, and curiosity. The *"Motiversum" we have* developed does the same thing—albeit with partly different terms that seem more suitable for our purposes, namely the classification of customer needs.

With the six fields of the *"Motiversum"*, we have thus identified the six central motives into which the needs of customers can now be vividly classified. At first glance, this appears to be a simple process: a life insurer would probably place its customers in the motive field "Safety & Security", while a manufacturer of outdoor wear would probably place its customers in the motive field "Excitement & Risk". This sounds plausible at first, but it does not necessarily have to be correct, because it is not the product alone that automatically determines customer needs, but rather, as we will show, the actual positioning of the company. Therefore, the identification of the central needs as well as the underlying motive structures is one of the essential challenges of the positioning process: In order to find access to the motive structures, the question must be answered as to why the loyalty-drivers, which prove to be highly relevant for the customers in the *Fan Traffic Signal*, are so important for the emotional bond. In practice, it has proven useful to follow up a classic *quantitative standardized* customer survey with a *qualitative* analysis phase to gain a sound understanding of the central needs. Alternatively, this can take the form of focus groups or in-depth interviews. The key guiding questions here are:

- Why are certain loyalty-drivers so important for customers? What motives and associated emotions are behind them?
- Where within the customer journey are they experienced?
- What causes a company to be perceived by customers as strong or weak in terms of these loyalty-drivers?

Based on the results of the qualitative study, the "Motiversum" then makes it possible to clearly assign the core customer needs (i.e., the loyalty-drivers) to the six basic motive and emotion structures and the associated typical behavior patterns. This facilitates both the alignment of positioning with the relevant motivational structures and targeted Orchestration.

Let's explain this in more detail by going back to the fictitious company in the IT industry. Being a customer of a market-leading company proved to be a key loyalty-driver for its customers. Let's assume that further qualitative analysis would have revealed that this is an expression of the motto: "If we buy from this provider, nothing can go wrong". From this, one could conclude a strong anchoring in the motive area of *security*. Typical behavior patterns are the pursuit of stability and, consequently, the avoidance of any change.

Given this knowledge, our sample IT company could more precisely align its positioning and, of course, its orchestration process with these key security motivations of its customer companies.

4.1.4 Instruments III: Understanding Identity: The Identity Workshop

Positioning will only be successful if the corporate competencies, corporate strategy, and self-image as well as corporate management, culture and values create the necessary basis for this. In this context, we again recall the negative example of *Deutsche Bank* (cf. Sect. 3.1), which successfully identified relevant customer needs in the relationship with a bank and focused on them in its positioning, namely a striving for "autonomy & power" and for efficiency as well as a strong performance orientation but was not culturally positioned internally to fulfill these needs. To prevent this from happening and to ensure the necessary alignment, management should develop and document a sound, shared self-image of the company, examine the suitability of this self-image for fulfilling positioning options, and self-critically assess the acceptance of these options among management and the workforce. In this

Source: Own illustration

Fig. 4.4 Identity workshop—question grid

way, potential hurdles in the positioning process can be identified at an early stage and targeted countermeasures can be taken. In our project work, the identity workshop with top management has proven its worth as a format for developing the self-image. A typical underlying question grid can be found in Fig. 4.4.

Discussions with top management often reveal that the decision-makers involved have different goals, have different views of customer needs, or do not pursue a uniform set of values. We observe the same pattern when we mirror the self-image of different hierarchy levels in separate Identity Workshops. A uniform self-image both at the top management level and among different management levels is elementary for the success of positioning, since the process of Orchestration based on Positioning can only work if all managers are moving in the same direction, because in the language of the *Fan Principle*, they are the "stars" of the employees, i.e., they provide them the necessary orientation.

4.1.5 Instruments IV: Checking Identity: The Employee Survey

To check how well managers are succeeding in providing employees with a consistent and correct orientation, the findings of the identity workshop should be reviewed from the employee perspective. The most suitable instrument for this is an employee survey. It shows how well the company management succeeds in making core values

4.1 Positioning

and processes, which are essential for fulfilling the tangible positioning: Let's take a fictitious company as an example, whose positioning focuses on making life easier for customers. The company knows from the customer's perspective that smooth, integrated, uniform communication is perceived as a relieving factor and thus contributes to the fulfillment of this Positioning. To achieve this, a culture of openness and an excellent exchange of information across departments are key prerequisites. If employees do not perceive this as being lived or implemented in this way, these are significant hurdles to the successful implementation of the Positioning.

As with the customer survey, we would also like to take a closer look at two aspects of the employee survey that repeatedly emerge as relevant to success:

- **Which employees should be interviewed?**
  Since *FANOMICS is* about the Orchestration of all processes and measures, the entire workforce is affected. This is because every employee is either in direct contact with customers or is an internal service provider for departments or colleagues who have direct customer contact. Thus, everyone influences the perception of customers at touchpoints in the customer journey either directly or indirectly. Therefore, we recommend surveying all employees. If this is not feasible, managers should definitely be surveyed, as they are key multipliers and opinion leaders who carry their self-image into the company and pass it on to the employees they manage. Employees with customer contact, i.e., sales and service units, are also particularly important, as their self-image has a direct impact on customers. If an employee survey is not possible at all, the required validation can also be carried out in workshops with management and employee groups.
- **What topics should be highlighted?**
  In essence, there are three main blocks of issues:
  1. How do managers and employees currently identify with the company? Do core needs and perceived company characteristics match? To answer these questions, we measure the *Fan Indicator* and the *Fan Rate* in the workforce according to the same logic as for customers (cf. Sect. 4.3.5)
  2. Do the perceptions of top management and the workforce regarding the company's profile of strengths and weaknesses coincide? What are the general attitudes of managers and employees toward value-based corporate management?
  3. Are the values relevant for the fulfillment of an (optional) Positioning also lived in the company? For this purpose, there are question grids that we use again and again to identify central contradictions and resistances and to incorporate them into the evaluation of positioning options. Such questions are, for example:
     (a) Does values-based behavior have a high significance in everyday work?
     (b) Are the specified values known?
     (c) Do employees believe that the values add up to success?
     (d) Are the values actually lived?

4.1.6 Instruments V: Checking Processes in Customer Management: The *Maturity Check*

The customer survey is the central starting point of *FANOMICS*, since it provides information about the core needs of the customers and about the strengths/weaknesses profile of the company from the customer's point of view. For the positioning process as well as later for the orchestration process, it is necessary to better understand the reasons for the evaluation by the customers. This is because the causes provide information regarding the effort required to create a fit with the core customer needs and where exactly the levers need to be applied. In practice, the maturity check format has proved its worth in checking the extent to which the processes in customer management are already suitable for successful implementation of the positioning and in determining how the relevant processes can be continuously optimized.

As an example, let's think again about the fictitious company that has set itself the goal of making life easier for its customers. To achieve this goal, centralized, sound, and up-to-date information about customers, including a comprehensive order and contact history, is essential. If the result of such a maturity check for this company is that the available customer data does not meet this requirement to a sufficient degree, then improvements would have to be made at this point.

The customer management maturity check can be conducted in the form of expert interviews with relevant decision-makers from management or as a workshop. A topic grid of such a maturity check developed by us can be found in Fig. 4.5. The CURRENT situation is initially assessed for a total of eight dimensions, including aspects such as "Positioning & Customer Management Strategy," "Customer Analysis," and "Processes and Tools" in five maturity levels each. In the comparison with a target maturity level derived from the targeted Positioning, particularly relevant hurdles and thus fields of action are identified. In the example shown, this would be the dimension "customer interaction", as this is where the actual and target maturity levels differ most.

4.1.7 Instruments VI: Identifying Opportunities for Differentiation: The Communication Analysis

The instruments presented so far are used on the one hand to comprehensively illuminate the customer perspective and in particular to identify core customer needs, and on the other hand to compare this customer perspective with the internal view of the company. The information required for successful positioning is complemented by a look at the competitive environment and the resulting opportunities for differentiation.

Since customers of relevant competitors are also surveyed as part of the customer survey, the *Fan Traffic Signal* also provides information on who is rated better in terms of key loyalty-drivers: Your company or one of the relevant competitors. However, this does not indicate which positioning is occupied by which key

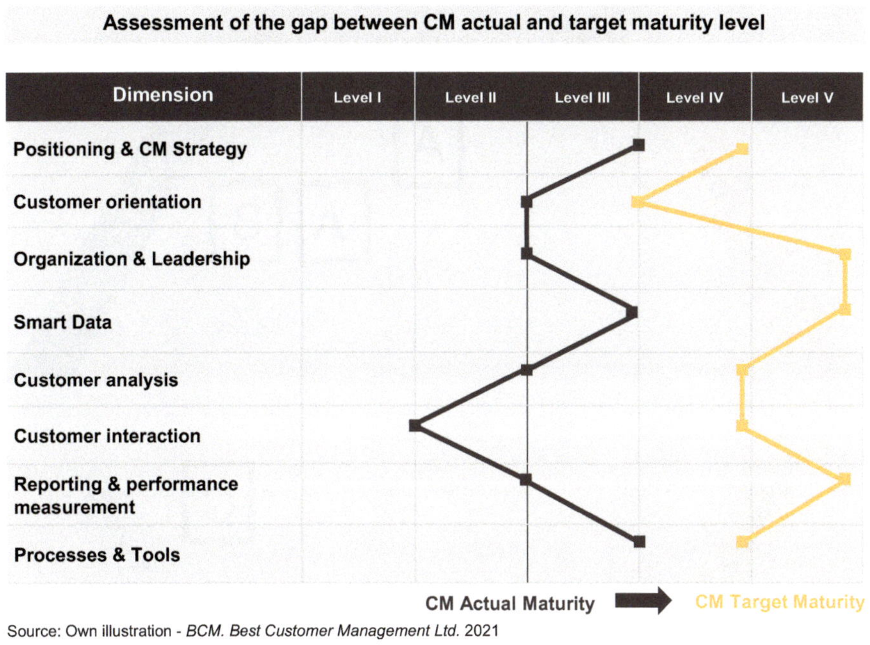

4.1 Positioning

Assessment of the gap between CM actual and target maturity level

Dimension	Level I	Level II	Level III	Level IV	Level V
Positioning & CM Strategy					
Customer orientation					
Organization & Leadership					
Smart Data					
Customer analysis					
Customer interaction					
Reporting & performance measurement					
Processes & Tools					

CM Actual Maturity → CM Target Maturity

Source: Own illustration - *BCM. Best Customer Management Ltd.* 2021

Fig. 4.5 Topic grid maturity check

competitor. To make it easier to identify opportunities for differentiation and to assess positioning options in terms of their suitability for differentiation, we recommend the instrument of communication analysis. It can be used to answer the following questions:

- How does your company position itself in terms of communication in comparison to its key competitors in addressing customers?
- Which needs relevant to your customers are communicated by which competitor and to what extent?

From the results, it is possible to deduce where there may be unoccupied relevant subject areas that offer opportunities for differentiation.

Review and analyze available communication material such as website, brochures, advertisements and presentations. Bundle this communication content by assigning it to the *motive* segments in our "Motiversum". In this way, you identify the communicative focal points. The example in Fig. 4.6 initially shows in which motive fields the three competitors of a fictitious company X from the banking sector position themselves. The motive fields of "autonomy & power" (company A), "structure & control" (companies A and B), and "safety & security" (company C) are played on. If, for example, there is an option for company X to position itself in the "ease" motive field because this is where the core needs of its customers are located, we would have identified a differentiation option in the direct competitive

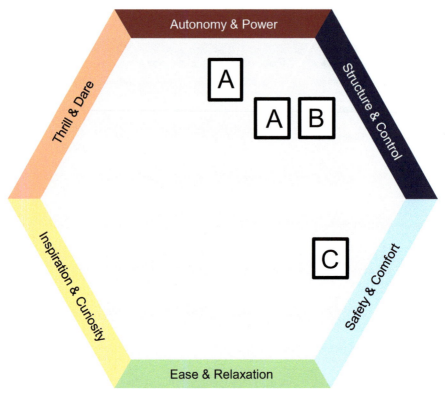

Source: Communicative competitive analysis, own illustration

Fig. 4.6 Example of communicative competition analysis I: The three competitors A, B and C of company X position themselves in the motive fields "autonomy & power", "structure & control" and "safety & security"

environment, since this motive field is not currently addressed by any competitor in terms of communication. This would then also mean that company X would have to realign its communications, since its focus is currently on the motive fields of "Structure & Control" and "Safety & Security" (the focus areas can be identified by the size of the circles, cf. Fig. 4.7) and thus competes in particular with Company A and Company B.

Unfortunately, such differentiation opportunities cannot always be uncovered with the analyses described. In fact, the search for a previously unoccupied positioning option which also creates a fit with core customer needs is very often fruitless since several suppliers are competing for existing customer potential in the relevant motive fields. However, if an opportunity for differentiation arises and it is not recognized and exploited, this would be associated with major economic success.

In most cases, however, where multiple vendors focus on the same motive field, more consistent Orchestration will determine who has a monopoly in the minds of their customers, turning more customers into Fans.

4.1 Positioning

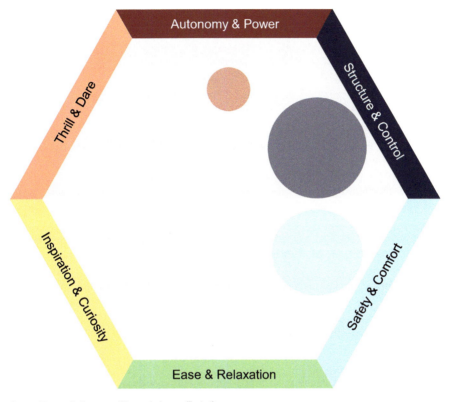

Source: Communicative competitive analysis, own illustration

Fig. 4.7 Example of communicative competitive analysis II: Example company X currently positions itself in the motive segments "Structure & Control" and "Safety & Security"

Sound Analyses and Information Are the Basis for a Secure Positioning Decision

1. The customer survey serves to identify core needs as well as the highly relevant touchpoints. Key analysis tools are the *Fan Traffic Signal* and the *Touchpoint Traffic Signal*. With the *Fan Traffic Signal,* we identify the central loyalty-drivers as well as the degree of fit and differentiation from the competition. With the *Touchpoint Traffic Signal, we determine* the highly relevant touchpoints.
2. Based on the loyalty-drivers, the *"Motiversum"* enables us to identify the core motives in which customer needs are located. This enables us to identify behavioral patterns and corresponding needs.
3. The identity workshop with top management, the employee survey, and the customer management maturity check examine from the company's point

(continued)

of view which core needs and motivational structures can be successfully orchestrated based on the strategy, the culture, and the strengths/weaknesses profile, which potential for improvement must be tapped for this purpose, and to which customer needs the company cannot create a fit due to its framework conditions. This analysis step makes it possible to distinguish suitable from less and not at all suitable positioning options.
4. The communication analysis shows which motives are currently being communicated by competitors and identifies differentiation potential by detecting previously unoccupied fields. At the same time, it helps to identify potential competitors for positioning options that address the same customer needs.

4.1.8 Derivation of Positioning

The previous explanations have shown that sound information is necessary to make the best possible positioning decision. This implies that there are different positioning options for most companies. We will explain the reasons for this in more detail with four examples:

- **Example 1**
  Very few companies are clearly positioned. As a result, they acquire customers with different core need structures over time. We will illustrate this using the example of banking institution A, which is exclusively active in retail banking. The *Fan Traffic Signal shows a* total of four highly relevant loyalty-drivers, namely "is very competent", "is very personal", "is very modern" and "offers favorable conditions". Through the subsequent qualitative analysis, these four loyalty-drivers could be assigned to two central motive fields as shown in Figure 4.8: Thus, there are two main positioning options for this company, one in the motive field "structure & control", the other in the motive field "ease & relaxation". To put it simply, this is because in the past, in its communication and at the touchpoints of service provision, banking institution A has made it possible to experience fit in the direction of both "structure & control" and "ease & relaxation". We are therefore dealing here with an "eierlegende Wollmilchsau": an egg-laying wool-producing lactating sow (jack of all trades) or also the decathlete pattern i.e., the desire to serve several potential customer needs and thus to bind a wide variety of customer groups in the long term (cf. Sec. 3.1). The decision in favor of one of the options will therefore help this company to take a more focused approach to reach potential customers with a clear profile and at the same time save resources.

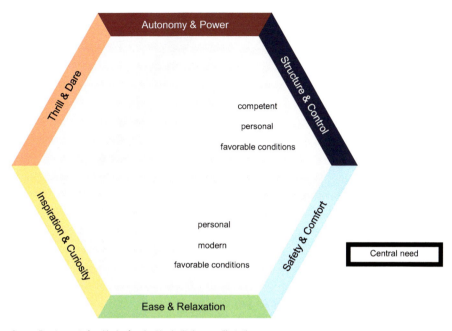

Source: Development of positioning for a banking institution, own illustration

Fig. 4.8 Location of the central needs of a banking institution in two motive segments: "Structure & Control" and "Ease & Relaxation"

- **Example 2**

  Bank A opens the door to another reason why there is often no *single* Positioning: Because even if the highly relevant loyalty-drivers could be clearly assigned to one motive field—let's assume for a moment that this is the motive field "ease & relaxation"—then it can make a big difference in terms of the prospects of success whether bank A positions itself within this motive field primarily as "modern," as "personal," or as "low-priced." A closer look at the *Fan Traffic Signal* shows that bank A is perceived in a poor light by customers when it comes to the loyalty-driver "is very personal" and thus has difficulty creating a fit there—a strong argument for not placing this loyalty-driver in the foreground in positioning. A comparison of competitors shows that there are competitors who are on a par with Bank A in terms of "is very modern", which is why a perceived differentiation could only be achieved with a great deal of effort.

- **Example 3**

  In the B2B environment, customers can be positioned in several motive fields if contacts with different needs are involved in the decision-making process. Let's look at this using Company B from the manufacturing sector. In the *Fan Traffic Signal, a* total of four company characteristics prove to be highly relevant loyalty-drivers, which could be positioned in the motive fields of "autonomy & power",

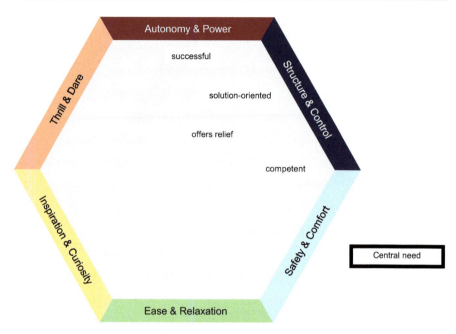

Source: Quantitative status analysis for a B2B company in the manufacturing sector, own illustration

Fig. 4.9 Location of the core needs of the customers of a company from the manufacturing sector in the *"Motiversum"*

"structure & control" and in between based on the following qualitative analysis (cf. Fig. 4.9). The result reflects the diversity of the interviewed contact persons from the client companies, who have different needs for Company B owing to their responsibilities: The managing directors opt for successful providers because this corresponds with their self-image, the purchasers primarily expect solution orientation in order to be able to work as efficiently and cost-effectively as possible, and the production manager looks for competent providers because he himself brings a high level of expertise to the table. Under these circumstances, a sound understanding of the decision-making process in the customer companies is important to be able to make the best decision for one of the positioning options. This is because, in the best case, positioning should create a sense of "fit", especially for the central decision maker.

– **Example 4**
This example opens up the view of another typical case with several positioning options: The loyalty-driver "offers relief" is so complex that it equally affects the motive fields of "autonomy & power", but also "structure & control": This means: In order to create an optimal feeling of fit with customers with this complex claim, it makes sense to emphasize certain facets in the positioning,

4.1 Positioning

for example those that go hand in hand with particular strengths or the opportunity to differentiate in the competitive environment.

Correspondingly, most companies have various options for positioning themselves. The first question is how to find these positioning options? In the logic of *FANOMICS*, the basic prerequisite for any successful positioning is the focus on a core customer need. If this is not the case, the feeling of fit and thus emotional connection can never be created. Positioning options which do not address sufficient customer potential with suitable core needs are therefore fundamentally ruled out.

We would like to explain this in more detail using the third example just described: However great the temptations may be for our example company B from the manufacturing sector to position itself in the "inspiration & curiosity" motive field because (a) the company is rated as excellent with regard to the loyalty-drivers "modern" and "creative" located in this motive field and (b) the communications analysis reveals that no competitor has yet positioned itself in this motive field and that there would therefore be a theoretical possibility of differentiation. Nevertheless, the company would fail miserably with this positioning. This is because there is simply *no* customer potential for this positioning approach. In this context, please think again of the DIY chain *Praktiker* (cf. Sect. 3.1): *Praktiker*, too, had the seemingly best conceivable starting position with its positioning on "low-price offers" and the legendary claim "20% on everything except pet food". This enabled *Praktiker* to generate a monopoly position in the minds of consumers, who believed that they were *really* buying cheaper at *Praktiker,* even though this was not true. But even if factual strengths and the clear differentiation option in the DIY market environment spoke in favor of this, *Praktiker* failed with this positioning because "low-price" is not a relevant core need of DIY customers.

So don't be tempted! Instead, focus on the core customer needs when searching for the positioning opportunities relevant to you. So, once you have (a) understood your customers' key loyalty-drivers and (b) mapped them to the underlying motive fields, you will have a clear view of the positioning options that are conceivable for you.

Once you have clarity in this regard, the next key step is to identify the most promising positioning variant among the assorted options. To do this, you now need all the information you have gathered from the customer perspective, the internal view, and the view of the competition. Figure 4.10 shows an overview of those criteria that should be considered and evaluated in the comparison of positioning options to make the best possible decision. They reflect the model idea and the definition of *FANOMICS*. We will present the seven criteria in more detail below and then illustrate the decision-making process for you using a concrete example.

1. *Target group relevance*: Positioning must be relevant to the target group(s) to be addressed. This criterion is of a rather theoretical nature, as we only subject positioning options that are highly relevant to customers to an in-depth examination. It is therefore a prerequisite. We take the necessary information regarding the loyalty-drivers from the *Fan Traffic Signal*, i.e., the customer survey. As the

Source: Own illustration

Fig. 4.10 Criteria for evaluating the positioning options

basis for a reliable assignment to *motive* segments in the "Motiversum", we draw on in-depth information from the qualitative analyses, which we use to examine the relationships between the various loyalty-drivers more intensively.

2. *Positioning Fit*: Positioning must create a fit between the actual strengths of your company and the motives of the customers, because only then can emotional loyalty develop. A look at the *Fan Traffic Signal tells* us whether this is the case. In addition to the relevance of the various company characteristics for emotional attachment, it also shows how the company is rated by customers regarding these characteristics. Only if high relevance is accompanied by a good rating is the prerequisite for the perception of fit given.

3. *Differentiation*: Here we distinguish two sub-aspects.
   a. The positioning must create a feeling of uniqueness, because only then, according to the definition of *FANOMICS*, will the monopoly position be

created in the customer's mind, which will turn him into a Fan. We also take the information required for this from the *Fan Traffic Signal*, namely the comparison of the results from the customer and the competitor customer survey. If the company differentiates itself positively from its competitors in this comparison, this requirement is also fulfilled. The *Fan Traffic Signal* then switches back to green.
   b. Positioning must enable differentiation from the competition. To assess this, we look at the result of the competitors' communications analysis. If a positioning opportunity lies in a motive field that has not yet been occupied by any relevant competitor in terms of communication, this enables differentiation from the competition.
4. *Congruence*: Here again, we distinguish between two sub-aspects. The criterion takes up the core idea of Orchestration along the customer journey and distinguishes between service delivery and communication.
   a. The positioning must be tangible in the *service delivery* at the key touchpoints. The answer is provided by the *Touchpoint Traffic Signal* for service delivery, based on the results of the customer survey. If the company is rated well by customers at the touchpoints that are of particular importance for fulfilling the positioning, the *Touchpoint traffic signal* switches to "green", i.e., the criterion of congruence is fulfilled on the performance side.
   b. The positioning must be tangible in *communication* at the key touchpoints. The *Touchpoint Traffic Signal* for communication provides us with the answer, again based on the results of the customer survey. If the communication channels that are of particular importance for fulfilling the positioning are rated well by the customers, the *Touchpoint Traffic Signal* switches to "green"—the criterion of congruence in communication would then be fulfilled. In addition, one also checks the result of the communication analysis for one's own company. This shows on which of the positioning options the communicative focus currently already lies. This information is not a substantial criterion for the decision-making process, but it does help to estimate the effort that will be required if communication is to be orchestrated following the decision-making process: The less the previous communication has paid attention to the topics relevant to positioning, the more effort it will take to realign it.
5. *Conciseness*: Of course, it is important to communicate a positioning in such a way that the benefit conveyed and thus the fit-inducing stimuli are clearly and intuitively recognized by customers. If you do not yet have a clear solution for this, a concept or name test with existing and potential customers can help secure the decision.
6. *Future Relevance*: Positioning must be fit for the future and must specify a mission. We have already pointed out that a positioning should indicate the direction in which a company wants to develop for a long period of time, since the essential power for increasing emotional loyalty lies in constant repetition. Thus, the success of strong positionings is explained precisely by the fact that they stand for the same promise for a long time and consistently, also keep this

promise again and again, and thus offer their customers a reliable identification platform. Imagine for a moment if *BMW* did not stand for "driving pleasure" for more than 50 years and reliably make this driving pleasure tangible again and again both in its performance and in its communication. Instead, *BMW* would have initially decided to rather address drivers for whom the choice of car brand is strongly driven by the motives of "autonomy & power" (like *AUDI* with "Vorsprung durch Technik"), and then serve drivers who are driven by strong pleasure/comfort motive when buying a car (like typical Mercedes drivers, for example). Certainly, the company would not be as successful. So, when deciding on one of the positioning options, you should also think about future relevance. In our experience, many companies have enough expertise to come to a resilient conclusion on their own. If you're unsure, you can research specific industry trends, such as those often presented at leading industry trade shows. Or you can talk to industry experts or relevant scientists who can help you sharpen your own impressions.

7. *Cultural Fit*: Positioning must fit the strategic orientation, culture and self-image of the company. Only then will the company succeed in creating a feeling of fit and thus increase emotional customer loyalty. In our experience, many positioning approaches fail particularly on this criterion because the corporate decision-makers either do not have sufficient reliable information or do not want to acknowledge it. Imagine, for example, a medium-sized company owner who, despite the overwhelming amount of information from the identity workshop and the employee survey, does not want to accept that the necessary willingness to look after customers "around the clock" does not exist in his workforce. However, this is precisely a key prerequisite for successfully implementing the positioning option he has prioritized. You can probably imagine the result—the positioning will fail due to a lack of cultural adequacy. So, create a sound information basis for such central decisions, and then also be open to the factually best decision.

Based on these seven criteria, a decision grid emerges that does not always allow for such unambiguous decisions as Fig. 4.11 shown: The medium-sized industrial company from the electronics sector had gone through a positioning process together with an advertising agency. Strongly communicative and creatively driven, the company decided on positioning in the motive field of "Inspiration & Curiosity," namely "Our Passion for Electronics." However, the hoped-for successes did not materialize, neither in relationship quality nor in business terms. A comprehensive stocktaking (customer survey, identity workshop, employee survey, competitors' communications analysis) explained why: Neither were the core customer needs located in the motive field of "Inspiration & Curiosity" (see in Fig. 4.11 under the heading "Target group relevance"), nor did the company succeed in creating a sense of fit among customers with this positioning. The decisive reason for this was that the cultural anchoring in the company was not given.

Based on the *Fan Traffic Signal,* the core customer needs were located in the motive field of "autonomy & power" and "structure & control". In conjunction with

4.1 Positioning

Criteria	"Our passion for electronics"	"Our expertise for energy efficiency"
1. Target group relevance	-	++
2. Fit	0	++
3. Differentiation		
a. Uniqueness	0	+
b. Communication	++	-
4. Congruence		
a. Services	-	+
b. Communication	0	0
5. Conciseness	0	+
6. Future reference	-	++
7. Cultural adequacy	0	+

++ very strongly fulfilled   + strongly fulfilled   0 more or less fulfilled   - little fulfilled

Option that performs better on the corresponding dimension

Source: Own illustration

Fig. 4.11 Success criteria for positioning alternatives using the example of an industrial company

the findings from the identity workshop and the employee survey, it was possible to build on this and develop an alternative positioning option with the working title "Our Competence for Energy Efficiency," which created a much better fit and was already highly tangible for customers (see in Fig. 4.11 the criterion 4a. "Congruence/Performance"). The high level of cultural competence could be identified as a major cause of this: The company, which is dominated by engineers, has always defined itself in terms of high competence and a pronounced efficiency mindset. Since less significant criteria such as conciseness and future relevance were also clearly in favor of the alternative positioning option, the decision was not difficult. The Orchestration (see Sect. 3.2) also worked, so that clearly measurable successes were achieved: The *Fan Rate increased* by 13% within four years.

There are cases where the decision between two or more positioning options is not as clear-cut as in our case study. We would like to provide you with tips from our consulting experience for three frequently encountered constellations:

- If an option is particularly attractive from the perspective of target group relevance and differentiation, but the current fit is low, it is advisable to first work concertedly on the deficits at the performance level until the customers have a feeling of fit. Only then should the positioning be actively communicated. Do not promise anything in communication that you cannot deliver to the customer in your service provision.
- Frequently, the criterion of differentiation cannot be met for any of the positioning options. This is because the relevant motives in which substantial customer potential can be located are manageable. This is particularly true for B2B customer relationships and whenever the choice of provider is of little importance

to customers. For example, when deciding on insurance—as the word already implies—the motive of security is very powerful for many customers, so they are found in the motive field of "safety & security". Correspondingly, many of your competitors are also active in this area. However, this should not prevent you from positioning yourself there as well, as long as many other criteria speak in favor of it. The prerequisite is that you differentiate yourself in the perception of customers in the long term through consistent Orchestration (see Sect. 3.2). Since the overwhelming number of providers follow the "more is more" philosophy and do not focus consistently, the chances of this are promising, if you set yourself realistic time goals: Be patient and think of one or two success stories—for example, that of *AUDI*. There, too, the consistent focus on "Vorsprung durch Technik" and the motive field of "Autonomy & Power" addressed by it took years to take hold—but then produced the desired successes on a sustained basis.

- If management is unable to reach a decision, it has proven useful to include the market perspective in the decision-making process in the form of a potential analysis. As the name suggests, this involves determining for the competing positioning options how large the potential of suitable customers in each case actually is. For example, a car manufacturer who, taking into account all the relevant positioning options, would have equal opportunities with customers with "Safety and Power" motive would opt for the positioning option that addresses the motive that is more frequently encountered among car drivers and thus offers greater growth opportunities.

After you have gone through all these steps, you have created a central basis for successful management with *FANOMICS* by deciding on a Positioning. Ideally, your Positioning fulfills the requirements formulated at the beginning of the chapter: It is consistently aligned with the core customer needs, brings them in line with your own strengths and competencies, and creates a perceived differentiation from the competition.

Our description of the process of deriving the Positioning is ideal-typical and presupposes your willingness to invest time and resources accordingly. In our experience, one should plan at least six months for this—assuming that management is willing to make decisions. If you do not want to invest this time and resources, you can also shorten the process. In the final analysis, you can make all the necessary decisions in management even without comprehensive analyses if you are certain that you know exactly about customer needs, customer perceptions and your position in the competitive environment and can also assess the views of your managers and employees well. Provided this is the case, isolated positioning decisions can be made by management in a single workshop—but with a higher risk of error.

Although it has already been mentioned several times in the comments on the derivation of the Positioning, it should be stated again here in all clarity: Even if *FANOMICS* is initially aimed at existing customer relationships, its effect and the benefits of its implementation extend far beyond existing customers and make themselves felt in the acquisition of new customers.[4] This applies to Positioning: It is also of paramount importance in the development of new customers, because it creates orientation. Who has a clear and intuitively recognizable profile, wins customers not only more easily, but above all wins the correct customers—namely not new Mercenaries, which bring only short-term business, but customers, which are ready to enter long-term commitments. After all, only when the customer's decision made in favor of a new provider proves to be correct, because they get exactly what they were looking for, does the investment in customer acquisition pay off. After all, this customer is not a "flash in the pan," but remains loyal.

Finally, we would like to look at another level of impact of successful positioning, namely the dovetailing of customer and employee perspectives. The positive effect of positioning also becomes clear when we look at the company, and we would like to emphasize two aspects in particular at this point[5]:

- The first aspect describes the effect of Positioning on employee motivation. We have already mentioned several times the resource-saving effect of questioning the benefits of new and ongoing projects, instruments and measures for positioning and not starting or discontinuing them in the first place. This consistent "more yes to no" philosophy saves money and conserves employee resources. It is immediately obvious that employees who can concentrate on the essentials as a result are more motivated—with positive effects on emotional customer loyalty. Let us illustrate this with an example: Let's assume that the telephone service center of a mail order company had previously formulated 20 criteria based on which the quality of telephone calls with customers was evaluated. The telephone calls are orders, and the average duration of the call is five minutes. How well do you think employees will be able to focus on core customer needs if, on the one hand, they don't know them and, on the other hand, they have to meet 20 quality criteria formulated far away from customer needs instead? And what effect will it have on the motivation of the service center employees and on the contact satisfaction of the ordering customers if these employees know the essential needs of the customers and concentrate on these, instead of drumming through meaningless quality specifications (such as calling the customer's name several times) empty of content?
- The second aspect particularly concerns large, internationally positioned companies, because Positioning creates clear and binding orientation for further (international) growth. This is of decisive importance not only regarding corporate culture, but also for the increasingly global customer markets: How is the identity of a supplier to be clearly recognizable for a customer if he experiences something completely different in the business relationship with the German subsidiary than with the headquarters in the USA?

---

[4] For information on the use of FANOMICS in new customer business, cf. Sect. 5.2.
[5] For a comprehensive discussion of interactions, see Sect. 4.3.

4.2 Orchestration

Fans want, indeed they need, repetition: they want to experience over and over again what once made them fans. That is the nectar of every fan relationship. Just recall some of the examples we presented at the beginning: From Leonard Nimoy, who could never discontinue the role of *Mr. Spock,* to *Udo Jürgens,* who could not leave the stage without the encore in his bathrobe. To *Neil Young,* who finds himself condemned to play "Heart of Gold" over and over again (cf. Sect. 1.2). They are not only stars—they are also "hostages" to their fans. The latter's demand for repetition of the fan experience forces the stars to deliver this repetitiveness—that is, to be what corresponds to the image of the star in the fan's mind at every point of contact with the Fan. And only to those stars who deliver this call for repetition do fans swear eternal loyalty—since only they seem not to betray the values they share. "Repeatability" is therefore the central mechanism with which stars bind their fans—and the instrument with which they hold their fan community together. What is important is that this repeatability mechanism only works if the fan experience is also offered in an authentic and credible way. So, to take up the example of *The Who* once again, it is not enough just to have the image of a "guitar smasher"—you then have to actually smash guitars regularly if you want to keep the fans in line (cf. Sect. 1.2).

It is clear how this mechanism can be transferred to customer relationships: Companies that want to create and retain Fan customers must offer them this constant *repeatability.* They must convey their central messages, tailored to the customer's needs, over and over again and make it possible to experience them. Only from this will customers perceive that their provider serves their needs better than the competition. This means that companies must not only present themselves accordingly in advertising and communications but must also make this central message tangible and tangible at all points of contact that the customer has with the company. In the entire provision of services and in every form of communication. Only those who "play" the central fan message again and again at *all points of* contact offer a ritual, recurring reinforcement for the fan that they have made the right decision, and thus maintain identification with the company and its offerings.

Orchestration as *the* central mechanism *of FANOMICS* thus has three facets: First, it is about the *frequency of contact* (1), because if contacts are lost or made more difficult, this weakens the relationship base with fans; there is simply a lack of opportunities for repetition. Second, it is about the necessary *fit of* all contact experiences of customers along their customer journey, which must be orchestrated both across the board (2) and contact-specific (3). We will turn to these three facets in the following.

4.2.1 The Importance of Contact Frequency and Measures to Increase

You may object that the transfer from the Fan relationship to corporate relationships in this context was only theoretical and metaphorical—but in fact the correctness of

4.2 Orchestration

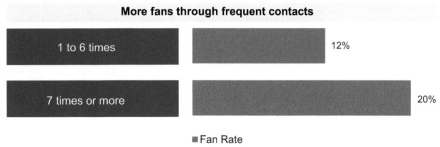

Fig. 4.12 The *Fan Rate* increases with contact frequency, since contacts enable the repeated experience of fit

the consideration that repeated matching contact experiences increase customer loyalty can be empirically proven. As one of countless examples confirming the connection derived from fan research, consider a study commissioned by a national bank. We surveyed how often customers had cross-channel business contact with the bank in the last twelve months and how this contact was evaluated. We also collected the *Fan Indicator* and overall satisfaction and were thus able to classify the customers in our *Fan Portfolio*. The results in Fig. 4.12 clearly show that the more contact experiences the customers had, the higher the *Fan Rate*. We find this correlation in virtually every customer study, knowing full well that it equally reflects the fans' increased need for contact with their provider and is an expression of the emotionalizing effect of repeat contact.

This realization poses great challenges for companies, but also offers equally great opportunities. This is particularly true for companies in industries where contacts are rarely initiated by customers, such as the electricity industry, insurance companies and banks, IT companies, and health insurance companies. What all these industries have in common is that most customers are not particularly involved, and customers usually only seek contact on an ad hoc basis. Here, companies need active contact strategies with relevant content; purely promotional contacts or contacts that do not generate any concrete benefit for customers quickly lead to so-called wear-out effects (Craig et al. 1976; Blair 1988; Bass et al. 2007), that is, to rejection reactions that make it increasingly difficult or impossible to establish contact and thus damage emotional customer loyalty more than they strengthen it.

The fact that contact strategies with relevant content are worthwhile can be explained by using the example of a governmental health insurance company. To do this, one must know that the most attractive target groups of health insurance companies are the young, healthy, and working members who pay premiums and either make no or hardly any use of services. For these members, health insurers are viewed as "a necessary evil" that costs unnecessary expenditures and provides little benefit. The mercenaries' share and fluctuation are correspondingly high; especially since comparison portals have made it much easier to change health insurers, which

Per n=1,000	Initial measurement	Impact measurement		Profitability calculation		
	Fan Rate	Fan Rate	Termination-quote	Effort/customer	Benefit/customer	Δ
Group 1	20%	25%	12%	5€	7€	2€
Group 2	20%	30%	10%	10€	9€	-1€
Group 3	20%	35%	8%	15€	21€	6€
Group 4	20%	45%	5%	30€	28€	-2€
Control group	20%	20%	15%	0€	0€	0€

Source: 2HMforum. customer comissioned research for a health insurance company

Fig. 4.13 Optimization of support concepts in the multi-channel by measuring the *Fan Rate* and the profitability

used to be a time-consuming process. The governmental health insurer in our example has set up a contact concept for this economically particularly attractive customer group and actively contacted them twice a year—adapted to their respective circumstances. In the process, suitable offers relating to wellness, fitness and prevention were placed or "simply" information about corresponding topics was provided. The appropriate topics were determined in advance as part of target group surveys.[6] As a result, this measure almost doubled the *Fan Rate* compared to a control group without corresponding "holding contacts" and halved the proportion of cancellations in this target group. In terms of the cost-benefit ratio, this approach, which at first glance appears to be quite costly, proved to be highly efficient due to the enormous leverage.

In another example—also for a health insurance company—various contact topics and strategies involving a wide variety of contact channels, some of them digital, were specifically examined in terms of their cost-benefit ratio (cf. Fig. 4.13). As a basis for decision-making, the increase in the *Fan Rate* and the churn rates within the groups were measured for a total of four different campaigns and a control group that did not participate in any of the campaigns as part of an initial measurement before the campaign start and an impact measurement at the end of the campaign. It is true that Campaign 4 proved to be the most effective because it resulted in the largest increase in *Fan Rate* as well as the lowest churn rate. However, when comparing effort and benefit per customer, campaign 3 generated the highest

---

[6] Cf. also Sect. 4.2, which shows how the needs-based design of offers and services works within the framework of FANOMICS.

4.2 Orchestration

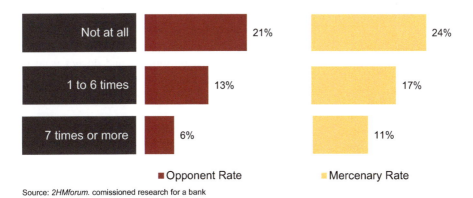

Fig. 4.14 Failure to experience fit due to insufficient contact frequency increases Opponent and Mercenary Rates

contribution margin and thus proved to be the most efficient. Campaign 3 was consequently applied to all customers. Despite what at first glance appears to be considerable effort, such approaches are very well suited to spreading the right topics in the right dosage and via the right channels without unnecessarily wasting resources.

Excursus: Lessons from the Corona Era: The Impact of Contact Bans and Restrictions

The Corona crisis made the relationship between contact frequency and emotional commitment particularly explosive: as a result, customer potential has been redistributed in dimensions never experienced before. As a result of the contact bans and restrictions, customers no longer buy or buy less frequently, and they use services less frequently. This weakens the basis of the relationship with the customer because there are simply no opportunities for the all-important repeat business. The fact that these theoretical considerations are also empirically well-founded can be seen in turn from the commissioned study for a bank customer cited earlier: The fewer contacts customers have, the greater the proportion of Opponents and Mercenaries, i.e., customers with a low level of emotional attachment (cf. Fig. 4.14).

The learning from the Corona crisis can be applied well to all industries that generally struggle with low contact frequencies: Companies can cushion the negative impact on customer relationships by developing and implementing multi-channel concepts. Digital channels are also very well suited to maintaining the necessary contact frequency. Prerequisite: The messages are relevant and establish the necessary fit with the core customer needs. The whole thing has a nice side-effect: done well and orchestrated with the other channels, companies save resources by using digital channels compared to cost-intensive personal contacts. In general, and in detail, we address the topic of how digital channels can be used to increase the *Fan Rate* in Sect. 4.3.

The Cross-Touchpoint Orchestration Process
The underlying basis for a promising orchestration process is a current positioning, whether from a systematic derivation within the framework of *FANOMICS* or from some other source. If you do not have a formal positioning and do not want to develop one, you will at least need well-founded insights into the central loyalty-drivers that you have taken from the *Fan Traffic Signal for the orchestration process.*

We wish to illustrate the concrete approach to Orchestration again with the *ALDI-example:* You will certainly remember that the central loyalty-driver for *ALDI customers* is "fast" (cf. Sect. 3.4). For the sake of simplicity, we will assume in the following explanations that this is the starting point for the orchestration process at *ALDI.*

The next step is about the objective of Orchestration: It always revolves around the overall tenor that is created by the coordinated interaction of all—and transferred to customer relationship management, revolving around answering the question of which coordinated measures companies can be used *across touchpoints* and in a *touchpoint-specific* manner to make the positioning promise tangible.

Many of these measures can achieve a large effect with a small outlay, i.e., they have a leverage effect. Let us first take a closer look at the cross-touchpoint levers. These levers are, on the one hand, cultural and structural framework conditions that not only have an effect at *one* touchpoint, but also influence employee behavior in a concerted manner across the entire customer journey. These can be the value mission statement, leadership principles, leadership behavior, processes, and the available infrastructure (for example, the CRM solution used). On the other hand, the skills and competencies of employees are also frequently effective starting points for Orchestration across touchpoints (cf. Fig. 4.15).

To be able to proceed as efficiently as possible, you need an inventory as well as a well-founded assessment of which of these levers offer particularly great opportunities for optimizing Orchestration in your company. We have had particularly good experience with examining a few important touchpoints more closely in regard to the positioning promise. We have identified these with the *Touchpoint traffic signal.* You remember the *ALDI example*: For the perception of *ALDI*'s speed, the checkout, the price, and the layout of the stores are particularly important.

What is the idea behind this approach? Of course, there are countless touchpoints between a company and its customers; depending on the business model, there may even be several hundred (Petifourt 2019). Ideally, Orchestration should work across all of these touchpoints, but in fact it is not purposeful to examine them all, as in our experience the main impact on the customer comes from a few. If we select the most important ones as a proxy for all of them, we can assume that the cultural and structural framework and the hurdles to Orchestration are sufficiently well captured. Thus, the basis for efficient Orchestration across all touchpoints can be developed.

4.2 Orchestration

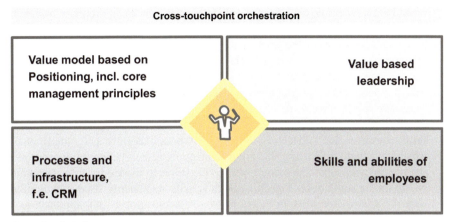

Fig. 4.15 Orchestration dimensions

Let's take the example of *ALDI and* consider what such a process might look like for the central touchpoint "checkout".

The first step is to formulate a target image for this contact point that describes what a particularly positioning-compliant experience should look like for the customer: The customer wants to leave the checkout as quickly as possible: To achieve this, on the one hand the waiting time should be as short as possible, and on the other hand the actual "checkout" including the payment process should be as quick as possible. Once this has been clarified, the next step is to ask what is preventing *ALDI from providing* the customer with this positioning-compliant experience of fast service at the checkout. In the following, we will take the waiting time as an example[7]:

- It could be too long because too few employees are on duty at *ALDI stores* and therefore too few checkouts can be opened, especially during peak hours. This would be a personnel resource and deployment planning issue.
- Another effect on waiting times is that additional checkouts are not staffed quickly enough by employees, even though they would be available in the store. Why is this the case? The answer is not trivial. Available employees may not have heard the call to open another register. This would be a classic infrastructure issue: (more) loudspeakers would need to be installed, or employees could wear headsets through which they could be reached directly. Also conceivable: The employee has heard the call but does not respond because they are busy unloading a delivery. They obviously prioritize their current activity higher than the checkout service. This could be because they are not even aware of how important it is for fulfilling the core customer needs to take over the checkout. It

---

[7] Cf. also the detailed explanation of the implementation of "fast" at *ALDI checkouts* in Sect. 3.4.

could be a new employee who has not yet been taught the appropriate basics. If so, this is a communication deficit that urgently needs to be remedied. Finally, they could be aware of the importance and still decide to finish the current job before opening another checkout. This, in turn, could be owing to a number of reasons: For example, because there is a bottleneck in deliveries due to waiting trucks, which puts the employee under pressure. In that case, the logistics processes would have to be checked. Or the employee doesn't like working at the checkout, they much prefer unloading goods, so the cause is rooted in their skills, competencies, and talents. There are two possible solutions for this, both of which have to do with leadership and organization: Either *ALDI* introduces work-sharing processes that allow employees in the stores to work only at the checkout or only in the warehouse, depending on their skills and talents. If you are familiar with the day-to-day work in the store of a discount grocer, this approach to a solution seems unrealistic. It is more likely that an employee who does not see his or her talents and abilities in working at the checkout should be encouraged to find a job other than at a discount grocery store.

– It is equally conceivable that the employee enjoys working at the checkout, but they do not see why they should interrupt their existing work just to quickly fill the checkout, even though they are aware of the relevant work instructions. We are obviously dealing with an attitude issue, i.e., a classic culture issue: it is possible that the employee observes similar behaviors in the store manager, and their disregard for the work instructions is not sanctioned either. In this case, it is a leadership issue. If, on the other hand, the store manager exemplifies the values of *ALDI-*, the question arises as to whether the employee really fits in with *ALDI*. Then we are dealing with a personnel recruiting issue. It is no coincidence that the motto "train for skills, hire for attitudes" applies.

– After all, it has an impact on waiting times if the employees at the checkouts do not "process" a customer's purchase quickly enough. On the one hand, this can also have something to do with skills and competencies, which can of course be trained, but certainly only to a certain extent. Then one must state evenly that not everyone is equally suitable for this fast conversion, as it is demanded with *ALDI* at the checkout, in order to follow the dogma of speed. And, you've probably already guessed, of course this is where the issue of friendliness at the checkout comes into play, which we have already explained in detail elsewhere (see Sect. 3.4): If *ALDI-* employees are particularly friendly at the checkout, this may imply a more positive shopping experience for individual customers, but according to generally known basic rules of interpersonal communication, it is then also understood by these customers as a call for small talk—which leads to longer waiting times for the vast majority of all other customers and thus violates the core customer needs that *ALDI-* wants to serve. If an *ALDI-* employee at the checkout is nevertheless conspicuously friendly, this can have two causes: Either they do not know better, then it is a switching problem, or they know better, but do not comply, because it does not, for example, correspond with their mentality. Then we are again dealing with an attitude problem.

All these measures, which we have derived using the highly relevant touchpoint "checkout" as an example, have a positive effect on the perception of *ALDI*'s speed across all touchpoints. We would also like to explain this briefly using a few examples:

- The lack of or incorrect staffing has implications for restocking empty shelves with fresh merchandise: for the typical *ALDI customer*, who finds grocery shopping a chore, this can mean waiting due to missing items or having to make an unnecessary additional purchase—both of which are avoidable time expenditures that result in the positioning promise not being met.
- Better communication among employees through infrastructural improvements—such as wearing a headset—also have a positive effect in escalation situations, for example, when a very specific employee or the branch manager is needed.
- Consistently communicating the importance of speed, especially to new employees, raises awareness of customer communications at all other touchpoints.
- The focus in recruitment on employees who fit in with *ALDI* and its positioning also has a positive effect on the overall customer journey. This also applies to the selection of managers who, because of their role model function, bear responsibility for the behavior of employees in the stores that is in line with the positioning.

This illustrates what we mean by the topic of Orchestration, but also how companies can implement Orchestration pragmatically and efficiently. Based on our experience, there are always relevant hurdles in companies across touchpoints that stand in the way of effective Orchestration. Focusing on measures to eliminate them creates the aforementioned leverage through enormous synergies, because they work not only at one, but at many touchpoints along the customer journey.

What is absolutely essential for successful Orchestration is a corporate management that creates the necessary conditions and is prepared to act as part of the "orchestra" itself. If, at board level, departments such as sales, service and human resources are distributed among different decision-makers (which corresponds to the reality in many companies), these decision-makers are required to synchronize their activities, speak with one voice and also, for once, assume the role of the triangle player who takes a step back and works toward his or her relevant assignment. We are aware that this cannot always be reconciled with the typical profile and self-image of top decision-makers.

4.2.2 The Touchpoint-Specific Orchestration

Owing to the significance of some touchpoints or due to the high organizational requirements for the cross-touchpoint orchestration process, it may be expedient for companies to initiate additional specific orchestration measures at the key touchpoints as an alternative or in parallel. In the touchpoint-specific orchestration process, attention is paid to all measures which, although they only take effect at the touchpoint itself and have a direct impact there, influence the overall perception and thus promote or inhibit the orchestration. The advantage is that, in the best case, only one decision-maker responsible for the touchpoint is required for implementation, and thus decisions can be made, and measures implemented quickly. The disadvantage is that with touchpoint-specific measures, aspects that can only be optimized across touchpoints are neglected and then not or only insufficiently taken care of, and the feeling of fit for the customer thus remains incomplete.

Allow us to explain this as before using the example of *ALDI* and the highly relevant touchpoint "checkout". The basis for a touchpoint-specific orchestration process is again an elaborated positioning or at least knowledge of the core customer needs. So at *ALDI, it is all about being* as fast as possible at the checkout. *ALDI* has made numerous touchpoint-specific decisions accordingly, three of which are exemplified below:

- There is no merchandise collection area at *ALDI* check out so that customers cannot "temporarily park" their purchases because this slows down the process for waiting customers. The clear requirement derived from this is therefore to design checkouts accordingly.
- Another specific influencing factor is the payment process. For a long time, *ALDI* did not allow cashless payment because transactions took too long. Today, *ALDI* offers *cashless* payment, which is so fast that it no longer creates a disadvantage compared to paying with cash.
- Special competencies of employees are particularly relevant at the checkout. For example, in the past, when scanning was not yet used, they knew the prices for all products by heart to optimize the payment process.

The list could be extended to include several other points that also contribute specifically to speeding up the checkout process for customers. Nevertheless, the question arises—a rhetorical one after the comments on the orchestration process—whether *ALDI* has done everything possible to ensure that customers can pay quickly with this bouquet of Touchpoint-specific measures alone. The answer is no, because cross-touchpoint measures also make a significant contribution. What good is the optimized payment process if the checkout is not manned because *ALDI* has failed to communicate to employees how important "speed" is for customers and that it is important under all circumstances to open another checkout as quickly as possible when the appropriate call is made?

With all cultural and structural topics, i.e., when it comes to value-oriented leadership, personnel selection and development, or communication, several decision-makers and company divisions are often involved, making decisions more difficult to make and implement. Therefore, it is purposeful, because it is pragmatic and can be implemented quickly, to start with the touchpoint-specific orchestration process. If possible, start with a highly relevant touchpoint. Why? Because measurable successes will then be achieved more quickly and effectively, not only at the

4.2.3 Management Instrument: The Follow-Up Feedback Survey

Just as for the successful positioning process, we also need resilient information for the touchpoint-specific orchestration process that helps us to identify the appropriate levers at the individual touchpoints and then to check the effectiveness of initiated measures. Now, as part of the positioning process, we have already presented to you the customer and competitor survey that generates the necessary insights, for example, to create the *Fan Traffic Signal* and the *Touchpoint Traffic Signal*. So, we have already generated information on the perception of the touchpoints with this survey. But if we need more in-depth insights on the performance at individual touchpoints to efficiently design the orchestration process, the findings from the customer survey are not yet sufficient. To illustrate this, we would like to return to a practical example from Sect. 3.1, namely that of *Deutsche Bahn* and *Deutsche Lufthansa*.

You will recall that we showed that *Deutsche Lufthansa* is perceived to be much more punctual than *Deutsche Bahn*. We substantiated this with survey results, which we would now like to discuss in more detail (Becker and Lang 2013). They come from a "classic" customer study, namely a representative survey of regular and occasional users on the punctuality and reliability of both transport companies. In terms of methodology, therefore, this study corresponds to the customer and competitor customer surveys that we used to derive the Positioning. They are characterized by the fact that they allow statements to be made about all customers, regardless of frequency of use or last use. In this general survey on punctuality and reliability, *Deutsche Bahn* falls more than 30 points behind the comparison group of *Lufthansa customers on* a 100-point scale (cf. Fig. 4.16). However, to conclude from this result alone that *Deutsche Bahn* has a more serious performance problem with punctuality than *Deutsche Lufthansa falls* short of the mark.

To illustrate this, we would like to present another alternative survey instrument: As part of our own basic research, we asked 460 customers of *Deutsche Bahn* (long-distance travelers only) and *Lufthansa* (domestic flights only) immediately after their arrival at train stations and airports, respectively—how satisfied they were with the punctuality of their trains and flights, respectively, on this *specific trip*. *This survey* technique, in which the statements do not relate to all customers but only to customers who have recently been in contact with a company, is known as follow-up feedback. The advantage of this approach is obvious: the customers' assessment reflects the service provision they have just experienced. Distorting aspects of the service perception, on the other hand—namely general prejudices about this service provision—are largely hidden at this moment. Figure 4.17 shows the result for our example: The travelers' judgments hardly differ. To air passengers, flights appear just as unpunctual as trains do to rail passengers.

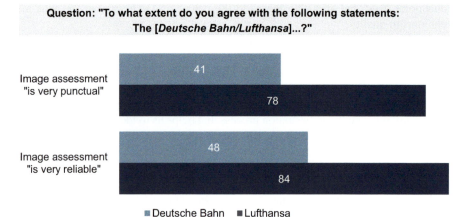

Fig. 4.16 The general assessment of punctuality and reliability is strongly influenced by brand perception: *Deutsche Bahn* lags far behind *Lufthansa*

Fig. 4.17 Only the follow-up feedback provides an unfiltered view of perceived punctuality: *Deutsche Bahn* and *Lufthansa* hardly differ

What can be concluded from this? The cause of *Deutsche Bahn*'s problem with punctuality compared to *Deutsche Lufthansa* is primarily not a performance deficit. After all, in the assessment of performance, *Deutsche Bahn does* not do well, but it is practically on a par with its flying competitor, *Lufthansa*. The causes are therefore more to be found at the level of perception: Both companies are equally punctual—or unpunctual, if you will. Nevertheless, they produce completely different perceptions among their customers. We do not want to go into the causes in more detail; we have already done that elsewhere (cf. Sect. 3.1). Rather, we are concerned here with another insight: namely, that the type of customer survey and the time of measurement influence the result and that it is therefore decisively a matter of the objective when selecting the measurement instrument.

The example of *Deutsche Bahn* and *Lufthansa* has shown that the customer's assessment, generally queried, is inevitably always influenced by brand perception. Such a query is the subject of the "classic" customer survey from the "bird's eye view", which we use in the context of deriving the positioning in order to generate general statements about core customer needs, the relationship quality and its key influencing variables. However, if a company wants to have the actual performance at key contact points evaluated from the customer perspective, this "classic" survey technique will lead to considerable distortions. This is because for the majority of customers surveyed, their last contact with the provider was some time ago. Owing to the time gap and the associated dwindling ability of the customer to remember concrete contact situations, it is difficult to obtain valid judgments about the actual service provision. However, these are central to the optimization of touchpoints.

Anyone wishing to obtain customer feedback in order to derive reliable approaches to sharpening service provision with regard to core customer needs must therefore ask customers directly at the "touchpoint". On the one hand, the ability to remember is then still very high due to the temporal proximity, which makes a very detailed query possible. On the other hand, brand influences can then be virtually ruled out.

Conversely, such follow-up feedback is not suitable for supporting the strategic orientation of the company, as the overall picture is very much shaped by the last contact to which the survey relates. If the strengths and weaknesses of the survey approaches are considered, this results in a meaningful interplay: the classic customer survey is needed to identify central loyalty-drivers and, based on these, the relevant touchpoints. The follow-up feedback takes up this information and deepens the findings as a basis for the touchpoint-specific orchestration process. This is also illustrated by the *ALDI example* (cf. Fig. 4.18): Based on the results of the classic customer study, we were able to derive the *Fan Traffic Signal* and thus identify the central loyalty-driver, namely "*ALDI* is very fast". In turn, we used this central loyalty-driver to derive the highly relevant touchpoints. At *ALDI,* the checkout proved to be the most important touchpoint for the perception of "fast." The follow-up feedback at the "checkout" touchpoint can now be used to understand the perception of performance at the checkout more precisely and to derive findings for its consistent alignment with core customer needs.

What exactly do customers rate in follow-up feedback, and why? To answer this question, let's take another look at its goals:

In terms of a successful orchestration process, we are interested in the overall evaluation of the touchpoint by customers with a concrete contact experience. We capture this through the overall satisfaction with the concretely experienced contact, as it is a performance evaluation. For successful Orchestration, it is critical that customers rate the contact at a highly relevant touchpoint with a score of "1", because only then does the feeling of fit occur. We can see this when we correlate the touchpoint rating with the *Fan Rate*. As we can see in Fig. 4.19, the *Fan Rate* of customers with a perfectly fitting contact experience far exceeds the *Fan Rate* of all

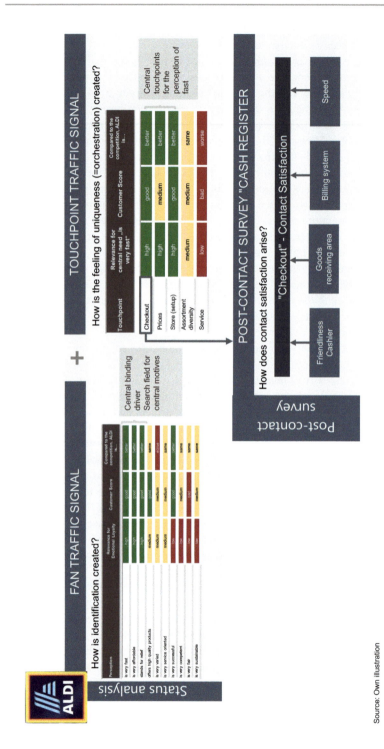

Fig. 4.18 The relationship between "Classic customer survey" (of all customers) and "Follow-up feedback" (at the relevant touchpoint immediately after contact)

Source: Own illustration

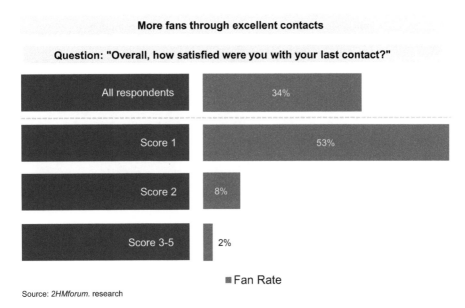

Fig. 4.19 Only the score "1" counts: When customers feel a fit during a contact experience, the *Fan Rate* increases

customers—regardless of a contact experience. But even when the experience at the touchpoint is rated "2", the *Fan Rate drops* significantly below that of all customers. This means that even if a contact is rated "2" or worse, the contact has damaged the relationship quality. This finding can be replicated time and again across all studies for all companies in all industries. We have therefore decided to use the proportion of customers who rate a contact as "1" as a relevant control variable for the degree of Orchestration at a touchpoint.

Overall contact satisfaction is therefore the key parameter for understanding how well alignment with core customer needs at touchpoints is working and how measures to improve the fit over time affect customer feedback. So, measurement is best done on an ongoing (random) basis so that changes in results can be responded to quickly. Detailed information on implementation can be found in Chap. 6.

The question now arises as to how we can identify the relevant factors of this contact satisfaction to be able to work on increasing it in a touchpoint-specific, targeted, and efficient manner. A major advantage of the follow-up feedback survey is that, owing to the proximity in time between the contact experience and the survey, we can also query details to identify the relevant influencing factors.

For a more detailed understanding of the approach, let's take a look at the example of a savings bank that would like to focus even better on the personal consultation in the branch. As part of upstream workshops with the responsible employees as well as qualitative surveys of customers, we were able to identify aspects such as the customer orientation of the employees, the conduct of the

Fig. 4.20 Determining the driver effect in advisory meetings: Satisfaction is most strongly influenced by customer orientation

conversation, solution competence, accessibility/availability, and speed as potentially relevant for the evaluation of the advisory discussions. These aspects were therefore included in the follow-up feedback, "translated" to concrete customer experiences. For example, the degree of customer orientation was recorded by means of statements such as "The consultant was always friendly" or "The consultant took an interest in me".

In order to understand how important the individual aspects are, their so-called driver effect for overall satisfaction with the counseling sessions is determined (this is done mathematically by regression calculations). The result for our example of personal counseling sessions at the savings bank branch is shown in Fig. 4.20 is shown: Customer orientation turns out to be the most important driver, followed by conversational skills and solution competence. Obviously, speed, on the other hand, is less important, as this topic proves to be the least important. The results are then used for the optimization process and help to deploy resources correctly.

4.2.4 Example VIII: DiBaDu: Perfect Orchestration in Telephone Customer Contact

In our benchmark study Fanfocus Deutschland, *ING* is the market-leading bank with the highest *Fan Rate* in Germany (cf. Fig. 4.21). A finding that may surprise one or the other reader at first glance. After all, *ING is* a direct bank, which means it does not have the opportunity to recharge the relationship through the personal contacts at

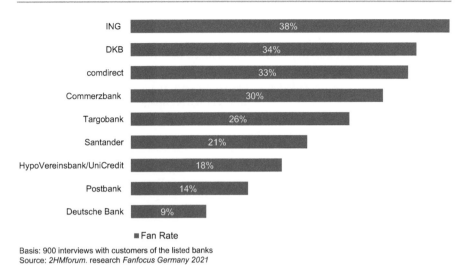

Fig. 4.21 *Fan Rates* of banks in comparison

the local branch, which are regarded as particularly emotionalizing. In addition, *ING* still has the image of being the interest rate leader, having advertised heavily with interest rate advantages, especially in the early years on the German market. And customers won over by such offers behave—to use the language of our *Fan Portfolio*—in a mercenary fashion. So apparently a difficult starting situation for turning customers into Fans.

Under these circumstances, how does *ING* achieve first place in terms of customer relationship quality among all the market-leading banks in Germany? The answer: by consistently focusing on central customer needs. In the following, we would like to explain this to you based on telephone customer care. To do this, we first want to answer the question of where the central need of *ING customers* lies, on which it is important to focus. Those who consciously decide in favor of a direct bank and thus against the advice-intensive services offered by the branches obviously do not attach much importance to personal on-site advice. Very often, these are customers who have a broad basic financial knowledge and are therefore not dependent on time-consuming and cost-intensive advisory services. They are looking for a bank that can address their concerns as quickly and easily as possible. They want to decide for themselves whether and when to contact their bank and then expect their concerns to be dealt with quickly and conclusively.

Maximum accessibility is essential to meet these customer needs. This is easy to achieve on the Internet, but what happens if a problem cannot be solved there? Then *ING is available to* its customers by telephone 365 days a year, seven days a week and 24 hours a day. But theoretical availability is one thing, factual availability is another. Well-aware of how important reliable implementation is for meeting core customer needs, *ING*'s telephone customer service has set itself high targets in this regard: it aims to answer at least 95% of calls overall—and 80% of calls within

20 seconds. *ING* has been pursuing this goal for years—because it knows that it is serving an essential customer need here.

But maximum accessibility is only one side of the coin; customers also expect their concerns to be processed quickly and conclusively. How can this be guaranteed? *ING* has concluded that the employees play a decisive role in this: they must not only have a high level of professional competence, but in particular the ability and motivation to understand and solve customer needs. The bank has drawn some astonishing conclusions from this:

1. In contrast to other banks, *ING* relies primarily on its own employees for telephone customer service and not on external call centers, even though this may entail higher costs. This is because the bank's own employees feel and convey motivation more strongly because they identify more intensively with "their" company and its goals. This motivation is felt by customers as a pronounced service orientation and has a positive effect on the perceived quality of contact and thus on emotional customer loyalty.
2. In line with the motto "Train for skills, hire for attitudes!", the direct bank pays less attention to technical skills than to a pronounced customer-oriented attitude when selecting its employees for customer service. Even the way employees are approached when recruiting on the job market conveys—as Fig. 4.22 illustrates this view. Technical competencies are then imparted to the selected employees in training courses.

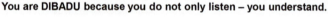

Fig. 4.22 Customer orientation as a personality trait: addressing *ING* for employee recruitment. (Courtesy of © ING AG 2014. All Rights Reserved)

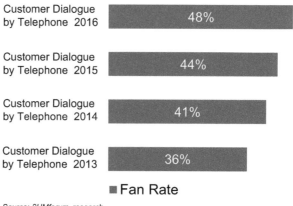

Fig. 4.23 Result of consistent Touchpoint-specific Orchestration: Increase in *Fan Rate* over time

3. Since the final processing is crucial for the customers, *ING* refrains from any productivity-oriented sanctioning. In other words, there are no specifications as to how many calls an employee must make within a given time window or how long a call may take on average.
4. Instead, the target systems and training measures are consistently geared to what really counts in the end, namely the customer's perception. Regular customer feedback is the prerequisite here. In other words, training modules and evaluation tools are not created based on theory, but based on the customers' assessment of the conversations and sound analyses that determine what influences the customers' assessment.

These findings and their implementation are a process that takes years and is continuously reviewed and readjusted by follow-up feedback. The fact that considerable success is achieved with so much consistency can be seen in Fig. 4.23. The *Fan Rate* among callers to *ING's* telephone customer advisory service is shown. The proportion increased by 12 percentage points between 2013 and 2016—the period when the above measures were introduced—and so did the value through the telephone customer dialog.

4.2.5 Orchestration of Individual Touchpoints

In this section, we will now take a closer look at the Orchestration process at those touchpoints which prove to be highly relevant in many companies and industries:

1. Experience has shown that designing a product or service offering to meet customer needs is a major challenge for many companies. On the other hand, this touchpoint offers enormous opportunities to save resources by consistently focusing on customer needs. After all, it is rarely the breadth of the offering that creates the fit for customers. On the contrary, an excessive range of products is

often not only immensely expensive in development, production, and warehousing and difficult to communicate to sales, but is also not desired by the customer at all. Therefore, in the following chapter, we want to give you concrete advice on how to realize a needs-based offer—and how this approach can be transferred to other touchpoints, such as the optimization of the website as well as the communication content.
2. Great overarching potential is also offered by optimizing prices. A key finding is that many companies do not consistently skim off customers' willingness to pay prices because they allow themselves to be strongly influenced by the screaming minority of Mercenaries when setting prices and do not consistently link and communicate prices with the central customer benefit. We also want to provide you with an overview of how direct effects on corporate success can be achieved by optimizing pricing.
3. Even though *FANOMICS* aims to turn highly satisfied customers into fans, the *Fan Portfolio* also identifies a group of customers who are (still) emotionally loyal but (currently) not satisfied, namely the Captives. As a rule, these are fans who, however, have been disappointed on the performance side and have therefore become dissatisfied. Accordingly, this type can very often be traced back to inadequate complaint management. The same applies to Opponent customers: Although the situation is more complex, since Opponents are not emotionally loyal, complaint management also plays a role in the development of Opponents. Therefore, this touchpoint also deserves a closer look.
4. Many companies consider the degree of innovation of their products and services to be a key driver of customer satisfaction and loyalty. However, if innovations are used and communicated incorrectly, they can significantly disrupt the customer's experience of fit and even lead to churn. We will also explain why this is the case and how innovations can be used in a targeted manner to increase the feeling of fit in a separate section.
5. Finally, we want to address a topic that has become a central challenge for most companies at the latest as a result of the Corona crisis, namely digitalization. In doing so, we want to explore the central question of whether and how contacts via digital channels also contribute to increasing emotional loyalty.

4.2.6 Touchpoint I: Demand-Oriented Offers and Services

Offers and Services as a Relevant Point of Contact

The needs-based design of a company's offers and services is of foremost importance, as this is usually a central touchpoint of companies with their customers. In the narrower sense, offers and services refer to the products and services of a company, which are also the initial focus of the following explanations.[8] The design of needs-

---

[8] In a broader sense, however, offerings and services also include other output that is useful to customers, such as information and/or communication. An outlook on this will be taken up in this section.

based products and services ensures that companies can experience their core promise at this touchpoint. Nevertheless, many companies tend to obscure the view of those offers and services that are linked to the core promise by an exuberant "more is more" of accompanying offers, in the sense of: "The customer will already find the right services for him. " What the right offers, and services are for the customer is for the company to decide, based on what it knows about the core customer needs. Anything else leads to a dilution of the corporate image and thus prevents the monopoly position in the minds of customers and thus the exploitation of potential.

The Wild Growth and Its Causes
Time and again, our studies show that portfolios of offerings and services are not consistently designed to meet needs. In many companies, service portfolios have historically grown considerably. In many cases, the reason for this is an increasing differentiation of products and services over time with the aim of (1) picking up on trends and thus wanting to exploit market opportunities without reflection, (2) wanting to achieve growth by winning new customers in fragmented markets, (3) wanting to conceal uncertainty about the true needs of customers by offering a wide variety of products and services, and/or (4) wanting to serve customer segments with lower customer value. This development is additionally fueled when a company has free capacities. In other words, an inflated portfolio is often the result of chasing opportunities and thereby betraying its own values.

This phenomenon is even more common in times of economic success. Thus, many companies offer a large quantity of products and services to win every customer and keep them in the life cycle. This also makes sense from the point of view of short-term growth and stability through customer diversification—however, this approach falls short: Not only do customer relationships generated in this way often not bring stability. They are also bought at a high price, namely in the sense of investments that are not placed in line with requirements. And many managers shy away from (regular) streamlining of such historically grown portfolios, as the fear of losing individual customers to the competition is too great. So, what is well-intentioned quickly becomes "too much" and prevents the necessary needs-based alignment of offerings and services—and thus sustainable corporate success.

Negative Consequences for the Company
While it is questionable whether an overflowing portfolio of offerings and services on the market has any kind of positive effects, the flip-side is indisputable: it has immediate negative effects for the company. For example, an increasing number of offerings and services is always associated with an increase in complexity costs. If you understand complexity as the opposite of simplicity, you quickly arrive at a low level of manageability, controllability, and plannability. The fact that this has a detrimental effect on employees in terms of time and psychology is in no way surprising. Managing a large portfolio, for example, is a challenge for employees, starting with requirements analyses, development and production of product variants and extending to marketing and sales. As we will show, for sales in particular, as the

interface to the customer, a large variety is often more of a burden than a blessing if the core customer need is not recognizable as a bracket for possible sales arguments. And managers are faced with the thankless task of having to master or coordinate this complexity in addition to all the other challenges. Corresponding reflexively created structures and processes to supposedly cope with the situation then make it even more complex in many cases. For example, extensive documentation is created for all products, some of which must also be continuously maintained by the employees to give them back the feeling of control that they first lost due to the over-complexity.

But even detached from the consequences for the everyday work of employees, a move away from more offerings and services is advisable: With increasing product diversification, the batch sizes of each individual variant or of the parts decrease, so that economies of scale are lost. Or service providers need more staff to bring expertise in-house for additional services. Ultimately, product diversification quickly results in degressive revenue growth with disproportionate cost increases, so the economic success of expanding the portfolio of products and services should always be examined. The example of *Märklin*, the market leader among European model train manufacturers, which went into insolvency in 2009, precisely shows this effect as the cause of the company's difficulties. *Märklin* rolled out its product range more and more, the catalog eventually comprised over 500 pages—to serve the collectors, male buyers from the age of 40 upwards. Customer growth, on the other hand, was not on the cards, nor was it a central strategic goal. As a result, the products cannibalized each other on a large scale, because the new products were not bought in addition, but the demand for the previous products merely shifted to far more products. Sales thus remained the same, but costs rose: This is because *Märklin* had to fill its warehouses with a variety of parts to be able to manufacture the individual variants. The small batch sizes for the many end products had significant consequences: More effort for development, production and sales, economies of scale disappeared, storage costs and thus capital commitment increased. This development threatens many companies that fill their portfolio of offerings and services purely on the basis of products and innovations without paying attention to customers and potential demand.

Negative Consequences for Customers
Even the (potential) customers are not left unscathed by an excessive range of products and services. Essentially, two aspects can be named that are problematic and torpedo the "customers to Fans" approach:

1. For Fan Customers specifically, an arbitrary "more" is not desirable at all: because this ultimately dilutes the core of why customers are ardent supporters of the company in the first place. In the medium to long term, even a strong customer relationship erodes if offers and services are not clearly and obviously related to the central need due to their design. As a result, fan customers gradually question whether the provider is still their true home, the one that creates the fit. For example, the German consumer goods company *Beiersdorf,* with its Nivea

brand that has been in business since 1905, was able to experience what a deviation from the brand's core values by introducing complementary products can mean. The Nivea brand, with its core product, the cream in the familiar flat blue can, is in the field of skin-care cosmetics. The brand's basic promises are naturalness/looking natural, care and mildness. In search of growth options, the decorative cosmetics market appeared attractive to the company in the 1990s. The trend toward naturalness in the decorative cosmetics market at the time, reflected in classic, natural colors, and subtle makeup, encouraged the decision-makers at *Beiersdorf* to introduce a complementary product line under the Nivea brand in 1998. A sub-brand was created under the name Nivea Beauté. The aim was for the new line to benefit from the positive image of the parent brand, which is characterized by care, naturalness, quality, trust and a rather modest appearance. At the same time, the parent brand Nivea was to be protected from possible negative repercussions by using a subsidiary brand. Initially, business went quite well, but sometime after the launch of Nivea Beauté, the market continued to evolve, "Looking natural" gradually lost ground in the color cosmetics market, and the products could not continue to be successfully marketed via the care aspect. As a result, the Nivea Beauté brand kept picking up on current trends in the market, creating such a diffuse image that the brand essence and thus the core promise of the parent brand were in danger of being diluted. To protect the parent brand from further damage, namely the disappointment of its core clientele, the Nivea Beauté line was finally withdrawn from the market in 2010.

2. An overflowing service portfolio—irrespective of the lack of a content bracket—also results in complexity costs for customers. They quickly lose track of what they are looking for, which leads to frustration and ultimately to an erosion of emotional loyalty. If, on the other hand, the customer gets involved in the multitude of services and offers, then he faces an even greater challenge in his decision-making behavior. So, in the end, the large offer does not lead to great joy, but to gigantic disappointment. Because of the sheer mass, the decision for and against individual offers and services can no longer be made with sufficient certainty and without regret—which often ends in a non-purchase. At first glance, this sounds somewhat counter-intuitive, as the idea of sheer unlimited choice seems quite tempting. But companies and customers alike often underestimate the effort it takes to choose from a wider range of offers.

A field study by the psychologists Iyengar S and Lepper M (2000) dealt with the so-called selection paradox: Using the example of a selection of jam varieties, they showed that an increasingly large assortment has a demotivating effect with regard to purchasing. For this purpose, customers of a supermarket were presented with different numbers of jam varieties on different days: 24 and 6 choices. With the large selection, about 60% of the customers considered showed interest in the products, but only 3% of the customers expressed an intention to buy. In the smaller selection of six varieties, the proportion of interested parties was lower than in the large selection, at about 40%, but ultimately 30% of customers also bought a jar of jam.

How *ALDI*-Does It
Let's take up our *ALDI example* again—because the company shows along the touchpoint "offers and services" that it has understood exactly the problem just described. The company consistently considers "speed" as a central promise in the design of its product range and thus also avoids the challenges of a loss of time resulting from diversification, which is counterproductive in terms of the core customer needs. The company's philosophy states that *ALDI* focuses on the essentials and has set itself the task of offering only products that provide consumers with the greatest possible benefit (needs-based approach). In its concentrated product range, *ALDI-Süd* sells around 1600 basic items. And in the definition of its rational sales system, *ALDI-Süd* describes its requirements for the presentation of products as "clearly laid out" and "identical in every store." This, it says, is intended to keep search costs down for its customers. Dieter Brandes, ex-managing director of *ALDI*, stated the following in an interview: "Above all, complexity is to be avoided. [...] At Aldi it is called [...]: Avoid superfluous things" (Langer 2004).

The Reference to FANOMICS
By focusing on core customer needs, the management of a company according to the basic rules of *FANOMICS* offers the possibility of selecting the essential, i.e., needs-based, components from among the possible offers and services. Companies usually approach this target state from two different directions:

1. The product portfolio is not sufficiently developed to create a sense of fit for customers, and further services are needed. In this case, the initial focus is on the development of offerings and services, in which the group of fans should play a constructive role (cf. Sect. 2.1). The services developed in this way must then be examined to determine whether they meet the needs in the context of the overall portfolio, i.e., the existing services and offerings.
2. The portfolio is to be thinned out so that companies can make enormous savings by not offering more—combined with the possibility of being able to deploy resources in much more beneficial places in order to be able to increase emotional loyalty among customers. For those responsible, it is particularly important to be able to make decisions about streamlining the portfolio with a high degree of certainty. Consequently, reliable information is required about which offers and services are particularly important against the background of core customer needs or as "hygiene factors". Hygiene factors refer to offers and services whose absence may lead to migration, but whose existence in turn is not a driver of fan loyalty (cf. Herzberg 1959; Matzler and Bailom 2004). We explain more about this later in this section. With a consistent orientation of the offer design based on the *Fan Portfolio* and the core customer needs, companies thus implicitly ensure that they say *yes* to the "right" services and *no* to the "wrong" ones.

Problems in Determining Needs-Based Offers and Services
Now, differentiating among needs-based and thus more or less preferred offers and services by customers is anything but trivial. Decision-makers try to do this time and

again based on objective criteria, such as sales figures. The knowledge about which offers and services were used to what extent should then enable a reliable statement about customer preferences. However, individual offers and services are not claimed by certain customers for many reasons (personal, situational, financial, technological), even if there is a clear preference for them. For example, the German car manufacturer *Mercedes-Benz* works with its brand promise "The Best" and decided to revive the Maybach product brand for this reason, among others: as a premium product above the S-Class. The products are marketed profitably, but the market share in the relevant target group is extremely low. Nevertheless, the product plays an important role in credibly communicating the brand promise and conveying the claim to leadership in the premium automotive sector—even and especially to customers who buy the manufacturer's cheaper product lines. Consequently, surveying customers is still the most valid instrument for determining the offers and services that meet their needs. But how do you get differentiated statements from customers during a survey about what is more important and therefore more in line with their needs than others? Caution is indeed called for here: The classic scale-based survey, which asks for agreement with regard to the importance or liking of various offers and services, ultimately leads to an inflation of wishes and importance. The respondents then usually mark all the listed offers or services as important. If a company were to orient itself to such results, it would in turn become the much-cited eierlegende Wollmilchsau (egg-laying wool producing lactating sow)—which it does not want to be.

Decision-Based Method for Preference Measurement as a Solution
Decision-based methods should be used to answer this question. Customers are presented with real decisions as part of a quantitative survey. The aim is for the respondents to select the most important and least important alternatives from several presented, thus making a real trade-off. This then results in valid preference profiles of customers, which indicate the differentiation in product perception that is actually present on the market along the lines of utility. These methods allow preferences to be determined not only for the aggregate of all respondents, but also for individual customers. This trade-off procedure is particularly important for Fans, as this customer group is characterized by the fact that it tends to consider all the services offered by its provider. On this basis, it is then possible to derive how relevant individual services in the portfolio are compared to other services.

Application Taking into Account the Perceived Fit
If a portfolio of offers and services can and must actually be thinned out in the sense of Orchestration, two aspects are relevant for the decision on the central offers and services to continue to be offered, namely to identify those offers and services that (1) increase the perceived fit with the company and (2) prevent churn, especially among mercenary customers, for the time until the emotional bond is successfully increased. This is because Mercenaries primarily buy offers and services, while Fans buy the company or brand. Consequently, there may be offers and services that do not directly increase emotional attachment but can be regarded as a hygiene factor.

Accordingly, depending on the question, it makes sense to look at the specific offer and service preferences of the segments from the *Fan Portfolio*. The Fan Customers are of particular importance here since they have maximum fit and can make well-founded statements with their extensive knowledge of the company and its services.

If the importance that Fan Customers attach to components of a provider's offer should be identified—since they create a high level of fit at this touchpoint—decision-based methods must be applied. This applies in general to the determination of individual and/or group-specific preferences.[9] We will illustrate how this works and what results it leads to using the example of a hotel chain. This chain sees itself as a "budget design brand". In 2000, it was still strongly oriented towards the competition, operated hotels in peripheral locations and offered an interchangeable product with which it wanted to be successful through price. But the company gradually emancipated itself from the original budget approach by understanding the key needs of today's fan clientele better and better and consistently taking this into account in its implementation. In the course of this, the provider shifted its locations to the vicinity of city centers and primarily served German cities and European metropolises. The success speaks for itself: in the meantime, the company has increased its sales tenfold. But what exactly did the hotel chain do in terms of needs-based offerings? The company focused its offers on the essentials and not much more, consistently and to this day putting the central value driver "design" in the foreground. The results of a decision-based process for uncovering fan customers' preferences, in this case a MaxDiff analysis, brought to light the relevant offer specifications for experiencing the core customer needs. The results then helped to focus on the essential facets and selectively trim less relevant aspects of the service package.

It can be intuitively seen (cf. Fig. 4.24) that for Fan Customers, the brand essence of "design" is in the forefront and must be made tangible in the perception of the product. In addition, Fan customers are concerned with the location in the urban environment and thus with the immediate "downtown" immersion after leaving the hotel. In contrast, the size of the breakfast buffet or the room amenities are not relevant to Fan Customers. And that is how every visitor knows it: Compared to other hotels, the breakfast buffet is rather spartan. Even having breakfast in the lounge takes some getting used to for some visitors. The real Fan Customer, however, literally looks for it, the morning stay in the design environment. The rooms are also sparsely equipped. For example, guests will look in vain for a coffee machine, and there is no minibar in the rooms either. However, this is of no importance to the Fan Customers. They are looking for the evening experience in the urban and design-oriented lounge with integrated bar.

---

[9]A regression-based method is not an option here for methodological reasons. This is used, for example, to identify the really important ones for the experience of the core customer needs for all customers across all touchpoints.

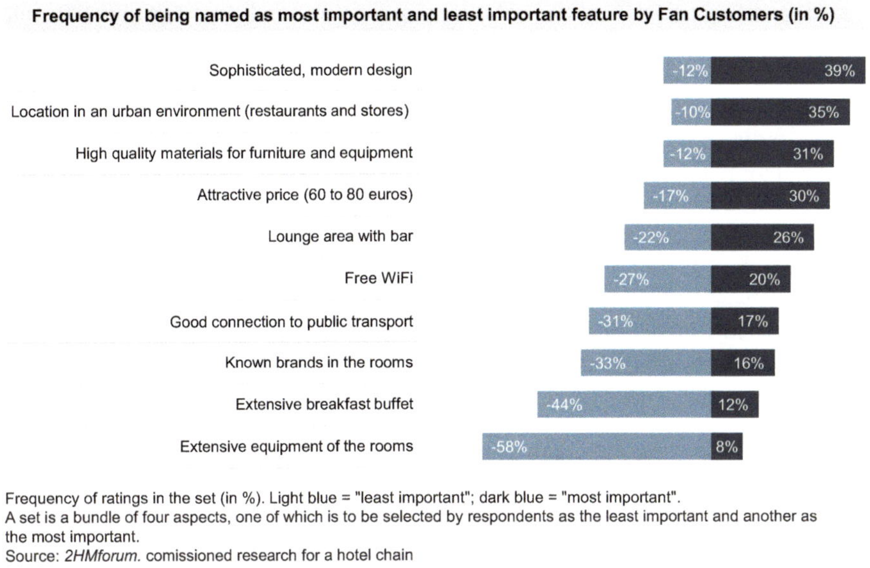

4.2 Orchestration

Frequency of being named as most important and least important feature by Fan Customers (in %)

Feature	Least important	Most important
Sophisticated, modern design	-12%	39%
Location in an urban environment (restaurants and stores)	-10%	35%
High quality materials for furniture and equipment	-12%	31%
Attractive price (60 to 80 euros)	-17%	30%
Lounge area with bar	-22%	26%
Free WiFi	-27%	20%
Good connection to public transport	-31%	17%
Known brands in the rooms	-33%	16%
Extensive breakfast buffet	-44%	12%
Extensive equipment of the rooms	-58%	8%

Frequency of ratings in the set (in %). Light blue = "least important"; dark blue = "most important".
A set is a bundle of four aspects, one of which is to be selected by respondents as the least important and another as the most important.
Source: *2HMforum.* comissioned research for a hotel chain

Fig. 4.24 Identifying relevant hotel chain supply specifications for experiencing core customer needs

Applicability to Other Marketing Tools

A needs-based portfolio of offers and services pays off on core customer needs and is thus a valuable lever for developing customers into Fans and keeps customers from other segments, such as the Mercenaries, throughout the lifecycle. It does so while conserving resources. As a result, this approach increases company return on investment and frees up financial resources to ensure a fully orchestrated customer journey.

4.2.7 Touchpoint II: Prices in Line with Demand

Status Quo

When optimizing their offers and services, companies must inevitably also think about the consideration paid by the customer: As a rule, this is the price to be paid. In practice, we see the following picture time and time again: when setting prices, companies focus on particularly price-sensitive segments—often on the screaming minority of Mercenaries. In fact, price is the only marketing instrument that has a direct impact—which makes many a decision-maker weak. However, the opposite position to "As cheap as possible!" is "What costs nothing is worth nothing!" And it is precisely this credo that is shared above all by convinced customer segments such as Fans and Sympathizers, who therefore have a different view of the price—namely, they never see it in isolation from the "fit" of the products or services. Undoubtedly, many of these customers also look at the price—but it is less a question of "cheap" and more a question of price value and price fairness. After all, Fan Customers are ready and willing to pay an appropriate price for useful offers and services. But they don't want to be taken advantage of. Optimizing customer benefits is then—with correspondingly successful communication—directly linked to a corresponding willingness to pay a price. Customers' price perception and willingness to pay is the result of their experiences at all points of contact between the customer and the company. Consequently, successful Orchestration is highly relevant for the perceived value of products and services. Our fundamental *FANOMICS* research (cf. Sect. 2.1) shows, for example, that conditions are evaluated more positively by a large proportion of Fans and Sympathizers and that price satisfaction is significantly higher than among the other groups in the *Fan Portfolio*. The background to this is that for Fans and Sympathizers, prices and conditions are simply decoupled from the product to a considerable extent; rather, they are measured by their high fit with core customer needs. "We sell a lifestyle—the motorcycle comes free," as *Harley-Davidson* used to say (Delekat 2015).

Orientation on the Benefit for the Fans
When designing services and service portfolios, companies must primarily orient themselves to the Fan segment. Accordingly, it makes no sense for companies to let their Mercenaries dictate the prices when specifying services and service portfolios. A service that is aligned with the core need has an immediate high value for Fan customers, as the fit between customer and company is essentially manifested in the service. Consequently, Fans are also prepared to pay an *appropriate* price. The Fan's perception of the benefits is therefore decisive for pricing—the more needs-oriented offers and services are, the higher the estimated value. But how should companies deal with the fact that Fans regularly associate a higher benefit with the offers and services of their provider, which in turn leads to a higher price? This is because the prices for offers and services are higher than the willingness to pay of individual customer segments. But this is not wrong, it is correct, since the service is usually made for the fan. What is needed is an approach that enables companies to meet the benefit-based price expectations of the other segments. This is made possible by various forms of price differentiation, i.e., different ways of implementing different prices on the market:

- qualitative/performance-related price differentiation
- quantitative price differentiation
- time-based pricing
- spatial price differentiation

By thoughtfully applying these various approaches to differentiation, Fans can be offered special perks, while justifying lower prices for segments such as the Mercenaries—without taking advantage of the other groups. The Fan receives a fully customized service, provided with the appropriate and adequate price demand. For the Mercenaries, who combine the same service with a lower benefit, a modified variant can then be assembled with just a lower price (qualitative price differentiation)—but always with the view of a not overflowing variety. In order not to dilute Fans' perceptions of their brand, decision-makers should work here with differentiated (sub)brands if necessary. Lower prices can also be offered by reducing the unit price as the quantity purchased increases in accordance with a discount scale or by implementing loyalty programs (quantitative price differentiation). The price can also be reduced at certain times (time-based price differentiation) or in certain regions or sales channels (spatial price differentiation). Individual customers can then decide whether they want to accept certain inconveniences in return for a lower price.

If we think of various instruments for implementing price differentiation that we encounter repeatedly in practice, the following are among those that should be noted: Introduction of product variants, customer cards with loyalty rewards as well as coupons, vouchers, and special offers. It is crucial that the design of these instruments is consistently geared to Fan Customers, as they should be the measure of all things in the customer portfolio.

1. The introduction of product variants is aimed at performance-based price differentiation. Here, it must be unmistakably clear that the service designed to satisfy the core need—and thus tailored to the Fan—is the standard. If, for example, companies want to offer a slimmed-down version for the Mercenaries, it must at least be made clear through communication that the "small" version is a good solution, but not the optimal one. This can be made clearer by using a kind of modular system: the "large" service is offered as standard with all the necessary elements, but the customer then has the option of deselecting individual elements. For example, the Fan Customer appreciates comprehensive consulting and after-sales services from his provider because he values every contact with the company. The Mercenary, on the other hand, is more price-sensitive and in many cases has no interest in contact with the provider and thus not in the service wreath just mentioned. In connection with comprehensive products and services, for example, companies work with the metaphor of the flagship. In many cases, this is also the latest product in each case, but this is by no means necessarily so. However, it immediately gives the customer the impression that they are getting the best product here. In the case of the "small" performance as standard, on the other hand, the Fan customer would have the feeling of having to upgrade their product toward the optimum for more money and would implicitly feel misunderstood for their needs.
2. Loyalty cards with loyalty rewards are an instrument that is already implicitly geared to the attitude of the Fan or Sympathizer toward its provider. This is because the Fan has a higher purchase frequency and/or purchase volume compared to the Mercenaries, for example. Consequently, the Fan also benefits more than other segments. And even if this were not the case, loyalty rewards should be designed with a clear fit in the direction of Fan Customers: for example, rewards should not primarily be accumulated bonus points that can then be redeemed as discounts on the products usually purchased. This would turn Fans into price-sensitive Mercenaries and give away valuable profit margins. Instead, the Fan

customer should benefit in that the reward gives them the opportunity to immerse themselves more fully in the world of their provider, such as exclusive news, attractive and exclusive services, access to an exclusive community, company tours or the like, if the customer has achieved an appropriate score. This idea is also reflected in the concept of the customer card of the international fashion label *ESPRIT*. The "Friends" customer card distinguishes between three levels that customers can achieve through their purchasing behavior: (1) Basic, (2) Gold, and (3) Platinum. The respective level of a customer depends on the turnover within a calendar year. While customers at level (1) receive a number of basic benefits, such as discount coupons, the higher levels offer additional emotional benefits, such as VIP shopping from the Gold level and professional style advice from *ESPRIT* employees from the Platinum level.

3. If the company decides to work with the category "coupons, vouchers and special offers", it is also crucial to orient itself towards the Fans. For example, coupons should be geared less toward increasing customers' purchase quantities of products and services they have already bought in the past, but should induce cross-buying—a behavior that is closer to the Fan anyway, but also makes the Mercenaries more monetarily valuable to the company.

Pricing Methods

The basis for pricing products and for various segments is ultimately the needs-based nature or benefits of the services and offerings. But how can the price be determined on this basis? A direct query of the willingness to pay in a customer survey leads to strategic response behavior and to an underestimation of the customers' willingness to pay. Therefore, (1) multidimensional or (2) decision-based queries are suitable. Van Westendorp's Price Sensitivity Meter is a multidimensional query that does not focus on the one price a customer is willing to pay. Rather, four price points are of interest here, namely, at what price is the product "too expensive," "expensive," "cheap," and "too cheap." Price preferences can then be derived from this. The method is also advantageous when customers' ideas about the product are fuzzy or there are simply no price anchors, as is the case with innovations, for example. Decision-based methods, on the other hand, place the respondent in the situation of a choice decision.

The Gabor-Granger method and Conjoint Analysis should be mentioned here as well. When using the Gabor-Granger method, a valid derivation of a price-sales function and thus of price elasticities is possible through a series of decisions for or against individual price points. The more far-reaching variant of decision-based procedures for preference measurement is conjoint analysis. The idea of this "deconstructing" method is to present respondents with several product alternatives in the context of trade-off decisions. These alternatives are described on the basis of central characteristics and an overall price. Now the respondent has to decide again and again for one of several alternatives and also against the others. In this way, (a) price sensitivity, (b) the utility of individual product features and (c) the willingness to pay for individual product features and overall products can be determined. The starting point of the analysis is the company's Fans, since in order to optimize offers, the benefit and price perception of the central customer segment must first be understood. The remaining segments, especially Sympathizers and Mercenaries, are then examined. The findings about the Fans are then contrasted with the findings about the other segments. In this way, product characteristics that are of less importance to Mercenaries, for example, can be identified, and decisions on price adjustments for "smaller" product variants can be made. The essential "guard rail" here is the Fans' perception, as the optimal offer is to be put together for them. The price differences between the optimal and the smaller product should therefore also reflect the Fans' different perceptions of the benefits of these two products, while bringing the smaller product into the region of Mercenaries' willingness to pay in terms of price.

4.2.8 Touchpoint III: Reducing Shortfalls Through Needs-Based Complaint Management

For most companies, the primary goal is not to turn dissatisfied customers into satisfied ones, because they have already achieved this goal. They need a concept of how to emotionally bind their satisfied customers and thus turn them into customers with high customer value. This is exactly where *FANOMICS* comes in.

But this does not mean that the basic ideas of *FANOMICS* cannot also be used to turn dissatisfied customers into satisfied ones. However, the approach is fundamentally different from that of satisfaction management. It is oriented to the question of how to effectively increase customer satisfaction where it is necessary, without falling prey to the "more is more" paradigm of satisfaction management, or, to stay in the language of this book, without becoming that "eierlegende Wollmilchsau"/jack-of-all trades pig. It is not worthwhile to invest across-the-board in services that are already rated above average by customers. When implementing *FANOMICS* in the context of service provision, it is much more a matter of clearly focusing on the core customer needs—i.e., under certain circumstances, even critically reflecting on the question of whether less service is not also sufficient or whether a different design would not be more purposeful in order to strengthen the relationship quality with the customers.[10] In other words, the scope and nature of service provision are not ends in themselves, and distinct aspects of service provision do not stand side by side in isolation. Rather, the task is to orchestrate the individual aspects of service provision in such a way that, in the end, the *overall picture* is suitable for the customer in terms of his or her expectations.

Let us illustrate this again with a concrete example, and again we look at *ALDI* and the highly relevant touchpoint "checkout". If ALDI-understood *its* performance as an end in itself, and considered individual aspects in isolation instead of in its orchestrated effect, the consistent "no" to friendliness and a customer-friendly merchandise collection area would be unthinkable. Rather, one would work

---

[10]Cf. the detailed explanations on needs-based benefit design in Sect. 4.2.7.

separately and in isolation to improve individual aspects of performance. One would try to increase the friendliness of the employees at the checkout by changing staff recruitment and intensive training. By replacing or rebuilding the infrastructure, one would offer customers a merchandise collection area like at other supermarkets. But *ALDI* does not do that. Because *ALDI looks at* the individual aspects of service provision from the comprehensive perspective of the effect on relationship quality. This means that service provision is not an end in itself but becomes a means to an end. In the end, only the overall impression on the customer is what matters, and this in turn *cannot be* determined from the sum of the individual services. This example should open our eyes to what service provision—and thus customer satisfaction—is really all about in the end.

But what do we do with customers who are really dissatisfied? In this case, it is a matter of increasing satisfaction. Even if the proportion of these customers is manageable for most companies (see Sect. 1.6), we offer an effective approach for this as well within the framework of *FANOMICS*. This is because *FANOMICS* is not an approach exclusively for companies that have already reached a high level of maturity in customer relationship management but is particularly suitable for companies that are just getting started: We promise you that if you follow our advice, the investment required to increase customer satisfaction will be limited, and success will come quickly. Profit from the mistakes of others who have laboriously worked their way forward with a watering can and bought their improvements in customer satisfaction at far too high a price, in the best sense of the word. There is *only a* real need for action in the sense of a compellingly necessary improvement in performance if shortfalls occur at contact points that are highly relevant for customers. This is illustrated by two examples:

- **Example 1**
  What happens if the performance shortfall does *not* affect a highly relevant point of contact? As already explained in detail, the *ADAC* has survived the crisis about the manipulated vote on the "Yellow Angel" practically unscathed, hardly any member has turned away from the *ADAC* since the core need regarding the *ADAC* is precisely shaped by roadside assistance and not by surveys on the most popular car (cf. Sect. 3.1).
- **Example 2**
  What happens, on the other hand, if the performance shortfall does affect *one or more* highly relevant contact points? This is shown by the example of the car manufacturer *Mercedes Benz*, which had to make the opposite experience to *ADAC a* few years ago. Like no other brand, *Mercedes* stood for quality and reliability. This image was impressively reinforced by advertising campaigns in which, for example, the Mercedes-driving husband arrives home late—and apologizes with a car breakdown. What does the angry wife do? She gives him a resounding slap in the face and shouts angrily, "What? With a Mercedes?" (YouTube 2023). The quality claim of the *Mercedes* brand was so proverbially and naturally positioned in public opinion that the company could afford to write skits about this in the manner described and to flirt with the self-evidence of the

image. But then came the moose test: The new *Mercedes* A-Class tipped over during a test simulating swerving in front of an obstacle that suddenly appeared on the road, due to so-called rocking. Although this incident was not the only cause, it is fair to say that it had a lasting effect on customer loyalty. Many loyal customers turned away in disappointment. Sales figures—especially of the new A-Class—fell far short of expectations. The economic damage was enormous (Kaiser 2017). Later, it was said that comparable models from other manufacturers had failed the moose test just as badly as the *Mercedes*. But this rumor—amazingly for many—hurt sales of the competitors' models far less than it did for *Mercedes*. The reason is obvious: No other car manufacturer was positioned as sustainably on its quality promise as *Mercedes*—which is why this quality deficit hit the Swabians much harder than the competition.

We learn from these examples that performance shortfalls only really become a threat to relationship quality when they touch on customers' central needs. Companies must then take countermeasures quickly and efficiently. The essential prerequisite for this is a functioning complaints management system. Because of their high level of involvement, emotionally loyal customers will articulate their dissatisfaction if it really touches on aspects that are essential to them. This feedback from customers on performance shortcomings offers every company great opportunities in two directions: on the one hand, the company can respond individually to the complainant and even trigger positive effects in terms of relationship quality through perfect complaint handling. On the other hand, the company can identify significant performance deficits through a systematic evaluation of incoming complaints and actively take countermeasures.

What sounds so simple proves to be a major challenge for many companies in practice. As our own basis and our contracted research confirms time and again, there is no other discipline that is evaluated as critically by customers as complaint management—with fatal consequences for relationship quality (cf. Fig. 4.25): Already for customers with a complaint satisfaction rating of "3" on a grading scale from "1" for "very satisfied" to "5" for "very dissatisfied," the *Fan Rate* is significantly lower and the Opponents rate significantly higher than for customers who do not complain; and this effect is further exacerbated for complaint satisfaction ratings of "4" and "5." The result is damage to relationship quality that is often irreparable.

You may be asking yourself, what exactly is this damage? Customers, who become Opponents as a result of complaints not being handled as required, are very likely to leave sooner or later. But that is the lesser damage. Because Opponents—as their name suggests—actively work against their provider through negative word of mouth. It has long been known that dissatisfied customers pass on negative experiences to other existing and potential customers. Our studies also confirm this. This has always been a problem because it unsettles current customers and deters potential customers from purchasing. However, the potential threat has increased exponentially in the age of digitalization.

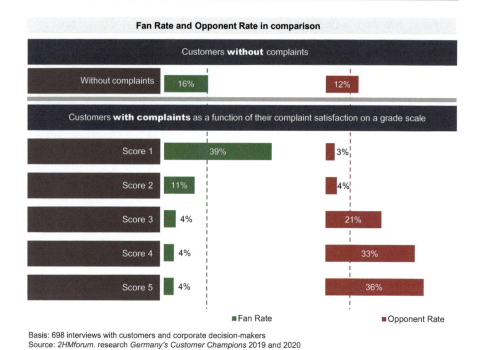

Basis: 698 interviews with customers and corporate decision-makers
Source: 2HMforum. research *Germany's Customer Champions* 2019 and 2020

Fig. 4.25 Super-GAU complaint: How Fans Become Captives or Opponents

A particularly impressive and frequently cited example of this is that of Canadian country musician David Carroll. In his song *United Breaks Guitars, he* describes how he himself had to witness the destruction of a 3500-dollar Bob Taylor guitar by rough baggage handlers during a flight with *United Airlines*—as well as the subsequent odyssey through the complaint instances at *United*—with the result that the guitar was not replaced. The refrain of the song is: *I should have flown with someone else, or gone by car, because United breaks guitars*. The video for the song was published on YouTube on July 6, 2009, and as of 05/31/2021 has been clicked over 20 million times (Youtube sonsofmaxwell 2009). It is an example of how much power a customer has in the age of social media and exactly how this power unfolds:

– It went viral on social media (by watching, sharing, and commenting on the video)
– A so-called spill-over effect took place: The classic media took notice, with virtually every renowned U.S. TV station picking up the story. This "spill-over" from the digital to the media world contributes to the further acceleration of dissemination.

4.2 Orchestration

Fig. 4.26 Complaint satisfaction of complainants is very low

- In the end, United even reacted, but much too late, because significant negative effects on the stock price had occurred, not to mention the damage to its image (Kupillas 2009).

Examples like this are repeated all the time. They show how dangerous it is when companies do not align their complaint management to meet needs. Now you might think that this only affects a small minority of complaints, since companies have their complaint management under control. Far from it! In our fundamental research (cf. Fig. 4.26), 45% of customers say they are not satisfied with complaint handling (this corresponds to grades 3 to 5).

There are numerous reasons for this, but the causes are by no means exclusively anchored in the product, as is commonly assumed. Figure 4.28 shows that around half of the complaints are attributable to shortfalls in logistics, service, or information and communication. This means that complaint situations can occur at a wide variety of touchpoints in the value chain, but practically represent a separate touchpoint with very specific requirements. Thus, in many companies, it has proven expedient to bundle complaint handling to enable an equally needs-based and efficient approach. There are three reasons for this: First, the necessary high level of commitment for the customer in a complaint situation can only be ensured by a central contact person who, as the customer's advocate in the company, brings about a need-based and binding solution. Secondly, it is only through centralization that information can be bundled and systematically evaluated and thus learning effects can be achieved. The third argument in favor of centralizing complaint management concerns the skills and type of employees who are suitable for handling complaints. Since emotionally charged situations are involved, a unique way of conducting conversations geared toward de-escalation is necessary, as well as a balancing temperament. This contradicts the talents according to which employees in sales and customer service are selected, who are otherwise the addressees of the complainants. In addition, the confrontation with subjectively perceived grievances of the customer triggers resistance especially when the customer's own performance is under discussion: This is the case, for example, when a customer complains to the service department about a lack of accessibility or competence in the processing of the complaint.

If this bundling of competencies is not possible or desired, employees with corresponding talents should be comprehensively empowered and sensitized. As end users, each of your employees is a customer several times a day. Use this background of experience to build empathy and thus enable your employees to put themselves in your customers' shoes. In addition to appropriate training measures, this also includes clearly formulated scope for action, in which cases and to what extent employees can act accommodatingly to bring about a final solution to the problem.

For your complaint management to be able to satisfy core customer needs in a focused manner, these organizational framework conditions are not enough. A complaints culture is just as necessary:

- It is not you who decides which complaints are justified or not, but the customer. For example, the "improper" use of a product or the "failure to follow instructions" are not an expression of misconduct on the part of the customer, but of communication on the part of the provider that is not in line with requirements (cf. Fig. 4.27).
- Make it easy for customers to articulate problems and shortcomings that arise. If customers have the impression that they either must go to immense lengths to report problems to their provider or that their feedback is not taken seriously, they will "vote with their feet", i.e., they will leave at the next opportunity. The great opportunity for effective deficit reduction is then lost. So, create ample

Fig. 4.27 Understanding the causes of complaints and eliminating them if possible

opportunities for customers to articulate themselves. It is important that customers who are dissatisfied with your services contact you, thus giving you a chance to respond. The proportion of these so-called complainants should be a central control parameter in the context of shortfall reduction.

If you implement this advice consistently, you will have equally sufficient and optimal access to the "horizontal movement" in the *Fan Portfolio* with a functioning complaints management: You will find out precisely where performance deficits occur and how you can systematically get to grips with them. In your efforts to increase customer satisfaction, this approach to shortfall reduction prevents you from falling into the "more is more" philosophy of classic satisfaction management, which has already been identified as problematic several times. Instead of fulfilling any customer needs in anticipatory obedience beyond what is necessary and wasting financial and human resources in the process, you pursue a strictly minimalist approach and invest only where performance shortfalls touch on your customers' core needs.

4.2.9 Touchpoint IV: Deploying Product Innovations in Line with Demand

"The main thing is that it is new" seems to be the motto of many companies when it comes to placing their innovations on the market. In the following, we would like to explain to them how you can increase the success rate of innovations through needs-based alignment.

Germany is traditionally a country full of innovators. Technology and innovation are at the heart of many companies, and there are over 180,000 companies that regularly produce innovations for the global market. Now, however, the "flop rate" for innovations is around 70%. This has nothing to do with the fact that the products are not technologically mature, but rather it is because the specific benefits of an innovation are inadequate or often not communicated sufficiently, so that customers rarely adopt these innovations as planned by the companies.

You may be familiar with the phrase from *Charles Revson* (the founder of the *Revlon* brand): "In the factory we produce cosmetics, in the store we sell dreams" (Gebhardt 2010). This is an excellent example of how innovation is about being benefit-oriented—in this case with reference to beauty—and not about technical functionality.

It is true that some companies are now able to move from the feature-oriented definition of their offerings in communications to the benefit-oriented definition:

- In the pharmaceutical industry, it is no longer "We produce new drugs", but "We contribute to even better health".
- IT system houses do not develop "new software", but they "reduce costs".
- An energy company no longer says, "We produce oil," but argues "We provide energy."

What we notice, however, is that when it comes to innovations, many companies often go back to the classic feature-oriented definition. This is because companies often must explain their innovations to themselves, especially in digitalization and deviate from the learned benefit-oriented definition and jump back to the classic property-oriented definition.

To prove this, we examined 30 ads on innovative products and services and found that the innovative products and services in over 50% of the ads are unspecific or insufficiently positioned—and thus ultimately difficult for the reader to process. To explain this in more detail, we want to use the proven model of the *"Motiversum"* (cf. Sect. 4.1): The values "innovation" or "new" are not plotted there because they are not clearly assigned to any motive, but are divided into different benefit aspects, depending on what kind of person the observer is and in what role they are currently acting.

Let's take an example of this for an innovation in mechanical engineering. Imagine that we want to sell the new machine to a decision-maker whose motives are based in the "inspiration & curiosity" field, then we don*'t have to* say, "the product is new", but "the product offers completely new possibilities, the innovative design is unique". If, on the other hand, we want to address decision-makers from the "Autonomy & Power" motive field precisely, then it would have to be "We have developed the strongest and most powerful machine available on the market" for the same new machine. For a decision-maker with the motive "Safety & Security", it is again a question of us giving him security with our product innovation. Here, we would have to position the new machine with the statement "You can play it safe with this, you can't go wrong". And if the decision-maker is driven by the motive of "structure & control", the message we should put behind an innovation is: "This is the most economical solution, we have calculated everything for you down to the smallest detail".

It is therefore important to understand that "new" in itself does not address any core customer needs. So, if you rely on the message "new" without translating it in a benefit-oriented way and encounter a customer from the motive field "safety & security" who wants to play it safe, then you actually create uncertainty, because "new" is intuitively a change to the current and is perceived as a threat by a customer with a strong security orientation. This not only leads to a failure to process the innovation idea, but in the worst case even causes reactance. To determine the degree of fit and acceptance for innovations, the classic instrument of follow-up feedback, as we use at other touchpoints, is not suitable. For innovations, we need evaluation models that check the corresponding suitability for demand even before the costly implementation. We need market research approaches that are suitable for positioning innovation ideally from the customer's point of view. Answers to the following questions are helpful here:

4.2 Orchestration

- How must the innovation be communicated to trigger maximum fit with core customer needs?
- How big is the potential, how many customers are likely to take up the innovation if it is communicated appropriately?
- What are the reasons why the innovation is not perceived by certain customers as meeting their needs? If you know the reasons, how can you take targeted countermeasures to increase the potential of the innovation?
- How high is the willingness to pay for the innovation designed to meet demand? How high is the needs-based price? And how can the price be optimally adapted to the customer's needs to realize the maximum willingness-to-pay?
- What does all this mean for your cost-benefit calculation? Will the innovation be profitable? Is the potential and willingness-to-pay sufficient to compensate for the investment in research, development, and market launch?
- And finally, which touchpoints are relevant to bring customers into contact with the innovative product, the innovative service, and thus to develop the desired effect of the innovation in the customer world?

4.2.10 Touchpoint V: The Emotionalizing Effect of Digital Channels

What for years, even for a whole decade, was often just a buzzword or a catchphrase, has become true due to a small virus: the digital revolution. Practically from one day to the next, we were all forced to rethink. Because personal relationships with customers, business partners and employees were massively curtailed. Examples of this are the retail trade, the catering trade, banks, and also industry, which previously contacted their customers primarily via trade fairs and on-site visits by field staff. And now: no familiar greeting ritual, sometimes no eye contact at all—and if so, then only from a distance via camera, no tea or coffee together at the important meeting, no handshake after signing the contract. The emotional bond, the closeness, the connection through personal contact was abolished by decree (Becker 2020).

But is this really the case? After all, that is only one side of the coin. On the other side, the use of contactless, digital channels exploded irrevocably in the wake of the covid crisis: What many previously perceived as cumbersome and insecure turned out to be fast, transparent, safe, and hygienic. Best of all, we know from more than 20 years of fan research that it doesn't matter whether direct on-site or face-to-face contact occurs between customers and employees (i.e., in person or over the phone). Users of digital channels can also experience tangible emotionalization. The decisive factor is that customers have a choice and are not forced into a particular channel—and that digital contacts are perceived as appropriate by customers in the same way as face-to-face contacts. As already explained generally for contacts (cf. Sect. 4.2), this means that customers must also rate the contact via a digital channel as "1" in the scoring logic. Only then does the *Fan Rate* increase. How strongly, illustrates Fig. 4.28—the rate of increase of digital contacts is even higher than that of the classic analog channels. Even at grade 2, the *Fan Rate* falls below that of customers who have had no contact at all. So, the opportunity has been lost.

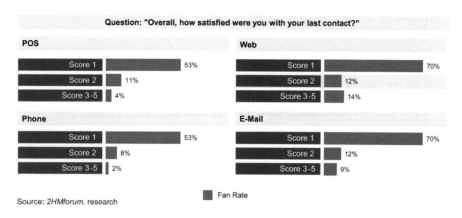

Fig. 4.28 Perfectly orchestrated customer contacts increase the *Fan Rate*—also via digital channels

What is often overlooked, especially in the digital upheaval: is that digital channels will only make a lasting contribution to corporate success if companies have done their homework. Anyone who does not have a sound understanding of customer needs, customer perceptions, and opportunities for differentiation from the competition, and who does not systematically implement these insights at all points of contact with the customer, will not be successful in the digital channels either. Here, many responsible parties simply confuse cause and effect. It is not the digital channels that create loyalty and increase the *Fan Rate*, but the other way around, a high *Fan Rate* is the guarantee that digital channels as additional contact, orientation and sales channels will increase the company's success.

This means especially in times of crisis, when everything has to happen quickly: Those who act with a watering can or "shotgun approach" before they have established sound foundations will not benefit, but on the contrary: they damage the relationship and destroy resources.

4.3 Employees as Fan Makers

The core idea of Orchestration puts employees at the center of successful business management with *FANOMICS*. It is no coincidence that people talk about the brand "wearing shoes". This means that employees play a key role in conveying the positioning—i.e., the fit between the core customer needs and the perceived company performance. One reason for this is that the importance of the service industry, where the employee is the "product" for which the customer pays, has grown increasingly in recent decades. The role of the "Company Lifeblood Factor" employee also becomes intuitively clear when we consider the enormous frequency and intensity of contact between employees and customers. The fact that the "Company Lifeblood Factor" is not only about personal contacts, but also about

4.3 Employees as Fan Makers

contacts via digital channels, is suggested by what we have said so far (cf. Sect. 4.2). We will go into this aspect in more detail below.

First, however, let us turn to the fundamental question of how the effect of employees on emotional customer loyalty can be described, and what positively influences it.

4.3.1 The Customer Orientation of the Employees

The success of *FANOMICS* depends very fundamentally upon the consistency and culture of the company and of each individual employee to align themselves with customers and their central needs. The ability and willingness of employees to recognize and engage with core customer needs is what we call customer orientation. Customer-focused employees succeed in creating a sense of fit at points of contact. They do exactly what meets the customers' central needs.

Contrary to the understanding frequently encountered in theory and practice, we do not equate customer orientation with a particularly friendly and courteous approach to customers (Homburg 2001). As our *ALDI South* example impressively shows, this unspecific understanding of customer orientation is not purposeful; it can even result in employee behavior that runs counter to core customer needs (cf. Sect. 3.4).

To demonstrate the importance of employee customer orientation for emotional customer loyalty, we developed a customer orientation index based on these considerations, incorporating four questions that can be asked in both customer and employee surveys:

1. Employees feel personally responsible for customer satisfaction.
2. Employees find it easy to put themselves in the customers' shoes.
3. Employees are aware that their salary is paid by the customers.
4. Employees find frequent customer contact pleasant.

The first two statements measure the ability and willingness to engage with the customer and his or her central needs, the last two measure the customer-oriented attitude of the employees. The extent to which the customer orientation of employees measured in this way has an impact on emotional customer loyalty is shown in Fig. 4.29.

We can thus use the customer orientation index to accurately measure the effect of employee customer orientation upon emotional customer loyalty. The chart illustrates, based on customer surveys in B2C and B2B, that the customer orientation of employees is rated best by Fan customers (with an index value of 90 (out of a possible 100) points(B2C) and 94 points (B2B) respectively). It then drops successively and reaches its absolute low point among the Opponents in B2C with 34 points. But what influences the perceived customer orientation of the employees? We will now go into this in more detail and present measures that are appropriate to the causes.

Values: Mean values on a scale from 0 (no customer orientation) to 100 (maximum customer orientation)
Basis: B2C: 9,167 customer interviews, B2B: customer survey of 263 corporate customers of a company in the manufacturing sector
Source: B2C: *2HMforum.* research *Fanfocus Germany* 2018, B2B: *2HMforum.* comissioned research

Fig. 4.29 Customer orientation index by *Fan Portfolio*

4.3.2 Factors Influencing Customer Orientation

As the upper part of Fig. 4.30 illustrates, we distinguish between three main factors influencing customer orientation:

1. Employees have the necessary knowledge about customers (= customer insights).
2. Employees have the knowledge and the necessary skills.
    These two influencing factors incorporate whether employees *can* behave in a customer-focused manner to create a sense of fit at points of contact.
3. Employees *want to behave in a* customer-oriented manner, which depends strongly on identification with the job and with the employer, i.e., the internal relationship quality: how well do companies succeed in turning their employees into fans?

Even though we focus on external relationships in this book and devote ourselves to answering the question of how customers become fans, we still want to take a cursory look at this aspect for two reasons: firstly, because we are convinced that a large proportion of our readers, as corporate managers, are responsible for both thrusts, and secondly, because only by choosing the right starting point, namely the customer perspective, can activities to increase the *Fan Rate* among employees move in the right direction. We will explain this in more detail below.

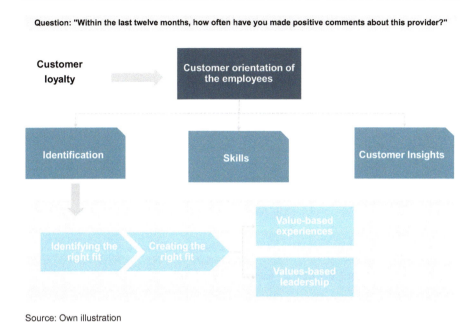

Source: Own illustration

Fig. 4.30 Factors influencing customer orientation

4.3.3 Influencing Factor 1: Knowledge and Information About Customers (Customer Insights)

Time and again, we experience in companies that the prerequisite for customer-oriented behavior of the employees is not a given: The employees do not know the core needs of the customers. Then they simply *cannot ensure the* perception of fit, at least not consciously and systematically. There can be two reasons for this: Either their employers do not know the customer expectations themselves, in which case we recommend the Sect. 4.1 "Positioning", which explains the procedure for deriving them. However, if we assume that most companies dealing with *FANOMICS* have done their "homework", then very often the necessary comprehensive and correct communication of customer insights is missing. Thus, it is by no means sufficient to present the findings of a customer survey regarding the core customer needs to the employees within the framework of a results presentation. However, it is necessary to solidify and deepen the findings so that employees can integrate them into their daily practice with customers: They need to know the key contact points, and they need to understand the relevant levers they can use to create fit. In order to trigger sustainable behavioral changes among employees, workshop formats have proven successful that offer employees the opportunity to provide input and to reflect together on approaches that generate fit—and that, based on the workshop results, enable the development and communication of a target concept that is binding for all.

Let's run through this process again using *ALDI* as an example: Only the consistent communication of the core customer need for "speed" enables *ALDI* employees *to* question intuitively correct, but in terms of the core customer need wrong behaviors, for example, friendly and courteous customer communication. It is therefore necessary that *ALDI* makes this essential clarification and communicates it to the employees. What this means in concrete terms for the employees in the stores and their behavior in everyday work is not yet clear. For this, it is necessary to explain to the employees at which contact points it is particularly important to be quick, for example at the checkout. Only then can employees prioritize their resources correctly. But they still don't know how specifically to establish the perception of "fast" at the checkout. To this end, *ALDI* has developed behavioral guidelines and training measures—based on comprehensive analyses and feedback loops with employees—which have been continually sharpened and optimized over the decades.

4.3.4 Influencing Factor 2: Employee Skills

A lack of skills can also be responsible for employees not being able to create the necessary fit with customer needs. For example, not everyone intuitively has the motor skills necessary to enable *ALDI* customers to experience the "checkout" point of contact as sufficiently fast. How can companies counteract this if employees' skills fail? The most logical measure is training and education because it is through instruction and constant repetition that we improve our skills. As already mentioned, *ING* has even made a virtue of this (cf. Sect. 4.2). This is because skills are teachable, whereas attitudes are not. Therefore, when recruiting for telephone customer dialog, ING tends to rely on employees who have the necessary attitude toward customer orientation and have already proven this in previous jobs, for example in tourism or the hotel industry. The necessary technical skills for telephone calls in the call center of a direct bank are then taught to the employees in intensive courses before they start their job. *ING* also relies on a so-called multi-skill concept, which enables employees to continually acquire new skills in addition to basic skills and thus to handle additional call and contact occasions.

4.3.5 Influencing Factor 3: Identification with the Employer—Fans Among Employees

Employees must *want to* behave in a customer-oriented manner, and it has long been assumed in research and practice that only satisfied employees make satisfied customers (Homburg and Stock-Homburg 2012; Nagl 1997). But readers of this book already suspect it, the connections are not that simple, even if the basic idea that there is a connection between the relationship quality of companies with their customers on the one hand and with their employees on the other hand is not wrong: We have explained in detail in this book that customer satisfaction is not

4.3 Employees as Fan Makers

the essential control variable of customer value, and so employee satisfaction is also not the decisive indicator of internal relationships. We will explain this in the following.

To this end, it is obvious to apply *FANOMICS* to the relationships between companies and their employees. After all, in recent years, valuable internal relationships have become at least as important as external ones for corporate growth and success: For years, companies have been vying for the best brains, and demographic developments and the shortage of skilled workers ensure that the demand for high potentials exceeds the supply many times over. Under these circumstances, many companies are united by the same question: How do we manage to attract and retain employees who will go through thick and thin for us, who are highly motivated and committed to the stated goal? Often, employers only focus on the performance level in order to satisfy their employees, for example through good pay, additional and social benefits, further training opportunities and flexible working hours. These are all important aspects. And that's why companies believe that if they invest in these performance aspects, employees will also become fans and show a corresponding level of loyalty. But this is a misconception. Similar to customers, the performance aspects lead to an increase in satisfaction; but satisfaction says nothing about the degree of emotional attachment.

To determine the *Fan Rate* among employees, we use the same model as for customers: We form a *Fan Indicator* from the statements on identification ("My employer is made for someone like me") and perceived uniqueness ("For me, my employer is the most attractive employer") and correlate this with overall satisfaction with the employer. The result is the *Fan Portfolio* for employee relations, which differs from the *Fan Portfolio for* customer relations only in terms of characteristic behavior patterns and thus also the naming of two groups:

- Employees with high satisfaction and low emotional attachment do not behave in a Mercenary fashion; on the contrary, they feel good, have sufficient income and try to keep their workload low. We therefore speak of corporate residents.
- Employees with low satisfaction and high emotional attachment are disappointed. If the causes of their disappointment cannot be eliminated, they are more likely to change employers. That is why we speak of the disappointed.

As with customer relations, we also conduct a regular baseline study on employee relations. Employees subject to social insurance contributions in Germany are surveyed. The *Fan Portfolio* across all employees shows a similar picture as for customers: Among employees, too, the overwhelming majority, 71%, are highly satisfied, but only a small proportion, 21%, are Fans of their employer (cf. Fig. 4.31). Even though these data refer explicitly to employees in Germany, various international comparative studies also show a low relationship quality of employees to their employers for many other countries, so that we can confidently assume a similar starting situation in the other industrialized nations (Gallup 2022; Kram and Isabella 1985; Rawlins 1994).

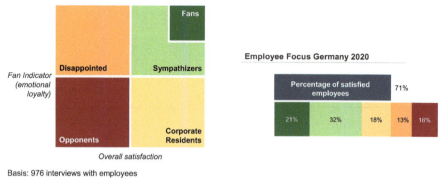

Basis: 976 interviews with employees
Source: *2HMforum.* research *Employee Focus 2020*

Fig. 4.31 *Fan Portfolio*: Not all satisfied employees are also emotionally loyal

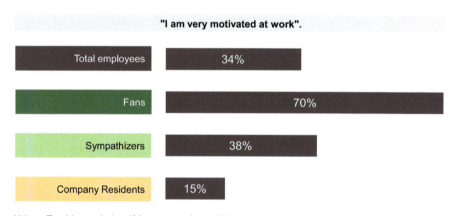

Values: Top 1 boxes (value 100 on a scale from 100 (completely agree) to 0 (not at all agree)).
Basis: 976 interviews with employees
Source: *2HMforum.* research *Employee Focus Germany 2020*

Fig. 4.32 Three out of four Fan employees are highly motivated in their work

Together with Fan Customers, fan employees represent the greatest capital for success for companies: They are more productive, they recommend their employer to others and—especially important in terms of customer relationship quality—they are above-averagely motivated and customer-oriented and therefore the perfect Fan Makers of customers.

Let's take a closer look at the latter. Figure 4.32 shows the correlation between the highly satisfied groups from the *Employee Fan Portfolio and* work motivation. While 70% of the Fan employees are highly motivated, this is only true for 15% of the company residents. And this is even though these two groups hardly differ in terms of their satisfaction with the employer. The same tendency emerges when we look at the connection to employees' customer orientation (and from the perspective of the employees themselves): More than half of the fan employees claim to feel

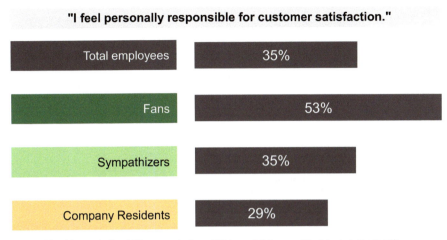

Fig. 4.33 Fans carry the "Company Lifeblood Factor" and are customer-oriented

personally responsible for customer satisfaction, but only just under a third of the corporate residents share this assessment.

And the fact that employee motivation has an impact on emotional customer loyalty can be illustrated by our example of the DIY chain with its stores, which you already know from Sect. 3.1 (cf. Fig. 4.33). As an additional dimension, in addition to emotional customer loyalty and profitability, we now show the average employee motivation of the best and the worst 25% of the illustrated stores in each case, in the form of an index value from 0 (minimum motivation) to 100 (maximum motivation) (cf. Fig. 4.34). Employee motivation is almost twice as high at the stores with the highest emotional customer loyalty and the best profitability as at the worst stores. We will discuss in more detail below how such fluctuations can occur between individual stores in the same DIY chain.

Emotional employee loyalty therefore increases emotional customer loyalty. But what leads to an increase in emotional employee loyalty? How do companies turn employees into Fans? To answer this question, let's first consider what a company needs fan employees for—namely, to turn customers into Fans and thus achieve sustainable success and growth. You may object that this falls short because Fan employees also have many other valuable qualities. That's true, but it is no use if you have the "wrong" fans among your employees.

What do we mean by "wrong" Fans? Employee Fan relationships are based on the perceived fit between core requirements of an employer and an employer's "offer" that can be experienced again and again, where "offer" includes the framework conditions of working in a company, i.e., culture/philosophy/values, leadership

Source: 2HMforum. research

Fig. 4.34 Motivated Fan employees turn customers into fans and thus increase economic success

model, communication. However, it is also crucial how these framework conditions make themselves felt in everyday working life, whether they are really lived.

If, for example, an employee strives for autonomy, i.e., as much independence as possible, and this is precisely what his employer offers him, he becomes a Fan employee of his employer. However, the question remains unanswered as to whether his employer will also be successful with an autonomy-oriented workforce as long as the customer perspective has not been illuminated and it has not been clarified that precisely this cultural basis is suitable for making the core customer needs tangible. If, on the contrary, a tight corporate management with little freedom for each individual employee were necessary to create the fit in the direction of the customer, this company would fail, no matter how high the *Fan Rate* among the employees might be. The decisive factor in determining whether a company has the right or the wrong fans among its employees is therefore what the framework conditions are that turn employees into fans, and whether these framework conditions benefit the implementation of *FANOMICS* in the direction of the *customer: If* they are suitable or, in the best case, even specifically designed to serve core customer needs, then this company is turning the right employees into fans. If this is not the case, this company can have as many fans among its employees as it likes, it will not be successful because it is not able to turn sufficient customers into Fan.

This realization is both drastic and momentous, as it shows that, contrary to the lived practice in many companies, sustainable success is only possible if customer and employee relationships are managed in a synchronized manner, and that in doing so, customer relationships define the direction in which employee relationships must be developed. Let us illustrate this with a few examples:

4.3 Employees as Fan Makers 251

- Let us first imagine a specialist surgical clinic; the customer there is the patient who has to undergo an operation. Now let us imagine that in this hospital a free-spirited chief physician likes to surround himself with like-minded doctors and nurses. During the operation, a heated discussion arises above the patient's open abdomen as to whether, in view of the correct clinical picture that presents itself, the originally planned operation should be carried out or whether another therapy should be preferred. It was decided to interrupt the operation for a workshop and then to vote on the further course of action. Certainly, this approach would contribute to a perceived fit for the physicians and nurses, but certainly not for the patient who has bled to death in the meantime. Of course, this is a very unrealistic example. But it illustrates, by implication, why wherever life and limb are at stake for the customer, there can only be strictly hierarchical cultures. Every intern in a clinic and every pilot can tell you a thing or two about this.
- Let's imagine an owner managed B2B service provider whose owner has prescribed a value mission statement for the company that is strongly focused on creativity and diversification and thus corresponds to his own personality profile. This attracts appropriately profiled executives and employees; the *Fan Rate* in the workforce is above average compared to the industry. However, it is known from customer studies that the core customer needs are located in the "structure & control" motive field. Key loyalty-drivers are the reliability, competence and speed of the provider. How easy do you think it is for this company, with its cultural framework imposed by the owner, to turn customers into Fan? Confronted with this question, the owner replies "Then we'll just look for the customers who fit our profile". Good for him who can afford to do that. In this context, consider the example of the *Praktiker* DIY chain, where failure to meet actual customer needs led to insolvency.
- Especially for the business customers of many industrial companies with complex products that require explanation, it is important to have simple, understandable solutions that take the pressure off them. However, such companies are traditionally often led by decision-makers who are engineers themselves and have an almost neurotically exaggerated intimate relationship with their products (ExBa 2003). They surround themselves with their peers and develop a culture in which product infatuation is lived out. Product innovations are then characterized by what is technically feasible, not by the contribution to customer benefits. A decision-maker once formulated this in a conversation with the authors as follows: "We can now build scales that measure accurately to the twelfth decimal place. Unfortunately, there is no application in the world for this type of scale that requires more than five decimal places. And our competitors can do that for half the price." This is another example of a company that generates a high *Fan Rate* internally but is unable to survive because of a lack of cultural fit with core customer needs.
- The banking world is in a pronounced transformation phase, accelerated by pandemic-related contact restrictions. More and more typical branch bank customers are realizing that online banking is not only secure, but also fast, flexible, and available at any time. This realization is changing customer

Perception	Relevance for Fan Indicator
is very innovative	high
is very flexible	high
is very agile	high
is very reliable	high
is well positioned for the future	medium
is a very safe employer	medium
is very credible	medium
is very serious	medium
is very sympathetic	medium
is very successful	low
is very fair	low
is very competent	low

Source: 2HMforum. comissioned research for a savings bank

Fig. 4.35 The *Fan Traffic Signal* shows the highly relevant loyalty-drivers of the employees of branch bank I and thus enables the alignment with the positioning-based mission statement

expectations of branch banks as well. The technical challenges may still be the least of the problems. But what about the core staff of a typical branch bank with a traditionally above-average *Fan Rate*, which has distinguished itself over decades by values that create a fit with security-oriented customer needs? What will happen to the internal *Fan Rate* if, due to the necessary change process, more flexible, faster and more autonomous managers and employees are now needed to remain competitive? Conversely, what happens if these banks do not change, thus maintaining the high *Fan Rates* in the workforce?

From these examples, it is possible to derive the essential steps that companies should address step by step in order to optimally dovetail customer and employee relationship quality (cf. also the part below on the Fig. 4.35):

1. Companies need a positioning-based corporate culture, i.e., a mission statement derived from core customer needs, and this mission statement must be communicated to the workforce in a sustainable manner. This is because the central function of corporate culture is to create the guard rails and guidelines for an orchestrated alignment of the company with core customer needs.
2. Companies should check the fundamental "fit" of their employees with this positioning-based mission statement: What is important for the company, what is important for the employees? The relevant instrument for this is the employee

4.3 Employees as Fan Makers

survey (cf. Sect. 4.1). You can use the *Fan Traffic Signal* instrument, which you are already familiar with from the derivation of the positioning, to check which of these values are particularly relevant for the emotional loyalty of the employees. In principle, two result scenarios are conceivable:

– The highly relevant loyalty-drivers of the workforce match the essential attributes of the positioning-based mission statement. An example of this can be found in Fig. 4.35. The branch bank I described here has succeeded in the transformation process on the part of its employees, because the necessary alignment of the mission statement with the increasingly digitally active customer, with its growing demands for flexibility, speed, and availability, is supported by the employees. There is therefore a fit between the core needs of the workforce and the positioning-based mission statement. Such companies can move on to step four.

– The highly relevant loyalty-drivers of the workforce do *not* match the essential attributes of the mission statement. An example of this can be found in Fig. 4.36. The branch bank II described here has *not* yet succeeded in the transformation process on the part of its employees, because the necessary alignment of the mission statement with the increasingly digitally active customer, with its growing demands for flexibility, speed, and availability, is not supported by the employees. Traditional values such as "security," "integrity," and "reliability" continue to be of the utmost importance for the emotional commitment of the

Perception	Relevance for Fan Indicator
is very serious	high
is very reliable	high
is a very safe employer	high
is well positioned for the future	medium
is very innovative	medium
is very credible	medium
is very sympathetic	medium
is very flexible	low
is very successful	low
is very agile	low
is very fair	low
is very competent	low

Source: *2HMforum.* comissioned research for a savings bank

Fig. 4.36 The *Fan Traffic Signal* shows the highly relevant loyalty-drivers of the employees of the branch bank II and thus enables the alignment with the positioning-based mission statement

workforce. There is therefore *"no fit"* between the core needs of the workforce and the positioning-based mission statement.

3. Companies should establish a basic fit in terms of the positioning-based mission statement through a mix of persuasion, recruiting employees who fit, and separating employees for whom the company's offering does not establish a fit.
4. Companies should strive for individual fit, especially at management level. The result of the *Fan Traffic Signal* always shows an aggregated picture of the entire workforce. Even if the aggregate picture indicates a high level of fit, this does not mean that all employees experience fit. One way to refine the picture is to ask specific questions within an employee survey, such as "I identify with my employer's philosophy and goals." You can see that the *Fan Rate is* enormously high when there is a high level of agreement with this statement and decreases massively as agreement falls (cf. Fig. 4.37). Alongside this, the distribution across the groups in the employee *Fan Portfolio* gives a more detailed insight into how strong the agreement and resistance are regarding the corporate culture. Since these results are collected and analyzed on an anonymous basis, you cannot conclude on the fit of individual managers and employees. Supplementary workshops or individual discussions are then recommended for this purpose. With regard to measures, we refer you to step 3: persuasion, recruiting suitable employees and separating them from employees who do not fit. You should bear in mind that at management level, the aim should be to achieve 100% commitment because, according to the model idea of the *Fan Principle,* managers are the "stars" to whom employees orient themselves. At the level of employees without management responsibility, a company also keeps a certain proportion of employees who do not fit. These may, for example, be indispensable due to certain skills or be needed to handle tedious routine work.

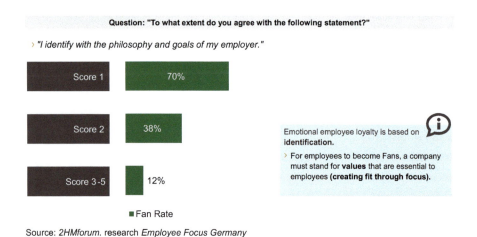

Fig. 4.37 With identification, the *Fan Rate* among employees increases

4.3 Employees as Fan Makers

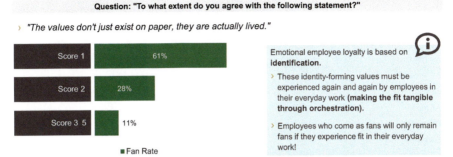

Source: 2HMforum. research *Employee Focus Germany*

Fig. 4.38 If the *identity-forming* values can be experienced again and again in everyday working life, the *Fan Rate* increases

5. Make the "fit" be experienced again and again, i.e., create orchestrated, value-based employee experiences. In other words, do the right employees repeatedly experience what makes them fans? The status can be checked as part of the employee survey, initially and explicitly by asking: "The values don't just exist on paper, they are actually lived." The result illustrates how important lived values are for the emotional commitment of employees. Even agreement with a score of "2" reduces the *Fan Rate* by more than half (Fig. 4.38).

In addition, the employee survey specifically asks about aspects where "fit" should be experienced, such as the perception of the supervisor, communication and information, cooperation in the team or the professional perspective. For these aspects (analogous to the approach taken with customers for the touchpoints), relevance can be determined regarding the value drivers. We call the result the *Fan Traffic Signal* because it provides information about the key drivers for turning employees into fans of their employer and thus into Fan Makers of customers, namely by orchestrating the experience of fulfilling their own central needs for the employer. To put employee ratings into perspective, we recommend surveying not only our own employees, but also employees of comparable companies (for example, in terms of industry and company size). We provide representative comparative values of employees from the same industry (e.g., for a financial services provider) as part of our employee studies. You can find a simplified Fan Maker *Traffic Signal* in Fig. 4.39.

A key factor in orchestrating employee experiences is values-based leadership, for the following reasons:

– Managers play a central role as identification figures and role models. We can prove that the relationship with the direct superior has a positive effect on the *Fan Rate* of employees.

Perception	Relevance to central need "is very reliable".	Employee evaluation	Benchmark FDL
Leadership	high	medium	bad
Working time	high	good	same
Communication	medium	bad	same
Cohesion	medium	good	same
Payment	medium	bad	same
Perspective	low	medium	better
Equipment	low	good	same

Source: *2HMforum.* comissioned research

Fig. 4.39 The *Fan Traffic Signal illustrates* which aspects are of particular relevance to employees with regard to their central loyalty-driver "is very reliable"

- The relationship quality between employer and employee is significantly influenced by the perception of information and communication. This, in turn, depends decisively upon leadership: A company can define as many communication processes or install as many tools as it likes. If managers do not use these to convey information, to live values, these will not be well-received by the employees.
- Orchestration can only be experienced by employees through the collaboration of management teams and the resulting implementation competence of management, as employees often move between the areas of responsibility of different managers in their daily work.

Managers should be fans themselves, i.e., feel a "fit" between their own core expectations and what their employer has to offer, to turn Employees, as Fan Makers, into fans, who turn customers into fans. That sounds simple, but in reality, many companies are far from achieving this. Our *Employee Focus Germany* shows (cf. Fig. 4.40) that in German business, even at the first and second management levels, fewer than one in four managers are fans of their employer . Even if one includes the Sympathizers, only around one in two top managers in Germany is emotionally loyal and satisfied—and thus fulfills his role as Fan Maker. At the level of department and team leaders, we find roughly the same result, but with a serious difference: the proportion of Opponents is 17%, which is 10 percentage points higher than among top managers. Instead of being Fan Makers and part of the company's management, these executives at the interface with the broader workforce act like class representatives and collaborators, aligning with employees against the company's management. Why is this so? Why is the Opponents' rate so high, especially among middle managers? The reasons are manifold:

- Often, managers are also unclear about the orientation of their companies and the corporate culture. If we ask top management in workshops what their own company stands for, we often get as many different answers as there are managers

4.3 Employees as Fan Makers

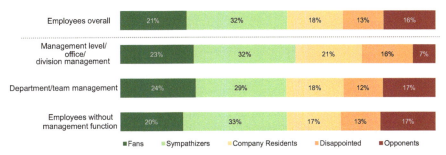

Source: 2HMforum. research *Employee Focus Germany 2020*

Fig. 4.40 The *Fan Rates* of the executives hardly differ from the *Fan Rates* of the employees. This suggests a lack of identification on the part of the executives

present. You can certainly imagine what this means in terms of deriving and communicating a uniform mission statement, and some of you know it from your own experience: affected employees from companies with an unclear corporate culture describe a pronounced silo thinking, a culture of mistrust, a collection of companies within the company.
– The orientation of the corporate culture is not consistently from the customer but, as in one of our examples, by default of the owner. The employed managers recognize the contradiction to customer needs, and more so the closer they are to the customer, but do not intervene, often because of an established culture of unconditional approval.
– Managers become leaders simply based upon special technical competencies and not on the basis of special leadership-specific competencies such as distinctive communication skills, empathy or strategic strengths (ExBa 2008, 2009). This often results in a lack of ability, which in turn leads to frustration on the part of the managers and thus to a decline in commitment.
– The first management level (or the founder level) does not see itself as part of the system, but as standing above the system, and therefore does not adhere to the defined rules of the game in the form of the mission statement and the leadership model. All measures and attempts to make fit tangible for the downstream management levels in such companies fail because of the poor role models and their insufficient credibility.

This exemplary list of possible causes in turn results in a list of countermeasures. We recommend:

– Begin at the management level. Measures at a subordinate level will then take better effect.
– Establish the necessary commitment, i.e., the feeling of fit between your own needs and the employer's offer. Then empowerment measures, for example leadership and communication training, or training in conducting employee interviews, have a greater chance of having a lasting effect.

- Start with structural issues. Clarify why so many executives overall are not emotionally loyal and address these structural deficits. For example, by implementing and communicating a positioning-based mission statement which is binding for all and a leadership model before starting with individual executives.
- Do not build the company culture "around their leaders" (that's a phrase we hear more often in our projects) but replace leaders who don't feel a fit. In most cases, this is a redemption for both parties. Conversely, the damage to your company is immense, since our experience shows that in addition to the affected executives themselves, most of the employees they lead are not fans of the company.

4.3.6 All Employees Are Fan Makers

If the previous comments on the role of Employees as Fan Makers focused on customer-facing areas such as Sales and Customer Service, this is not to say that all other employees do not equally influence emotional customer loyalty as Fan Makers. In the networked world of work, all employees have an indirect effect on customer relationship quality and/or they influence the emotional attachment and motivation of colleagues who have a direct or indirect effect on the customer. Let's illustrate this with a few examples, and we'll fall back on the *ALDI example* again for this:

- Imagine *ALDI* wants to deliver on its promise of fast shopping in its stores, but the goods fail to arrive because the employees responsible for purchasing the goods did not reorder in time, did not pay the invoices, or did not have a handle on the logistics.
- The advertising and communications department called out the wrong products for the weekly promotions, causing customers to show up at stores for the wrong products.
- HR has not been able to get replacements quickly enough for employees who leave the company, or employees are not adequately trained for their jobs and therefore do not have a handle on the processes. Then the promise of "fast" will not be fulfilled.
- The IT department does not adhere to the agreed schedule when introducing a new module of the EAP system. As a result, online orders cannot be processed with the promised speed.

The importance of employees who are not in direct contact with customers for emotional customer loyalty can be explained particularly impressively using the example of contacts via digital channels. These have become enormously more important because of the pandemic. Now, one might assume that employees who are responsible for such contacts do not have to be customer-focused to the same extent as employees on the "front end," i.e., in sales, distribution, and customer service. In fact, this is also consistent with recruiting practices in many companies: While employees in direct customer contact are specifically looked for corresponding key skills such as empathy, communication skills or sociability, employees for the design and management of digital channels continue to be selected based on their specialist IT skills.

We have discovered that employee motivation and customer orientation play just as significant a role with digital channels as they do with employees who have personal contact with customers. Visitors to websites or web stores have a very keen sense of whether a company's employees are oriented toward the customer when designing and maintaining digital channels. They can evaluate aspects such as "Those responsible find it easy to put themselves in the shoes of visitors/users" very precisely and in a differentiated fashion. And these aspects have a decisive influence on whether, in the end, the already quoted "1" appears in the grading scale for contact via a digital channel. What does this mean if the responsible employees in digital customer service were recruited for their technical and professional skills and not for their strong customer orientation? These employees are often unaware of how their actions affect the customer. Often, employees from "classic" service units are better trained and also better suited: So a rethink is needed here, both in the design of job profiles and in the development of employees responsible for digital channels.

What does this currently mean in the crisis and generally for the digital revolution that is now in full swing? With the growing importance of digital channels, you should pay even more attention to customer orientation, even among those responsible for digital channels, and strengthen them accordingly by means of special attitude training. To the same extent, it is important to strengthen employees who were previously deployed primarily in personal contact with the customer in dealing with digital channels that are far removed from contact.

It is obvious that the development of employees into Fan Makers must not be limited to those sub-organizations that traditionally work close to the customer but should ideally be understood as a challenge for the entire company. Conversely, this does not mean that it is not worth starting just because the entire company is not involved from day one. On the contrary, we have repeatedly found that it pays to start with areas that are close to the customer and are responsible for a large part of the impact on the customer, and then to move on to other areas step by step as successes occur.

4.4 Customer Value-Based Control

So far, we have always considered the various customer types in the *Fan Portfolio* as an aggregate. We have looked at their typical characteristics, described their customer value, and explained general measures for targeting individual types with the aim of either increasing the *Fan Rate* or making the most of fan potential. The benefits of these insights are enormous but remain reduced to general measures in the context of Positioning and Orchestration.

How would it be now if we could clearly assign each individual customer according to their customer value and thus also prioritize and initiate measures to increase the *Fan Rate in a targeted manner*—namely according to the characteristics of "their" customer group? Be it within the framework of target group-specific or even individual measures? This would open completely new possibilities for working with *FANOMICS*, all customer-related processes from service to sales specifically could be aligned to these findings—and thereby significantly increase the efficiency, but especially the effectiveness of all activities. Let us illustrate this with two concise examples:

- Captives are highly emotionally loyal but currently dissatisfied, as we have shown elsewhere, often due to an unsatisfactorily processed complaint. The appropriate action here is to specifically understand and address the perceived performance deficit.
- Mercenaries, on the other hand, are highly satisfied but not emotionally loyal. So here, any measures to improve performance perception would be a waste of money. Instead, it is about increasing emotional loyalty. Since we know that contact frequency is very important for emotional customer loyalty and that Mercenary customers have less contact than, for example, Sympathizers and fans, we could target the Mercenaries with appropriate campaigns instead of—as it were with the watering can—acting over all customers.

In the following, we will first look at how the area-wide assignment of customers in the *Fan Portfolio* is possible. Then we will look at the question of which groups we should address and with what priority, and which measures are suitable for initiating targeted increases in relationship quality among the various groups in the *Fan Portfolio*.

4.4.1 Personalized Assignment in the *Fan Portfolio*

The personalized assignment of customers in the *Fan Portfolio* can be done with two different variants

- In **variant 1,** the customer is *explicitly* asked for the information required for the unique assignment. The time required for customers to answer the three questions that enable a unique assignment in the *Fan Portfolio* amounts to a few seconds. This is preceded by a process in which it is defined at which contact points or via which channels the query is made and who carries it out. A wide variety of constellations are conceivable here, e.g., in the case of particularly valuable customers, the information is requested at regular intervals by telephone from an external call center, while less attractive customers receive an e-mail with a questionnaire. Depending on how many customers your company has, and which method of data collection proves to be most effective, explicit querying can be quite costly. This expense is reduced by using highly automated apps that are deployed at a wide variety of touchpoints and can be easily activated, for example, via a QR code. In conjunction with a unique customer number, fast,

4.4 Customer Value-Based Control

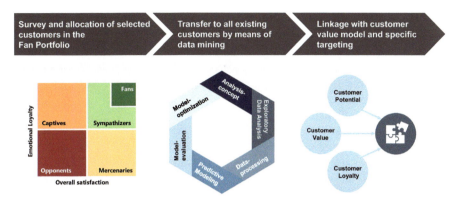

Source: Own illustration

Fig. 4.41 Data mining model for personalized allocation of customers in the *Fan Portfolio*

unambiguous, and thus cost-effective personalized assignments are therefore possible.
- For companies that consider the effort of explicit allocation to be too high, we have developed **variant 2**, in which the allocation of customers in the *Fan Portfolio* is carried out implicitly using an analytical approach. This variant also starts with a personal survey of a sample of customers and their classification in the *Fan Portfolio*. By linking this with available data from the *CRM and data warehouse* on the transaction and contact history of the customers, the basis is created for the development of so-called *data mining models*. The aim is to identify relevant patterns within the purchasing and usage behavior as well as the contact history, which will enable the classification of even the non-surveyed customers in the *Fan Portfolio* based on the developed *data mining model* (for an illustration of the process cf. Fig. 4.41). Since the classification is based on a mathematical formula, not all customers are correctly assigned. This disadvantage is far outweighed by the added value of the target group-specific targeting of measures, even for many customers. However, this so-called implicit approach is tied to a decisive premise: Sufficiently comprehensive, differentiating and up-to-date characteristics must be available from your *data warehouse* or CRM system, or it must be possible to enrich your customer addresses from external data sources.

For companies with a large customer base, the implicit approach is the method of choice, as explicit allocation is too costly. However, hybrid methods are also conceivable, in which the particularly important customers are explicitly queried and assigned at regular intervals, while the remaining mass of customers are assigned implicitly by analytical means, which is not completely error-free. It is also conceivable to start with analytical allocation across all customers, because it delivers results quickly, so that the target group-specific customer approach can be started across the board. The explicit query verifies the results at routine contact points, saving resources, or supplements them—as just described—with direct personal queries of particularly high-value customers.

For both variants, it applies that—as a prerequisite for practical implementation and everyday work—the result of the *Fan Portfolio* assignment must be reflected in your CRM system and maintained there on a regular basis. The necessary modifications can be made with little effort in any common *CRM software.* What is generally true when dealing with *CRM* also proves to be imperative for this application: Define how the maintenance and updating of the collected data in the database should be done. Specify responsibilities, timelines and process descriptions.

Avoid one widespread mistake: The individual classification of all customers in the *Fan Portfolio*, carried out by means of an explicit or implicit procedure, must not be the basis for determining the *Fan Rate* as a control variable, as we explain in Sect. 6.3, nor can it replace it. The different objectives of the two methods argue against this:

Control with the *Fan Rate* is about scientific precision, resilience, and traceability, whereby the anonymity of the survey can be an essential prerequisite. For the alignment of customer-related processes, on the other hand, personalization is imperative. For this, one accepts certain inaccuracies: as already described, the implicit approach produces "false" assignments for a certain percentage, but the explicit variant will also produce distortions—for example, due to the query directly by the provider. As a basis for a target group-specific approach, such uncertainties in the data can be accepted, since the added value of a 70% accurate classification is already immense. On the other hand, an error rate of this magnitude would be fatal and unacceptable for a central control variable such as the *Fan Rate,* which is used as the basis for all corporate activities. The classification of individual customers cannot and must not replace the regular empirical survey of the *Fan Rate.*

4.4.2 Customer Value Specific Measures and Prioritization

In this section, we show you how you should prioritize your activities to increase customer value according to the personalized mapping in the *Fan Portfolio.* Or, in other words, clarify the question: How attractive are the individual target groups in the *Fan Portfolio* for you? Fans are left out of this consideration; they have already reached the highest status. And this section is about increasing relationship quality. So, let's turn to the remaining four customer groups:

- **The Sympathizers**
  The most attractive of the remaining four customer groups are the Sympathizers. On the one hand, you can achieve the intended movement toward fan customers with comparatively little effort, and the benefits are enormous (cf. Chap. 2): Fans are the better ambassadors, have the higher expertise, and as a rule, the monetary customer value is also higher. Secondly, the group of Sympathizers is often the

largest customer group, so you have a corresponding leverage effect if you start with them. The procedure for identifying measures is the same for all customer groups: Based on the results of the customer study, you compare the results among the different groups of the *Fan Portfolio*. Regarding Sympathizers, too, there are some patterns that can be detected repeatedly in such reappraisals: Compared to Fan customers, Sympathizers have significantly fewer matching contacts that they rate as "1" and more often contacts that they rate as "3" or worse. Thus, a significant emotionalizing effect is missing. In addition, inviting Sympathizers (together with Fans) to exclusive events or VIP clubs has proven to be effective in further strengthening identification.

- **The Captives**
  The second highest priority should be given to measures to increase the relationship quality with Captives. This is because remedying the causes is not very time-consuming or resource-intensive, since the basic prerequisite of a good "fit" exists among Captives' customers. Frequently, these are disappointed Fans. In addition, there is a certain urgency to prevent the Captives from slipping into the group of Opponents sooner or later out of annoyance. Because of the fundamental fit, Captives customers offer the opportunity for sustainable deficit reduction in shortfalls by eliminating common problems. Captive *ALDI customers* would, for example, complain about the excessively long waiting time at the checkout in a particular store and thus provide *ALDI with* an important indication of where to take countermeasures. The key starting point with Captives customers is to reduce the performance shortfall. The prerequisite—as with Opponent customers—is a well-founded root cause analysis in a personal or telephone conversation by the responsible customer service representative. If you suspect that he or she is the cause of the perceived performance deficits, you should involve a complaints specialist. This is followed by an individual, quick, and accommodating measure to reduce the shortcomings and "make amends". Since these are former Fans or Sympathizers, i.e., there is basically a high degree of fit, this will lead to a rapid reactivation of the existing Fan potential.

- **The Mercenaries**
  Mercenary customers come third in our priority list. They are indeed a relevant group in many companies, and their perception of performance is comparable to that of Sympathizers. However, measures to increase relationship quality are more time-consuming and resource-intensive than for Sympathizers, and stray losses are to be expected in the process, as we have repeatedly experienced that Mercenaries also include customers who were acquired as part of price campaigns but who do not really fit the company. Examples of this are the promotions of branch banks, where new customers receive a bonus for opening a salary account, or *ALDI casual shoppers* who only ever buy certain special offers from the non-food range there but buy their groceries from *a competitor with a wider range. It* is unlikely that these customers will ever identify with the selected bank or with *ALDI.* Time and again, we have been able to show that, due to the lack of fit, Mercenary customers can also become Opponent customers in the medium term, who then eventually leave. Therefore, the expected successes with

Mercenaries are not as great as with Sympathizers or Captives. In the case of Mercenaries, this makes it even more valuable to look at the target-specific results of the customer study. After all, a typical feature of Mercenary customers is their low frequency of contact and, as a result, their low level of knowledge regarding the product and service offering. It is worth specifically targeting Mercenary customers since full knowledge of offerings very much increases emotional connection, provided that the offerings are in line with requirements. A significant lever is also the low estimation of contact quality. The extent to which this is an expression of contact-specific deficits or is due to the fundamental lack of fit of the Mercenaries, who expect something that is not offered to them by the provider, can only be found out through continuous accompanying measurement and comparison of the customer groups: If all customers rate the same contact points critically, it is probably due to the performance; if only the Mercenaries (and the Opponents) rate these aspects critically, it has more to do with the lack of fit.

- **The Opponent Clients**
  Many corporate decision-makers consider Opponent customers to be the most important target groups. This is probably due to fear of loss. This is understandable, because a large proportion of Opponents leave the company. Nevertheless—or precisely because of this—this is the least attractive target group, which consequently comes fourth and last in the list of priorities. Let's explain this in more detail: increasing the relationship quality of Opponents is time-consuming and resource-intensive, because the basic prerequisite of fit is often *not met* in this target group. Opponent customers of *ALDI,* for example, are customers who want friendlier cashiers and gentler handling of purchases through a merchandise catchment area. This means that you must expect large scatter losses among Opponents: If the "fit" is not sufficient, all measures will not be effective. In addition, because of their unclear fit, you can hardly learn anything from the Opponents that will help with sustainable reduction of shortfalls. For example, what can *ALDI* do with complaints about unfriendly cashiers from opponents—other than the fact that opponents reject them?

References

Barden P (2013) Decoded: the science behind why we buy. Wiley, West Sussex
Bass FM, Bruce N, Majumdar S, Murthi BPS (2007) Wearout effects of different advertising themes: a dynamic Bayesian model of the advertising-sales relationship. Mark Sci 26(2): 179–195
Becker R (2020) Alles digital, alles gut? Kundenbindung in Krisenzeiten, kommunikationsmanager 4-2020. F.A.Z.-Institut für Management-Markt- und Medieninformationen GmbH, Frankfurt, pp 50–51
Becker R, Lang J (2013) Wohin will der Kunde wirklich? QZ Qualität und Zuverlässigkeit 58(12): 30–34
Blair MH (1988). An empirical investigation of advertising wearin and wearout
Craig CS, Sternthal B, Leavitt C (1976) Advertising wearout: an experimental analysis. J Mark Res 13(4):365–372

References

Delekat T (2015) Ein Lebensgefühl – das Motorrad gibt es gratis dazu. Welt.de (07.06.2015). https://www.welt.de/print/wams/hamburg/article142062302/Ein-Lebensgefuehl-das-Motorrad-gibt-es-gratis-dazu.html. Accessed 2 July 2021

ExBa (2003) Benchmarkstudie zur Excellence in der deutschen Wirtschaft. Gut. Besser. Excellent! Published by forum! GmbH marketing + communication. DGQ – Deutsche Gesellschaft für Qualität 3:30–33

ExBa (2008) Benchmarkstudie zur Excellence in der deutschen Wirtschaft. Qualität bewegt. Kapitel Kundenfokussierte Unternehmensführung, Kapitel Mitarbeiter motivieren, Motivierte beflügeln, Kunden begeistern. Hrsg. Forum! GmbH marketing + communication. DGQ – Deutsche Gesellschaft für Qualität 8:42–45, 46–51

ExBa (2009) Benchmarkstudie zur Excellence in der deutschen Wirtschaft. Erfolgreich in starken Zeiten. Kapitel Menschen machen Erfolge – ExBa zieht Bilanz. Hrsg. Forum! GmbH marketing + communication. DGQ – Deutsche Gesellschaft für Qualität 9:46–51

Faßbender R-R, Thanhoffer M (2011) Kreatives Projektmanagement. Mit Projektinszenierung innovative Ergebnisse fördern. Springer Gabler, Wiesbaden

Gallup (2022) State of the Global Workplace: 2022 Report

Gebhardt P (2010) Kosmetik-Karriere: Lack mich! Spiegel.de (28.05.2010) https://www.spiegel.de/geschichte/kosmetik-karriere-a-948943.html. Accessed 2 July 2021

Häusel H-G (2016) Brain View: Warum Kunden kaufen. Haufe-Lexware, Freiburg

Herzberg F (1959) The motivation to work. Wiley, New York

Homburg C (2001) Kundenzufriedenheit, 4th edn. Gabler Verlag, Wiesbaden

Homburg C, Stock-Homburg R (2012) Der kundenorientierte Mitarbeiter: Bewerten, begeistern, bewegen, 2nd edn. Gabler Verlag, Wiesbaden

Homburg C, Kuester S, Krohmer H (2013) Marketing management: a contemporary perspective. McGraw Hill, New York

Iyengar SS, Lepper MR (2000) When choice is demotivating: can one desire too much of a good thing? J Pers Soc Psychol 79(6):995–1006

Kaiser H (2017) 20 Jahre Elchtest: Der Tag an dem Mercedes aus der Spur kippte. Stern (20.10.2017). https://www.stern.de/auto/news/mercedes%2D%2D-20-jahre-elchtest%2D%2Dals-der-autokonzern-aus-der-spur-kippte-7668094.html. Accessed 13 September 2021

Kotler P, Armstrong G (2020) Principles of marketing. Pearson Education, London

Kram KE, Isabella LA (1985) Mentoring alternatives: the role of peer relationships in career development. Acad Manag J 28:110–132

Kupillas J (2009) YouTube-Song zwingt Fluglinie zum Handeln. Welt. (24.07.2009) https://www.welt.de/wirtschaft/webwelt/article4186258/YouTube-Song-zwingt-Fluglinie-zum-Handeln.html. Accessed 31 May 2021

Langer K (2004) Das Prinzip Aldi, manager magazin. https://www.manager-magazin.de/unternehmen/karriere/a-288791.html. Accessed 31 May 2021

Matzler K, Bailom F (2004) Messung der Kundenzufriedenheit. In: Kundenorientierte Unternehmensführung, 4th edn. Gabler Verlag, Wiesbaden

Myers DG (2014) Psychologie, 3rd edn. Springer, Berlin

Nagl A (1997) Kunden- und Mitarbeiterorientierung in der lernenden Organisation. In: Handbuch Lernende Organisation. Gabler Verlag, Wiesbaden, pp 275–280

Panksepp J (1998) Affective neuroscience: the foundations of human and animal emotions. Oxford University Press, Oxford

Petifourt S (2019) Kunden hören und ihre Bedürfnisse verstehen. Quick Guide Agile Content-Produktion. Springer Gabler, Wiesbaden, pp 13–32

Rawlins WK (1994) Being there and growing apart: sustaining friendships through adulthood. In: Canary DJ, Stafford L (eds) Communication and relational maintenance. Academic Press, New York, pp 275–294

Scheier C, Held D (2007) Was Marken erfolgreich macht. Neuropsychologie in der Markenführung. Haufe, Freiburg

Scherer KR (2005) What are emotions? And how can they be measured? Soc Sci Inf 44(4):695–729

YouTube, Fremdgehen mit Mercedes - Eine Panne - witzige Werbung 90er. https://www.youtube.com/watch?v=oVIWrXzjVI4. Accessed 12 January 2023

YouTube, sonsofmaxwell, United Breaks Guitars (2009, July 07). https://www.youtube.com/watch?v=5YGc4zOqozo. Accessed 31 May 2021

FANOMICS: More than Controlling Relationship Quality

5

In Chap. 4, we dealt extensively with the question of how we can apply the *Fan Principle specifically* to the relationship between companies and their customers in order to increase the *Fan Rate*. But the *Fan Principle does* much more. Over the years, we have repeatedly discovered and developed new application possibilities for corporate management in basic research and in customer projects, three of which we would like to present to you in more detail below.

1. First of all, we are talking about the use of the *Fan Portfolio* for customer value-based segmentation: Many companies are looking for tools that they can use to segment and target their customers. In Sect. 4.4, we have already explained that it is possible to assign customers in a personalized manner in the *Fan Portfolio*. In this section, we will now look at how this assignment can be used to provide differentiated and prioritized support to customers along the value chain and how this approach can be dovetailed with other common segmentation approaches.
2. *FANOMICS* deals with the management of existing customers. But what about potential customers and customers of competitors? The *Fan Portfolio* also offers solutions for optimizing sales and communication with non-customers, which help to minimize waste and increase the chances of success.
3. For some years now, an approach to measuring and managing relationship quality has been enjoying increasing popularity. It is particularly impressive for the simplicity of its measurement and is therefore also suitable for cross-national comparative measurements, namely the Net Promoter Score (NPS). The approach is based on a single question in customer surveys, namely about the willingness to recommend a company to others. We have now bridged the gap between the NPS and *FANOMICS'* control approaches in some companies and called the result *NPSplus Insights*. It enables companies to continue the intuitive and simple measurement of NPS and at the same time to benefit from the holistic control possibilities of the *Fan Principle*.

5.1 Customer Value-Based Segmentation with the *Fan Portfolio*

Many companies still manage their customers according to the non-targeted "watering can principle" or "shotgun approach" regardless of their customer value: Profitable customers are managed just as (expensively) as customers who are unprofitable and thus (partially) eat up the profits from profitable customer relationships. By segmenting based upon the Fan Portfolio, customers can be supported in a differentiated and graduated manner according to their profitability at all touchpoints of the customer journey.

General findings on customer value make up the initial basis for this, as well as the characteristic features of the groups in the *Fan Portfolio*, which we have compiled in Fig. 5.1. For example,

- that the intention to maintain a long-term customer relationship is clearly above average among Fans and Sympathizers, but below average among Mercenaries and clearly below average among Opponents,
- that the price sensitivity of the Fans is very low, the Sympathizers low, the Mercenaries high and the Opponents very high,
- that the contact frequency of Fans is high, Sympathizers average and Mercenaries low.

The key point is the personalized assignment of customers (see Sect. 4.4) and the implementation of this information in the CRM system. In our experience, this can be implemented in any common CRM system with little effort. There are even CRM

	Fans	Sympathizers	Mercenaries	Captives	Opponents
Intention to establish lasting customer loyalty	++	++	-	+	--
Purchase volume/ order probability	++	+	0	+	-
Cross-buying willingness	++	+	0	0	--
Low price sensitivity	++	+	-	0	--
Recommendation	++	0	-	0	--
No negative word of mouth	++	+	+	+	--
Involvement	++	+	-	+	-
Perception of performance quality	++	+	+	-	--
Perception of contact quality	++	+	0	?	?
Perception of contact frequency	+	0	-	?	?
Customer value	++	+	0	0/+	--

++ very significant/ very positive, + significant/positive, 0 more or less significant/average, - not very significant/negative, -- not at all significant/very negative
Source: Own illustration

Fig. 5.1 *Fan Portfolio*: Overview of the customer value of the different customer groups

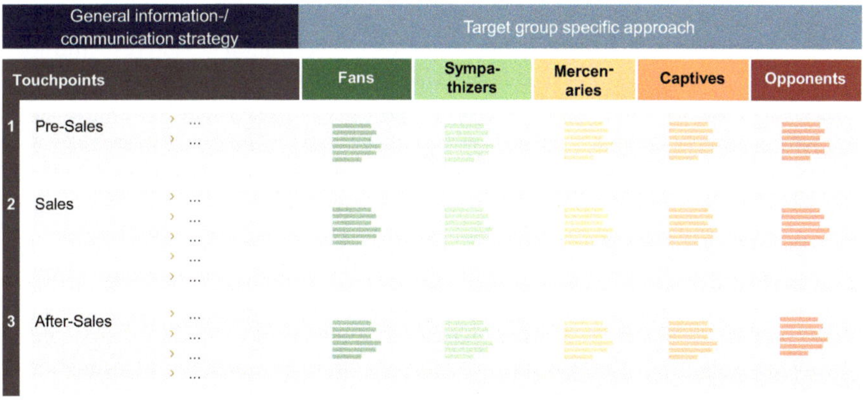

5.1 Customer Value-Based Segmentation with the *Fan Portfolio*

Fig. 5.2 Target group-specific alignment of customer-related processes along the entire customer journey

solutions in which the necessary questionnaire for querying overall satisfaction and the *Fan Indicator* are already integrated in the system, so that the assignment can be automated and carried out in real time.

Now it is a matter of defining the graduated approach, based on the general information about the groups of the *Fan Portfolio* along the customer journey at each touchpoint. This is found in a TARGET concept, which you will find depicted in Fig. 5.2 diagram. The target group-specific approaches at the individual touchpoints are described there in matrix-form.

What exactly is the added value of this TARGET concept? What exactly does the target group-specific alignment of all customer-related processes look like? These questions can be answered only individually for each company, and by taking the specific products and offerings, available resources, processes, and customer structures into account. However, the core idea is always the same, namely that customer value-based, target-group-specific addressing generates positive effects equally for your use of resources and for the effectiveness of the initiated measures. We would like to explain this with a few examples.

– Mercenaries are customers with high performance satisfaction but minimal loyalty. Our research findings suggest that their low contact frequency compared to the other customer groups is a key explanation for this. How can companies benefit from this insight? Let's say an automobile manufacturer knows which of its customers are Mercenaries and knows the term of their vehicle financing. The financing term for the customer's current model is now coming to an end. In the industry, this is a very good indicator that a new purchase is imminent. At this point, the car manufacturer can counter the Mercenary customer's particular threat of switching brands with orchestrated campaign management. In addition to centrally coordinated measures—mailings about current models and, in particular, price advantages (which, as we know, particularly appeal to Mercenaries)—it is necessary, in terms of Orchestration, to involve the local dealer. The latter can invite the fickle Mercenaries to presentations and test drives, thus specifically establishing additional points of contact and building a closer relationship. This catalog of measures in the pre-sales phase only makes sense for Mercenaries customers. For Fans and Sympathizers, the effort would not be necessary, for Captives it would hardly be promising, and for Opponents it would be wasted time.

– Let's stay with the example from the automotive industry for a moment. Despite intensive efforts (or perhaps because focused and target group-specific support has not taken place), customers migrate to another car manufacturer when the financing expires. The question then arises as to whether it is worthwhile to maintain contact with the lost customers over a period of three years to then—with the next new acquisition—get back into the game. The reasons for the churn are decisive for assessing the chances of success of this cost-intensive further processing of a former customer: Was it an Opponent customer who was very dissatisfied with the service provision and therefore churned? Or was it a highly satisfied Mercenary customer who could not resist a competitor's more attractively priced offer for a comparable vehicle model since they lacked the necessary emotional attachment to the original vehicle brand? As you can see, a truly reliable decision is made easier if you can clearly distinguish between Opponents and Mercenaries based on the allocation in the *Fan Portfolio*.

– Let's now look at a classic question from after-sales regarding the care of Captive and Opponent customers: Imagine you are confronted with a customer complaint, and you must decide whether to remove the cause of complaint on a goodwill basis or whether to reject it. If it is a Captive, you should consider the elimination very specifically, because the Captive is originally a Sympathizer or even Fan who is still emotionally connected to you. This is a customer for whom the identity between their needs and your offerings is to be taken as given. So, their complaint probably revolves around an issue of lasting relevance to other emotionally loyal customers as well. It is precisely the generous treatment of their complaint that could lead to their performance satisfaction rising again and them "moving towards" their original position in the *Fan Portfolio*. If, on the other hand, the complaint comes from an Opponent customer, you should carefully consider whether the investment is really worth it. This customer has concluded with you anyway, you will hardly be able to prevent their churn and may not even want to prevent it. There is also the question of whether this customer is a good fit for you at all. To understand this, the subject of the complaint can be revealing: If, for example, an *ALDI* customer were to complain about the inadequate goods collection area at the checkout, it is already apparent from the subject of the complaint that this customer is obviously not a good fit for *ALDI*. So, giving in would not only be a wasted effort, it would also send the wrong signal in terms of *focusing on* the central needs of other customers.

– Imagine you are scheduling the resources of your sales staff in an industrial company and cannot answer all incoming inquiries at the same time during a boom phase. Which inquiries would you process with which priority? The highest priority would be the inquiries from fans, due to the very high order probability, the very low-price sensitivity and the very high cross-buying readiness, followed by the Sympathizers, then the Captives, finally the Mercenaries and then the Opponents. In what can the prioritized processing of a request manifest itself? Of course, in the basic question of whether or not you make an offer, then in the question of who makes the offer (surely you would deploy your best staff to inquiries with the greatest potential), finally the question of how elaborately briefings are designed and how intensively you respond to customers' special requests.

– Finally, let's look at a particularly sensitive topic, namely target group-specific pricing. One thing to start with: Some companies take the realization that Fan customers are less price-sensitive than other customer groups as a call to charge Fans higher prices for the same services (cf. Sect. 4.2). This is a gross misunderstanding and inevitably leads to a serious breach of trust and damage to the Fan relationship. Nevertheless, both sides can benefit from this fan status. Those offering—by providing simple package offers to the Fan—thereby creating special, exclusive adjustments to price which the Fan particularly appreciates. The Mercenary customer is completely different. Here, since these customers show high price sensitivity, providers should offer their service in a modular fashion with maximum transparency and freedom of choice. To illustrate this with an example from the automotive industry: While the Fan prefers to buy a vehicle in full equipment including full leasing with integrated service and the manufacturer may even offer him an exclusive premium model that is not available for other customers to buy, the Mercenaries should be offered the vehicle in basic equipment at the lowest price, because he will compare. All accessories and special equipment then count as additional services—so the chance of winning is greatest.

5.1.1 Fan Marketing: How to Turn Fans into Profitable Customers

Time and again, companies ask us: "What is the most important customer group in the *Fan Portfolio*?" For all readers of this book, the answer is clear: Of course, these are the fan customers, because they explain a large part of the company's success (see Chap. 2). But instead of making a special effort to look after their most valuable customers, companies try to save on support—with the justification that fans are in a stable relationship situation, which is why there is no need to look after them more intensively. By focusing on the relationship quality of the fans, many companies miss out on great opportunities. After all, the greatest opportunity of addressing the customer types from the *Fan Portfolio in a* target group-specific, differentiated manner lies in optimally tapping the potential of fans through targeted fan marketing and turning them into particularly "profitable" customers. This can be explained with a few striking examples:

Consistently Harnessing the Expert Potential of Fans
Their immense knowledge of their provider's products and their high level of involvement make Fans valuable sparring partners in product and process optimization. Why? The essential premise for successful work with *FANOMICS* is the consistent focus on core customer needs. Who better than the Fan to check innovative ideas for their contribution to fulfilling needs and their suitability for everyday use? Companies can take advantage of this potential and specifically involve Fans in an early, conceptual phase of product development or process optimization. This has four positive effects: First, with their expert-like knowledge, Fans will ensure that developments go in the right direction at an early stage, which saves considerable costs for misguided developments "bypassing the market." Second, Fans will be the pioneers who are the first to purchase the newly developed products, and thus the forerunners of any innovation. Thirdly, as early users, Fans will not communicate any need for optimization to the outside world in a way that is detrimental to sales but will contact their provider and thus give the opportunity for early improvements. They act as beta testers of any innovation, so to speak. And fourthly, Fans will inspire further customers by recommending them to others, thus boosting sales.

Meanwhile, companies have recognized this enormous innovation potential of fan customers and are using it in the context of crowdsourcing, crowd testing, co-creating or open innovation. What these approaches have in common is that the involvement, identification, and expertise of fans are used to further develop and optimize products, offerings, services, or processes, or to procure exclusive information—and generally without demanding a fee. Some frequently cited examples of this are (Schmidt 2018):

– The new development of the *FIAT 500*: Fans were involved in product development in the run-up to the launch of the new *FIAT* 500 and thus had the opportunity to co-create "their" car. There were more than 10 million clicks on the website and over 170,000 designs in the first few months. These included the interior, the design of the exhaust, the design of the side mirrors and much more. Parts of the advertising for the new *FIAT* 500 were also generated using crowdsourcing.
– *LEGO Ideas*: On the ideas platform, LEGO *fans* can present their own designs, which can become a real *LEGO set* if supported by the *LEGO community* (Oliver 2020).
– *Red Bull Streets*: *Red Bull* was missing data from independent retail stores (e.g., addresses) in a region. Fans referred to by *Red Bull* as "Streetspotr" identified previously unknown retailers and provided photos and geodata. The quality of the data was ensured by georeferencing, plausibility checks and manual checks. The results—600 previously unknown retail outlets—were reported within 24 hours and forwarded to *Red Bull*.
– *The parcel service provider DHL* offers innovation workshops in which best practices are shared and use cases in and outside the industry are discussed, as well as thinking about the future in the logistics industry. In the "Idea Generation

Workshops," customers work with *DHL to* develop ideas for new products, services, and processes. Another workshop offered is the so-called "Trend Workshop". In collaboration with *DHL* experts, customers define their own personal trend radar based on their industry requirements.
– *Coca-Cola Freestyle*: *Coca-Cola* has developed vending machines specifically for the food service industry that allow customers to create their own flavor (Coca-Cola 2019). Around 300 such vending machines are currently in use in Germany. For the restaurateur, this has the advantage that he can offer a very large number of beverages. For this, it is not necessary to rent extra storage space, since the vending machine requires hardly any space and only a water connection, and the different flavors are created from cartridges. Certainly, the vending machine itself can be seen as a new product that has gone through the various stages of new product development with customer participation (*Burger King stores* as a test phase). More interesting here, however, is the perspective of seeing the *Coca-Cola* Journey from an individual point of view and considering the respective beverage with a personal flavor as a new product (at least for the customer). According to this, the concept development phase can first be identified for *Coca-Cola Freestyle*, in which the consumer's idea for a flavor forms the product. From the customer's point of view, the product development phase is (provisionally) complete when he or she has put together the preferred flavor(s). The implementation phase is complete when the customer receives the beverage.

Likewise, there are examples of industrial companies that identify their Fan Customers as a matter of course and use their expert potential by getting suggestions during product development, safeguarding decisions, and thus saving enormous development costs.

Finally, we want to address a very special aspect of Fan Customers' expertise: Imagine a complaint is received in a company's customer service department. They recognize that it is a Fan customer. Then this complaint deserves special attention in two respects. First, a Fan is not complaining to gain an advantage or to harm you. Rather, he only wants your best; he acts as a mystery shopper, so to speak. So, you can be sure that there is a really serious problem behind the complaint. Moreover, due to his expert-like status, the Fan recognizes problems earlier and more frequently than other customers. So, if you react quickly and draw the right conclusions, you will save yourself many more complaints, from customers where the relationship quality is far from stable—and where, as a consequence, the entire business relationship could be called into question if you were confronted with the same problem.

Unlocking the Cross-Selling and Upselling Potential of Fans
Fans are the customers with the highest cross-selling potential. In no other target group is the willingness to buy other products and services from a provider so pronounced. Providers can benefit from this, provided they know their fans: Imagine you are a car dealer, and a customer is sitting in front of you with whom you are currently discussing the configuration of his new vehicle. You are unsure how much

additional equipment you can offer him, and the consultation is time-consuming. If you now know it's a fan, then you can confidently draw from the full range. So, this is where your time investment in cross-selling and up-selling pays off—while with the other customer types, the chances of success are lower.

Or a second example: A mail order company has a particularly exclusive product on offer—in small quantities, but with extremely attractive margins. Advertising across the board via catalogs would not be effective, because the wastage would be immense. On the other hand, addressing fans directly with a mailing proves to be particularly promising. Advances in CRM, data warehousing, and data analytics are making it easier and easier to provide fan customers with new offers tailored to their needs, to exploit value chains, and to skim off price willingness. We all know how targeted Amazon repeatedly provides us with suitable follow-up offers once we have left our digital fingerprint.

Although these measures are obvious, this cross-buying potential of fan customers is often not exploited. Why? There are two reasons for this: First, even fan customers are unfamiliar with some offerings—a phenomenon we encounter more frequently the more insignificant the product or service is to the fan customer. One such area with low customer involvement is the banking sector, where even fan customers are unaware of more than half of the services offered, although this puts fans well ahead of the other customer groups in the *Fan Portfolio*. This means that the lower the level of customer involvement, the more important intensive product communication is. The second reason is that the products on offer are not attractive even to the Fan customers—and thus do not meet their needs. To prevent this, Fans should be involved in the product development process as described.

Leveraging the Referral Potential of Fans

A special characteristic of Fan customers is their potential for recommendation (cf. Chap. 2). They act as "salespeople" without you having to activate them to do so. However, the recommendation rate of fans from different industries varies greatly, and this is essentially related to two factors.

First, the degree of involvement also plays a key role here. A car enthusiast will recommend his brand more often than a driver for whom a car is primarily a means to an end. And an *Apple fan will* recommend his iPhone more often than a Fan customer will recommend his bank. So the less involvement your customers have, the more important it is to activate their recommendation potential. Let's use an example to explain how activation can take place: You work in customer service at a bank. You have just had a consultation with a Fan, and you sense how positive he found this conversation. Then you point him specifically to your Facebook page on the Internet. You can be sure he will follow your lead. There he will tell others about his positive experience—and thus become a valuable reference and orientation for prospective customers.

Second, fans need opportunities to recommend their provider to others. This plays a role wherever customers do not constantly come together and exchange information about their providers. We will use two examples to explain how such opportunities can be created.

- **Example 1**
  You are the sales manager of a software company. You are planning a roadshow at which you want to present your new IT solution to prospective customers. Then find some Fan customers from your CRM who are located at the respective roadshow sites and invite them. You will see how inspiring their participation is to the other attendees and prospects. The high credibility combined with the excellent expertise makes the Fans your most valuable salespeople.
- **Example 2**
  To communicate the competencies of a consulting company, look for suitable references. The Fan customers will be the first ones who will gladly report about their positive experiences in joint projects, also in a publicly visible way. The authentic voice of the Fan customer in conjunction with their expert-like knowledge of success effectiveness will have more radiance on potential customers than any self-promotion. At the same time, you offer the Fan customer a stage to present themselves and the joint successes. Thus, they reach potential customers and become a valuable promoter, which would otherwise hardly have been possible for them, since the fan does not originally know and contact their potential customers.

Exploiting the Potential of Fan Customers During the Crisis
The Covid pandemic and the accompanying crisis in many industries and companies have clearly shown how uncompromisingly Fan customers stand by their provider and how creatively and selflessly they support it. We would like to illustrate this with a few examples:

- The restaurant industry was particularly hard hit by the Covid-related contact restrictions. To help, active platforms formed all over Germany, locally, regionally, and nationwide, which enabled Fan customers to purchase vouchers to be redeemed at a later date. Many restaurants also sold these vouchers on their own, improving their liquidity. What is special about this form of a "loan" is that, since these are often small and micro businesses, every customer is aware that their investment can quickly fall victim to insolvency. Nevertheless, the level of trust and emotional attachment is so great that many millions of euros have been invested, often by people who themselves do not have large financial reserves. This example shows why many Fan customers state in surveys that they cannot imagine a world without their favorite company (Spitznagel 2020).
- There have been comparable campaigns in many other areas, which have one thing in common: they have a broad fan base:
  - With donations and pre-sold ticket purchases for the time after Covid, fans helped to cover at least part of the costs of artists, cultural workers, and cultural venues.
  - Travel bookers did not reclaim the deposits they had already made for package tours, but used them as credit for a future trip, thus helping the very hard-hit tourism industry to secure liquidity.

- And finally, the customers of sports clubs were also affected, especially season-ticket owners. Faced with the option of having the money they had already paid for events cancelled due to Covid refunded, converting it into a voucher for merchandising items or donating it to the clubs, the majority made use of the last option. Here, too, it should be noted that the donations often came from people with little economic success and were essentially used to finance the multi-million salaries of top athletes—without triggering any real feelings of disruption among Fans.

Fan customers are equally unconditionally loyal to their provider even if the crisis is self-inflicted (see Sect. 4.2). Fans defend their provider, even when they make mistakes, and they feel connected to them. This type of "true" loyalty ends only when the values of the Fans are betrayed, i.e., the fit between the central needs and the company services is no longer experienced in the long term. A striking example of this is the car manufacturer *VW; as a result of* the communication deficits following the emissions scandal, Fan customers turned their backs on the company because their core values could no longer be experienced (cf. Sect. 3.1).

You can see how diverse the possibilities are to profit from Fans and their characteristics if you really know your Fans and can also address them personally. If this is not the case, you will have to "pour out the described measures on all customers with a watering can", willy-nilly. This costs a lot more money and time, and above all, the desired effect will turn into the opposite in the worst case: Surely you can imagine how joyfully an Opponent customer will respond to your call to promote you. However, their messages will hardly be in your interest.

5.1.2 Potential-Based Segmentation Versus Segmentation with the *Fan Portfolio*

Now we want to outline a possible use of the *Fan Portfolio* in the context of customer value determination. The *Fan Portfolio* segments customers not only according to their relationship quality, but also regarding their customer value. The explanations in Chap. 2 have illustrated that the Fan customer has a significantly higher value for companies than other customer groups. However, the underlying valuation dimension differs fundamentally from typical customer value analyses and classifications. The Fan customers' value is based less on their classic economic success potential, which is used in many companies in the sense of an ABC customer logic. The value of Fans should not be reduced to their total sales since the true value of the Fan manifests itself in its maximum emotional customer loyalty and the resulting behaviors. If this second perspective is neglected in customer value-based segmentation, fatal misjudgments can result:

- On the one hand, Fans with less purchasing power are considered unattractive. In the medium term, the accompanying neglect in customer care can lead to Fans' love turning into the opposite, and they become bitter Opponents. This is a major

reason why approaches that propagate a separation from unprofitable customers have proven to be a misguided path. Almost always, the underlying profitability considerations are based on purely revenue-based customer value considerations and therefore lead to wrong decisions.
– On the other hand, Mercenaries with high purchasing power are automatically considered attractive. The resulting elaborate measures lead nowhere, because it is difficult to generate attractive returns with Mercenaries due to their high price sensitivity, and they jump ship at the first aggressive price offer.
– Such misjudgments are a thing of the past when the necessary expansion takes place with the allocation in the *Fan Portfolio*. The one-dimensional view of customer value becomes a two-dimensional view of customer value, in which classic segmentation by means of economic success criteria is accompanied by segmentation according to relationship quality.

For the sake of an easily manageable classification, we do not use the *Fan Portfolio* for this two-dimensional control approach, but the *Fan Indicator*. This does lead to a certain loss of information. However, since customer value is primarily described by emotional commitment (this corresponds to the vertical movement in the *Fan Portfolio*—cf. Fig. 3.1) and only to a small extent by satisfaction (this corresponds to a horizontal movement in the *Fan Portfolio*), the essential information is retained and we can present this modified customer value-based classification from the combination of customer potential and relationship quality unchanged in a descriptive form as a two-dimensional matrix (cf. Fig. 5.3).

The X-axis marks the degree of relationship quality from 1 to 3, the Y-axis marks the economic success from A to C. The cells are numbered from A1 to C3. By drawing arbitrary boundaries, a matrix with a total of nine cells is created, which are numbered from A1 to C3. This is the information basis for defining differentiated strategies per customer group for all customer-related processes. The use of resources is no longer determined one-dimensionally based on economic success, but the relationship quality is also included as a key criterion. This means that resources will not be concentrated unilaterally on A customers, but B1 and, if necessary, C1 customers will also be included. Conversely, differentiated answers will be given to the question of adequate effort for A3 customers: Since they are highly attractive to the provider but do not have a strong relationship, the focus here will be on relationship-strengthening measures to create the basis for higher revenues.

5.1.3 Allocation of B2B Customers in the Context of Value-Based Segmentation with the *Fan Portfolio*

To conclude this chapter, we would like to address a question that arises in B2B when we are dealing with more than one decision maker per company and we have to determine whether we make the allocation in the *Fan Portfolio* for each individual decision maker or for the entire company: Since the assignment in the *Fan Portfolio*

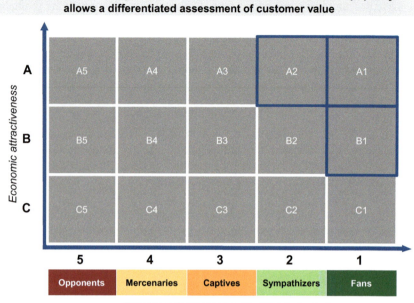

Fig. 5.3 Customer value-based classification

refers to the relationship level, an assignment exclusively on the individual decision-maker level makes sense. Assuming this is the case, it is possible that different contact persons from the same customer company may subsequently be assigned to different segments of the *Fan Portfolio*. The question then arises as to the extent to which differentiated support, addressing, and treatment of the various contacts from one and the same customer company can lead to conflicting goals or subjectively perceived disadvantages—and if so, how to counteract them.

In this case, too, maximum effectiveness and efficiency of measures are ensured by consistent adherence to the TARGET concept for target-group-specific customer care (cf. Sect. 4.4). Borderline cases or exceptions must be considered when developing the TARGET concept. Some examples of this are described below, whereby we also address the interaction of potential-based segmentation of the entire company based on economic success (macro level) and on the basis of individual decision-makers and their allocation in the *Fan Portfolio* (micro level).

- You are planning information events on your product range and want to invite your customers to them selectively based on customer value-based segmentation. In this case, the assignment of the decision maker in the *Fan Portfolio*, i.e., the micro level, determines the type of target group-specific treatment. You have

5.1 Customer Value-Based Segmentation with the *Fan Portfolio*

Participation in events for product/performance information

Fans	Sympathizers	Mercenaries	Captives	Opponents
› Not a priority, because fans are already well informed on products and services › Integration into a "VIP Club" is more effective.	› Not a priority, because sympathizers are already well informed on products and services. › Integration into a "VIP Club" is more effective.	› Important, because there are deficits in knowledge about products/services.	› Not a priority, the cause for dissatisfaction with product/services needs to be cleared up first. › If the problem is a lack of knowledge – then participation is important.	› Not effective, as there is usually no interest in constructive discussion of the product/service offering. Events could be used to damage the company.

Source: Own illustration

Fig. 5.4 Excerpt from the TARGET concept for addressing a specific target group for a selected touchpoint

worked out what the basic target group-specific approach looks like in your TARGET concept, which could look, for example, as shown in Fig. 5.4.

These specifications of your TARGET concept also apply if several decision-makers from the customer company can be invited (e.g., different production managers). In such a case, it would be conceivable for Fans and Sympathizers to be invited by mail, while the Mercenary target group prioritized for such information events would receive a letter and then a phone call. In this case, the potential-based classification of the company at the macro level has no influence on your segmentation strategy.

- You think about your target group-specific pricing. Then the assignment of the requesting decision-maker in the *Fan Portfolio* is decisive. This also applies if potentially several decision-makers from the customer company can make requests. Only the amount of the prices and the price structures should be designed uniformly for all decision-makers from the same company, in the sense of credibility and transparency. This also applies to price campaigns. The potential-based classification of the company has an impact on the base price level. For example, discounts granted can be based on the total sales of the customer company in the last fiscal year.
- You consider who you invite to a fan club—for example, to get lasting input from customers for your product innovations. The allocation of the decision-maker in the *Fan Portfolio* determines the target group-specific suitability. Accordingly, you concentrate on your fan customers and invite Sympathizers selectively to enhance their status. This also applies if there are several decision-makers in the customer company. There is no "discrimination" between Mercenaries and Opponents, and they do not perceive it that way: Mercenaries are not interested in a corresponding invitation due to their low emotional attachment to you, possibly they would even perceive it as an imposition. Captives would first expect a solution to their current problem and are therefore not open to a fan club

invitation. The classification of the company at the macro level has no influence on the target group-specific invitations for the fan club. If you want to include the companies with particularly high potential in a "VIP program," this requires a different format with different goals than the fan club.

You can see from these examples that the intuitive concerns regarding both the combination of customer value-based segmentation at decision maker and company level can be dispelled, as can those regarding the assignment of decision makers from the same company to different *Fan Portfolio* categories. The prerequisite is that you stick consistently to your TARGET concept and regulate potential borderline cases in a binding manner.

5.2 FANOMICS as an Instrument for Efficient New Customer Acquisition

FANOMICS focuses on relationship quality and ways to improve it. It therefore builds on existing customers. We assume that fans of a company are also customers of that company. However, we also know fans from sports or culture who do not have an active customer relationship with their "star". For example, there are fans of soccer clubs who live out their fan relationship by watching the weekly sports show or the highlights of the games on the Internet, by reading Web articles, in regional daily newspapers, or by talking to colleagues during the break at work, but who do not buy merchandising articles or go to the stadium. Likewise, there are fans of musicians who watch concert recordings on YouTube or on Spotify, read posts about their "star" and exchange ideas with other fans in forums, but do not buy CDs (or other formats) of their "star" and also do not go to concerts. This can have personal reasons, but also financial ones.

We asked ourselves whether there are fans who are not customers of their "beloved" provider, and if so, what the reasons are. Our instrument set allows us to identify the degree of fanhood even of non-customers by asking the two established questions on perception of unique position and fit, thus measuring the *Fan Indicator*. In the absence of an active customer relationship, we cannot ask about the customer's own satisfaction. Instead, we ask how satisfied the provider's customers are overall in the perception of the respondent, and in this way we can also assign the non-customers in our *Fan Portfolio*. The result is shown below as an example for two selected companies (cf. Fig. 5.5), namely for the car manufacturer *AUDI* and the market-leading insurer,*Techniker Krankenkasse*.

On the one hand, we can see that the *Fan Rate* among non-customers *of the two sample companies* is low, at 7% in each case. However, if we consider the underlying markets and thus the absolute figures, the picture looks different:

– Let's look at *AUDI* as an example. The current market share is about 6.8% of the 48.2 million passenger cars registered in Germany, i.e., there are about 3.28 million registered vehicles of the *AUDI* brand (Baumann 2021). If we subtract

5.2 FANOMICS as an Instrument for Efficient New Customer Acquisition

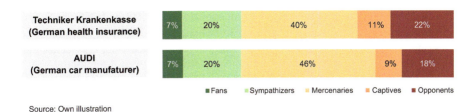

Source: Own illustration

Fig. 5.5 The *Fan Portfolio* for non-customers, using the example of *AUDI* and *Techniker Krankenkasse (TK)*, shows that there are Fans and Sympathizers among them as well

these from the 48.2 million, we are left with about 45.4 million vehicles. If we equate this number of vehicles with the number of non-customers for the sake of simplicity, then 7% of the 45.4 million non-customers, i.e., approx. 3.2 million, are *AUDI* fans. If we now consider the Sympathizers of *AUDI* among the non-customers, this amounts to another 9.1 million vehicles. What do these figures show us? Even if the proportion of Fans and Sympathizers among non-customers is small, the absolute figures are enormous and describe at first glance an enormous growth potential.

But why don't these people buy an *AUDI*, even though they are so fond of the brand? We also got to the bottom of this question: For the majority, the price plays the decisive role: They cannot (or do not want to?) afford such an expensive vehicle as an *AUDI*. This is where *AUDI* comes in: On the one hand, this may be due to life phases, for example, students or trainees who cannot (yet) afford an *AUDI but* may be able to later after starting their careers. So it might be worthwhile to build up a relationship now in order to "strike" at the right time. On the other hand, they could be potential customers with less purchasing power in general. In this case, it would be possible to expand the model range to include less expensive models (as *AUDI* has done time and again in recent decades), always weighing up whether this would have a negative impact on drivers of *AUDI premium models*, for whom exclusivity is a key purchasing factor.

– Let's look in the same way at the example of the *Techniker Krankenkasse (TK)*. For them, too, the *Fan Rate* among non-customers is a modest 7% at first glance. However, let's look at the absolute figures here as well: Currently, *TK* is the largest public health insurer in Germany with approximately 10.7 million insured (krankenkassen.de 2021). A total of around 73.4 million Germans has public health insurance. If we subtract the 10.7 million insured by *TK, we are* left with 62.7 million non-customers. Of these, 7%, or about 4.4 million, are fans among the insured non-customers, plus 20% Sympathizers, or another 12.5 million insured persons. As you can see, there is huge growth potential for *TK*. Here, too, we investigated the question of what is currently keeping these non-customers, who have strong emotional ties to TK, from becoming *TK customers*. Here, by far the most frequent citation is "I am a customer of another provider out of habit." This is not surprising, since health insurance tends to be a topic of low involvement, especially for the large mass of healthy people. This, combined with the unchanged prevailing opinion that switching health insurers is very costly, leads to a low willingness to switch. So, if *TK* wants to continue to grow and attract new members, it would have to specifically advertise the simplicity of switching and offer even more active support in switching.

These examples impressively show how attractive it is for companies to determine the *Fan Rate* among their non-customers and to specifically identify the hurdles that are currently preventing fans among non-customers from becoming customers. Because based on this information, which can be obtained by means of market research, companies can initiate measures to attract attractive new customers with little wasted coverage and optimized impact. These measures are of a general nature, such as the possible expansion of the product range in the *AUDI* example and the further lowering of switching barriers in the case of *TC,* since they are aimed at all non-customers.

This approach can be optimized further if the measures can be addressed specifically to the Fans (and, where appropriate, the Sympathizers) among non-customers. This means that companies must identify non-customers who are particularly inclined toward them. The methods of target group-specific allocation of non-customers in the *Fan Portfolio* do not differ from those used for existing customers (cf. Sect. 5.1). Here, too, we distinguish between an explicit and an implicit approach.

In the explicit approach, non-customers are surveyed, and the clear assignment is then made based upon the two questions on emotional attachment and the question on perceived customer satisfaction. This approach is time-consuming, even if it can be integrated into routine contacts in the sales process or into campaigns using appropriate tools. If large numbers of non-customers are involved, the implicit approach using data analytics is recommended, as with existing customers. However, this requires a further analysis step compared to the existing customers: The existing internal data of the customers from the *CRM is* enriched with further external information from marketing databases, i.e., for example, on age, purchasing power, and family structure. Based on this internal and external customer data in conjunction with the random assignment in the *Fan Portfolio,* potential customers can be identified who are very similar to fans or Sympathizers in terms of their characteristics. This is therefore referred to as the lookalike approach (Donahue and Hajizadeh 2019; Heineman 2016).

If we want to refine the picture even further in the context of lead qualification, we can add a further perspective, namely regarding the current relationship quality of these non-customers toward their current provider. This is because wherever a low level of emotional attachment to the current provider, i.e., in the case of Mercenaries and Opponents customers, corresponds with fantasies about another provider, the willingness to switch is at a maximum. This knowledge facilitates the efficient use of resources in sales, and wastage is reduced many times over.

5.3 Dovetailing of NPS and *FANOMICS* to Form "*NPSplus-Insights*"

In some companies, dissatisfaction with satisfaction measurements and satisfaction management has made the so-called Net Promoter Score (NPS) the preferred control variable for customer relationship quality, as the NPS is assumed to correlate with company growth and success. To calculate the NPS, the proportion of promoters and detractors among customers is first determined by asking a single question: "How likely is it that you will recommend company/brand X to a friend or colleague?" (Reichheld 2003). Responses are measured on a scale from 0 (unlikely) to 10 (extremely likely). Customers who answer with 9 or 10 are referred to as Promoters. Detractors, on the other hand, are those who answer with 0 to 6. Customers who answer with 7 or 8 are considered "passives". The NPS is then the difference between Promoters and Detractors (in % in each case). The value range of the NPS is thus between plus 100 and minus 100.

Now you may wonder what these remarks about the NPS are doing in this book. In fact, at first this seems to be a contradiction to our approach. After all, the NPS is indeed widespread, and companies receive a useful diagnostic tool regarding customer relationship quality with the NPS. However, the approach is not suitable for managing customer relationships because it takes the same wrong paths as satisfaction management. In the following, however, we do not want to join the legion of critics of the NPS, nor do we participate in current speculations that predict an exit of the majority of companies in the next few years (Gartner 2021). Those who wish to delve deeper into this are referred to the relevant literature (Lisch 2014; Baehre et al. 2021). Rather, we are interested in explaining how the NPS and the basic ideas of *FANOMICS* can be meaningfully dovetailed with each other as "*NPSplus Insights*" so that companies that have to use the NPS owing to group requirements can also benefit from *FANOMICS*.

The advantage of the NPS lies in its simplicity: It enables an intuitive and user-friendly determination of relationship quality. Management can assess how the company compares to the competition and how individual markets, divisions or departments compare. In contrast to elaborate satisfaction measurements, the NPS question is also inexpensive and meets with a high level of willingness to participate among customers owing to its brevity. It is therefore easy to understand why companies that have once taken this route and possibly also included the NPS in their target agreement systems shy away from the effort involved in introducing a different measurement instrument. The interaction with *FANOMICS* offers these companies an opportunity to compensate for the two central weaknesses of the NPS:

The *first central weakness* is the reduction of relationship quality to the question of willingness to recommend—and thus to an indicator of (emotional) customer loyalty (cf. Sect. 2.2). However, emotional connection is not the only influencing factor; the degree of satisfaction also influences relationship quality. A look at the *Fan Portfolio* impressively demonstrates the partially contradictory mechanisms of action of attachment and satisfaction: Mercenaries are highly satisfied but not emotionally loyal, and it is exactly the opposite with Captive customers; they are

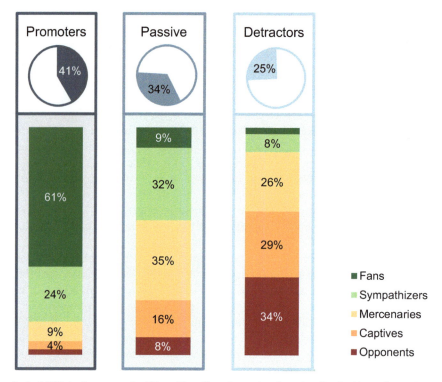

Basis: 9,612 interviews across the G7 countries with customers from the automotive, banking, online retail, grocery stores
Source: *2HMforum.* research

Fig. 5.6 Allocation of customers based on NPS is sharpened by interaction with the *Fan Portfolio*

not satisfied but emotionally loyal. This differentiation is completely lost in the one-dimensional view of relationship quality by the NPS. We will illustrate this with two examples. For this purpose, based on data from *Fanfocus Germany,* we have depicted the three groups of the NPS according to their distribution in the *Fan Portfolio* (cf. Fig. 5.6).

1. In addition to the dominant group of Fans, the Promoters also include a larger proportion of Sympathizers, although we were able to show that the Sympathizers tend to be the "silent connoisseurs" who rarely recommend others (cf. Sect. 2. 2.2)—the classification of the Sympathizers as promoters thus raises expectations that the Sympathizers do not live up to.
2. According to the reading of the NPS, Passives are the group from which new promoters could potentially be recruited. This suggests that Passives only need a small impulse to become Promoters. This impetus is then often provided by the company in terms of performance improvement (e.g., quality, service, or price). In fact, however, the largest group among Passives are Mercenary customers. As

5.3 Dovetailing of NPS and *FANOMICS* to Form *"NPSplus-Insights"*

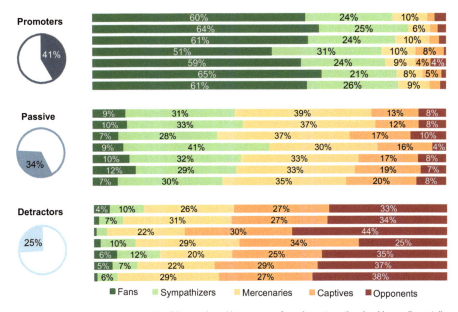

Basis: 9,612 interviews across the G7 countries with customers from the automotive, banking, online retail, grocery stores
Source: *2HMforum.* – research study

Fig. 5.7 International data in country comparison: comparison of the three NPS groups according to *Fan Portfolio* segmentation

we have already shown, they do not become referrers through increased performance. What is needed here is an increase in emotional customer loyalty.

3. More than half of the customers identified as "Detractors" by means of the NPS score are recruited from Mercenaries and Captives, i.e., from customer groups that are both only moderately willing to recommend to others, but for fundamentally different reasons. Moreover, the blanket NPS classification of "Detractors" as customers who are dissatisfied and speak negatively about their provider does not do justice to either Mercenaries or Captives.

The data from our international comparative study make it clear that these correlations exist in a similar form for all countries (cf. Fig. 5.7):

1. The percentage of Sympathizers among Promoters who quietly enjoy is at least 21 percent in the U.S. and at most 31 percent in Japan.
2. The percentage of Mercenaries among Passives who can become Promoters only by increasing retention ranges from 30% in Japan to 39% in Germany.
3. The percentage of Mercenaries and Captives to whom blanket attribution to Detractors does not do justice is at least 45% for Canada and peaks in Japan at 63%.

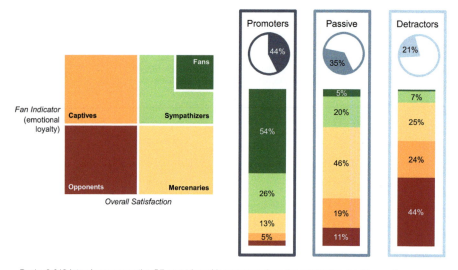

Basis: 9,612 interviews across the G7 countries with customers from the automotive, banking, online retail and grocery stores
Source: 2HMforum. research

Fig. 5.8 The example of *ALDI illustrates* how the assignment of NPS groups is sharpened by the interaction with the *Fan Portfolio*

Linking the NPS information with that of the *Fan Portfolio* provides clarity about the actual relationship quality; the potential of Passives and Detractors is much higher than imagined based on the NPS measurement *alone*. For example, it becomes clear that between 26% (in Italy) and 41% (in Japan) of Critics are more satisfied than average with their provider (Fans, Sympathizers or Mercenaries). And even among the passive customers, there is considerable sales potential. These customers do not recommend but are loyal and/or highly satisfied. This pattern is found in this form—with some shifts—in all the markets studied (cf. Fig. 5.7) and industries (cf. Fig. 5.8). This means that the simultaneous measurement of NPS and *Fan Portfolio* facilitates the precise identification of groups with different relationship quality—and thus also the derivation of measures befitting the cause. If you want to segment customers according to their relationship quality and thus their customer value, you cannot avoid the *Fan Portfolio* (see Chap. 2).

You will see that the additional survey time of about 30 seconds required for this can easily be saved elsewhere when we look at the second central weakness of the NPS system, which can be compensated for by interacting with *FANOMICS*: Companies that not only want to measure customer value, but also systematically increase it, need not only a "diagnostic tool", but also levers with which they can achieve a targeted increase in customer value by improving relationship quality.

The NPS is clearly oriented toward diagnosis. As described in detail in Sect. 1.6, the willingness-to-recommend is not an indication of emotional loyalty, but a consequence. It is not because customers recommend that they are emotionally

5.3 Dovetailing of NPS and *FANOMICS* to Form "*NPSplus-Insights*"

loyal, but because they are emotionally loyal that they (tend to) recommend. The argumentation of the NPS developers is therefore also based merely on an empirical correlation between the NPS and company growth. They fail to provide a causal analysis in the sense of a model idea as to why certain customers recommend more frequently and others less frequently. Accordingly, the recommendation as to how the NPS and thus the relationship quality can be increased is also limited to a purely empirical approach. Following the question on willingness to recommend, respondents are asked to state why they (do not) want to recommend the company. Based on the feedback, targeted and individual countermeasures are then taken, particularly with the Detractors, to eliminate the causes for the lack of willingness to recommend the company. This is classic compensation for shortcomings, as we know it from satisfaction management (see Sect. 2.1).

This means that although the NPS is a loyalty indicator, the thought model is clearly focused on increasing satisfaction "The damage done by bad profits comes in large part from the Detractors they generate. Detractors are customers who feel badly treated by a company-so badly that they buy there less, switch to competitors if possible, and warn others about the company in question...Customers who feel ignored or badly treated find ways to get back at the company" (Reichheld and Seidensticker 2006, p. 6). The drivers for good profits and thus for growth are (using the example of *Toyota* in Germany) "first and foremost an outstanding product policy, but also excellent service if repairs should nevertheless be necessary" (Reichheld and Seidensticker 2006, p. 7). So it is crucially about turning bad profits into good profits by turning dissatisfied customers into satisfied customers. The NPS is therefore essentially concerned with the question of how increased horizontal movement in the *Fan Portfolio* (cf. Fig. 3.1) can be triggered—in other words, how dissatisfied customers can be turned into satisfied customers. It is clear to all attentive readers of this book that the objective of the NPS thus contradicts the objective of *FANOMICS*. In order to prove this with data, we will take a closer look at the connection between NPS and *Fan Portfolio* in the assignment of customers, using the discount grocer *ALDI* as an example, and in particular compare the strategies of the two concepts (NPS and *FANOMICS*) for increasing customer loyalty. In Fig. 5.8 we show for this purpose the distribution of *ALDI* customers in the *Fan Portfolio* separately for the three groups of the NPS. It can be seen that the Promoters are largely composed of Fans and Sympathizers, so the two approaches largely agree on this point. The picture is quite different for the Detractors: Here we find a quarter of highly satisfied customers without attachment (Mercenaries), 24% of emotionally loyal customers who are dissatisfied (Captives), and 44% of Opponents customers who are neither satisfied nor emotionally loyal. It is obvious that the condensation of relationship quality to one dimension is accompanied by considerable loss of information—with far-reaching consequences for the initiated measures.

The central requirement of the NPS for *all* critics is to query the reasons for the lack of willingness-to-recommend and to counteract this individually. This query technique primarily brings to light more or less relevant perceived performance shortfalls. This is exactly how the creators of the NPS intended it: "'It is important to give dissatisfied customers the opportunity for constructive feedback. You can ask these customers if they would like to talk to one of your employees, who will try to better understand the disappointment and solve their problem. If this is not possible, you can supplement the survey with another question, "What is the main reason for the rating you just gave us?"'(Reichheld and Seidensticker 2006).

In this way, you provoke negative feedback from about a quarter of Detractors (by adding Mercenaries, Sympathizers and Fans), although these customers are highly satisfied. One such *ALDI* customer might state at this point that it is always too cold in his or her favorite *ALDI store*. Derived measures are not purposeful, since these customers are already highly satisfied and further investments in increasing satisfaction are in line with the "more is more" mantra of satisfaction management. The actual cause of the low relationship quality of a large proportion of these customers, the Mercenaries, namely the low fit, cannot be solved in this way. It may even happen that the elimination of the deficits subjectively perceived by Mercenaries harms the relationship quality of *ALDI* with its customers, namely if the Mercenaries do not fit *ALDI* at all (Sect. 1.6/Sect. 4.4).

Let's look further, namely at the Opponent customers. Here it is quite clear that the fit is not given in most cases. As already illustrated elsewhere (Sect. 1.6/Sect. 4.4), these customers would, for example, denounce the unfriendliness of the staff at *ALDI*, thus triggering measures in accordance with the NPS logic which definitely run counter to the focus and Orchestration and thus damage the relationship quality with the customers with high emotional attachment. Only in the case of Captive customers and thus in the case of only about one fourth of the Detractors does it make sense to query the performance deficits and to take targeted countermeasures—after all, these deficits at the performance level are responsible for the fact that these customers have (temporarily) "slipped out" of the segment of Fans or Sympathizers with high emotional attachment. This means that at the grocer ALDI, the NPS-compliant approach of compensating for perceived deficits leads to the destruction of resources for around three fourths of the critics and can additionally even endanger the relationship quality with loyal customers.

This finding applies to all sectors to varying degrees (cf. Fig. 5.9). In addition, the approach to root cause elimination in the context of the NPS does not help to answer the two key questions, namely firstly about the core customer needs and secondly about the highly relevant touchpoints.

What conclusion can we draw from this? Only in interaction with the core ideas of *FANOMICS do* the desired successes occur when the NPS is used as a measuring instrument: The relationship quality increases, and with it the customer value.

How can this be implemented in concrete terms? To derive the positioning and for consistent Orchestration, you need information about the loyalty-drivers and the highly relevant touchpoints. You, therefore, resort to the analysis tools of the *Fan Traffic Signal* and the *Touchpoint Traffic Signal* explained in detail in Sect. 3.4. You use the *Fan Indicator* or, if this is not feasible, the NPS question as an explanatory variable for customer loyalty in the *Fan Traffic Signal*. You create the basis for a fully comprehensive control by means of *FANOMICS* in terms of Positioning and Orchestration. You measure the success of the initiated measures at regular intervals with the NPS. If you do not ask the open question about the causes of the evaluation,

5.3 Dovetailing of NPS and *FANOMICS* to Form *"NPSplus-Insights"*

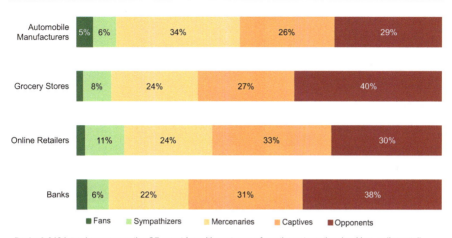

Fig. 5.9 The *Fan Portfolio* within the "Critics" NPS group

which is very time-consuming especially in coding and individual post-processing, the total effort will hardly change. Since *FANOMICS* enriches the NPS approach with the necessary insights regarding the core customer needs as well as the highly relevant touchpoints, we have chosen the name *NPSplus-Insights* for this approach.

Finally, we would like to discuss an application of the NPS that we strongly advise against. Basically, the NPS measures one aspect of relationship quality. Accordingly, the approach is unsuitable for measuring the quality-of-service provision. The same applies to the *Fan Indicator* (cf. Sect. 4.2). To explain this, imagine the person responsible for telephone customer dialog at an insurance company. In their target system, the NPS score is stored as an essential control variable. They are thus measured by how insurance customers respond to the NPS question about willingness to recommend following a telephone call with their employees. The response is influenced not only by the performance of the call agent, but also by the general perception of the insurance company, its image and previous experiences. This form of control not only causes great frustration for the manager, but also makes it impossible to make reliable statements about the quality of the telephony and about cause-adequate measures for improvement. Incidentally, this also applies to specified queries such as: "Would you recommend the call center of insurance company XY to a friend or acquaintance? " Even with this form of question, brand perception and overall performance will always play a role in addition to the call center's performance. The best way to measure performance is in a follow-up feedback survey with overall contact satisfaction as the central parameter (cf. Sect. 4.2). You can also ask the NPS question in follow-up feedback, but not to measure the quality of the service, but to understand how much the perceived service quality affects the relationship quality. To do this, you can compare the touchpoint-specific measured NPS in the follow-up feedback survey with the touchpoint-unspecific NPS

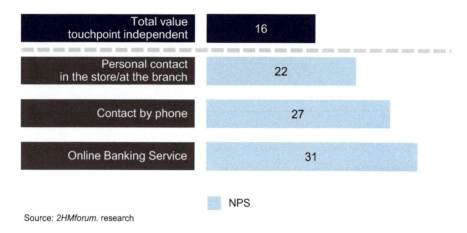

Fig. 5.10 NPS values for three different touchpoints of a branch bank

across all customers (see Fig. 5.10): It can be seen that, in the case of a branch bank, contact at the branch hardly contributes at all to increasing the NPS, whereas both telephone contact and, in particular, online banking have a very positive effect on the willingness-to-recommend.

Incidentally, NPS author Reichheld (Reichheld and Seidensticker 2006, p. 58) also recommends using the question of contact satisfaction for touchpoint-specific quality measurement, using the American car rental company *Enterprise* as an example.

In summary, we can state that by combining this with the control ideas of *FANOMICS,* companies with NPS histories are enabled to segment customers based on customer value in addition to pure measurement, and that the efficient further development of relationship quality is more successful than if these companies rely solely on NPS.

References

Baehre S, O'Dwyer M, O'Malley L, Lee N (2021) The use of net promoter score (NPS) to predict sales growth: insights from an empirical investigation. J Acad Market Sci 50:1–18

Baumann U (2021) Kfz-Bestand 2020 Fast 67 Millionen Fahrzeuge zugelassen. https://www.auto-motor-und-sport.de/verkehr/kfz-bestand-2020/. Accessed 5 July 2021

Coca-Cola (2019) News: Coca-Cola baut Freestyle-System in Deutschland weiter aus. https://www.coca-cola-deutschland.de/media-newsroom/coca-cola-baut-freestyle-system-in-deutschland-weiter-aus. Accessed 5 July 2021

Donahue L, Hajizadeh F (2019) Artificial intelligence in cloud marketing. Artificial Intelligence and Machine Learning for Business for Non-Engineers. CRC Press, Boca Raton, FL, pp 77–88

Gartner (2021) Gartner predicts more than 75% of organizations will abandon NPS as a measure of success for customer service and support by 2025. https://www.gartner.com/en/newsroom/press-releases/2021-05-27-gartner-predicts-more-than-75%2D%2Dof-organizations-will-. Accessed 26 July 2021

References

Heineman F (2016) Driving performance with programmatic CRM. In: Programmatic advertising. Springer, Heidelberg, pp 243–254

Krankenkassen.de (2021) Die größten Krankenkassen: Zahl der Versicherten 2021. Euro-Information, Berlin. https://www.krankenkassen.de/krankenkassen-vergleich/statistik/versicherte/aktuell/. Accessed 5 July 2021

Lisch R (2014) Measuring service performance - practical research for better quality. Routledge, London, pp 152–155

Oliver (2020) LEGO Ideas 2.0: LEGO World Builder offiziell gestartet. https://www.stonewars.de/news/lego-world-builder/. Accessed 5 July 2021

Reichheld F (2003) The one number you need to grow. Harvard Bus Rev 81(12):47–54

Reichheld F, Seidensticker FJ (2006) The ultimate question. With the net promoter score to loyal customers and profitable growth. Carl Hanser Verlag, Munich

Schmidt S (2018) Erfolgreich Neues: Crowdsourcing. https://www.schwarmorganisation.de/2018/02/15/erfolgreich-neues-crowdsourcing/. Accessed 29 July 2021

Spitznagel A (2020) Mit diesen Projekten werden Restaurants und Geschäfte in der Corona-Krise unterstützt. https://social-wave.de/2020/04/mit-diesen-projekten-werden-restaurants-und-geschaefte-in-der-corona-krise-unterstuetzt/. Accessed 5 July 2021

Success Factors of *FANOMICS* 6

In this final chapter, we will address success factors of *FANOMICS* that have emerged over and over again in the many years of working with the approach in more than one hundred customer projects. In doing so, we want to focus on three particularly relevant aspects:

1. **Building Awareness and Acceptance**
   FANOMICS is a holistic management approach that can always be used successfully if all managers in particular, and in the best case all employees as well, are integrated at an early stage and recognize the personal benefits for their own work. For this to succeed, there are some specific measures that we would like to present to you.
2. **Measuring customer value**
   The implementation of *FANOMICS* is associated with investments. The question of benefit is completely justified. The most important currency for its determination is customer value. In this chapter, we will take an in-depth look at the options available for measuring customer value, the advantages and disadvantages of the various approaches, and how you can keep internal willingness-to-invest high.
3. **Continuous measurement and goal systems**
   Impact measurements are indispensable for tracking the progress of your efforts in emotional customer loyalty. The more regularly and continuously these impact measurements are carried out, the more present the topic is in the company and the more consistently work is done on the defined topics. Continuous impact measurement is also an essential prerequisite for formulating goals: If you want to use *FANOMICS* because you are convinced that you will make your company more successful in the long term in this way, you will not be able to avoid a concrete objective in connection with a monetary or non-monetary incentive. The two topics are closely interlinked and should be dealt with together (cf. Sect. 6.3).

© The Editor(s) (if applicable) and The Author(s), under exclusive license to Springer Nature Switzerland AG 2023
R. Becker, G. Daschmann, *FANOMICS*®, Future of Business and Finance, https://doi.org/10.1007/978-3-658-41239-5_6

6.1 Building Awareness and Acceptance

FANOMICS is a management program. The previous explanations may already have made clear that after implementation, many things will no longer be as they were before. We are talking about a paradigm shift, which can be identified by some characteristic points:

- In the future, it will no longer be a matter of "more is more," but of doing the right thing in a focused manner—and thus also of refraining from doing things. Specifically, the "more yes to no" principle described in the examples of *ALDI* and *Miele* poses major challenges for management, staff and organizations. The fear of losing customers as a result is too widespread.
- Cherished behavioral patterns, such as the tendency to focus on weaknesses and their compensation, must be reconsidered and corrected.
- The launching of new projects and measures requires constant reflection and review to see if there really is tangible added-value for customers.
- With *FANOMICS*, customer orientation is no longer just the subject of a few specialist departments; it affects the entire organization, especially those responsible for strategy and operations, who in the future will (should) no longer be measured (exclusively) by monetary indicators from accounting, but also by their specific contribution to turning customers into Fans and thus ensuring the sustainable economic success of the organization.
- In addition, detailed analyses of the "customer journey" and in particular of the highly relevant contact points will quickly give you a feeling that the necessary focused alignment to customer needs can only succeed if not only the customer-related processes such as sales, service, communication and marketing act according to the basic ideas of *FANOMICS,* but also all back office and staff departments. For example, what good is it if a bank's customer service representative processes a customer's loan application quickly, but then the application is stuck in the credit department for several weeks? Everyone in the company must become a Fan Maker.

This list could be extended at will, and you will certainly have noticed other aspects while reading the book that allow us to speak with justification of a change process that affects the entire organization, the management as well as the workforce. From this, some factors for successful corporate management with *FANOMICS* can be derived:

- What applies to all change processes is also essential for the introduction of the *FANOMICS* management system: In phases of change, people seek orientation. In companies, this orientation is primarily provided by the company leadership and the entire management. This means for you: If you are the top decision-maker, you should be at the forefront of the movement and make it unmistakably clear in your organization that you are introducing *FANOMICS* as an essential building block for securing sustainable corporate success. If you are not part of

6.1 Building Awareness and Acceptance

the top decision-makers, enlist your executive contact to be a "project sponsor" for *FANOMICS*. This will increase the chances of a successful introduction.
- When it comes to building awareness and acceptance, it is important to convey the message in two stages: first to management and then to the workforce, with the close involvement of management. In many companies, the *FANOMICS workshop format has proven its worth* in this respect, as it makes the underlying *Fan Principle*, the mechanisms of action and, in particular, the benefits for the company and for each individual tangible. Finally, the individual steps in the implementation should be explained, responsible persons named, and time schedules clarified. The workshop character offers sufficient scope, particularly in the design of the implementation, but also in the decision on responsibilities, to encourage and involve executives and employees directly in shaping the process. In this way, the most important initial questions can be clarified:
  - What are the specific framework conditions in the company?
  - Where does the company currently stand in customer management, what are its strengths, what are its weaknesses, and what are the causes?
  - Where does the competition stand?
- Just as important as the soundness of the teaching of *FANOMICS* is its sustainability. Various factors can contribute to this:
  - If you implement the *Fan Rate* as a key performance indicator for corporate management in addition to business indicators, this will automatically entail continuous reflection on the significance of the *Fan Rate* and the model idea behind it (cf. Sect. 1.5).
  - If you use the *Fan Portfolio to segment* your customers according to their relationship quality (and thus according to their customer value), you will create the basis for aligning all customer-related processes with specific target groups. This will also contribute to a sustainable anchoring of *FANOMICS* in your company. Nothing has such a motivating effect as feeling the success at two points at once: achieving more impact with customers through differentiated addressing and, at the same time, saving resources through the measures tailored to specific target groups (see Sect. 4.4).
  - The implementation of the *Fan Rate* as a control variable and the segmentation with the *Fan Portfolio* require a high level of penetration and acceptance among management and employees. For this reason, it has proven helpful to establish so-called "fan ambassadors" in the company, especially during the implementation phase, who report on the introduction process with regular contributions in internal corporate communications and in routine management meetings as well as in customer-oriented departments. In addition, the fan ambassadors should channel problems and, if necessary, identify and discuss any resistance that arises with those responsible to ensure the sustainable success of the implementation process. It has proven to be very effective if one of the fan ambassadors acts as a fan conductor—alluding to the central challenge of Orchestration. He has a particularly intensive theoretical training

and ideally also practical experience in working with *FANOMICS*. He or she defines which implementation steps are to be tackled and in what sequence, trains and coaches the fan ambassadors, regularly measures successes, coordinates the interfaces with other ongoing projects in the company, and reports directly to the company management.

Which brings us to the last question of this chapter, namely how responsibilities should be organized. *FANOMICS* is not an instrument of a specialist department alone. As a management program, it affects strategic and operational managers in equal measure. Therefore, responsibility should also be broadly distributed. A *FANOMICS steering committee is* conceivable, in which at least one member of the management and three to four decision-makers from the operational management level (e.g., sales/marketing, human resources, service, segment managers) as well as members from the circle of fan ambassadors are represented. The fan conductor chairs this FANOMICS steering committee. The responsible specialist departments, e.g., Marketing or Market Research, can then be responsible for implementing individual operational measures, e.g., status analysis or continuous measurement of the *Fan Rate*, in the proven form.

Our advice on building awareness and acceptance is based on two decades of consulting experience around the analysis and optimization of customer relationships. As already mentioned, the insights derived from this cannot be transferred one-to-one to every company. Find your own way how to introduce and design *FANOMICS*. Let us, but also other companies, share your experiences: Use the platform www.fanomics.de/en, where we provide information and materials, e.g., to support fan ambassadors. In addition, we offer you the opportunity here to exchange ideas with other companies that are also steering with *FANOMICS* or are just starting to do so.

The Most Important Tips for the Introduction of *FANOMICS*

1. Implementing the *Fan Principle* is a change process that affects the entire organization: make it a top priority!
2. Involve the entire management early on and have them actively participate in the implementation.
3. Ensure sustainable institutionalization and communication. Fan ambassadors can be a valuable help here. The fan conductor coordinates all implementation activities and creates interfaces with other projects in the company.
4. Anchor overall responsibility in a *FANOMICS steering committee* that integrates key operational decision makers in addition to senior management.
5. Take advantage of the experiences of other companies that have also decided to use *FANOMICS for* corporate management and take part in the exchange.

6.2 Validation of Success Effectiveness by Measuring the Customer Value of Fans

We have proven the connection between *Fan Rate* and economic success both through our basic research and through commissioned projects and have presented the corresponding findings in detail (cf. Chap. 2). This should motivate your company to also look for evidence of these correlations in its own data as part of customer studies, because it proves to increase acceptance if management recognizes the growth effect of an increasing *Fan Rate* in its own company when introducing *FANOMICS*. We want to present alternative approaches to validate the relationship between *Fan Rate* and economic success in the following and specifically address advantages and disadvantages of the different approaches. In doing so, we distinguish between customer-specific approaches and considerations of customers in the aggregate.

In the case of the customer-specific approaches, the comparison of the various customer groups provides evidence that Fan customers have a higher customer value than the other customer groups in the *Fan Portfolio*. It can be deduced from this that the higher the *Fan Rate*, the higher the overall customer value—and thus also the company's success. One such customer-specific approach is to correlate various indicators of the respondent's customer value with the customer groups from the *Fan Portfolio*. In concrete terms, this means as part of a customer survey, you ask the three questions that enable classification in the *Fan Portfolio*, as well as other questions that indicate customer value. Examples are purchase frequency and volume, duration of the customer relationship, price willingness (price sensitivity and price elasticity), cross-buying willingness, willingness-to-recommend and factual frequency of recommendation or social media activity (cf. Chap. 2).

The advantages of this approach lie initially in the high validity of the measurement regarding the correlation between relationship quality (based on the *Fan Portfolio*) and the intended behavior and secondly in the simple, low-cost implementation. In contrast, there are two disadvantages: First, the validity of the measurement in terms of actual behavior is difficult to assess. In other words, does what the customer states in the interview actually match his or her actual behavior? For example, can the customer really assess and reflect in the interview how often he has really recommended his provider to others? And secondly, it remains unclear for B2B companies to what extent the responses of interviewees from customer companies can be extrapolated to the provider as a whole. For example, if a production manager is surveyed and is identified as a Fan, the company may still behave in a mercenary way, for example if the purchaser in the company decides on the supplier and the latter is precisely a Mercenary. Despite these limitations, this approach proves to be deliberate in many companies since it is equally easy to implement, and the results reflect sufficient credibility to achieve the desired acceptance assurance.

Another method of analyzing the correlation between *Fan Rate* and economic success on an individual customer basis addresses a weakness of the first approach, namely that customers' behavioral intentions do not necessarily reflect their actual behavior. Therefore, in the second approach, a correlation is formed between the direct monetary customer value of the respondent (or the company it represents) and its allocation in the *Fan Portfolio*. This approach provides high validity in terms of the correlation between relationship quality and actual purchase behavior. Implementation is simple and cost-effective, provided that resilient customer-specific indicators for direct monetary customer value (specifically transaction data, purchase volumes, contribution margins) are stored in CRM. In concrete terms, you can imagine this approach as follows: You enrich the customer addresses for the survey with the transaction data from your CRM. In the survey, you then ask the relevant questions for the assignment in the *Fan Portfolio*. The information from the CRM can then be correlated with the assignment in the *Fan Portfolio* (see Sect. 5.1). For all its advantages, this procedure also has disadvantages:

– Since only transaction data is usually included, it is not possible to operationalize the indirect customer value of fans. This is significant because it does not capture the value of less affluent but extremely active multipliers among the fans. The solution is to include the questions on indirect customer value directly in the empirical survey, as in the first approach.
– As with the first approach described, the measurement is carried out at the individual level. In the case of customer companies from the B2B sector, it therefore remains unclear to what extent the assignment of the decision-maker surveyed can be extrapolated to his company.
– If there are contractual ties between the provider and the customer under investigation, the effect of relationship quality on purchasing behavior may be weakened or superimposed: typical examples are contracts with mobile phone providers or with banks in the context of lending. The customer may, for example, be strong in sales or profitable without this necessarily being an expression of high relationship quality. It may also be due to the predicament of not being able to terminate a long-term contract.
– A major problem with all validation methods that compare factual transaction data with data on relationship quality is the different time frames of the data: Whereas the transaction data figuratively resembles a look in the rear-view mirror (for example, the sales per customer from the last twelve months are included), the relationship quality query focuses on current and future behavior. In concrete terms, this means that if we want to correctly understand the effect of a high relationship quality on the immediate monetary customer value, it is useful to look at the behavioral data for the future. The effects of an increase or decrease in relationship quality can often only be seen with a time lag of one to two years (and depending on the customers' freedom of action). From this perspective, it is advisable and pragmatic to cross-reference relationship quality data collected one to two years ago with current factual sales data at the individual data level to identify and correctly attribute effects.
– In certain industries, customers' transaction behavior is shaped not only by their "want" but also by their "ability": Imagine classic retail customers of a bank. Owing to low financial margins, these customers may be eager to take advantage

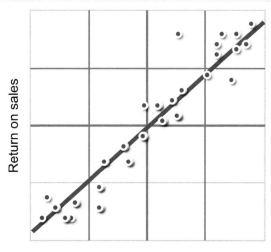

Fig. 6.1 The relationship between emotional customer loyalty and return on sales

of further savings services from their bank, but the plan fails due to a lack of creditworthiness. In such a case, even the corresponding measurements of the direct monetary customer value will not show the desired result. If, on the other hand, we focus on wealthy private banking customers in this analysis, the expected correlations become apparent, as this customer group has sufficient financial resources to engage in cross-buying.

In practice, this procedure has always proved advantageous when resilient and reliable data material was available from CRM and the customer's transaction behavior was not at all or hardly restricted by the contractual or other framework conditions just described—which means that the degree of relationship quality influenced buying behavior without (significant) time lag.

Finally, let's look at an approach in which customers are considered in the total. This is done by comparing the economic success of the company and the *Fan Rate* or the *Fan Indicator* over time or by correspondingly comparing company divisions. This approach is illustrated in Fig. 6.1 illustrates. Using the example of a retail company, it can be seen how the relationship between emotional attachment and profitability is shown in the comparison of the individual stores. It appears simple and intuitive. If we compare the measured emotional customer loyalty with the return on sales across all the company's stores, we see that the higher the emotional customer loyalty, the higher the return on sales. The advantages of this approach are evident: it proves to be very practical for target agreements (in our example for the store managers), as emotional loyalty is directly correlated with the success of the company or the subunits (in our example the stores). In addition, this approach also considers the indirect effect of high emotional customer loyalty, e.g., recommendation—but only if this indirect customer value has a direct impact on the store business. If it has a cross-branch effect, for example through recommendation to an acquaintance who then buys at another store, this effect is not discernible, and the indirect customer value cannot be traced.

Those who believe that they have found the ideal way of validation underestimate the effort that must be expended for a reliable observation. For valid statements, "all other things being equal" conditions must be created, which in practice proves to be very time-consuming and involves high personnel and financial costs for implementation.

Requirements for Validation and Valid Statements
1. The target figure—be it the return on sales, the contribution margin or another business indicator for success or growth—must be standardized. This applies to cost structures, customer structures, the market and competitive environment, and singular effects (strikes, weather-related sales slumps, etc.).
2. Likewise, identical framework conditions must be created for the *Fan Indicator* or the *Fan Rate*. In particular, it is important to exclude sampling influences (selection, size) as far as possible: If, as in our example, we survey only 50 customers per store for validation (which, depending on the number of stores, can add up to a considerable number of interviews to be conducted), the statistical error spread is still ±5.5 points for the *Fan Indicator* and ±14 percentage points for the *Fan Rate*. It is hardly to be expected that the correlation with the business indicators will lead to the desired result under these circumstances. In addition, even with this approach, a dynamic view is expedient, because the effects on returns of a changing customer relationship quality in the aggregate occur with a time delay. As already explained, this applies in particular to long-term contractual commitments, as the effect of relationship quality on purchasing behavior may then be weakened or superimposed.
3. Finally, it should also be noted with this approach that the measurement of emotional commitment in the context of a survey takes place at the individual level. Thus, in the case of customer companies, it remains unclear to what extent the assignment of the surveyed decision-maker can be extrapolated to his company.

The explanations make it clear that this approach of validating the connection between emotional commitment and economic success is very intuitive, but the practical implementation is very complex, and the results are nevertheless controversial owing to the difficult to control influencing variables. This explains why most companies focus on one of the two approaches described above (or on a combination of these two) in the context of customer surveys.

6.3 Continuous Measurement and Goal Systems for Managing Success

The successful use of *FANOMICS* in your company requires that you sustainably position the central indicator, the *Fan Rate*, as a strategically and operationally relevant control variable. The goal is that your corporate management is henceforth based on two pillars: Your accounting system with its central business management indicators—this is like looking in the rear-view mirror—and the *Fan Rate* as a currency for the quality of your customer relationships. The *Fan Rate* not only allows us to look into the future, but also teaches us how we should manage that future to grow profitably. Do you share this idea of a two-pillar model of corporate management that is based equally on classic business management variables *and* those of relationship quality? Then this should also be expressed in equally weighted systems of key figures. This means that customer feedback must be measured and managed just as consistently as the economic success indicators.

Now you might object that the *Fan Rate* has already been measured in the *customer survey* (Sect. 4.1). This is true, but the classic customer *survey* is based on a sample that is deliberately kept small, since it aims to make statements at a high aggregate level in the search for the common denominator for positioning, orchestration, and focusing. Viewed in this way, the determination of the *Fan Rate* within the framework of this classic customer survey is *only* a side effect—at its core, however, is the analysis of the core customer needs and the relevant touchpoints. Thus, the *classic customer survey does* not meet the requirements for customer feedback in the context of *FANOMICS*. Let us look for a moment at the "established" pillar of every corporate management system, at accounting and its success factors, to understand what we can learn there for the design of an adequate customer feedback system.

- As a rule, the key business figures are not only available in aggregate form, but can also be evaluated in a differentiated manner, whether by individual operating units or cost centers.
- The key business figures are continuously updated. In modern accounting, rolling planning makes it possible to determine the exact status in real time—and thus to react quickly and appropriately to the causes.
- The business management ratios have proven their worth over decades. The techniques used to determine them are objectively comprehensible and reliable. Their high credibility is the basis for broad acceptance.

How can these success factors from accounting be transferred to the measurement of customer feedback? Let's first deal with the need for differentiated evaluations: Obviously, it is not sufficient to measure the *Fan Rate* only in aggregated form.

Because then the *classic customer survey* would be sufficient to *determine the status*. Only the differentiated measurement of relationship quality enables those responsible to react in a targeted manner. Moreover, this is the prerequisite for holding the responsible decision-makers accountable for the results achieved or not achieved: The managing director of an international industrial company in Germany, for example, will hardly allow himself to be measured by a *Fan Rate* that was measured for all of Europe as part of customer feedback. The same may be true for those responsible for specific product lines or business units. This means that the success of *Fan Rate* management will depend to a decisive extent on how differentiated the results are collected and made available.

However, when differentiating the results of customer feedback according to areas of responsibility and accountability, it must also be considered that the *Fan Rate* is not the right control variable for all purposes (Becker and Lang 2013). The explanations in Sect. 4.2 make it clear that one must distinguish between the performance perception of customers and their relationship quality. To recall briefly: Assessing the performance of a manager, who is responsible for an operational process such as customer service or internal sales, the *Fan Rate falls short* and often leads to demotivation. This is because process managers can only effectively influence customers' perception of performance in relation to *their* process, for example, customer service. Since the *Fan Rate expresses* the overall perception of the customer, many factors are included that the process manager cannot influence at all, for example, corporate communications and thus image-building measures. Think of the manager responsible for telephone customer service at an insurance company who, together with his team, delights every caller—and yet the *Fan Rate* is only average because claims processing by the company's own specialist department always drags on forever or because customer confidence has been damaged by reports of delaying tactics on the part of the insurance company. So, if he were measured by the *Fan Rate* (alone), this would trigger a feeling of powerlessness.

When differentiating customer feedback, a distinction should therefore be made between those responsible for relationship quality and those responsible for processes. While the *Fan Rate* is the adequate parameter for the former, process managers should be evaluated based on customer contact satisfaction, i.e., performance oriented. As discussed in detail elsewhere, follow-up feedback is conducted for this purpose immediately after the service has been provided (cf. Sect. 4.2).

How can the second success factor of accounting, namely always up-to-date, preferably rolling recording and control, be transferred to the measurement of the *Fan Rate*? Let's first consider why this is so important: If measurement were carried out once a year (or even less frequently), there would be a risk that attention would be focused only on the customer relationship in the short term. Now, one could object that even through target agreements and continuous campaigns, the topic of "customer" would always be on the agenda. However, practical experience in companies shows that the use of resources is strongly influenced by current impressions. Everyone can certainly form their own picture of what happens when a company's sales department communicates sales figures daily—but only communicates the *Fan Rate* once a year. A balanced presence of economic success and relationship quality indicators in day-to-day business is a prerequisite for the propagated two-pillar management model to really work. Regular surveys of the *Fan Rate* during the year are useful. Because current measurements have another major advantage: they allow a clearer assignment of cause and effect, thus accelerating the learning curves in the companies and enabling rapid countermeasures.

Timely recording brings us directly to the third success factor: the resilience and thus the credibility of data—in connection with the measurement of the *Fan Rate*, i.e., customer feedback. In this context, the sample size or the response rate is an essential aspect.

Ideally, customer feedback is based on a complete survey. If this is not possible—for economic success reasons or to avoid having to survey individual customers too frequently in a manageable population—the aim should at least be to have the largest possible samples per unit of analysis to generate reliable and selective results. Why this is important is illustrated by a concrete calculation example: We assume that we want to measure the *Fan Rate* per branch for a bank, assuming for simplicity's sake that each branch serves about 1000 customers. How reliable is the result for the *Fan Rate depending on the* selected sample? Let's assume there are only 50 feedbacks per store. The results show the *Fan Rate* in a selected branch to be 30%. As explained above, due to the margin of error in a 50-person sample, the actual *Fan Rate* of this store is in a resilient range between 16% and 44%.[1] What do you think, would the corresponding store manager agree to be measured against this inaccurate *Fan Rate* survey? Let's now assume that 300 customers per store were surveyed instead. Then the fluctuation range of the actual *Fan Rate is reduced* to ±5 percentage points—a result that should meet with significantly higher acceptance. Important for your considerations on the sample size is: You only need three answers for the clear allocation of your customers in the *Fan Portfolio*. For the customer, this is done in about 30 seconds. Due to the brevity, the costs per interview are therefore low—and larger samples can be financed.

One way to start saving resources is to focus on particularly attractive customers. However, as the explanations in Sect. 5.1 have made clear, this can also be misleading. This is because only customer segmentation in the *Fan Portfolio* makes it possible to see the true customer value. Anyone who selects customers to be surveyed based on typical classification approaches solely according to their economic success will regularly overlook valuable fan customers with small economic budgets.

This leads us to the last central prerequisite for decision-makers to accept the *Fan Rates* surveyed: namely, that the responses and the *Fan Rate* determined from them must be reliable. This is always questionable if you evaluate your decision-makers based on the *Fan Rate achieved*. Automatisms will then take effect, leading to a distortion of the results. Decision-makers will try to manipulate the results in their own interests, for example by influencing the respondents (from good coaxing and

---

[1] This results from the so-called 95% confidence interval of the sample. It indicates the range of values within which the so-called "true value" lies with 95% probability.

suggestion to bribery or the threat of sanctions) or the sampling (for example by selecting unrepresentative but particularly well-liked customers). Experience has shown that such effects can be better controlled if the data collection is carried out by a neutral institution. As in all areas of quality management, the same applies here: Do not let anyone collect the data themselves that is intended to provide information about their own performance and target achievement.

As we have already explained in detail (see Sects. 4.4 and 5.1), it is of elementary importance for sustainable work with *FANOMICS to be* able to assign individual customers in the *Fan Portfolio in a clear* and personalized manner. How can this be reconciled with the idea of an anonymous survey of the *Fan Rate* by a neutral service provider? Basically, by looking at and working on these two target systems separately: on the one hand, the anonymized survey for implementing the *Fan Rate* as a control variable, and on the other hand, the personalized assignment of customers in the *Fan Portfolio* as the basis for customer value-based control. And if you cannot resist the temptation—in terms of the synergy effect—and want to use the results of the first query in a personalized way after all: Let customers decide for themselves whether they prefer to answer anonymously or whether they agree to you using the results in a personalized way.

1. If you want to be successful with *FANOMICS*, you must measure and manage the *Fan Rate* as a central control variable just as consistently as the economic success indicators.
2. Differentiated measurement of relationship quality, for example by region, country or business unit, is necessary as the basis for targeted management. Only then can the responsible decision-makers be held accountable for the results achieved or not achieved.
3. Regular surveys of the *Fan Rate during the year* are necessary so that customer relations are constantly present in the perception of employees and the effect of initiated measures can be closely monitored.
4. The resilience and thus the credibility of data collected on customer feedback depend crucially on a sufficiently large sample and the response rate.
5. The reliability of collected data on relationship quality can be increased if a neutral institution is entrusted with the implementation.

Reference

Becker R, Lang J (2013) Wohin will der Kunde wirklich? QZ 58(12):30–34

More than "Just" Success: How *FANOMICS* Gives Meaning to Doing Business

A few years ago, during a conversation about *FANOMICS*, the head of communications for a leading household appliance manufacturer asked us what we thought of the following statement: "It's never been so easy to turn your customers into fans!" One is spontaneously inclined to agree, because that is exactly what the millions of "likes" given in social networks, which is equated with fanhood, and the inflationary affirmation of companies to want to turn "customers into fans" suggests to us. Nevertheless, we are convinced of the opposite. It has never been so difficult to turn your customers into fans.

In order to justify our statement, let us once again consider the two essential characteristics of the fan that we have identified from social science research: Fans are recognized by their identification with their star as well as by the subjective uniqueness they attribute to their star in fulfilling their core needs. These two characteristics explain why it is attractive for all companies to learn from fan relationships and transfer the underlying mechanisms to their relationship management. After all, companies, their products, and their services have long since ceased to be perceived by customers as unique.

But that was not always the case. In the past, it was enough to have the better product to differentiate oneself perceptibly for customers. The product differences were large and easy for customers to recognize. Customers knew only a few providers since the Internet was not available for comparison among providers worldwide and in real time. So it was enough to have the better products to differentiate, and thereby to turn customers into fans.

But product development progressed, products became more and more mature, and new suppliers were attracted by the profits, so that an increasing number of suppliers offered increasingly similar products in the perception of customers. So companies invested more and more in product-related services: in their infrastructure, their service, their employees. In this way, they were able to differentiate themselves and thus also turn their customers into fans—albeit at an increasingly high cost.

However, more and more suppliers followed suit when it came to investing in product-related services, with the result that companies no longer differentiated themselves in the perception of their customers in this respect either. Once this

© The Editor(s) (if applicable) and The Author(s), under exclusive license to Springer Nature Switzerland AG 2023
R. Becker, G. Daschmann, *FANOMICS®*, Future of Business and Finance, https://doi.org/10.1007/978-3-658-41239-5

point was reached, the price spiral spun faster and faster, because price was the only remaining performance feature that companies could still use to differentiate themselves perceptibly.

Since then, companies in all developed markets worldwide have been looking for a way out of this price competition, and we have discovered such a way out with *FANOMICS*. Because *FANOMICS* shows a way how companies can differentiate themselves in the perception of their customers despite interchangeable products, performances and services:

- The first step is to focus on core customer needs.
- Then it is about Orchestration of all customer touchpoints along the customer journey since that is the only way to create a sense of uniqueness. So it is not enough to optimize individual product or service aspects, and it is not enough for individual customer-facing departments to make a special effort. Everyone and everything must act in a focused and coordinated manner.

Although we have been using *FANOMICS* for several years to show a way for companies to escape price competition and thus become even more successful, by no means does every company seize the opportunity to implement it; despite the fact that almost all of them propagate a desire to turn their customers into fans. We have identified three central reasons why many companies find it so difficult to back up their words with action:

1. Surely it has to do with the necessary paradigm shift from the "more is more" mantra to focus and orchestration that keeps many companies from leaving their comfort zone with (still) acceptable success and getting on the road.
2. There is no doubt that German companies are in love with their products—and undeniably with some justification: It is no coincidence that "Made in Germany" is synonymous throughout the world with special quality and reliability. With regard to the successful management of customer relationships, however, these product-loving tendencies cloud the view of the essentials: Where products are so sophisticated that customers cannot tell the difference between identical services from different suppliers, more performance becomes an investment grave rather than a success factor. Where managers are so one-dimensionally convinced of the relevance of their products for success, a management model like *FANOMICS*, in which products are only one point of contact among many, is difficult to convey.
3. The misdirection of relationship management with its focus on compensating for short-comings is also due to a distorted perception; namely the overvaluation of negative messages: Anyone who is constantly confronted in the media with examples of the "service desert Germany" and who, as a decision-maker, receives mainly negative customer assessments from his management team, ultimately does not trust the positive feedback from market research—if he ever collected it at all. Even a few critical customer statements can outshine the positive impression of a comprehensive, empirically reliable customer survey that shows a proportion of satisfied customers of 80% or more. Companies are also so

intensively concerned with improving their performance because they overestimate the actual need for action and completely misjudge it. They have been confirmed for decades by marketing textbooks and by consultants who proclaim the "more is more" mantra of satisfaction management. So, there was a lack of alternative control variables and mechanisms.

As was to be expected under these general conditions, the hoped-for successes have not materialized in many companies despite considerable efforts and investments in customer relationships. But instead of questioning the control variables and instruments used, the existence of the connection between customer relationship quality and corporate success was fundamentally called into question. People were in tunnel vision mode and maintained it. Investments continued to be made, but the significance of relationship management shrank in many places to the level of an auxiliary discipline in marketing or sales. In other words, as a result of the faulty orientation, relationship management had failed to prove its importance for the company's success—with correspondingly far-reaching consequences for the hierarchical anchoring and budget allocation and thus for its status in the company.

FANOMICS has the potential to reverse this trend—as *the* gamechanger for relationship management. Because *FANOMICS* provides proof that valuable customer relationships are an essential prerequisite for sustainable corporate growth. The necessary condition is the departure from satisfaction as the sole control variable and from the corresponding control model—satisfaction management—with its "more is more" paradigm—and the insight that it is essentially *not* about increasing customer satisfaction.

In years of research and on the basis of several hundred thousand interviews with customers, we discovered the *Fan Principle* and developed *FANOMICS* and its implementation fields based on it. We were able to prove how a consistent focus on the *Fan Rate* and the *Fan Principle* makes companies more successful. We were able to show that this is due to the superior customer value of fan customers, who buy more and more often, are less price-sensitive, are very familiar with the offers and thus become the most valuable ambassadors of their provider. Using numerous examples from different industries, we have been able to repeatedly validate the explanatory and predictive value of *FANOMICS*' key performance indicators. We were able to show that companies that operate according to the principles of *FANOMICS* are the most successful in their industry and, conversely, how plausibly the failure of companies can be explained by violations of the rules of the *Fan Principle*. Another key finding from our many years of research and consulting work is that consistent focus on the control elements of *FANOMICS* does not entail additional costs; on the contrary. Through the consistent *Focus,* resources are used more efficiently, and the necessary investments are reduced. This means that those who strictly adhere to the principles of *FANOMICS* increase the relationship quality with their customers and save money at the same time. Both effects together explain the enormous growth spurt. As the last building block (for the time being), we have now been able to prove that these success-effective effects of *FANOMICS* apply to the central developed markets worldwide, irrespective of cultural influences.

We summarize: This book provides evidence that Fan customers have a higher customer value than other customer groups and, with the *Fan Rate,* offers companies a new, reliable currency to measure the status of their customer relationships. With the *Fan Portfolio,* all customers can be assigned according to their customer value and thus targeted precisely. And with *FANOMICS,* we provide the control system with which every company can increase its *Fan Rate.*

Therefore, we repeat our promise from the introduction (because fans love repetition) that—regardless of the industry, regardless of the size of your company, regardless of whether you are in the B2B or B2C sector, whether you are based with your company in Europe, Asia or North America—your economic success will increase when using *FANOMICS.*

But *FANOMICS* is basically much more than "just" a management program for economic success. It also has a meaningful effect since it aligns companies with the quality of human relationships.

Wilhelm von Humboldt once said: *"Basically, it is always the connections with people that give life its value."* This means that anyone looking for value or meaning in business does not focus primarily on economic metrics, but on the quality of the underlying human relationships. It follows suit: Instead of understanding growth exclusively as an end, instead of accepting growth as the fixed and starting point of all thinking and acting in management, instead of subordinating everything else to the primacy of growth, the *FANOMICS* model of thinking additionally offers a return to that sense-making which may have been lost in the process.

Now you may object that with *FANOMICS we* have just proved that relationship quality—in the sense of emotional connection—makes companies more successful, and that *FANOMICS* is therefore also a growth-oriented model. That is true, but in the implementation of *FANOMICS, the* objective is turned around: Because it is first a matter of putting oneself and one's own goals and wishes aside, of getting involved with the motives and needs of the customers and of aligning everything, but also everything, with these. Those who are willing to take this step will automatically be successful with *FANOMICS.* But this success becomes a positive side effect of an orientation towards human relationship quality.

This meaningful aspect also emerges from what the alignment with the ideals of *FANOMICS* triggers in the customers. Not only do they reward the consistent focus on their central needs and expectations along the customer journey in the truest sense of the word, not only monetarily, but also through unconditional trust and loyalty. What's more, customers experience these fit-focused relationships, which at their core offer the constant repetition of what they value and love, as the antithesis of stability, security, and affirmation in a meritocracy where we otherwise define ourselves by movement, change, success, and power. And they value this experience—indeed, they need it.

So, by turning our customers into fans, we not only become more successful in our own cause, but we also help to make our customers happier. And that makes sense—for customers and for the company. Because what applies to customers can of course also be applied to all other stakeholders of companies and organizations, to employees, managers, members, volunteers, and the public: consistently implemented, *FANOMICS* places people, their needs, and their relationships at the center of all actions—the return on this focus then arises virtually by itself. *FANOMICS* is thus not only the path to economic success, but also a meaningful relationship-oriented orientation of one's own actions for every company.